Essentials of American Government

ERNST B. SCHULZ *BERNHARD, 1896—*

PROFESSOR EMERITUS OF POLITICAL
SCIENCE, LEHIGH UNIVERSITY

REVISED

BARRON'S

EDUCATIONAL SERIES, INC.

WOODBURY, NEW YORK

☆ CONTENTS

PREFACE   iii

1. The Constitutional Foundation   1

2. Governmental Powers
   and Intergovernmental Relations   32

3. Individual Rights and Responsibilities   65

4. Elections, Political Parties, and Pressure Groups   112

5. The National Government: Unique Features   152

6. Congress   190

7. The Presidency   237

8. Administrative Agencies   275

9. The National Judiciary   317

10. State Constitutions   352

11. State Government: The Legislative Branch   379

12. State Government: The Executive
    and Judicial Branches   416

13. Local Government: Counties, Towns and Townships,
    Special Districts   455

14. Local Government: Municipalities   484

15. Public Expenditures and Revenues   517

APPENDIX
    Glossary   551
    Cases Cited in Text   565

Digest of Selected Supreme Court Cases 569
Examination Questions: Essay and Other Types 591
Suggested Supplementary Reading 609
Articles of Confederation: Excerpts 615
Constitution of the United States 620

INDEX 655

☆ PREFACE

TWO difficult decisions confront the author of an "Essentials of American Government." One is deciding what is essential; the other is determining the thoroughness of treatment to be accorded the topics selected for consideration. Debatable value judgments are unavoidable and the attainment of brevity requires omission of some material and curtailed discussion of many complicated problems.

This volume (revised in early 1972) is designed primarily for review purposes. It also may prove useful for courses in which a brief text is combined with several monographs dealing with various aspects of government in the United States.

Writing about government in the United States is easier in one respect today than it was forty or more years ago. A wealth of material is available to the author. Particularly helpful publications, in addition to many general and special studies of excellent quality, are *The Book of the States* (issued biennially), *The Municipal Year Book* (published annually), the yearly *United States Government Organization Manual,* and *Congress and the Nation, 1945–1964,* a large volume published in 1965 by the Congressional Quarterly Service.

Comparatively few of the countless books dealing with either general or special features of national, state, and local government are included in the bibliography of this text. Many of those listed are relatively inexpensive "paperbacks" which, having the merit of dealing briefly with particular subjects, are likely to be purchased and read by students with an inclination for supplementary reading.

I am indebted to Dr. H. R. Whitcomb and to the late Dr. R. J. Tresolini, both of Lehigh University, for various helpful suggestions and to Lois Brown and Margaret Dennis for the location of library materials.

ERNST B. SCHULZ

Correlation of This Review with Recent Textbooks

The first column shows the chapter numbers in this Outline. Read across to find the corresponding chapter numbers in six widely used textbooks, where you will find in detail the same material discussed in the Outline.

CHAPTERS IN THIS TEXT	BURNS & PELTASON	FERGUSON & MC HENRY	YOUNG'S OGG & RAY	HATHORN, PENNIMAN, FERBER	FISER, BROWN, GIBSON	IRISH & PROTHRO
1. The Constitutional Foundation	2, 3	2, 3, 4	1, 2	2, 3	3, 4	4
2. Governmental Powers and Intergovernmental Relations	4, 5	4, 5	3	4, 14 (269–274), 22 (440–442)	5	4
3. Individual Rights and Responsibilities	6, 7, 8	6, 7	4	5, 6	6, 7	13
4. Elections, Political Parties, and Pressure Groups	9, 10, 11, 12, 13, 27	8, 9, 10, 11	5, 6, 7	7, 8, 9, 10	8, 9, 10	5, 6, 7, 8
5. The National Government: Unique Features	3 (41–47), 13, 14, 15, 16	12, 14, 16	8	11, 12, 13, 15	4, 12	8, 9, 10, 12

6. Congress	16, 17	12, 13	9, 10, 11	14, 15, 16	11		9
7. The Presidency	14, 15, 21 (434–448)	14, 15, 18	11, 12, 20	12, 13	12, 29	10, 15
8. Administrative Agencies	18, 22–26, Epilogue (704–708)	15, 21–23	13, 15–21	19, 20, 22–28	13, 20–27	11
9. The National Judiciary	19	16	14	17, 18	14	12
10. State Constitutions	28	24	23		16	
11. State Government: The Legislative Branch	29	24	24		16	
12. State Government: The Executive and Judicial Branches	30	25, 26	25, 28	15, 16	15, 16	
13. Local Government	31, 34	27	29, 30		17	
14. Local Government: Municipalities	31, 32, 33	27	31, 32, 33	17, 18	17, 18	
15. Public Expenditures and Revenues	35	17, 28	22, 27	21	20	14

Reading Guide to Selected Textbooks
Consult chart

Burns, J. M. & Peltason, J. W. *Government by the People*, 8th ed., (Englewood Cliffs, Prentice-Hall, Inc., 1972)

Ferguson, J. H. & McHenry, D. E., *The American System of Government*, 11th ed., (New York, McGraw-Hill Book Co., 1971

Young, W. H., *Ogg and Ray's Essentials of American Government*, 9th ed., (New York, Appleton-Century-Crofts, 1964)

Hathorn, G. B., Penniman, H. R., & Ferber, M. F., *Government and Politics in the United States*, 2nd nat'l ed., (Princeton, D. Van Nostrand Co., Inc., 1966)

Fiser, W. S., Brown, S. G., & Gibson, J. S., *Government in the United States* (New York, Ronald Press Co., 1967)

Irish, M. D. & Prothro, J. W., *The Politics of American Democracy*, 5th ed., (Englewood Cliffs, Prentice-Hall, Inc., 1971)

The Constitutional Foundation

CHAPTER ☆ ONE

Colonial Political Institutions
    Types of Colonies: Corporate, Proprietary, Royal
    Colonial Governor
    Legislative Branch
    Judiciary
Declaration of Independence
First State Constitutions
Articles of Confederation
    Governmental Features
    Defects of the Articles
Constitution of the United States
    Main Body of the Constitution
        Preamble
        Articles I–VII
    The Amendments
        The First Ten
        Eleventh
        Twelfth
        Thirteenth, Fourteenth, and Fifteenth
        Sixteenth
        Seventeenth
        Eighteenth and Twenty-First
        Nineteenth

       Twentieth
       Twenty-Second
       Twenty-Third
       Twenty-Fourth
       Twenty-Fifth
       Twenty-Sixth
       Twenty-Seventh (proposed)
   Processes of Constitutional Change
     Amending Procedure
     Change by Interpretation, by Custom and Usage, by
       Auxiliary Legislation
   The Living Constitution

☆ ☆ ☆ ☆ ☆ ☆ ☆ ☆ ☆ ☆ ☆ ☆ ☆

The governmental system of the United States is based on a constitution which began its effective life nearly two hundred years ago. A combination of two opposing characteristics, rigidity in some respects and flexibility in others, accounts for the fact that an instrument of government devised in the late 18th century still meets the needs of a large, wealthy, and heavily populated country which has experienced continuous social transformation as a consequence of rapid population increases, urbanization, territorial expansion, and 19th and 20th century scientific achievements and technological innovations. Although significant constitutional changes have occurred, largely through interpretation, reinterpretation, and formal amendment, the life expectancy of the original constitution continues to be high. The Philadelphia convention of 1787 deserves credit for confining the Constitution's content to fundamentals, avoiding excessive detail, using many words and phrases of broad rather than narrow meaning, and providing a mode of amendment which is neither too easy nor extremely difficult.

As prepared in 1787 the Constitution's provisions were products of the experiences of the inhabitants of the thirteen original states. Then, as now, both ideas and events were major factors in the shaping of political institutions. Before examining the Constitution as it is today, brief consideration will be given to colonial government during the period immediately preceding the Revolutionary War, to the Declaration of Independence and the first state constitutions, and to the Articles of Confederation which were in effect from 1781 to 1789.

Colonial Political Institutions

The government of the British colonies varied considerably from the beginning to the end of the colonial period. Nevertheless, certain general features are identifiable as characteristic of the relations between the mother country and its dependencies in that part of the world which eventually became the United States. These features include legal subordination of the colonies to the King and Parliament, principally the former; colonial charters of several varieties; governments which in most cases were composed of agencies of the King or a proprietor in combination with an assembly representing the colonists; and varying degrees of colonial self-government, often greater in fact than as a matter of law.

Types of Colonies

Three types of colonies were functioning during the period immediately preceding the Revolutionary War, viz., corporate or charter, proprietary, and royal. The *corporate* colonies were Rhode Island and Connecticut which governed themselves under charters granted by the King to the *settlers or colonists as a group*. These colonies enjoyed far greater freedom from external control than colonies of the proprietary and royal variety. There were three *proprietary* colonies—Pennsylvania, Maryland, and Delaware. The distinguishing feature of this type of colony was that the King granted land and governing authority to a proprietor who, although owing obligations to the King and being subject to various restrictions imposed by the British government, was legally the dominant political figure in his colony. The *royal* colonies, most numerous at the time of the revolt against Britain, included New York, New Hampshire, New Jersey, Massachusetts, Virginia, North Carolina, South Carolina, and Georgia. Royal colonies were subject to direct control by the King who was represented by a governor possessing whatever governing authority was conferred on him by his commission and instructions, both original and supplementary.

Every colony had a governor; all but two (Pennsylvania and Delaware) a bicameral legislature; and all a judicial system composed of several levels of courts. Except in Rhode Island and Connecticut, the chief executive (governor) and the upper legislative chamber (the governor's council) were agencies of government representing the interests of either the King or a proprietor. The lower chamber of the legislature was an assembly whose members were chosen by an electorate composed of property-owning and tax-paying colonists. In Rhode Island and Connecticut, the elective legislative assembly was the most important and dominant organ of government, whereas in the other colonies neither the governor and his council nor the lower chamber of the legislature, which spoke for the colonists, was able to dominate the political scene. The government of most of the colonies was a house divided against itself.

The Colonial Governor

The governor in the royal colonies was appointed by the King and served at the latter's pleasure. As agent of the King he discharged various responsibilities, such as presenting reports to his superior, recommending legislation by the mother country in regard to the colonies, approving or vetoing acts of the colonial legislature, and transmitting approved acts of the latter for royal approval or disallowance. He served as a channel of communication between Britain and the colony and aided other royal officers assigned to colonial service.

As chief executive of the colony, the governor possessed important powers and performed a variety of functions. His involvement in the lawmaking process was based on the right to recommend and initiate laws, on an absolute veto over acts of the legislature, on control over the frequency and length of legislative sessions, and on authority to dissolve the assembly and order a new election. His executive powers were extensive, as evidenced by the power to appoint and remove all important colonial officials, to enforce the

laws and maintain order, to serve as commander-in-chief of
the military forces, to levy troops, and to grant pardons for
offenses other than treason and felonies.

The governor's legal authority, although impressive, was
by no means absolute. He was bound by the provisions of
his commission and supplementary instructions. His approval
of colonial laws was subject to British supervision and disallowance. Imperial control of the colonies was undertaken
for the most part by the Crown, but Parliament could and
did enact laws binding on the colonies, including navigation
acts, trade regulations, and the imposition of taxes. Furthermore, Parliament possessed authority to investigate colonial
affairs. As for internal restraints on the governor the advice
and sometimes the consent of the governor's council was
requisite to the taking of gubernatorial action. Probably the
most important local check on the governor's exercise of his
legal authority was the elective assembly's control of the
purse strings.

The foregoing account of the governor's powers and
responsibilities pictures the role of the governor in the royal
colonies. His position in the proprietary colonies was in
many respects the same, but his immediate superior was the
proprietor rather than the King. However, in the corporate
colonies, Rhode Island and Connecticut, the governor was a
comparatively weak official. He was selected annually by
the legislative assembly and placed in complete subordination to that body.

The Legislative Branch

With two exceptions, Pennsylvania and its adjunct, Delaware, the colonial legislatures were two-chambered bodies.

The upper chamber was the governor's council; the lower an assembly chosen by the small proportion of colonists who were qualified to vote.

In the royal colonies the council was appointed by the King from a list of persons nominated by the governor. The latter could suspend council members but only the King could remove them. In the proprietary colonies members of the council were designated by the proprietor and removable by him. As for Rhode Island and Connecticut, the personnel of the council was chosen by the freemen for a one-year term.

In addition to its lawmaking power, the council advised the governor and performed various administrative functions. It also sat with the governor as the colonial court of last resort. The Rhode Island and Connecticut councils shared executive powers and responsibilities with the weak governors of these colonies to so great an extent that the executive was in effect plural in type.

The assembly in all of the colonies was elective but its members were chosen by an electorate of limited size. Such qualifications for voting as ownership of property, payment of taxes, and sometimes additional religious and moral requirements had the effect of confining the voting privilege to a minority of the adult colonists, chiefly the well-to-do. Representatives were apportioned among towns, counties, and parishes, but little or no attention was paid to differences in population.

The assembly's role in the enactment of laws was equal to that of the council. Its greatest weapon in its relations with the governor was control over the financing of governmental activities. By refusing to authorize expenditures and levy taxes, it was often able to bargain effectively and exact concessions from a governor who, as spokesman for the King or a proprietor, represented the latter's interests rather than those of the colonists.

The Judiciary

The colonial judiciary was appointive, not elective. Appointment by the governor, commonly with the advice and sometimes the consent of his council, was the prevailing practice. In Connecticut and Rhode Island, members of the judiciary other than the governor's council were selected by the legislature.[1]

Justices of the peace, with jurisdiction limited to minor civil and criminal cases, constituted the base of the judicial hierarchy. Next in line were courts of quarter sessions and oyer and terminer. These were general trial courts with fairly broad original jurisdiction. Usually, the justices of the peace in a given district comprised the personnel of these courts. Above them was the court of last resort consisting of the governor and his council. Pennsylvania and Massachusetts had separate supreme courts appointed by the governor. Appeals could be carried in certain cases from the colonial courts of last resort to the Privy Council of the King.

The Declaration of Independence

Conflicting interests and claims of the mother country and the colonists eventually resulted in the Revolutionary War. The colonists demanded clarification of their relation

[1] See *supra*, p. 7, for the methods of choosing the governor's council in the royal, proprietary, and corporate colonies.

to the British government, particularly in regard to the appropriate field of external control and the desirable sphere of colonial self-government. They resented the King's treatment of the colonies and such Parliamentary legislation as the navigation laws, acts placing restrictions on trade and manufacturing, enactments imposing customs duties which worked to the disadvantage of the colonists, and tax-levying laws like the Stamp Act of 1765 which proved ineffective and was repealed early in 1766.

The colonists insisted that they were entitled to all of the fundamental rights of Englishmen and that one of these was "no taxation without representation." They desired self-government with respect to their internal affairs and were convinced that the British government was determined to exploit its dependencies for the benefit of the mother country.

The first part of the *Declaration of Independence* (drafted chiefly by Thomas Jefferson and adopted by the Second Continental Congress in 1776) sets forth the fundamental principles of government to which the colonists subscribed. Among a number of assertedly "self-evident" truths were (1) all men are created equal, (2) all are endowed by their Creator with certain unalienable rights, among them life, liberty, and the pursuit of happiness, (3) to secure these rights governments are instituted among men, deriving their just powers from the consent of the governed, and (4) whenever any government becomes destructive of these ends, it is the right of the people to alter or abolish it and to institute a new government, laying its foundation on such principles and organizing its powers in such form as shall seem most likely to effect their safety and happiness.

The second part of the Declaration submits "facts" in

support of the general charge that the history of the King of Great Britain, George III, is a record of repeated injuries and usurpations having the objective of establishing an absolute tyranny over the colonies. King George was accused of withholding assent to important laws beneficial to the colonies; of hampering the functioning of the colonial legislatures in various ways, e.g., by dissolving the elective assemblies and refusing for a long time to cause the election of others; of sending swarms of officers to harass the colonists; and of obstructing the administration of justice by making judges subservient to his will. Many other grievances were listed, some attributed to actions of the King and others to acts of Parliament, e.g., the imposition of taxes without colonial consent and cutting off colonial trade with all parts of the world.

The last paragraph of the Declaration contains the pronouncement that the colonies are, and of right ought to be, free and independent states, that they are absolved of all allegiance to the British Crown, and that all political connection between them and Great Britain is dissolved.

The First State Constitutions

During the years 1776 and 1777, ten of the original and self-proclaimed states drafted and adopted constitutions to replace their colonial charters. The Massachusetts constitution became effective in 1780. Connecticut and Rhode Island, instead of devising new constitutions, merely made a few changes in the charters under which they had functioned during the colonial period.

The Massachusetts constitution was drafted by a constitutional convention and ratified by the people. In the other states the constitutions were prepared by the assemblies and in most instances put into effect without submission to the voting population for approval. New Hampshire followed the Massachusetts procedure when it replaced its 1776 constitution in 1784. About half the states made no provision for an amending process different from the procedure for ordinary lawmaking. Most of the others provided for revision by special conventions; the remaining few established an amending procedure featured by special legislative action.

These first constitutions provided for three branches of government and included guarantees of various individual rights and liberties. As for the type of government, the language of the constitutions indicated adherence to the principles of separation of powers and checks and balances. However, the executive and judicial branches were placed in a position of subordination to the elected legislature which selected the governor in all but three of the states. The governor's powers were strictly limited, whereas few restrictions were placed on the policy-determining authority of the legislature. Terms of office, except in the case of judges, were short, usually a year, and qualifications for voting and for holding office included the ownership of property. Religious requirements were established in some of the states.

The only one of these original constitutions still in effect is that of Massachusetts. It has been amended more than eighty times. Five of the states replaced their first constitutions prior to the end of the eighteenth century (Delaware, Georgia, New Hampshire, Pennsylvania, and South Carolina) and three of these substituted a third constitution for the second during the same period (Georgia—1777, 1789,

1798, New Hampshire—1776, 1784, 1792, and South Carolina—1776, 1778, 1790). New York adopted a new constitution in 1801, but the other states adhered to their original constitutions, although with amendments, for a considerable number of years, viz., Virginia until 1830, New Jersey, 1844, Maryland, 1851, and North Carolina, 1868. Connecticut and Rhode Island replaced their modified colonial charters with new constitutions in 1818 and 1843 respectively.

The first constitutions proved satisfactory in some respects and unsatisfactory in others. Their sundry provisions, their declarations about fundamental principles of government, and especially the experiences of the states under them undoubtedly influenced the political thinking of the Philadelphia delegates who drafted the Constitution of the United States.

The Articles of Confederation

The Second Continental Congress appointed a committee in June, 1776, to prepare a plan for confederation. This committee submitted its report the following month but the proposed scheme of confederation was not adopted by Congress until November, 1777. The required ratification by *all* of the states was finally obtained in 1781.

The Articles of Confederation created a league or association of the thirteen states similar in its essential nature to the former League of Nations and the present United Nations. Its various defects led to the calling of the Philadelphia Convention of 1787 which drafted the still surviving Constitution of the United States.

Governmental Features

The principal organ of government created by the Articles was a unicameral Congress in which each state had but one vote, even though a state could send a delegation of no more than seven nor fewer than two delegates. Delegates were appointed annually by each state in such manner as its legislature directed and these delegates were recallable at any time. No delegate could serve more than three years during a six-year period. The Congress chose a presiding officer with the title "President" but no delegate could serve in this capacity for more than one year out of three. This President was not an executive officer in any sense of the term.

The powers of Congress were limited to the comparatively few that were *expressly* granted. Congress was authorized to manage foreign relations and to enter into treaties and alliances, to declare and conduct war, to build and equip a navy, to determine the size of the land forces which were to be furnished by the states on a quota basis, to appoint the commander-in-chief of these forces, to deal with the Indian tribes, to regulate the alloy and value of coin, to fix the standard of weights and measures, and to establish and regulate postoffices. Congress could borrow money and emit bills of credit, but the power to levy taxes remained in the hands of the states which were supposed to supply the funds requested by Congress to meet expenses incurred for the common defense or general welfare.

Congress was essentially an executive body, as indicated by the nature of the powers delegated to it. In addition to the powers so far mentioned, it was authorized to appoint such committees and civil officers as might be necessary for the management, under its direction, of the affairs of the United States. It also was empowered to appoint a Committee of the States consisting of one delegate per state. This Committee was to function during the recesses of Congress and execute such powers of the Congress as that body chose to delegate, subject, however, to an important restriction. Most of the major powers of Congress were exercisable only with the assent of nine states. These powers could not be delegated to the Committee of States.

The Articles made no provision for a national judiciary. State courts were relied upon for the adjudication of practically all disputes. Congress was authorized to appoint courts for the handling of prize cases and for the trial of piracies and felonies committed on the high seas. The only other exceptions to the settlement of controversies by state courts were jurisdictional disputes between states and cases involving different grants of land to private persons by two or more states. Congress was the last resort on appeal in disputes of this type but its function was to set up judges or commissioners for the settlement of each particular dispute.

Amendments to the Articles of Confederation required favorable action by both Congress and the states. Ratification by the legislature of each state was requisite. Although numerous alterations were proposed, the unanimity rule prevented adoption in every instance.

Defects of the Articles of Confederation

The Articles of Confederation had many serious defects which soon became apparent to its contemporaries. Since efforts to correct them by amendment invariably met with failure, a series of events finally resulted in the calling of the Philadelphia Convention.

The major weakness of the Confederation was the inability of the central government, viz., Congress and its subsidiaries, to act directly on the individual inhabitants of the states. It had to rely on state enforcement of its policies and lacked authority to compel the states to discharge this and other responsibilities. An attempt to coerce the states would have required resort to military force and that would have meant war. Such action was not sanctioned by the Articles. Furthermore, the land forces at the disposal of Congress were composed only of such men as the states were willing to provide. This arrangement was another defect of the Articles.

The same situation existed in regard to revenue. Congress depended on state contributions of money. If the states failed to provide the funds needed by the central government, no effective remedy was available. Congress possessed borrowing power but its credit was impaired because the power to levy taxes was not included among its delegated powers.

Failure to provide for national regulation of commerce was another serious weakness of the Articles. It resulted in interstate conflict and recrimination. Short-sighted state action was damaging to the country as a whole and to financial, commercial, and manufacturing interests in particular. Although Congress could regulate trade with the Indians and enter into commercial treaties with foreign countries, it was unable to deal with the problems of foreign commerce in other ways and had no control whatsoever over commerce among the states.

Other defects worthy of mention include (1) the requirement that an affirmative vote of nine of the thirteen states was necessary to exercise of the most important of the few powers granted to Congress; (2) the unanimity rule in regard to amendment of the Articles; and (3) failure to provide for a national judiciary. Lack of at least a national court of last resort meant that the courts of each state were final interpreters of acts of Congress and of treaties to which the Confederacy was a party.

Broadly speaking, the Articles proved unsatisfactory because of the weakness of the central government. Its limited powers and its inability to enforce conformity to its policies and to the provisions of the Articles gave rise to situations which led to the movement for a stronger union. The ineffectiveness of union under the Articles was foreshadowed by the following stipulation in Article II of this document: "Each State retains its sovereignty, freedom, and independence, and every power, jurisdiction and right, which is not by this confederation expressly delegated to the United States, in Congress assembled."

The Constitution of the United States

The Philadelphia Convention was held in 1787. It was called by Congress after considering a recommendation to that effect by the Annapolis Convention of 1786 which was attended by the delegates of only five states. A total of fifty-five delegates from all of the states except Rhode Island eventually assembled in Philadelphia and participated in the drafting of the Constitution of the United States.

The delegates considered various proposals for a stronger union, among them the Virginia and New Jersey plans, and the final product of their deliberations was derived from these and other sources, including the Articles of Confederation, the state constitutions, and the political institutions and experiences of the colonial period. Upon completion of its task of framing a constitution, the Convention submitted its handiwork to Congress and recommended that state conventions be held for the purpose of ratifying the proposed constitution. It also suggested that ratification by nine states be sufficient for placing the new constitution in operation.

Most of the delegates were in agreement with respect to the desirability of certain general features of the governmental system to be established, viz., a division of powers between the national government and the states; a stronger national government; guarantee of the supremacy of the constitution and national laws; and a national government, republican in form, organized in accordance with the doctrines of separation of powers and checks and balances. Various features of the new system were the products of compromise. The most notable of these was the Connecticut Compromise which provided for a bicameral legislature with strictly equal representation of the states in one house and representation according to population in the other.

Main Body of the Constitution

The main body of the Constitution, as drafted and as it now exists, consists of a preamble and seven articles. Comparatively few changes in the original provisions of these articles have been made.[2]

THE PREAMBLE   The preamble states the purposes which the framers had in mind, viz., a more perfect union, the establishment of justice, domestic tranquillity, common defense, promotion of the general welfare, and securement of the blessings of liberty. Neither the national government nor the states derive powers from the preamble.

ARTICLE I   Article I deals with the legislative branch of the national government. It prescribes the structure of Congress, the methods of selecting its members, terms of office, qualifications for membership, and other organizational features. Equally important are enumeration of the powers of Congress, stipulations concerning lawmaking procedure, and specific limitations on the powers of both Congress and the states.

ARTICLE II   The second article is devoted to the executive branch, in particular the Presidency and Vice Presidency. It designates the method of selecting the President and Vice President, their terms of office, and their required qualifications. Provision is made for removal of these and other civil officers of the United States through the impeachment process. Several parts of this article itemize the powers and responsibilities of the President.

ARTICLE III   The subject matter of Article III is the national judiciary. Judicial power is vested in one Supreme

[2] The amendments which have altered some of the original provisions are the 11th, 12th, 13th, 14th, 16th, 17th, 20th, 22nd, 23rd, 24th, 25th, and 26th,

Court and such inferior courts as Congress may establish. The method of selection and the tenure of office of judges are specified and the jurisdiction of the national judiciary is prescribed in detail. In addition to a definition of treason and certain requirements for conviction of this crime, a few procedural requisites for criminal trials in national courts are enumerated.

ARTICLE IV The fourth article, besides empowering Congress to admit new states into the union and to govern territorial possessions of the United States, establishes several obligations of the national government to the states and of the states to one another. An example of the first type of obligation is the duty of the national government to protect the states against invasion; of the second, the stipulation that each state shall give full faith and credit to the public acts, records, and judicial proceedings of every other state.

ARTICLE V Article V prescribes the process for formal amendment of the Constitution. A single permanent limitation on the amending agencies is included, viz., no state may be deprived of its equal suffrage in the Senate without its consent.

ARTICLE VI The most important provision of this article establishes the supremacy of the Constitution, national laws, and treaties over conflicting provisions of state constitutions and laws. Also, all officials of both the national government and the states are required to take an oath, or to make an affirmation, in support of the Constitution.

ARTICLE VII The final article, VII, is known as the schedule. It merely provided that the Constitution was to

become effective when ratified by the conventions of nine
states.

The Twenty-Six Amendments;
Twenty-Seventh (Proposed)

Of the twenty-six amendments, the first twelve were proposed and ratified during the period 1791 to 1804. Three
more were added from 1865 to 1870 inclusive. The remaining eleven became effective during the years 1913 to 1971.

THE FIRST TEN AMENDMENTS   The first ten amendments were proposed and ratified in fulfillment of an understanding, at the time state conventions were considering the
new constitution, that specific guarantees of individual rights
against invasive action by the national government would
be added through the amending process. Eight of these
amendments constitute what is known as the Federal Bill
of Rights and contain guarantees of both substantive rights,
e.g., religious freedom and freedom of speech, and procedural rights, e.g., trial by jury and the rule that no person
shall be compelled in any criminal case to be a witness
against himself. These amendments have always been construed as limitations on the national government rather than
on the states—an interpretation endorsed by the Supreme
Court in *Barron v. Baltimore*.[3] In recent years, however, the
provisions of many of these amendments have been "read"
into the due process clause of the Fourteenth Amendment
by the Supreme Court.[3a] The Ninth Amendment states that
the enumeration of certain rights in the Constitution shall

[3] 7 Peters 242 (1833)
[3a] *Infra*, pp. 79, 82.

not be construed to deny or disparage others retained by the people; the Tenth provides that powers not delegated to the national government, nor denied to the states, are reserved to the states respectively, or to the people. Instead of being a guarantee of individual rights, the latter amendment is a statement of principle concerning the division of powers between the national government and the states. Its purpose was to emphasize the fact that the national government possesses only such powers as have been granted to it.

THE ELEVENTH AMENDMENT   The Eleventh Amendment prohibits the national courts from exercising jurisdiction in cases instituted by citizens or aliens against one of the states. This amendment was a direct consequence of the case of *Chisholm v. Georgia*,[4] in which the Supreme Court had ruled that individuals could sue the states without the consent of the latter.

THE TWELFTH AMENDMENT   The election of 1800 resulted in a tie electoral vote between Jefferson and Burr. Jefferson, who was the Republican party's Presidential candidate, nearly lost out to his running mate, Burr, when the House of Representatives was faced with a choice between the two. To prevent a recurrence of this situation, the Twelfth Amendment provides for distinct electoral ballots for President and Vice President as a substitute for the stipulation in Article II that presidential electors are to vote for two persons and that the person with the largest majority shall be the President and the one with the next largest the Vice President. It also states that the House of Representatives is to choose one of the three highest as President, if no

[4] 2 Dallas 419 (1793).

person obtains a majority, and that the Senate is to select a Vice President from the two highest receiving votes for that position, provided no one secures majority support.

THE THIRTEENTH, FOURTEENTH, AND FIFTEENTH AMENDMENTS   The Civil War led to the adoption of three amendments. Slavery is abolished by the Thirteenth and disqualification for voting on account of race, color, or previous condition of servitude is forbidden by the Fifteenth. The Fourteenth Amendment defines United States and state citizenship. It also prohibits the states from abridging the privileges and immunities of United States citizens, from depriving any person of life, liberty, or property without due process of law, and from denying to any person the equal protection of the laws. The foregoing are the most important provisions of the Fourteenth Amendment.

THE SIXTEENTH AMENDMENT   The Sixteenth Amendment was added in 1913 because of the Supreme Court's ruling in 1894 that an income tax had to be apportioned among the states according to population. This amendment authorizes Congress to levy income taxes without apportionment among the several states.

THE SEVENTEENTH AMENDMENT   Amendment Seventeen provides for popular election of United States senators. From 1789 to 1913 members of the upper chamber of Congress were selected by the legislatures of the several states.

THE EIGHTEENTH AND TWENTY-FIRST AMENDMENTS   The Eighteenth Amendment established prohibition throughout the United States and all territory subject to its jurisdiction. This noble experiment was terminated by adoption of a repealing amendment, the Twenty-First, in 1933.

THE NINETEENTH AMENDMENT The Nineteenth Amendment prohibits both the national government and the states from denying the right of United States citizens to vote on account of sex. Although commonly referred to as a guarantee of woman's suffrage, this amendment affords protection for males as well as females.

THE TWENTIETH AMENDMENT The Twentieth Amendment changed the month of beginning of the terms of President, Vice President, and members of Congress from March to January. By specifying January 20th for commencement of the terms of President and Vice President and January 3rd for those of members of Congress, this amendment eliminates what was referred to as the "lame duck" session of Congress which had begun in December and ended on March 4th of the following year. It specifies January 3rd as the day on which the first session of Congress is to be held unless Congress, by law, establishes a different date. The amendment also designates who is to become President or act as President if the President-elect shall have died before taking office, or shall have failed to qualify, or if no President shall have been chosen prior to beginning of the Presidential term.

THE TWENTY-SECOND AMENDMENT The Twenty-Second Amendment provides that no person shall be elected to the office of President more than twice. Until Franklin D. Roosevelt was elected for four successive terms, the two-term tradition had been adhered to for 150 years.

THE TWENTY-THIRD AMENDMENT In 1961 the Twenty-Third Amendment was ratified. It authorizes the District of Columbia to appoint, in a manner determinable by Congress, the number of Presidential and Vice Presidential electors to which it would be entitled if it were a state, subject to the limitation that the District's electoral vote shall not exceed that of the least populous state in the union.

THE TWENTY-FOURTH AMENDMENT Amendment Twenty-Four concerns voting in a primary or other election for President or Vice President, for electors for President or Vice President, or for Senator or Representative in Congress. It prohibits both the national government and the states from denying citizens the right to vote in these elections by reason of failure to pay any poll or other tax.

THE TWENTY-FIFTH AMENDMENT The Twenty-Fifth Amendment was ratified early in 1967. One of its provisions pertains to a vacancy in the office of Vice President. The President is authorized to nominate a Vice President who shall take office upon confirmation by a majority vote of both houses of Congress. However, this amendment deals primarily with cases of Presidential disability. Its specific provisions will be summarized in a subsequent chapter.

THE TWENTY-SIXTH AMENDMENT The Twenty-Sixth Amendment became effective in 1971. It provides that the right of citizens of the United States to vote, if eighteen years of age or older, shall not be denied or abridged by the United States or by any State on account of age.

THE TWENTY-SEVENTH AMENDMENT (Submitted, 1972, to states for ratification) This proposed amendment stipulates that equality of rights under the law shall not be denied or abridged by the United States or by any State on account of sex.

Processes of Constitutional Change

The foregoing summary of the contents of twenty-six ratified amendments indicates the nature of the alterations which have been made in the Constitution as a document. Modifications also have occurred in ways not involving changes in the Constitution's wording, *viz.* by interpretation, by custom and usage, and by auxiliary legislation, sometimes referred to as statutory amplification. These processes of change will be explained and exemplified after consideration of the procedure for formal amendment.

The Amending Procedure

Amendments may be proposed either by Congress or by a convention called by Congress on application of the legislatures of two-thirds of the states. A two-thirds vote of each house of Congress, provided a quorum be assembled, is requisite for proposal by that body. As a matter of law, the President is excluded from participation in the amending process, but as a matter of fact he may be able to influence the action taken by the House and the Senate.

Proposed amendments become effective only if ratified by three-fourths of the states. Congress is authorized to specify which of two state agencies is to decide for or against ratification—either the state legislatures or state conventions. So far, all amendments have been proposed by Congress and all but one submitted for ratification to the state legislatures. In the case of the Twenty-First Amendment (which repealed the Eighteenth), state conventions were designated by Congress as the ratifying agencies. Under no circumstances may a state act through some agency other than a convention or its legislature, for example, by transferring the power of decision to its qualified voters.

The only exception to the procedure just described is that no state, without its consent, shall be deprived of its equal suffrage in the Senate. Unanimous rather than three-fourths approval is required for departure from strictly equal representation of the states in the upper house.

Established practice in connection with ratification is that a state which has rejected a proposed amendment may subsequently change its vote to the affirmative, whereas an affirmative vote may not be replaced by a later vote in the negative. Congress may establish a time limit within which ratification by the states must occur, as it did by designating a seven-year period when the Eighteenth, Twentieth, Twenty-First, Twenty-Second, and Twenty-Fifth amendments were submitted to the states. It is the sole judge of whether, by lapse of time, a proposed amendment has lost its vitality and is no longer ratifiable.[5] The child labor amendment, for instance, proposed in 1924 is still open to ratification by the states.

The amending process is difficult because of the requirement of extraordinary majorities for both proposal and ratification. It is easier than was the mode of altering the Articles of Confederation which required ratification by all of the states. Some advocates of simplification have suggested that ordinary rather than extraordinary majorities should be sufficient for both proposal and ratification. Other critics have

---

[5] *Coleman v. Miller*, 307 U. S. 433 (1939).

objected to ratification by legislatures or conventions. A direct popular vote on proposed amendments has been favored. One suggestion along this line was made many years ago, viz., that a majority popular vote in a majority of the states, together with a nation-wide popular majority, should be the requirement for ratification. Past proposals for change have been rejected and at the present time alteration of the amending process seems highly improbable.

The Supreme Court has held that there are no limitations on the subject matter of proposed amendments. Thus the Constitution may be amended to substitute Congressional selection of the President for choice by the electoral college, to provide for the election rather than the appointment of Federal judges, or, to give but one more example, to eliminate various guarantees of individual rights.

Change by Interpretation

The written handiwork of men, by reason of the limitations of language, commonly gives rise to controversy concerning the meaning of words and phrases. Consequently, change through interpretation and reinterpretation usually occurs, as it has in the case of the documentary Constitution of the United States.

The initiative in interpreting the Constitution lies with the active branches of the national government, i.e., the President and Congress, and, in the case of the states, with their legislative and executive agencies. Initially, Congress decides on the character and scope of the powers granted to it; the President does the same in regard to his constitutionally conferred authority; and the states, too, determine whether contemplated action falls within the scope of their "reserved" pow-

ers. Action follows interpretation and unless the issue of
constitutionality is raised in a court case, legislative and executive determinations of the meaning of the Constitution prevail. If the validity of governmental action is challenged in
the course of litigation, the courts have an opportunity to
decide whether violation of the Constitution has occurred.
The conclusions of the Supreme Court are customarily accepted as final.

Broadly speaking, the Supreme Court is possessor of the
authority of the last word. There are exceptions. Thus the
Constitution makes each house of Congress judge of the
election, returns, and qualifications of its members and authorizes each house to expel its members by a two-thirds
vote. Presumably, the door is closed to judicial review of the
decisions of each of the two chambers of the legislative
branch. Again, some issues arising under the Constitution
have been said to involve "political" rather than "justiciable"
questions. These are subject to final settlement by the political branches of the government, viz., the legislative and/or
the executive. However, the line of demarcation between
the political and the justiciable is drawn, and may be re-
drawn, by the Supreme Court.[6]

Throughout this text reference will be made to constitutional modification through interpretation and reinterpretation. Only one example will be presented at this point. Many
policies of Congress have been based on its conclusions concerning "valid" exercises of its power to regulate foreign and
interstate commerce. It relied on this power in enacting child
labor legislation in 1916. When this action was declared unconstitutional by the Supreme Court, it resorted in 1919 to

---

[6] See *Baker v. Carr*, 369 U. S. 186 (1962); *Wesberry v. Sanders*, 376
U.S. 1 (1964); *Reynolds v. Sims*, 377 U.S. 533 (1964).

its power to levy taxes. This second effort met with the same fate as the first, with the result that the Child Labor Amendment was proposed. The amendment remains unratified, but the need for it was lessened when, in 1941, the Supreme Court upheld the Fair Labor Standards Act of 1938 as a legitimate exercise of the commerce power.[7] In so doing the Court overruled its earlier decision in *Hammer v. Dagenhart*[8] which had invalidated the Child Labor Law of 1916 on the ground that its enactment constituted an abuse of the power to regulate commerce. Thus an important constitutional modification was achieved in 1941 merely by reinterpretation of the same words in the Constitution.

Change by Custom and Usage

Custom and usage have played an important part in the constitutional history of the United States. The written words of the Constitution fail to reveal what actually occurs in the functioning of the political institutions of this country. Two illustrations will demonstrate the point.

Selection of the President by the electoral college has worked out differently than anticipated by the framers of the Constitution. They expected presidential electors to exercise personal discretion in casting their ballots. However, the development of political parties had the effect of causing electors to vote for the nominees of their respective parties. Since departures from this custom rarely occur, the electoral college merely registers the result of the popular vote along partisan lines.

The role of the President in the governmental process is far greater than depicted by the Constitution. He functions

[7] *United States v. Darby*, 312 U.S. 100.
[8] 247 U.S. 251 (1918).

as a popular, party, and legislative leader and his influence is frequently so great that the legislative branch is placed in a position of subordination to the executive.

Change by Auxiliary Legislation

Listing "auxiliary legislation" as a mode of constitutional modification may create the impression that legislative alteration of constitutional provisions is permissible. Such is not the case. What is meant is that some parts of the Constitution require legislative action to make them operative. Self-executing provisions are distinguishable from those which are non-self-executing.

The Constitution provides for a Supreme Court but an act of Congress is necessary to fix its size which is alterable at any time. Congress, too, pursuant to express or implied constitutional authorization, is the creator of inferior courts and such administrative agencies as the major departments and the independent regulatory commissions. In providing for choice of the President by an electoral college, the framers of the Constitution specified that electors were to be appointed in such manner as the legislatures of the states may direct. So state legislation is requisite for the choice of electors. Although popular election of presidential electors is now provided for by all of the states, legislative selection of these electors was preferred by a number of states for a considerable period after the Constitution became effective. Another example of the need for auxiliary legislation is prescription of the times, places, and manner of holding elections for Senators and Representatives.

The Living Constitution

The primary function of a constitution is to establish the fundamental features of a system of government. But a documentary constitution does not commence living until placed in operation and once its life begins and continues, a reading of the document is insufficient to convey full understanding of the system which it has created.

The living constitution includes the document, all of the interpretations of its various provisions, modifying customs and usages, and auxiliary legislation. An instrument of government which "lives" undergoes transformation throughout its existence. That is why continuous examination of the constitutional foundation of a governmental system is essential. The framers of the Constitution of the United States, although unable to foresee future developments, undoubtedly anticipated that it would be transformed in one way or another in the course of its life. So it has been in the past and will be in the years ahead.

Governmental Powers and Intergovernmental Relations

C H A P T E R ☆ T W O

A Federal System of Government
   Supremacy of the National Government
Powers of the National Government
   Express and Implied Powers
      "Commerce" Power
      Taxing Power
      Treaty-Making Power
      War Powers
   Source of National Powers in Field of Foreign Affairs
   Limitations on the Exercise of National Powers
Powers of the States
   Reserved Powers
   Limitations on Powers of the States
Exclusive and Concurrent Powers
   Determining Factors
Powers of Units of Local Government
Obligations of the National Government to the States
   Respect for Territorial Integrity and Legal Equality
   Guarantee of Republican Form of Government
   Protection Against Invasion and Domestic Violence

Obligations of the States to One Another
    Full Faith and Credit Clause
    Rendition of Fugitives from Justice
    Privileges and Immunities of State Citizens
Obligations of the States to the National Government and
    the Union
Intergovernmental Cooperation
    National Services to the States and Local Units
    State Assistance to Local Units
    Interstate Cooperation
    Interlocal Cooperative Activity

☆ ☆ ☆ ☆ ☆ ☆ ☆ ☆ ☆ ☆ ☆ ☆ ☆

Governing authority in the United States, although extensive, is limited in various ways. The Constitution restricts the powers of both the national government and the states. Moreover, state governments operate under the additional restrictive provisions of state constitutions.

Governmental controls and services have been expanding steadily for a great many years, but this expansion has been due primarily to the more frequent and more extensive exercise of previously possessed powers than to an increase of power through the process of constitutional amendment. In the case of the national government, an increasingly liberal interpretation of its delegated authority enables it to do many things which at one time were thought to lie beyond the scope of its delineated jurisdiction.

A Federal System of Government

A federal rather than a unitary system of government exists in the United States.[9] Under the latter type of system, national authorities prescribe the powers exercisable by major and minor units of local government, whereas under the former, powers are divided by *constitutional provision* between the national government on the one hand and major governmental subdivisions on the other. Unlike a confederation, which is an association of independent states, a genuine federation transforms previously independent states into political components of a single state. It took a civil war in the United States to settle a long-standing dispute about the nature of the union created by the Constitution as drafted in 1787.

A number of features of the Constitution are conducive to preservation of the federal principle which is determinative of the respective roles of the national government and the states in the general governmental process. The Constitution is amendable only by joint action of the national government and the states; the states have a voice in the functioning of the national government, being represented in both houses of Congress and participating in the selection of a President; and the judicial settlement of constitutional controversies promotes respect for the Constitution as the supreme law of the land. The Supreme Court, an organ of the national government, is the ultimate deciding agency in

[9] The federal principle controls the relations between the national government and the states. As for the states, their governmental systems are classifiable as unitary inasmuch as state governments, with minor exceptions, possess authority to create units of local government and prescribe the nature and extent of their powers.

cases involving constitutional disputes. Although expected to deal impartially with disputes concerning the distribution of power between the national government and the states, this highest tribunal has been inclined to look favorably upon claims to power by the national government, largely because of social developments increasing the number and variety of problems of nation-wide concern.

Supremacy of The National Government

A fundamental precept of constitutional law is the supremacy of the national government within the sphere of its legitimate functions. Article VI of the Constitution provides: "This Constitution, and the laws of the United States, which shall be made in pursuance thereof; and all Treaties made, or which shall be made, under the Authority of the United States, shall be the supreme law of the land; and the Judges in every State shall be bound thereby, any Thing in the Constitution or laws of any State to the Contrary notwithstanding."

In various cases decided over the years, the Supreme Court has given effect to this supremacy clause. It has adhered to the rule that no state may interfere with or obstruct the valid instrumentalities and operations of the national government.

Powers of The National Government

In the field of domestic affairs, the national government possesses only such powers as have been delegated to it by the Constitution, either *expressly* or *by implication*. Few powers have been added to the original grant by formal amendment. The greatly increased authority of the national government is attributable to extremely generous interpretation of its various enumerated powers, particularly the power of Congress to regulate foreign and interstate commerce, to lay and collect taxes, and to make all laws necessary and proper for carrying into execution all powers vested by the Constitution in the government of the United States.

Broad and liberal interpretation has kept pace with changing social conditions. Matters which at one time were essentially of local significance have become matters of vital interest to the nation as a whole. The initial distribution of powers, prescribed in 1787 in consideration of 18th century conditions, remains suitable today only because of a decidedly progressive interpretation of the words and phrases originally used in specifying the sphere of authority of the national government.

Express Powers

Express powers are those listed, itemized, or enumerated in the Constitution, such as "Congress shall have Power to lay and collect Taxes . . . ; to borrow money on the credit of the United States," and "to regulate Commerce with foreign Nations, and among the several States. . . ." Some of the authority delegated to the national government is indicated by express grants of power to the executive and judicial branches, viz., the President "shall have Power, by and with the advice and Consent of the Senate, to make Treaties, provided two-thirds of the Senators present concur" and the judicial power "shall extend to all Cases, in

Law and Equity, arising under this Constitution, the Laws of the United States, and Treaties made, or which shall be made, under their Authority. . . ."

Implied Powers

Implied powers are those inferable from one or more express grants of authority.[10] The doctrine of implied powers accounts for a substantial proportion of the powers now recognized as exercisable by the national government.

The case of *McCulloch v. Maryland* [11] stands as a major milepost in the constitutional history of the United States because of Supreme Court endorsement of the doctrine of implied powers, broad interpretation of the expressly granted powers of Congress, and the principle of national supremacy. Two basic constitutional issues were involved in the case: (1) whether Congress, in the absence of an express grant of authority to do so, could incorporate a bank and (2) whether a state could tax an instrumentality of the national government.

Chief Justice Marshall, speaking for the Court, called attention to the constitutional provision authorizing Congress to make "all laws which shall be necessary and proper, for carrying into execution the foregoing powers, and all other powers vested by this Constitution, in the government of the United States, or in any department thereof." He subscribed to the view of the broad constructionists that "necessary and proper" meant appropriate, useful, and convenient,

[10] If the basis of inference consists of two or more express grants or the totality of expressly delegated authority, the power so derived is sometimes referred to as a "resulting" power. But it is merely an implied power with a broad basis of inference.

[11] 4 Wheaton 316 (1819).

rather than indispensable—as had been contended by the strict constructionists. Marshall maintained that the creation of a bank was an appropriate way of implementing such expressly granted powers as "the great powers to lay and collect taxes; to borrow money; to regulate commerce; to declare and conduct war; and to raise and support armies and navies."

The other issue in the *McCulloch* case, the constitutionality of the Maryland tax levy, was disposed of by calling attention to the supremacy clause of Article VI. Maryland's tax was declared unconstitutional as applied to the branch of the United States bank on the ground that the states have no power, by taxation or otherwise, to retard, impede, burden, or in any manner control, the operation of the constitutional laws enacted by Congress to carry into execution the powers vested in the general government.

The grants of power to regulate foreign and interstate commerce and to lay and collect taxes have enabled the national government to do many things by implication which are not even suggested by the express language of the Constitution. Among other important sources of implied powers are the power to declare war, raise and support armies and a navy, and enter into treaties with other countries.

The "Commerce" Power

The words "commerce" and "regulate" have been broadly construed. Commerce covers much more than buying and selling transactions. It includes navigation; transportation by railroads, busses, and aircraft; the transmission of electric power, oil, gas, and water; communication by telephone, telegraph, radio, and television; and other varieties of intercourse. If state lines are crossed, the commerce qualifies as "interstate," even if a particular act of commerce begins and ends in the same state. The phrase "to regulate" means more than prescribing the rules to be observed in carrying on interstate commerce. It also permits protection, promotion, restriction, and prohibition of various kinds of commerce. As liberally interpreted, for example, the commerce clause has been held to justify national legislation making it a federal crime to transport women across state lines for immoral purposes, to knowingly drive a stolen automobile from one state to another, and to carry a kidnapped person across state borders.

Among the subjects concededly falling within the scope of the reserved powers of the states are manufacturing, agriculture, mining, labor-management relations, and intrastate commerce. The Supreme Court has ruled that the first four do not constitute commerce and that the last one is not included within the meaning of the phrase "interstate commerce." Nevertheless, all of these matters, under certain circumstances, are subject to national control. Outstanding examples of the far-reaching implications of the commerce power are afforded by two comparatively recent cases, viz., *United States v. Darby*[12] and *Wickard v. Filburn.*[13]

In the *Darby* case the constitutionality of the Fair Labor Standards Act of 1938 was challenged. The *Wickard* controversy involved the Agricultural Adjustment Act of 1938 which endeavored to stabilize agricultural production. Wickard had exceeded the wheat acreage quota assigned him and

[12] 312 U. S. 100 (1941).
[13] 317 U. S. 111 (1942).

contended that his excess wheat production was to be consumed only on his farm and not shipped in interstate commerce.

Although conceding that manufacturing, labor conditions, and agriculture fall outside the meaning of "commerce," the Supreme Court upheld the constitutionality of both acts of Congress. It asserted that the power of Congress to regulate interstate commerce extends to the control, through legislative action, of intrastate activities which have *a substantial effect* on that commerce or the exercise of Congressional power over it.

The Taxing Power

The power to lay and collect taxes also has opened the door, by implication, to national activity not expressly authorized by the Constitution. Even though the national government lacks general authority *to legislate* for the purpose of promoting the general welfare, it is explicitly authorized *to levy taxes* in furtherance of this objective. The taxing power provides a constitutional basis for the adoption of policies which otherwise may only be established by the states. A significant example is the Social Security Act of 1935 and its subsequent amendments. In cases challenging the constitutionality of the unemployment insurance and old-age benefit features of the act,[14] the Supreme Court held that the tax levied is for a public purpose; no unlawful invasion of the reserved powers of the states is involved;

---

[14] *Steward Machine Co. v. Davis*, 301 U. S. 548 (1937)—unemployment insurance; *Helvering v. Davis*, 301 U. S. 619 (1937)—old-age benefits.

and the states are neither compelled to participate in the security program nor coerced into abandoning governmental functions which they are not permitted to surrender.

The grant of power to raise and spend money for public purposes provides constitutional justification for federal grants-in-aid to the states and local units. Although states and local governments are not legally obliged to accept these grants, the social and political pressure in favor of acceptance is great. If the grants-in-aid are conditional, as so many of them are, the accepting governments are bound to conform to the purposes designated by Congress and also to such standards of performance as the national authorities prescribe. In this way the national government is able to achieve objectives which fall outside the scope of its delegated regulatory authority, e.g., hospital construction, education, including school-lunch programs, and urban re-development.

Congress sometimes levies taxes for the purpose of regulating matters not included within its granted lawmaking authority. Its primary objective may be moral, economic, or social in character, as exemplified by the taxing of sales of marihuana and the taxation of transfers of machine guns, sawed-off shotguns, and silencers. Generally speaking, the Supreme Court will uphold regulatory and destructive taxes if a tax is "on its face" a revenue measure, regardless of the Congressional motive in levying the tax. However, if the Court concludes that a particular tax is a penalty, it will declare it unconstitutional, as it did when Congress imposed a tax of 10% on the annual net profits of mines, factories, and other establishments employing child labor in disregard of standards established by the national government.[15]

[15] *Bailey v. Drexel Furniture Company*, 259 U. S. 20 (1922).

The Treaty-Making Power

The treaty-making power is another grant of authority which permits national control of matters normally falling within the reserved powers of the states. Treaties may deal with any matters which are an appropriate subject of international agreement, e.g., the rights and duties of aliens of a particular nationality residing in the United States. The provisions of such a treaty supersede conflicting state legislation. *Missouri v. Holland* [16] is a case pertinent to the subject under consideration. The Supreme Court upheld a 1918 act of Congress providing protection for migratory birds *in pursuance of a treaty* entered into with Great Britain for that purpose in 1916. Earlier legislation by Congress in 1913 had been declared unconstitutional by the lower federal courts on the ground that control of bird life was not covered by the powers granted Congress.

The War Powers

This consideration of implied powers will be terminated by reference to Congress's expressly granted powers to declare war, raise and support armies, and provide and maintain a navy. These powers enable the national government to do many things not expressly authorized by the Constitution, e.g., the establishment of compulsory military service, and when the United States is engaged in war, the powers of the national government, by implication, come close to being unlimited. A case in point is the placement of United States citizens of Japanese extraction in "war relocation

[16] 252 U. S. 416 (1920).

centers." This military evacuation program was upheld as constitutional in *Korematsu v. United States.*[17]

Source of National Powers in Respect of Foreign Affairs

Until rather recently, it was commonly believed that the national government possessed only such powers as have been *delegated* to it either expressly or by implication. The Supreme Court has concluded that there is a single exception to this general rule. In *United States v. Curtiss-Wright Corporation et al.,*[18] it asserted that a fundamental difference exists between the powers of the national government in respect to foreign or external affairs and those pertaining to domestic or internal affairs. In the field of internal affairs, the doctrine of delegated powers is categorically true. Not so, in the area of foreign affairs. Said the Court: ". . . the investment of the federal government with the powers of external sovereignty did not depend upon the affirmative grants of the Constitution. The powers to declare and wage war, to conclude peace, to make treaties, to maintain diplomatic relations with other sovereignties, if they had never been mentioned in the Constitution, would have vested in the federal government as necessary concomitants of nationality. . . ."

Limitations on the Exercise of National Powers

In exercising its many powers, the national government must abide by various expressed and implied limitations on

[17] 323 U. S. 214 (1945).
[18] 299 U. S. 304 (1936).

its authority. Examples of restrictions specifically stated in the Constitution are the following: no tax or duty shall be laid on articles exported from any state; Congress shall make no law respecting an establishment of religion, or prohibiting the free exercise thereof, or abridging the freedom of speech or of the press; no persons shall be deprived of life, liberty, or property without due process of law; and private property shall not be taken for public use without just compensation.

Implied limitations on the powers of the national government are comparatively few in number. National authorities may not exercise powers reserved exclusively to the states or use their delegated powers to attain unconstitutional objectives, such as requiring the states to pay taxes that have the effect of directly burdening or substantially interfering with the discharge of *governmental functions* by state governments and their instrumentalities.[19] Nor may Congress deprive particular states of the legal equality which all of the states are entitled to under the Constitution.

Powers of The States

The Tenth Amendment states: "The powers not delegated to the United States by the Constitution, nor prohibited by it to the states, are reserved to the states respectively, or to the people." More accurately, since some powers are concurrent, the states may exercise powers which have not been

[19] Although officials and employees of state and local governments no longer enjoy immunity from the payment of federal income taxes on their salaries, the owners of state and municipal bonds are still exempt from federal taxation of the interest earnings of such bonds.

denied them or granted *exclusively* to the national government.

Reserved Powers

Except for a few express grants of authority, the powers of the states are correctly described as "reserved" or "residual" because of the understanding at the time of the Constitution's framing that the states retained all powers other than those denied them or granted solely to the national government. No enumeration of state powers was therefore necessary. State authority extends to numerous matters. Some of the many subjects falling within the reserved jurisdiction of the states are criminal law, property and contract rights, inheritance, marriage and divorce, education, conservation, public health, police and fire protection, highway construction and maintenance, manufacturing, mining, agriculture, traffic regulation, intrastate commerce, and local government.

The reserved authority of the states includes what is referred to in legal parlance as "the police power." It is definable as the right to impose restrictions on individual liberty and on the use of property in order to safeguard or promote the public health, safety, morals, convenience, and general welfare. The police power is by no means absolute. Particular exercises of this power must satisfy the requirements of due process of law and equal protection of the laws, as well as other constitutional limitations. Generally speaking, this power justifies only reasonable restraints on individual behavior; arbitrary, capricious, and unduly oppressive governmental action is precluded.

Most of the few powers conferred on the states by express constitutional stipulation pertain to the organizational features of the national government. Examples are the right of the states to appoint presidential electors in such manner as their legislatures direct and the right of the people of each state to select members of Congress. In addition, state legislatures are authorized to apply to Congress for the calling of a national constitutional convention; the states are to decide on the fate of proposed amendments to the Constitution; and the consent of the legislatures of the states concerned is required for the creation of new states within the jurisdiction of any state or by the junction of two or more states or parts of states.

Limitations on the Powers of the States

Among express denials of power to the states are the following: no state shall enter into a treaty, alliance, or confederation; coin money; emit bills of credit; pass any law impairing the obligation of contracts; abridge the privileges or immunities of United States citizens; deprive any person of life, liberty, or property without due process of law; or deny to any person within its jurisdiction the equal protection of the laws.

There are also implied limitations. The states may not interfere with the legitimate operations of the national government, tax its instrumentalities, or exercise their powers within the boundaries of other states of the union. Nor may states secede from the union which, according to the Supreme Court, is an indestructible union composed of indestructible states.[20]

[20] *Texas v. White*, 7 Wallace 724 (1869).

Exclusive and Concurrent Powers

Some powers are exercisable only by the national government, others only by the states, and still others by both the national government and the states. Whether particular powers are *exclusive* or *concurrent* depends on a number of considerations.

Determining Factors

First, the Constitution may state expressly that a specific power is exercisable only by a designated government. The sole provision which does so is the one which authorizes Congress to exercise *exclusive legislation* over the seat of government of the United States, viz., the District of Columbia, and over places purchased with state consent for the erection of forts, magazines, arsenals, dock-yards, and other needful buildings.

Second, the exclusiveness of a certain power may be due to grant of the power to one government and denial of the same power to the other. Thus the national government is authorized to coin money, whereas this power is expressly denied to the states.

Third, in one instance the concurrent character of a power is based on an express grant of precisely the same power to both the national government and the states. State legislatures are authorized to prescribe the times and manner of holding elections for Senators and Representatives, but Congress may make or alter such regulations.

Fourth, the exclusive or concurrent character of a power may depend entirely on inferences drawn from the nature of the power, the nation-wide jurisdiction of the national government, and the limited territorial jurisdiction of the states. Ultimate determination of the impliedly exclusive or concurrent character of powers rests with the courts.

Powers granted the national government fall in the "exclusive" category *by implication* if uniformity of policy throughout the country is deemed necessary and the states, by reason of their restricted territorial jurisdiction, are obviously unable to deal effectively with problems of nation-wide rather than essentially local significance. National powers which are exclusive by implication include, *among others*, authority to establish a uniform rule of naturalization; power to dispose of and make all needful rules and regulations respecting the territory or other property belonging to the United States; the admission of new states to the union; and control over foreign affairs.

The powers of the states which are exclusive by implication are those which lie outside the scope of powers expressly or impliedly vested in the national government. Examples are control over education, the private property rights of citizens, and local government.

Concurrent powers are exercisable by both the national government and the states. Except for the single instance noted above, all of the powers falling in the "concurrent" category have been placed there by implication. An excellent example is the taxing power. Express delegation of this power to Congress has not been construed as prohibiting exercise of the same power by the states. The states never intended to deprive themselves of authority to raise the revenue necessary to discharge of their governmental responsibilities. Other illustrations of powers considered concurrent by implication are the enactment of bankruptcy laws, the regulation of weights and measures, exercise of the power of eminent domain, and the establishment of courts for the adjudication of disputes.

The question of whether the regulation of foreign and interstate commerce is a concurrent power has been, and still is, a controversial subject. State regulation of local aspects of such commerce with respect to which diversity of policy is considered either unobjectionable or necessary has been upheld by the Supreme Court, e.g., *Cooley v. Board of Wardens of the Port of Philadelphia*,[21] but the disputed question is whether the states are merely exercising their police power, and in so doing taking action which affects interstate and foreign commerce, or whether they share the commerce power to a limited extent with the national government. Clearly, however, if Congress exercises its power, conflicting state policies are superseded, and even if Congress has failed to act, the states lack authority to deal with those aspects of foreign and interstate commerce which, in the judgment of the Supreme Court, require uniformity of policy throughout the United States.[22] Furthermore, any state action which unduly burdens or obstructs foreign and interstate commerce is unconstitutional.

The general rule in regard to concurrent powers is that national action, when taken, supersedes conflicting state policies. A notable exception is that the rule does not apply

[21] 12 Howard 299 (1852).

[22] An Arizona law prohibited the operation of trains of greater length than seventy freight or fourteen passenger cars. No act of Congress limited train lengths. In *Southern Pacific Co. v. Arizona*, 325 U. S. 761 (1945), the Supreme Court declared the Arizona statute unconstitutional. If the length of trains is to be regulated at all, national uniformity in the regulation adopted, such as only Congress can prescribe, is practically indispensable to the operation of an efficient and economical national railway system.

in connection with taxation. Both the national government and the states may simultaneously levy the same taxes, e.g., on personal income.

In summary, the national government possesses only such powers in the field of domestic affairs as have been delegated to it either expressly or by implication, whereas the states may exercise any powers not exclusively granted to the national government or denied them by express or implied constitutional provision. In regard to foreign affairs, the powers of the national government are considered a concomitant of the status of the United States as a sovereign state. Some powers are vested exclusively in the national government, others exclusively in the states, and still others are concurrent and consequently are exercisable by both the national government and the states. Within the sphere of its delegated authority, either exclusive or concurrent, the national government enjoys supremacy and its policies prevail, in the event of conflict, over action taken by the states, subject to an exception in the levying of taxes.

Powers of Units of Local Government

In a later chapter the subject of local government will receive consideration, but at this point it seems advisable to complete the discussion of governmental powers by brief mention of the source and scope of the powers exercisable by minor political subdivisions like counties, townships, cities, and special districts. These units of local government, legally speaking, are creatures of the states. As such, they possess only such powers as the states confer upon them. Local units derive no authority from the Constitution of the United States, but they, like their creators, i.e., the states, are duty-bound to abide by the Constitution as the supreme law of the land.

Obligations of The National Government to the States

Obligation to Respect the Territorial Integrity and Legal Equality of the States

The national government is required to respect the territorial integrity of the states. This obligation is set forth in the clause authorizing Congress to admit new states into the Union. The power of admission is qualified by the stipulation that no new state shall be created within the jurisdiction of any other state or by combining two or more states or parts of states, without the consent of the legislatures of the states concerned as well as of Congress.

Respect for and maintenance of the legal equality of the states is an implied obligation of the national government. This duty is inferred from the federal character of the governmental system established by the Constitution and from the fact that no provision of the Constitution, as originally drafted and subsequently amended, draws any distinction between the powers of one state as compared to the others. Congress, having power to admit new states, may establish the conditions requisite to admission and deny admission until these conditions have been met by the territory desirous of becoming a state. Once admitted, however, any conditions which conflict with the principle of state equality in the *possession of governmental powers* cease to be binding.[23]

A judicially recognized exception to the general rule that conditions requisite to the attainment of statehood may be disregarded after admission is that the states are bound by agreements of a business nature or by contracts pertaining to property. Thus an agreement not to tax lands sold by the United States, until after elapse of a designated period of time, is binding after admission upon a state which, as a territory, subscribed to this agreement in order to secure Congressional approval of its application for statehood.

Guarantee of a Republican Form of Government

The national government is directed to guarantee to every state a republican form of government. By "republican" the framers of the Constitution meant a government of the representative type. No specific criteria of such a government were specified and the Supreme Court has taken the position that the issue is "political," i.e., non-justiciable.

The Constitution does not indicate the steps to be taken in the event of establishment of a non-republican government in one of the states. By implication, Congress may refuse to seat the Representatives and Senators chosen by that state or, if more drastic action appears necessary, authorize the President to use the armed forces of the country to carry out the constitutional guarantee. In 1912 the government of Oregon was claimed to be non-republican because of that state's establishment of the initiative and the referendum—instruments of direct legislation by popular vote. The Supreme Court, in *Pacific States Telephone &*

[23] *Coyle v. Smith*, 221 U. S. 559 (1911).

Telegraph Co. v. Oregon,[24] ruled that the courts are bound by the stand taken by the political branches of the government. Since Congress had seated Representatives and Senators from Oregon, its action indicated that the Oregon government was considered republican in form despite provision for the initiative and the referendum.

Protection Against Invasion and Domestic Violence

In express terms, the Constitution imposes two additional obligations on the national government with respect to the states. First, it shall protect them against invasion and second, on application of the state legislature or of the executive (when the legislature cannot be convened), against domestic violence.

Invasion occurs if forces external to the United States attack one of the states; in that event the United States is also attacked. The term "invasion," furthermore, comprehends attacks by one or more of the states upon another or others.

Protection against domestic violence refers to violent disturbances arising within a state, such as an uprising against the government of a state, forcible resistance to the enforcement of state law, mob violence, and other cases of resort to violence within a state for whatever reasons motivate the persons relying on force for attainment of their objectives. Ordinarily, the constituted authorities of a state are able to deal with such situations, and are expected to do so, but if the legislature or the governor, when the former cannot be convened, request federal assistance, the national government is constitutionally authorized, although not compelled, to intervene.

[24] 223 U. S. 118 (1912).

Many persons labor under a misconception concerning the right of the national government to deal with situations involving domestic violence. They apparently believe that a state request for help is *always* requisite. Such is not the case. The national government may act in instances of domestic violence whenever such violence interferes with its legitimate activities, endangers its property, or prevents or threatens to prevent the exercise of rights guaranteed to individuals by the Constitution and laws of the United States.

In the comparatively recent violent attempts to prevent desegregation in public educational institutions, the national government acted within the scope of its constitutional authority in sending military forces, on its own initiative, to the scenes of domestic violence in Arkansas (1957) and Mississippi (1962). As interpreted by the Supreme Court, the equal protection clause of the Fourteenth Amendment establishes a right against segregation based on race or color which the states are under obligation to respect and which the national government is duty-bound to enforce.

Obligations of The States to One Another

The Full Faith and Credit Clause

Article IV establishes a *rule of evidence* by requiring each state to give full faith and credit to the public acts, records, and judicial proceedings of every other state. "Public acts" includes statutes and ordinances; "records" comprehends recordings of deeds, wills, mortgages, marriages, divorces, births, and deaths; and "judicial proceedings" covers the judgments and proceedings of courts in *civil* cases.

Generally speaking, if persons *subject to the jurisdiction of a state* acquire rights and duties based on either its laws or judicial decisions in civil actions, another state wherein the aforesaid rights and duties become a matter of controversy is under obligation to recognize their validity, even if in conflict with the provisions of its own laws. Such is the meaning of the full faith and credit clause. It does not give the laws of a state extra-territorial effect and make them binding on persons in general outside as well as within its territorial limits.

A valid marriage in one state, if neither polygamous nor incestuous, must be accorded recognition in other states; so too, with respect to divorces. But in both cases full faith and credit must be given only if the state in which the marriage occurred or the divorce was granted had jurisdiction over the parties concerned. Again, a will drawn up in conformity with the law of a particular state in which the decedent was domiciled must be given full faith and credit in other states in determining disposition of the decedent's property. To cite but one more example, a contract entered into under the laws of a state, or a court judgment of that state concerning the rights and duties of parties to the contract, is entitled to full faith and credit in other states in which action is brought to compel fulfillment of the contract or adherence to the court decision.

Interstate Rendition of Fugitives from Justice

As provided in Article IV of the Constitution, "a person charged in any state with treason, felony, or other crime, who shall flee from justice, and be found in another state, shall, on demand of the executive authority of the state from which he fled, be delivered up, to be removed to the state having jurisdiction of the crime." The purpose of this provision is to prevent the several states from becoming havens of refuge for persons accused of crime in a particular state. Its wording appears to be mandatory but the Supreme Court, in *Kentucky v. Dennison*,[25] took the position that the clause was merely declaratory of a moral obligation and that there was no way of compelling a state executive to abide by this obligation. The consequences of this interpretation have been alleviated to some extent by an act of Congress of 1934 which made it a crime to flee across state lines for the purpose of escaping prosecution.

A person is a fugitive from justice if a crime has been committed in the state demanding his return; if he was present in the state at the time this crime occurred; and if he has either been accused or convicted of the crime and thereafter is found in another state. Should an asserted fugitive from justice be kidnapped by public officials or private persons and taken to the state which has charged him with criminal misconduct, he may, despite his forcible removal, be placed on trial in that state.[26] Although Congress in 1932 made kidnapping involving the crossing of state lines a federal crime, this law does not prevent state prosecution of kidnapped fugitives from justice, even though the national government may prosecute and convict the kidnappers.

Privileges and Immunities of State Citizens

"The citizens of each state shall be entitled to all privileges and immunities of citizens in the several states." This pro-

[25] 24 Howard 66 (1861).
[26] *Mahon v. Justice*, 126 U. S. 700 (1888). This case has not been overruled.

vision of the Constitution establishes a "golden rule" addressed to the states, viz., "Treat the citizens of other states as you treat your own." Its purpose is to prevent discriminatory legislation directed against the citizens of other states.

A state may expand or contract the privileges and immunities of its own citizens and, consequently, those of the citizens of other states subject to its jurisdiction, inasmuch as equality of treatment is all that the Constitution requires. Citizens of a particular state are not entitled, in other states, to the same privileges and immunities which their state has conferred on them. The fact, for instance, that citizens enjoy special privileges at home, e.g., permission to engage in certain professions, the right to hold offices, and the privilege of voting in elections, does not compel other states to grant them the same privileges. Only unreasonable discriminations based on state citizenship conflict with the constitutional clause here under consideration. Corporations, according to the Supreme Court, are not "citizens" within the meaning of this constitutionally imposed obligation of the states to refrain from discriminatory legislation.

The privileges and immunities in regard to which equality of treatment is mandatory are those of a *fundamental character* which are common to the citizens of a particular state. Among them are protection against illegal action, access to the courts, the acquisition, use, and disposal of property, traveling within or through the state, residing there, and engaging in trade, agriculture, and other *ordinary* business under substantially the same conditions as apply to the state's own citizens. A state may not levy discriminatory taxes on the citizens of other states, e.g., taxing the property of the latter at a rate higher than payable by its own citizens.

The equality of treatment rule does not compel a state to

grant citizens of other states the same privileges accorded its citizens in the enjoyment of what the courts have referred to as "the common property" or "the important resources" of the people of the state. However stated, this principle warrants state denial of hunting or fishing privileges (in inland waters) to the citizens of other states and also exclusion of such citizens from a state's parks, other recreational facilities, or public institutions like homes for the indigent. A state need not admit citizens of other states to a state university or other public educational institution. If it does, as is the common practice in the case of universities, it may charge a higher tuition than is payable by its own citizens.

The purpose of the privileges and immunities clause is to outlaw classifications based on state citizenship. Generally speaking, discriminatory legislation and treatment is prohibited, but there are exceptions—exceptions which in the judgment of the courts are "reasonable."

Obligations of The States to The National Government and The Union

With one exception, no article of the Constitution deals specifically with obligations of the states to the national government and the union. The exception is the supremacy clause which stipulates that judges of the several states shall be bound by the Constitution, laws in pursuance thereof, and treaties, anything in the state constitution or laws to the contrary notwithstanding. Other obligations are implied. Several of these have been mentioned in the preceding pages, e.g., the duty of the states to avoid interference with the legitimate operations of the national government, the obligation to maintain a republican form of government, and the duty to refrain from exercising powers not reserved to the states by the Constitution.

Moreover, states are obviously under obligation to select members of the two houses of Congress, to prescribe voting qualifications (subject to constitutional restrictions), to appoint Presidential electors, and to consider proposed constitutional amendments submitted to them for ratification. In addition, there is the obligation to remain in and never secede from the Union.

Intergovernmental Cooperation

A discussion which emphasizes legal arrangements with respect to the allocation of governmental powers and intergovernmental obligations is likely to create a false impression of the way in which the governmental system of the United States operates. To a considerable and steadily increasing degree, the several levels of government in this country cooperate with one another in solving problems that have national, regional, and local aspects. What has been referred to as "cooperative federalism" is the outgrowth of circumstances resulting from the facts of social life. Comparatively few problems can be solved satisfactorily by the national government alone, by the states alone, or by local units functioning within the limits of their legal authority.

Intergovernmental cooperation takes place in various ways and to varying degrees. A limited exposition will serve the purpose of demonstrating that the national government, the states, and local units do more than is required of them by constitutional or statutory provisions of the compulsive variety.

National Services to the States and Local Units

The national government collects and disseminates information of a statistical character and publishes reports embodying the results of a diversity of research projects. Many of its agencies furnish expert advice and render consultative and other services at the request of state and local officials. In various instances, national, state, and local authorities collaborate in solving particular problems and in administering policies which fall in functional fields of mutual interest. To cite but one example, the task of dealing with crime has assumed such proportions that state and local governments are unable to discharge it effectively without help from the national government. Congress has enacted a series of laws which extend national authority to certain types of crime. This kind of legislation provides a legal basis for co-operation on the part of the FBI and local police forces in the apprehension and prosecution of criminals.

The most important way in which the national government assists state and local governments is by providing necessary funds. Grants-in-aid were discussed earlier in this chapter and it was pointed out that states and local units are legally free to reject offers of financial assistance. However, acceptance almost always occurs. Conditional grants-in-aid result in coercive controls, but since acceptance is not legally compulsory, the submission of states and local units to these controls is voluntary in principle if not as a matter of political fact.

State Assistance to Local Units

State governments, subject to controlling provisions of state constitutions, enjoy extensive legal control over units of local government. A combination of legislative and judicial control has characterized state-local relations from the earliest times, and still does, but greater reliance is now being placed than formerly on a supplementary type of control, viz., that exercisable by state administrative agencies.

State-local relations are truly cooperative in character only if local units are not compelled as a matter of law to submit to policies adopted by state authorities. Among the noncoercive activities of state governments which are intended to be of assistance to local governments are (1) the collection and dissemination of information, (2) the giving of advice, (3) the rendition of services of different varieties, e.g., the installation of accounting systems, (4) the investigation and inspection of local services at the request of local authorities, and (5) financial assistance, such as grants-in-aid and state-collected and locally shared taxes. Unconditional grants-in-aid fall in the non-coercive category, as do conditional grants of financial assistance, inasmuch as local units are legally free to reject them.

Interstate Cooperation

Cooperative activity among the states assumes a variety of forms and its results vary in effectiveness. The Constitution of the United States stipulates that "no State shall, without the consent of Congress, enter into any agreement or compact with another State." However, the Supreme Court has held that Congressional consent is not required for *all* agreements. The controlling principle seems to be that such consent is necessary only if a compact tends to increase the political power of the states which are parties thereto and may as a consequence encroach upon or interfere with the supremacy of the national government. Agreements of a non-political or business type may be entered into without Congressional approval.[27]

The kind of compact requiring Congressional consent is exemplified by the 1921 agreement between New Jersey and New York establishing the Port of New York Authority for the purpose of dealing with the planning and development of terminal, transportation, and other facilities in the port of New York district and promoting and protecting the commerce of this district. Another example is the compact creating the Interstate Oil Compact Commission which is concerned with the conservation of oil and gas by the prevention of physical waste. This commission is composed of the representatives of thirty-three states.

Many arrangements for promoting voluntary cooperation have developed among the several states. The most important of these is probably the Council of State Governments. This Council serves as a clearing-house for information and research, endeavors to improve state legislative, administrative, and judicial practices, acts as an agency for cooperation among the states in the solution of interstate problems, and tries to facilitate and improve state-federal and state-local relations. A considerable number of interstate organizations are *affiliated* with the Council. Among them are the National Governors' Conference, the National Legislative Conference, the Conference of Chief Justices, the National Association

[27] For examples of such agreements see *Virginia v. Tennessee*, 148 U. S. 503 (1893).

of State Budget Officers, and the Association of Juvenile Compact Administrators. Various other cooperative organizations *collaborate* with the Council, e.g., the National Conference of Commissioners on Uniform State Laws.

Interlocal Cooperative Activity

The intergovernmental relations so far mentioned are those between the national government and both the states and their political subdivisions, between the states and their component local units, and between the states themselves. To complete the picture of intergovernmental relations, consideration of interlocal cooperative activity is necessary.

A proliferation of units of local government, especially in metropolitan areas, has led to state legislation permitting local units to collaborate in several ways. One form of cooperation is the joint enterprise characterized by a combination of two or more units of government for the purpose of dealing with some problem of common concern. Another type of cooperation is the rendition of service by one unit of government for others, usually on a contractual basis. A third type of cooperative action involves an exchange of services by participating local units.

Local units and their officials have formed a variety of associations designed to promote common interests. There are leagues of municipalities in nearly all of the states. These state leagues are constituent members of the National League of Cities (formerly the American Municipal Association) which renders informational and other services to aid the state leagues in functioning more effectively, conducts research programs, and sponsors an annual meeting. State associations of county officials are also functioning in most of the states. Their activities include the influencing of state legislation and the improvement of county administration by educating their members through such means as conferences, institutes, and publications.

Many national organizations of public officials provide services of importance to cities, counties, and other local governments. One of their functions is the provision of information and expert advice for local officials. A substantial number carry on research activities, issue publications, and conduct conferences, seminars, and in-service training programs. Examples of these organizations are the International City Management Association, the Municipal Finance Officers' Association, and the National Institute of Municipal Law Officers.

Various other professional organizations serving local governments have a membership comprised of both public officials and specialists in particular fields. For example, the American Public Works Association has a membership composed of public officials, educators, editors, consulting engineers, equipment manufacturers, and, among others, contractors.

Intergovernmental cooperation assumes different forms and involves national, state, and local governments. It has increased greatly during the last generation and probably will continue to do so in response to the needs of a dynamic society characterized by an extremely high degree of social solidarity. The territorial distribution of governmental powers by constitutional and statutory provision is now associated with a cooperative federalism that continues to develop as fewer and fewer problems remain soluble by the separate action of governments with legally restricted territorial jurisdiction.

Individual Rights and Responsibilities

CHAPTER ☆ THREE

United States and State Citizenship
   Acquisition of United States Citizenship
      By Birth
      By Naturalization: Collective and Individual
   Loss of United States Citizenship
      Involuntary Loss: When Unconstitutional
      Voluntary Expatriation Permissible
   State Citizenship
Rights Associated with Citizenship
   State Citizenship
   United States Citizenship
Rights Guaranteed to All Persons by the United States
      Constitution
   Major Rights against the National Government
   Major Rights against State Action
Significance of Various Fundamental Rights
   Writ of Habeas Corpus
   No Compulsory Self-Incrimination
   Unreasonable Searches and Seizures Prohibited
   Double Jeopardy Prohibited
   Death Penalty
   No State Impairment of the Obligation of Contracts
   Freedom of Speech, of the Press, of Assembly
   Freedom of Religion

Due Process of Law
Equal Protection of the Laws
Guarantees of Rights in State Constitutions
The Duties of Individuals

☆ ☆ ☆ ☆ ☆ ☆ ☆ ☆ ☆ ☆ ☆ ☆ ☆

The legal rights and responsibilities of individuals are prescribed by constitutional provisions (national and state) and by the body of national and state law, including legislative enactments, administrative rules and regulations, the rules of common law (judge made), and court decisions interpretive of the written law of the land. Some rights and responsibilities are associated with citizenship; others pertain to all persons regardless of their status as citizens, nationals, or aliens. A national is a person owing permanent allegiance to a particular country. Whether he also qualifies as a "citizen" depends on the law of that country. In the case of the United States, the inhabitants of annexed territories become nationals rather than citizens unless citizenship is conferred by treaty or by act of Congress.

United States and State Citizenship

Acquisition of the citizenship of a particular country may be by birth or by naturalization, i.e., by conversion of an alien into a citizen. Either or both of two general principles may be used in determining citizenship by birth. According to the principle of *jus soli* (law of soil), the controlling consideration is the place of birth. The other principle, *jus sanguinis* (law of blood), emphasizes the status of the parents at the time a child is born, no matter where the birth occurs. As for the acquisition of citizenship by naturalization, the process may be *collective* or *individual*. *Collective naturalization* occurs when citizenship is conferred on a group of persons, such as the inhabitants of a designated territory. The *individual procedure* requires a particular alien desirous of becoming a citizen to establish his qualifications in accordance with the process prescribed by law for this purpose.

Citizenship may be lost as well as acquired. At one time countries subscribed to the doctrine of indelible allegiance, i.e., once a citizen, always a citizen. Nowadays, bodies politic commonly permit voluntary expatriation. Involuntary loss of citizenship occurs under whatever conditions the laws of a particular country stipulate.

Acquisition of United States Citizenship

(1) BY BIRTH. The principle of *jus soli* is incorporated in the Fourteenth Amendment which provides: "All persons born or naturalized in the United States, and subject to the jurisdiction thereof, are citizens of the United States and of the State wherein they reside." With exceptions to be noted shortly, any individual who is born within the territorial limits of the United States (the fifty states, District of Columbia, and incorporated territories), regardless of his race, color, or the status of his parents, whether aliens or citizens, acquires United States citizenship solely because of the place of his

birth. This point was definitely settled by the Supreme Court in *United States v. Wong Kim Ark*.[28]

Exceptions to this general rule are due to the phrase "subject to the jurisdiction thereof." Examples of persons born within but not subject to the jurisdiction of the United States are the children of visiting heads of foreign countries, of ambassadors and other diplomatic representatives of such countries accredited to the United States, and of members of the armed forces of a foreign enemy in occupation of United States territory.

Congress, by law, has specified the circumstances under which a child born outside the United States acquires citizenship by birth. This law, which involves application of the principle of *jus sanguinis*, is too complicated to warrant a detailed account of its various provisions. Only a few illustrations will be given. An individual acquires United States citizenship by birth if born outside the United States and its outlying possessions, *both parents being citizens*, provided that one of them, prior to the birth, has resided in the United States or one of its outlying possessions; if *one parent is a citizen* and *the other a national*, the citizen parent must have been physically present in the United States or one of its outlying possessions for a continuous period of one year at any time prior to the birth; and if *one parent is a citizen* and *the other an alien*, fulfillment of the following condition is necessary to the acquisition of citizenship by birth, viz., the citizen parent, prior to the birth, must have been physically present in the United States or one of its outlying possessions for a total of at least ten years, not fewer than five of them after the age of fourteen. To retain the citizenship so acquired (in this last mentioned instance),

[28] 169 U. S. 649 (1881).

the child must come to the United States prior to attaining the age of twenty-three and remain at least five years, provided that such physical presence follows the age of fourteen and precedes the age of twenty-eight.

(2) BY NATURALIZATION. United States citizenship has been obtained through *collective naturalization* in a number of instances. Examples are Puerto Ricans in 1917, Indians in 1924, and Virgin Islanders in 1927. Such naturalization may be accomplished by special act of Congress or by the provisions of a treaty dealing with the acquisition of territory by the United States, e.g., Louisiana and Alaska.

Individual naturalization involves (1) an optional declaration of intention, (2) a mandatory application or petition for citizenship, (3) investigation and a preliminary hearing by the Immigration and Naturalization Service, (4) a final hearing by either a federal district court or a state or territorial court of record, and (5) if the findings are favorable, administration of the oath of allegiance and the issuance of letters of citizenship. Applicants must meet various qualifications established by law. These include a minimum age of eighteen; continuous lawful residence within the United States for at least five years prior to the granting of citizenship; ability to read, write, speak, and understand the English language; good moral character; no disqualifying political beliefs; and knowledge of the fundamentals of United States history and government. Some exceptions to the usual requirements are provided by law, e.g., a three instead of a five year residence is sufficient for the husbands or wives of United States citizens.

Loss of United States Citizenship

(1) INVOLUNTARY LOSS: WHEN UNCONSTITUTIONAL
Two recently decided cases require consideration in regard
to the loss of United States citizenship. One is *Beys Afroyim
v. Rusk*[29] (1967). The other is *Rogers v. Bellei*,[29a] a 1971
decision which limited the scope of the *Afroyim* ruling by
distinguishing between citizenship as defined by the Fourteenth Amendment and citizenship based solely on Congressional legislation. This case will be considered after a review
of the *Afroyim* and several other decisions.

In 1967 the Supreme Court decided that Congress has
neither express nor implied power to expatriate a citizen,
natural-born or naturalized, *without his assent*. This interpretation of the Constitution was proclaimed in the *Afroyim*
case. A majority of five justices overruled a contrary conclusion in *Perez v. Brownell*[30] which was decided in 1958
by a five to four division of the Court's membership. The
specific issue in both cases was the constitutionality of a
statutory provision prescribing loss of citizenship because
of voting in a foreign political election.

During the interval between the *Perez* and *Afroyim* rulings, several other Congressional stipulations concerning
involuntary expatriation had been declared unconstitutional.
In *Trop v. Dulles*[31] the Supreme Court disallowed the forfeiture of citizenship because of discharge from the armed
forces after conviction, by court martial, of desertion in
time of war. The five majority justices were unable to

[29] 387 U. S. 253 (1967)
[29a] 401 U. S. 815 (1971)
[30] 356 U. S. 44 (1958)
[31] 356 U. S. 86 (1958)

agree on reasons for the ruling of unconstitutionality, but four maintained that Congress lacked power to impose loss of citizenship as a punishment for crime and also that this penalty constituted cruel and unusual punishment—forbidden by the Eighth Amendment. In *Kennedy v. Mendoza-Martinez*[32] the Court decided that *automatic* loss of citizenship by statutory provision, because of departure from or remaining outside the country to evade military service, is invalid. The imposition of loss of citizenship, as a penalty, without prior and proper trial, violates the Fifth and Sixth Amendments. In *Schneider v. Rusk*[33] the Court set aside, as unconstitutional, legislation which deprived naturalized citizens of their citizenship because of residence abroad, either in their native country or in some other foreign land, in excess of specified periods of time. This provision constituted unlawful discrimination under the due process clause of the Fifth Amendment. Naturalized citizens (said the Court) may not be made "second class" citizens in comparison with persons acquiring citizenship by birth.

Presumably, citizenship acquired by naturalization may still be revoked if obtained illegally or by fraud. Examples of fraudulent attainment are a false statement about the period of residence in the United States; disloyal conduct subsequent to the granting of citizenship (construed as evidence of fraud); and membership in subversive organizations (likewise so construed).

The constitutional *reasoning* in the foregoing cases was replaced by the 1967 *Afroyim* pronouncement that Congressional imposition of involuntary loss of citizenship, *for any reason*, is prohibited by the Constitution. However, the application of the *Afroyim* ruling *has been restricted* by

[32] 372 U. S. 144 (1963)
[33] 377 U. S. 163 (1964)

the Supreme Court's 1971 decision in *Rogers v. Bellei.*

The *Bellei* case involved a citizen, Bellei, who was the son of an alien father and United States citizen mother. Bellei was born abroad but acquired citizenship by birth under Congressional legislation specifying the circumstances under which United States citizenship is conferred despite birth outside the United States. The law pertaining to a case like that of Bellei provides for loss of citizenship unless certain conditions are met, *viz.*, continuous physical presence in the United States for five years between the ages of 14 and 28. Bellei failed to fulfill these conditions and presumably lost his citizenship under provisions of the Nationality Act of 1952.

The Supreme Court upheld the constitutionality of these provisions. In so doing it limited the applicability of the *Afroyim* ruling to *Fourteenth Amendment citizens*—those born *in* the United States, naturalized *in* the United States, and subject to the jurisdiction thereof. It stated that the acquisition and/or loss of citizenship not covered by the Fourteenth Amendment is determinable by Congressional action.

As of early 1972, the constitutional situation appeared to be this: (1) the involuntary loss of *Fourteenth Amendment citizenship* is unconstitutional and (2) the loss of citizenship acquired by birth outside the United States (abroad) depends on Congressional policy. In the *Bellei* case the Court said that the *Schneider* v. *Rusk* and *Afroyim* rulings involved (were bottomed upon) Fourteenth Amendment citizenship.

The constitutionality of several statutory provisions pertaining to expatriation remains uncertain. These will be mentioned in the following section.

(2) VOLUNTARY EXPATRIATION PERMISSIBLE Voluntary expatriation is permissible. Among the ways of accomplishing it are by formal renunciation in a manner prescribed by law; by willingly becoming a naturalized citizen of another country; and by taking an oath of allegiance to a foreign state.

Congress has prescribed loss of citizenship under the following circumstances: conviction of treason or an attempt to overthrow the government by force; serving in a foreign military force without the consent of the United States government; and acceptance of employment by the government of a foreign state if eligibility for such service is confined to its nationals.

Some of these actions, perhaps all, are construable as voluntary expatriation by implication—a construction which the Court might have placed on the failure of Bellei to meet the five-year continuous physical presence requirement. Unless so construed, will the Burger court adhere to the rulings in the *Afroyim* and *Bellei* controversies and hold that the above-mentioned statutory stipulations specifying loss of citizenship are unconstitutional in the case of *Fourteenth Amendment citizens*?

One's status as a citizen, national, or alien is a matter of considerable importance with respect to legal rights and responsibilities. Although the national and state constitutions guarantee many rights to all persons (as do the provisions of statutes), some rights, privileges, and immunities are associated with citizenship.

State Citizenship

For many years prior to the adoption of the Fourteenth

Amendment, uncertainty prevailed regarding the relationship between national and state citizenship. According to one point of view, United States citizenship was derived from state citizenship; according to another, the reverse of this asserted relationship was inferable from the Constitution. The former position was favored by the Supreme Court in the Dred Scott case—decided in 1857.

This controversy was settled by the Fourteenth Amendment which stipulates that citizens of the United States are citizens of the state wherein they reside. United States citizenship is *primary;* state citizenship, *secondary*. Residence within a state is a matter of personal intent supported by some evidence in substantiation of the avowed intention of the individual whose claim to residence is questioned. The physical presence of the claimant within the state is unnecessary.

Most citizens of the United States are legal residents of one of the states. Many have been citizens of different states in the course of their lives. Some, such as those having their legal residence in the District of Columbia, in a territorial possession of this country, or in a foreign state, lack state citizenship.

Rights Associated with Citizenship

The rights associated with citizenship fall in two categories, viz., the rights of United States citizens and the rights of state citizens. Some of these rights are guaranteed by constitutional provision but the remainder are derived from laws established by the national and state governments in the exercise of their various powers.

Rights Associated with State Citizenship

Within the scope of their reserved powers, the states are free to determine the rights of persons subject to their jurisdiction. In doing so they may distinguish between citizens and aliens and confer rights on the former which are denied to the latter, provided that their action is consistent with the Constitution, laws, and treaties of the United States. As pointed out in the preceding chapter, a state is required to grant the citizens of sister states the same fundamental privileges and immunities which it confers on its own citizens, thereby relieving the former of the disabilities of alienage.

Examination of the constitutions and laws of the fifty states is essential to ascertainment of the rights of persons as state citizens. In many branches of law the rights of aliens are the same as those of citizens, but in regard to a variety of matters state citizens are given preferential treatment. Various states, for example, bar aliens from engaging in certain occupations, e.g., the practice of law or medicine, from employment on public works, and from receiving workmen's compensation benefits.

The advantages of being a state citizen rather than an alien are not as great as they probably would be if the discretionary power of the states were unlimited. Treaties entered into by the national government with foreign countries sometimes deal with the rights and duties of aliens in the United States. The provisions of these treaties prevail over conflicting stipulations of state constitutions and laws. So do acts of Congress which qualify as legitimate exercises of its delegated powers. Furthermore, all persons, aliens as well as citizens, are beneficiaries of a number of restrictions imposed on the states by the Constitution of the United States. The most important of these is the provision of the Fourteenth Amendment that no state shall deprive *any person* of life, liberty, or property without due process of law nor deny to *any person* within its jurisdiction the equal protection of the laws.

Access to the national courts is related to state citizenship in some categories of cases. The jurisdiction of these courts, as set forth in Article III of the Constitution, includes controversies between citizens of different states, between citizens of the same state claiming lands under grants of different states, between citizens of a state and aliens, and between a state and citizens of other states and aliens. Consequently, the *states* may not prohibit their citizens from seeking relief in the national courts in cases of the foregoing type. Congress, however, possesses authority to provide that such cases may be brought before state as well as national tribunals and may even confer exclusive jurisdiction on the former. The Eleventh Amendment prohibits the national judiciary from exercising jurisdiction over suits instituted by citizens or aliens against a state.

Rights Associated with United States Citizenship

Rights associated with United States citizenship are established by the Constitution, either expressly or by implication, by acts of Congress, and by treaties. Their number is small as compared to the legal rights conferred on all persons, whether citizens, nationals, or aliens.

In sundry matters Congress may, if it chooses, confine the possession of particular rights to citizens of the United States, provided that in so doing it does not disregard the conferment of rights by constitutional provision *on all persons*.

Examples are (1) the Homestead Act of 1862 which permitted only citizens or aliens who had declared their intention of becoming citizens to enter and reside on public land for the purpose of perfecting title and (2) legislation under which only citizens are eligible for appointment to the civil service of the United States.

Treaties entered into with foreign countries often deal with the rights of individuals. Thus the rights of United States citizens in a particular foreign state may be attributable to a treaty to which that state and the United States are parties.

Few provisions of the Constitution deal explicitly with the rights of citizens of the United States. Four amendments, the Fifteenth, the Nineteenth, the Twenty-Fourth, and the Twenty-Sixth, stipulate that the right of United States citizens to vote shall not be denied or abridged, either by the national government or by the states, on account of race, color, or previous condition of servitude (Fifteenth); sex (Nineteenth); failure to pay poll or other taxes—election of national officials only (Twenty-Fourth); or age, if eighteen years or older, in all elections (Twenty-Sixth). Only natural born citizens of the United States are qualified to serve as President or Vice President; and United States citizenship, for a designated minimum period of time, is a necessary qualification for membership in the two houses of Congress.

United States citizenship is referred to three times in the Fourteenth Amendment. Of principal importance are the definition of United States citizenship and the provision prohibiting the states from making or enforcing any law which abridges the privileges and immunities of citizens of the United States. The Amendment fails to identify these privileges and immunities.

In *The Slaughter House Cases*, decided in 1873,[34] the Supreme Court took the position that the privileges and immunities referred to are only such as owe their existence to the relationship between the citizen and the national government and to the provisions of national laws and treaties. It indicated clearly that these privileges and immunities *do not comprehend ordinary civil rights*. The latter remain subject to state determination, except insofar as the discretionary power of the states is limited by other constitutional stipulations. Since the Court, up to now, has adhered to the interpretation first established in *The Slaughter House Cases*, Congress, in passing the Civil Rights Act of 1964, relied on its power to regulate foreign and interstate commerce and to enforce the provisions of the Fifteenth, Nineteenth, and Twenty-Fourth Amendments, as well as the due process and equal protection clauses of the Fourteenth which place limitations on *state actions* as distinguished from those of private individuals.

In the *Slaughter House* and subsequent cases the Supreme Court has given examples of what it considers privileges and immunities of United States citizenship. Among them are the right to come to the seat of the national government to transact business with it, to seek its protection, to share its offices, and to engage in administering its functions; the right of free access to seaports and to use of the navigable waters of the United States; the right to become a citizen of any state by establishing a *bona fide* residence therein; the privilege of receiving the protection of the national government on the high seas or within the jurisdiction of a foreign government; protection from violence while in the custody of the national government; the right to travel from state to

[34] 16 Wallace 36.

state and to engage in foreign and interstate commerce; and rights conferred on citizens by valid national legislation.

The Supreme Court has never undertaken a comprehensive and final enumeration of the privileges and immunities of United States citizenship. Some of them are enjoyed by aliens in this country, not as a matter of constitutional right, but only by reason of courteous and generous treatment by the national government, which may withdraw them at any time.

Rights Guaranteed to All Persons by The Constitution of The United States

Most constitutionally guaranteed rights limit the exercise of governmental powers in dealing with *all persons*, aliens and nationals as well as citizens. Some guarantees of this type, such as those of the first eight amendments, merely curtail the exercise of power by the national government; a few apply only to the states, e.g., no impairment of the obligation of contracts or denial of the equal protection of the laws; and others are directed against both the national government and the states, as evidenced by duplicate provisions prohibiting the denial of due process of law, the passage of bills of attainder and *ex post facto* laws, and the granting of titles of nobility. The Supreme Court has concluded that the due process clause of the Fourteenth Amendment, by implication, prohibits state infringement of some of the same rights which the first eight amendments safeguard against invasive national action.

Rights guaranteed to individuals are assignable to two distinct categories—substantive and procedural. A substantive right is one which permits a person to do something, to act in

pursuance of a chosen objective. Freedom of speech, freedom
of religion, the right to marry, the right to work, the right
to travel, and the right to acquire, use, and dispose of property—all of these are rights of the substantive variety. Procedural rights, often referred to as adjective rights, are
conferred for the purpose of aiding or protecting the individual in the enjoyment of his substantive rights. The
rights of individuals to resort to specified procedures for the
redress of wrongs or to be dealt with in accordance with
prescribed modes of action are rights of a procedural type.
Examples are the right of access to the courts; the right of
a defendant to be notified, to be presented with the charges
against him, and to be tried fairly by a competent tribunal;
and the right to petition a court for a writ of *habeas corpus*.

Major Rights Expressly Guaranteed to All Persons against the National Government[35]

(1) PROCEDURAL RIGHTS

> No bill of attainder or *ex post facto* law shall be passed.
> Treason consists only in levying war against the United
>   States or in adhering to its enemies. Confession in open
>   court or testimony of two witnesses required for con-
>   viction.
> Unreasonable searches and seizures prohibited. Warrants
>   to be issued only on probable cause.
> Indictment by grand jury and public trial by jury re-
>   quired in criminal cases; accused to be informed of
>   charges against him, confronted with witnesses against

[35] The Second Amendment, a limitation of the powers of the national government, states that the right of the people to keep and bear
arms shall not be infringed. Its purpose is to prevent Congress from
disarming the state militia. Although the phrase "the people" suggests
all persons, aliens may be denied the right to keep and bear arms.
The power of the states to do so has been upheld—*Patsone v. Pennsylvania*, 232 U. S. 138 (1914).

him, have compulsory process for obtaining witnesses in his favor, and have assistance of counsel for his defense. Trial by jury in common law suits, if amount in controversy exceeds twenty dollars.

Double jeopardy prohibited.

No compulsory self-incrimination.

No excessive bail or fines; no cruel and unusual punishment.

Privilege of writ of *habeas corpus* may be suspended only when necessary to public safety in times of rebellion or invasion.

No private property to be taken for public use without just compensation.

No person to be deprived of life, liberty, or property without due process of law.

(2) SUBSTANTIVE RIGHTS

Religious freedom.

Freedom of speech and of the press.

Freedom of peaceable assembly.

Right to petition government for redress of grievances.

No slavery or involuntary servitude, except as a punishment for crime.

United States citizenship acquired by birth within the United States, if subject to the jurisdiction thereof.

No person to be deprived of life, liberty, or property without due process of law—a source of substantive as well as procedural rights.

No denial of equal rights because of sex

Major Rights Expressly Guaranteed to All Persons against State Action

(1) PROCEDURAL RIGHTS

No bill of attainder or *ex post facto* law shall be passed.

No person may be deprived of life, liberty, or property without due process of law.

No person may be denied the equal protection of the laws.

Full faith and credit shall be given in each state to the public acts, records, and judicial proceedings of every other state.

(2) SUBSTANTIVE RIGHTS

> No state shall pass any law impairing the obligation of contracts.
>
> No slavery or involuntary servitude, except as a punishment for crime.
>
> No person may be deprived of life, liberty, or property without due process of law.
>
> No state shall deny to any person the equal protection of the laws.
>
> No denial of equal rights because of sex

The due process and equal protection clauses are extremely important safeguards against state denial or infringement of individual and group rights, both substantive and procedural. These limitations have given rise to more litigation than any other provisions of the Constitution. The restrictive effects of the due process guarantee have been greatly expanded because of the Supreme Court's ruling that the "liberty" mentioned in this stipulation includes religious freedom, freedom of speech, freedom of assembly, and a number of other freedoms to be mentioned subsequently. As now interpreted, due process also requires the conferment of certain procedural rights which the states at one time were free to withhold, e.g., trial by jury in serious criminal cases.

The Significance of Various Fundamental Rights

The foregoing enumeration of the major rights guaranteed by the Constitution of the United States is enlightening only to a limited extent because few, if any, of these guarantees, as worded, are self-explanatory. Their meaning is determined from time to time by interpretation and application to particular situations. Although the several branches of government, national and state, participate in the process of interpretation, final interpretative rulings are handed down by the Supreme Court. Initial action by other agencies of government sooner or later gives rise to cases which are carried to this court of last resort.

Explanations of these rights have been presented in the opinions and dissenting opinions of the Supreme Court justices. Statements about the general meaning of various guarantees, although necessary and valuable, do not enable anyone, including members of the Court, to foresee with accuracy what the fate of a particular governmental act in a given situation will be if its constitutionality is challenged.

The Writ of Habeas Corpus

The writ of *habeas corpus* is an order issued by a court directing officials who hold a person in custody to appear before the court and show sufficient cause for their action. This writ is issuable on petition of the person held in detention.

Suspension of the privilege of the writ of *habeas corpus* by the national government is permissible only when, in cases of rebellion or invasion, the public safety may require it. This provision does not apply to the states. However, the policy of a state with respect to the writ of *habeas corpus* is challengeable under the due process clause of the Fourteenth Amendment.

The privilege of the writ of *habeas corpus* is an indispensable guarantee of personal freedom. It prevents governments in this country from holding persons in custody for whatever reasons seem sufficient to executive and administrative officials.

Self-Incrimination

The Fifth Amendment, binding only on the national government, provides that no person shall be compelled in any criminal case to be a witness against himself. This provision, as interpreted, also protects persons compelled to testify under oath before various official agencies, such as legislative committees and grand juries. In the case of the states, the Supreme Court has overruled earlier decisions and now maintains that the due process clause comprehends the privilege against self-incrimination.[36]

The rule against self-incrimination prevents the government from resorting to forcible measures, such as torture and threats of physical harm, to obtain confessions of guilt. It also prohibits the *compulsory* answering of questions and the *compulsory* producing of private papers and documents which might reveal facts that would subject the questioned person or owner of the papers to criminal prosecution.

Voluntary confessions are admissible as evidence, but difficulties arise in determining whether a particular confession was voluntary. Among the circumstances which may lead to a judicial conclusion that a confession was involuntary are denial of the immediate assistance of counsel; failure to warn a suspect of his right to counsel and his right to remain silent; questioning in the absence of counsel; questioning of prolonged duration; and the threat or infliction of physical harm.[37] Courts consider the "totality of circumstances" in determining *voluntariness*. Statements made to police by an

---

[36] *Malloy v. Hogan*, 378 U. S. 1 (1964).

[37] A landmark decision with respect to confessions was made in *Miranda v. Arizona*, 384 U. S. 436 (1966). Also see *Escobedo v. Illinois*, 378 U. S. 478 (1964).

accused under circumstances rendering the statements inadmissible to establishment of the prosecution's case are admissible for impeaching the accused's credibility, provided (1) that such statements are inconsistent with accused's trial testimony bearing directly on the crimes charged and (2) that the accused makes no claim that his statements were coerced.[37a]

Persons who invoke the rule against self-incrimination are not necessarily guilty of criminal misbehavior. A person may find himself in a compromising situation, despite his innocence, which could result in his prosecution and possibly his conviction if he were to divulge information which he alone possessed.[38]

By granting immunity from prosecution, the government is able to compel testimony by persons who otherwise would take advantage of the privilege against self-incrimination. If immunity has been granted properly, subsequent refusal to answer questions justifies the institution of contempt proceedings against a recalcitrant witness.

Unreasonable Searches and Seizures

The Fourth Amendment, directed against the national government, prohibits unreasonable searches and seizures of persons, houses, papers, and effects. It also specifies that warrants shall issue only on probable cause, supported by oath or affirmation, particularly describing the place to be searched and the persons or things to be seized. The Supreme Court has held that the due process clause of the Fourteenth Amendment also prohibits unreasonable searches and seizures

[37a] *Harris v. New York,* 401 U. S. 223 (1971)
[38] *Slochower v. Board of Education,* 350 U. S. 551 (1956).

by the states. Thus the Constitution provides protection against illegal arrests of persons and illegal search for and seizure of things by any government—national, state, or local.

Arrests without a warrant are reasonable and therefore valid if a person commits a crime in the presence of the arresting officer or if the arrest is based on probable cause or reasonable ground for believing that the individual has committed a crime. The fact that there may have been ample time in which to obtain a warrant does not, under such circumstances, invalidate the arrest. Arrests on mere suspicion are unconstitutional at both the federal and state levels; there must be probable cause or reasonable grounds.

Searches without a warrant qualify as reasonable if incidental to a valid arrest, e.g., search of the arrested person. Recently (1972) the Supreme Court held that police have the right to "stop and frisk" a suspect on the basis of an anonymous tipster's word that the suspect carried a hidden pistol and illegal narcotics. Until a few years ago a search of the premises without a warrant, when incident to a valid arrest, was permissible—subject to limitations which defied generalization. Since 1969 the search has been restricted to the arrested individual's person and to the area (such as the room in which the arrest is made) from within which he might have secured either a weapon or something that could have been used as evidence against him.[38a] How long this ruling will survive is a matter for conjecture. In the case of moving vehicles, such as automobiles, search without a warrant is legally justified if based on the probability that the vehicles contain "articles offensive to the law,"

[38a] *Chimel v. California*, 395 U. S. 752 (1969).

e.g., stolen goods, or that a person who has committed a crime is traveling in a vehicle.

Until recently, administrative officers, such as health or housing inspectors, had the right to search buildings without obtaining a search warrant if their objective was to ascertain the existence of conditions detrimental to the public health or safety. This exception to the general rule that search warrants are necessary to a valid search was *abrogated by the Supreme Court in 1967.* In *Camara v. Municipal Court of the City and County of San Francisco*,[39] the Court held that search warrants are required *even for such purposes.*

Evidence gathered on the occasion of illegal searches and seizures by public officials is inadmissible in a prosecution for criminal conduct. The Court first took this position in regard to prosecutions by the national government. A short time ago, 1961, in *Mapp v. Ohio*,[40] it ruled that the due process clause of the Fourteenth Amendment prohibits the use of evidence, so obtained, in state prosecutions for the commission of crimes prohibited by state law.

A relationship exists between the constitutional prohibition against involuntary self-incrimination and the barring of unreasonable searches and seizures. Although each guarantee is independent of the other in its sphere of influence, the two are complementary. The relationship has been stated to be that a search is unreasonable if its purpose or result is the securing of self-incriminating evidence. Compulsory procurement of a man's private papers and effects for use as evidence against him violates the guarantee that no person

[39] 387 U.S. 523 (1967).

[40] 367 U. S. 643 (1961). The *Mapp* case overruled *Wolf v. Colorado,* 338 U. S. 25 (1949), a case in which the Supreme Court had held that illegally acquired evidence is admissible in state actions instituted because of violations of state laws.

shall be compelled in any criminal case to be a witness against himself. Self-incriminating evidence secured by any search and seizure is barred from introduction, as evidence, in a criminal proceeding.

Uncertainties concerning the validity of searches and seizures are numerous. The reactions of courts to particular cases are so unpredictable that a seemingly sound generalization based on previous rulings is subject to modification at any time.

Double Jeopardy

The Fifth Amendment stipulates that no person shall be subject for the same offense to be twice put in jeopardy of life or limb. This amendment applies only to the national government. However, in 1969 the Supreme Court held that the double jeopardy clause of the Fifth Amendment is applicable to the states through the Fourteenth Amendment.[40a] It adhered to this ruling in 1970.[40b]

A person who has been tried and either acquitted or convicted of a criminal charge may not be tried or punished again for the *same particular act* which resulted in his first trial. He may, of course, be tried on charges of committing the same offense a second time, but this prosecution, being distinct from and unrelated to the first, would not amount to placing him in double jeopardy.

Just when placement in jeopardy occurs is a question that has given rise to controversy. In the case of a completed

[40a] *Benton v. Maryland,* 395 U. S. 784 (1969)
[40b] *Ashe v. Swenson,* 397 U. S. 436 (1970); *Harris v. Washington,* 30 L Ed 2d 212 (1971)

trial before a proper court, the defendant has clearly been put in jeopardy. So too, if proceedings have commenced before a court having jurisdiction and the jury has been impaneled and sworn. A person has not been placed in jeopardy by reason of preliminary examination by a committing magistrate; if a jury is discharged by the judge because of failure to agree on a verdict; if it be shown that the court in which the trial was conducted lacked jurisdiction; and, to cite another example, if dismissal of a case occurs at the request of the prosecutor on the ground of insufficient evidence.

The constitutional immunity against double jeopardy may be waived by the defendant in a criminal case. Such waiver occurs if the accused requests a new trial or, having been found guilty, appeals to a higher court. A subsequent trial under the circumstances indicated is considered a continuation of the initial proceeding.

Under the federal system of government of the United States, a particular act may be a crime according to national law and also under the law of a state. If both the national government and the state have jurisdiction over the offense and the person accused of committing it, the latter is subject to trial and conviction by each government. Since two distinct offenses have been committed by the same act, one under national law and the other under state law, the accused individual is not put in double jeopardy when separately prosecuted and tried by national as well as by state authorities.

The Death Penalty

As now imposed, the death penalty was declared unconstitutional by a five to four decision of the Supreme Court

(June 1972).[40c] There was no "opinion of the Court." Each of the judges prepared an opinion setting forth his position concerning the issue of constitutionality. Two justices of the majority apparently favored absolute prohibition on the ground of "cruel and unusual punishment"; one emphasized the point that the death penalty, when so seldom invoked, ceases to be the credible threat essential to influence the conduct of others; and two based their ruling against constitutionality on the ground, primarily, that the death penalty is inflicted discriminatively, selectively, and arbitrarily under prevailing legislation concerning capital punishment —a denial of equal protection of the laws. As remarked by the Chief Justice in a dissenting opinion, the actual scope of the Court's ruling is not entirely clear and the future of capital punishment in the United States remains uncertain.

Impairment of the Obligation of Contracts

No state shall pass any law impairing the obligation of contracts. Contracts are agreements in accordance with the provisions of which the parties thereof acquire rights and obligations. The phrase "obligation of contracts" comprehends not only the terms of a particular contract but also the duty to abide by them and the remedial rights available to the parties in the event of infraction, as this duty and these rights are prescribed by the law in effect at the time the contract was negotiated. In various cases the Supreme Court has stated briefly that the obligation of a contract is the law which binds the parties to perform their agreement and that laws which subsist at the time and place of making a con-

[40c] *Furman v. Georgia, Jackson v. Georgia, Branch v. Texas*, 40 Law Week 4923.

tract, and where it is to be performed, enter into and form a part of it, as if they were expressly referred to or incorporated in its terms.

States as well as individuals may be parties to contracts which are not subject to impairment by state law. For instance, charters which a state grants to a private corporation are contracts which may not be altered or repealed by its legislature unless the right to do so was reserved at the time the charter was granted. In the case of contracts to which only private persons are parties, a state law relieving an individual of his responsibility to discharge a contractual obligation, e.g., the duty of a debtor to pay back a loan by a creditor, or a law providing less effective remedies in instances of breach of contract than those available at the time a contract was negotiated, would constitute an unconstitutional impairment of the obligation of contracts. Changes in remedies which apply to future contracts may, of course, be provided for by legislative enactments.

In dealing with controversies involving the issue of impairment, courts are faced with the necessity of deciding whether a valid contract exists, what the obligations of the contract are, and whether impairment by state law has occurred. Invalid contracts are unenforcible. Even valid contracts remain subject to state control, despite the impairment clause, because private persons, by contract, cannot deprive the states of their authority to safeguard the vital interests of the general public. In the event of conflict between the "public interest" and "private interests," the latter must give way. Furthermore, certain governmental powers, e.g., the police power, cannot be contracted away by the government itself.

The contract clause is not an absolute and utterly unqualified restriction of the state's protective powers. Legislation addressed to a legitimate end, if the measures taken are reasonable and appropriate to that end, is not prohibited by the stipulation that no laws impairing the obligation of contracts may be passed.

Freedom of Speech, the Press, and Assembly

The First Amendment prohibits the passage, by Congress, of any law abridging freedom of speech or of the press or the right of the people peaceably to assemble. As for the states, the Supreme Court has asserted that these freedoms are included within the meaning of the term "liberty" as incorporated in the provision that no state shall deprive any person of life, liberty, or property without due process of law.

Freedom of speech, so essential to the democratic process of government, is not absolute. Abuses of this freedom may be forbidden. Two distinct and significant interests, both public, require balancing in determining the validity of restraints on freedom of speech, viz., the interest of the public in preventing evil behavior and the public's interest in preserving freedom of expression.

Freedom of speech is limited by the rights of other individuals and by considerations of public safety, decency and morality, health, and general welfare. To prevent abuses of this freedom, provision may be made for remedial action by individuals whose rights have been infringed by the statements of others; also, penalties may be imposed on persons convicted of unlawful exercises of the right of free speech. The first type of abuse is illustrated by libelous or slanderous remarks about an individual. A suit for monetary damages is the usual remedy. Examples of the second type are the use of profane or obscene language in public; falsely calling "fire" in a theater and causing the audience to stampede for the exits; and advocacy of the immediate overthrow of the government by force. Punishment by fine or imprisonment may be provided for in such instances.

Restraints on freedom of speech are constitutional only if in compliance with certain standards established by the Supreme Court in a line of cases involving this issue. These standards include the following: reasonable ground for fearing that the practice of free speech will result in a serious evil; reasonable ground for the belief that an asserted evil is serious; reasonable ground for believing that the apprehended danger is too great to leave the correction of evil counsels to time and full discussion; and the advocacy, in words, of unlawful action and not merely abstract doctrine.

The Supreme Court has not adhered consistently to every one of these standards. However, it has invariably stressed the necessity of a serious evil and good reason for considering a particular evil to be grave. Inconsistency has occurred primarily on the question of the degree and proximity of the danger that unrestricted speech will result in a major evil within the authority of government to prevent. Several tests of "danger" have been devised by the Court, viz., "clear and present danger"; "clear and probable danger"; and "bad tendency." *The one most commonly used is "clear and present danger."* Occasionally the Court has applied the "bad tendency" [41] and the "clear and probable" [42] danger tests. A probable danger is not necessarily a present or immediate danger. Consequently, this test attaches less importance to

[41] *Gitlow v. New York*, 268 U. S. 652 (1925).
[42] *Dennis v. United States*, 341 U. S. 494 (1951).

the time element than the "present" danger criterion. As for the "bad tendency" standard, it either disregards both time and probability or minimizes the significance of these factors. The danger may be remote and the degree of probability minor, without negating the contention that speech may be productive of a tendency towards evil.

Although the clear and present danger criterion continues to be the favorite of the Supreme Court, it still remains true, as remarked many years ago by Associate Justice Brandeis, that the Court has not fixed the standard by which to determine when a danger shall be deemed clear; how remote the danger may be and yet be deemed present; and what degree of evil shall be considered sufficiently substantial to justify resort to abridgment of free speech and assembly as a means of protection.

What has been said above applies to both freedom of the press and freedom to assemble. The right to assemble is closely associated with freedom of speech, inasmuch as people assemble for the purpose of discussing and giving expression to their views. A point not heretofore mentioned is that freedom of speech and of the press, as a general rule but not absolutely, prohibit governmental censorship in the sense of prior restraints on speech and publication. In *Near v. Minnesota*,[43] the Court stated that the chief purpose of the guarantee of freedom of the press is to prevent previous restraints on publication. However, it has been unwilling to ban all prior censorship, as evidenced by its pronouncements in controversies involving motion pictures and obscene literature. The Court's position seems to be that prior restraint or censorship, as distinguishable from subsequent punishment

[43] 283 U. S. 697 (1931).

for statements already made, is permissible *only in exceptional cases.*[44]

In the case of the Pentagon papers concerning Vietnam war policy-making, the Court denied an injunction restraining their publication on the ground that the United States government failed to show justification for imposition of a prior restraint of expression. It asserted that any system of prior restraint bears a heavy presumption against its constitutional validity.[44a]

In 1972, a year after the above ruling, the Court announced two important decisions. One declared that journalists have no right under the freedom of speech and press guarantees of the First Amendment to refuse disclosure of confidential sources of information to *grand juries.*[44b] In the other decision a ruling to the same general effect with respect to a *grand jury investigation* concerning re-publication of the Pentagon papers by the Beacon Press was applied to Senator Gravel and his aides.[44c] Despite the constitutional stipulation that neither Senators nor Representatives shall be questioned in any other place for speeches or debates in either House, the Court held that the *grand jury* had the right to question the Senator and his aides with respect to the source of the highly classified documents in the Senator's possession—as long as no legislative act was implicated in the questions. Immunity under the speech and debate clause is inapplicable to a grand jury investigation regarding criminal behavior.

[44] *Times Film Corporation v. Chicago,* 365 U. S. 43 (1961); *Burstyn v. Wilson,* 343 U. S. 495 (1952).

[44a] *New York Times Company v. United States; United States v. Washington Post Company,* 29 L Ed 2d 822 (1971)

[44b] *United States v. Caldwell, Branzburg v. Hayes, In Re Pappas,* 40 Law Week 5025.

[44c] *Gravel v. United States,* 40 Law Week 5053.

Freedom of Religion

The guarantee of religious freedom is based on the explicit stipulations of the First Amendment which is binding on the national government and on the due process clause of the Fourteenth Amendment which has been construed as prohibiting state action in denial of this important liberty. Neither the national government nor the states may enact laws respecting an establishment of religion or prohibiting the free exercise thereof. The purpose of this guarantee is to prevent governmental domination of the religious beliefs and practices of individuals and to close the door to the direction of governmental action by a religious sect—something which could occur if the establishment of an official religion and church were permissible.

Erection of a "wall of separation between church and state" was the purpose of the clause against *establishment of a religion*. It rested on "the belief that a union of government and religion tends to destroy government and to degrade religion" and also "upon an awareness of the historical fact that governmentally established religions and religious persecutions go hand in hand." The establishment of a state church or adoption of an official religion is banned even though no direct governmental compulsion may be involved and other religions are permitted to carry on their activities. In *Engel v. Vitale*[45] the Supreme Court held that the constitutional ban on the enactment of laws establishing a religion was violated by state authorization of daily recital, in school, of a prayer composed by New York state officials; and in *Abington School District v. Schempp*,[46] the same conclusion was

[45] 370 U. S. 421 (1962).
[46] 374 U. S. 203 (1963).

reached with respect to a Pennsylvania statute requiring the daily reading, without comment, of at least ten verses from the Holy Bible. A different position was taken in *Everson v. Board of Education*[47] with respect to a township board of education policy which authorized reimbursement to parents of money expended for the bus transportation of their children to school, including parochial as well as public schools. The Court held that the policy was intended to promote the welfare of school children and their parents rather than to provide financial aid in support of a religious institution or sect. Furthermore, a state may grant property-tax exemption to religious organizations if the legislative purpose is *not* aimed at establishing, sponsoring, or supporting religion and if the effect of the exemptions is *not* an excessive governmental entanglement with religion.[47a] Nor is federal aid to church-related colleges and universities for the construction of buildings and facilities prohibited, provided these are to be used exclusively for secular educational purposes and no time limit is placed on the government's interest in such federally financed projects.[47b]

Guarantee of the *free exercise of religion* bars legislation respecting religious beliefs and their expression. Violation of this freedom is predicated *on coercion*, whereas the element of forcible constraint may not be implicated in disregard of the ban against establishment of a religion. Religious freedom does not mean that all behavior based on religious doctrine is immune from restriction by law. In *Reynolds v. United States*,[48] the Supreme Court upheld the conviction of Reyn-

[47] 330 U. S. 1 (1947).

[47a] *Walz v. Tax Commission of City of New York*, 397 U. S. 644 (1970)

[47b] *Tilton v. Richardson*, 29 L Ed 2d 790 (1971)

[48] 98 U. S. 145 (1878).

olds, a Mormon, under an act of Congress making polygamy a punishable crime in the territory of Utah. In rejecting Reynolds's contention that his religious freedom had been abridged, the Court pointed out that this freedom does not include the right, in the name of religion, to commit acts of an immoral or criminal character. Generally speaking, no one is exempt from obedience to criminal law merely because of his religious convictions. Three cases have been selected to illustrate instances in which the Court has ruled that governmental restraints have interfered with the free exercise of religion.

In *Murdock v. Pennsylvania*,[49] a local ordinance required the procurement of a license and the payment of a fee by all persons canvassing or soliciting orders for merchandise of any kind or delivering such articles under orders so obtained and solicited. Jehovah's Witnesses engaged in such activity without obtaining the required license or paying a fee. The Supreme Court held that the ordinance was invalid in its application to the distribution and sale of religious literature. No tax can be levied on exercise of the right of religious freedom. In *West Virginia State Board of Education v. Barnette*,[50] the issue was the constitutionality of a *compulsory flag salute*. The children of Jehovah's Witnesses, having refused to salute on religious grounds, were expelled from school. To compel the giving of a salute and to subject the disobedient children and their parents to specified penalties violated the guarantee of religious freedom. By so ruling the Court reversed a decision rendered three years earlier in *Minersville School District v. Gobitis*.[51] In *Wisconsin v.*

[49] 319 U. S. 105 (1943).
[50] 319 U. S. 624 (1943).
[51] 310 U. S. 624 (1943)

Yoder[51a] the defendants were convicted of violating Wisconsin's compulsory school attendance law which requires a child's school attendance until age sixteen. Yoder and others contended that high school attendance was contrary to the Amish religion and way of life. The Court upheld their right to refuse sending their children to public or private school after graduation from the eighth grade. It stated that the state's interest in universal education is not entirely free from a balancing process when it impinges on other fundamental rights, such as those specifically protected by the free exercise of religion clause of the First Amendment which is binding on the states via the Fourteenth Amendment. Wisconsin had failed to show how its admittedly strong interest in compulsory education would be adversely affected by granting an exemption to the Amish.

The constitutional guarantees pertaining to religion have such restrictive effects as the following: no state church may be established and no official religion designated; no law may be passed aiding one religion or all religions; governmental participation in the affairs of any religious group or organization is prohibited; no taxes may be levied and public funds expended for the purpose of supporting religious organizations or activities; religious activities, as such, e.g., delivering a sermon, are completely immune from taxation; no one may be compelled to attend religious services or be prohibited from doing so; and no one may be forced to subscribe to any religious beliefs or disbeliefs.

A great variety of circumstances may give rise to litigation requiring judicial interpretation of the guarantees pertaining to religion. Application of these guarantees to specific situa-

[51a] 40 Law Week 4476 (1972)

tions has often revealed division of opinion within the Supreme Court and given rise, on occasion, to reversals and modifications of previous rulings, especially as the personnel of the Court has changed.

Due Process of Law

What is due process of law, without which neither the national government nor the states may deprive persons of life, liberty, or property? It has been said that "due process" is undefinable, but this statement is partially false and partially true. Its falsity is due to the fact that the general meaning of this restriction on governmental power has been indicated clearly enough in many cases in which due process has been the subject of consideration by the Supreme Court. Its truth is based on another fact, viz., that the general sense of this phrase cannot be stated so precisely and so comprehensively that one is able to forecast the outcome of litigation in which a denial of due process is claimed.

At first, due process was construed as a limitation only on procedure. The judicial view which now prevails and dates back many years is that the substance of governmental policies regulating behavior also is subject to the requisites of due process. Thus substantive as well as procedural rights are safeguarded by the process clause.

In regard to procedural rights, the general import of due process is that administrative and judicial proceedings must meet the tests of fairness and just treatment. The principal "due process" requirements in connection with adjudication by *administrative agencies* are adequate notice and a fair hearing. Among the elements which the Supreme Court has held necessary to due process in the settlement of controversies by the *judiciary* are proper notice to the defendant of the cause of action against him; an opportunity to be heard and the right to counsel in all criminal prosecutions, either for felonies or for misdemeanors, which may result in imprisonment;[51b] an orderly trial by an impartial tribunal having jurisdiction over the controversy; the right to confront and examine witnesses; the inadmissibility of illegally seized evidence; the exclusion of involuntary confessions in criminal cases; and the right to a speedy and public trial.

Of the procedural rights expressly guaranteed against the national government, several are considered unessential to due process and therefore not binding on the states. Examples are indictment by a grand jury and trial by jury in juvenile delinquency adjudications.

Until recently, trial by jury in both criminal and civil cases apparently could be dispensed with by the states. In 1968 the Supreme Court held that the due process clause of the Fourteenth Amendment comprehends the jury trial stipulation of the Sixth Amendment and requires state provision of jury trials in *serious* criminal (*Duncan v. Louisiana*)[52] and *serious* criminal contempt cases (*Bloom v.*

[51b] *Argersinger v. Hamlin,* 40 Law Week 4679 (1972). The Court in this case stated that indigent defendants are entitled to a court-appointed counsel, inasmuch as the right to counsel pertains to defendants in general in all criminal prosecutions which may eventuate in loss of liberty. In *United States v. Wade,* 388 U. S. 218 (1967), the Court ruled that the presence of counsel is a constitutional essential at *any critical stage* of the prosecution of an accused person, formal or informal, in court or out. However, in *Kirby v. Illinois,* 40 Law Week 4607 (1972), the Court held that the presence of counsel is unnecessary in a police station show-up which occurs before the defendant has been indicted or otherwise formally charged with a criminal offense. See *Infra,* pp. 588, 589.

[52] 20 L Ed 2d 491

Illinois).[52a] However, neither the national government nor the states are constitutionally obligated to provide twelve-man juries.[52b]

Two cases decided in May, 1972, upheld the right of the states to provide for jury verdicts by a "substantial majority" instead of by unanimous vote. In *Johnson v. Louisiana*[52c] a 9 to 3 vote was considered sufficient to convict a defendant charged with a crime necessarily punishable by hard labor. This case arose before the *Duncan* decision and the Court asserted that jury unanimity was never held to be a requisite of due process and that the equal protection clause was not violated by the Louisiana policy of requiring unanimity for conviction of some crimes, e.g., capital cases, but not for all. In *Apodaca et al. v. Oregon*[52d] a Court majority of five held that the Sixth Amendment guarantee of a jury trial, applicable to the states through the Fourteenth Amendment, does not require that a jury's vote be unanimous in criminal cases. However, one of the five maintained that the rule of unanimity is mandatory in *federal* criminal jury trials—as maintained by the four justices who dissented from the ruling that unanimity is not obligatory in state criminal trials. The result (perhaps temporary) of the *Apodaca* case is as follows: five justices agree that unanimity is required in federal trials but five, including one of the former group, maintain that unanimity is not essential to state criminal convictions. In neither the *Johnson* nor the *Apodaca* case was a distinction drawn between capital and non-capital criminal prosecutions.

[52a] 20 L Ed 2d 522
[52b] *Williams v. Florida,* 399 U. S. 78 (1970)
[52c] 40 Law Week 4524
[52d] 40 Law Week 4528

In 1969 the highest court declared that individuals in the military services cannot be tried by courts-martial except for *service-connected crimes*.[52e] Crimes against civilians by service-men on a military base are sufficiently service-connected to warrant trial by court-martial.[52f]

Many of the above-mentioned requisites of due process apply to juvenile as well as to adult court proceedings, e.g., the giving of notice, the right to counsel, the privilege against self-incrimination, and the right to confront and examine witnesses.[52g] Also, the guilt of a juvenile charged with a *serious* crime must be proved beyond a reasonable doubt and not merely by a preponderance of the evidence.[52h] However, the due process clause of the Fourteenth Amendment does not assure the right of trial by jury in the adjudicative phase of a state juvenile delinquency proceeding.[52i]

The general meaning of due process with respect to substantive rights, as stated by the Supreme Court, is that "regulation which is reasonable in relation to its subject and is adopted in the interests of the community is due process." Unreasonable, arbitrary, or capricious governmental policies imposing restraints on individual liberty or depriving persons of life or property are unconstitutional. Among the various factors considered by the judiciary in passing judgment on the reasonableness of laws are the purpose of legislation, the relation between the avowed objective and the means chosen for achieving it, and the circumstances that have led to regulatory legislative action. Reasonable men, including members

[52e] *O'Callahan v. Parker*, 23 L Ed 2d 291
[52f] *Relford v. Commandant*, 28 L Ed 2d 102 (1971)
[52g] *In Re Gault*, 387 U. S. 1 (1967)
[52h] *In Re Winship*, 397 U. S. 358 (1970)
[52i] *McKeiver v. Pennsylvania*, 29 L Ed 2d 647 (1971)

of the Supreme Court, may disagree concerning the reasonableness of particular restrictive laws.

Many governmental actions have been challenged on the ground of denial of due process. Some have survived the tests of reasonableness and/or fairness; others have not. The most appropriate closing observation is that any exercise of governmental power is reasonable or fair if considered so by a Supreme Court majority.

Equal Protection of the Laws

No state, according to the Fourteenth Amendment, shall deny to *any person* the equal protection of the laws. The national government is not subjected to an identical limitation but the Supreme Court has held that the concepts of due process and equal protection are not mutually exclusive and that arbitrary and unreasonable discriminations constitute a denial of due process. However, it has asserted that "equal protection of the laws" is a more explicit safeguard against prohibited unfairness than "due process of law." [53]

Both the due process and equal protection clauses are limitations *only on governmental action*. Individual invasion of individual rights is not the subject matter of these and other provisions of the Fourteenth Amendment. That is why restrictive *legislation* is necessary to prohibit discriminatory and otherwise reprehensible behavior on the part of individuals in their relations with one another.

The requirement of "equal protection" does not demand strict legal equality in the sense that every person is to possess the same rights and be subject to the same duties as every

[53] *Bolling v. Sharpe*, 347 U. S. 497 (1954).

other person. Classification is permissible, but all individuals in the same class must be accorded the same rights and be bound by the same obligations. A classification is valid if any state of facts may reasonably be conceived to justify it. Invidious discrimination, rather than all discrimination, is prohibited by the equal protection clause.

The determining factors are reasonableness and relevance to the purpose of legislation. Shortly before the end of the nineteenth century, the Supreme Court upheld a Louisiana statute which required railroads to furnish separate but equal accommodations for white and colored people. It asserted that a law authorizing or requiring separation of the two races cannot be considered unreasonable or obnoxious to the Fourteenth Amendment.[54] Nearly sixty years later, however, the Court ruled that segregation of children in public schools solely on the basis of race, even though the physical facilities and other tangible factors may be equal, is unconstitutional. This holding in *Brown et al. v. Board of Education*[55] was based on the view that "separate educational facilities are inherently unequal" and therefore prohibited by the equal protection clause. Segregation in schools of the District of Columbia was declared invalid in *Bolling v. Sharpe*,[56] but in this case the Court's decision was based on the due process clause of the Fifth Amendment, inasmuch as the equal protection provision of the Fourteenth applies only to the states and not to the national government. The Court stated that segregation in public education imposes a burden on Negro children that constitutes arbitrary deprivation of their liberty in violation of the due process clause.

[54] *Plessy v. Ferguson*, 163 U. S. 537 (1896).
[55] 347 U. S. 483 (1954).
[56] 347 U. S. 497 (1954).

The ruling in the *Brown* case was followed by decisions
banning segregation in various public facilities, including
transportation, parks, playgrounds, golf courses, and bath-
ing beaches. In 1971 the Court held that the closing of
swimming pools does not violate either the Thirteenth
Amendment or the equal protection clause of the Fourteenth, provided substantial evidence indicates that the closing is due to the conviction that pools cannot be operated
safely and economically on an integrated basis; that no
evidence shows an intention to aid covertly the maintenance
and operation of pools private in name only; and that there
is no state action affecting blacks differently from whites.[56a]
In *Reitman v. Mulkey*,[57] decided in 1967, the issue was the
constitutionality of a California constitutional amendment
prohibiting state and local legislation denying or limiting
the right of any person to *refuse* to sell, lease, or rent real
property for residential purposes to anyone to whom he did
not desire to sell, rent, or lease. This provision was declared
unconstitutional because it involved the state in racial discrimination inasmuch as *its effect* was to *authorize private
discrimination on racial grounds* in the housing market. In
James v. Valtierra[57a] (1971) the Court supported a California constitutional provision stipulating that no low-rent
housing project (defined as a development furnishing living

[56a] *Palmer v. Thompson,* 29 L Ed 2d 438. In regard to transportation see *Henderson v. United States,* 339 U. S. 816 (1950), *Gayle v.
Browder,* 352 U. S. 903 (1956), *Boynton v. Virginia,* 364 U. S. 454
(1960); public beaches, bath houses, *Mayor & Council of Baltimore
v. Dawson,* 350 U. S. 877 (1955); golf courses, *Holmes v. Atlanta,*
350 U. S. 879 (1955).
[57] 387 U.S. 369. Earlier cases prohibiting racial discrimination in
housing are *Buchanan v. Warley,* 245 U. S. 60 (1917), *Shelley v.
Kraemer,* 334 U. S. 1 (1948), and *Barrows v. Jackson,* 346 U. S.
249 (1953).
[57a] 402 U. S. 137 (1971)

accommodations for low-income persons) shall be developed, constructed, or acquired in any manner by a state public body until approved by a majority vote in a city, town, or county referendum. This provision was upheld on several grounds, *viz.*, (1) it did not violate the supremacy or the privileges and immunities clauses of the United States Constitution, (2) did not rest on racial distinctions, and (3) did not deny equal protection by singling out low-income persons for *mandatory referenda*—inasmuch as such referenda, which other groups have to face, have been required in California for the decision of various questions, among them the approval of constitutional amendments, general-obligation bond issues, and territorial annexations. The issue in *Moose Lodge No. 107, Appellant v. Irvis*[57b] was whether the granting of a state liquor license to a private club practicing racial discrimination constitutes discriminatory action by the state in violation of the equal protection clause. The Court held that the mere granting of a liquor license to such a club, *except as noted below,* does not implicate the state *sufficiently* to make the discriminatory practice "state action." Irvis had been refused service as an invited guest in the club restaurant. No question of the club's discriminatory membership policy was involved in the case. A three-judge federal panel had ruled in favor of Irvis. The discriminatory guest practice had been incorporated in the by-laws of the club after this decision. Pennsylvania's liquor board regulation requires that "every club licensee shall adhere to all provisions of its constitution and by-laws." The Court stated that this regulation, in effect, places state sanctions behind the discriminatory practices of the club. However, it held that enforcement of the regulation

[57b] 40 Law Week 4715 (1972)

should be enjoined only *to the extent that it requires the
club to adhere to its discriminatory practices*. Otherwise,
no *state* discriminatory action is involved in the granting
of a liquor license. In 1967 a Virginia law prohibiting marriages on the basis of a racial classification was declared
unconstitutional as an invidious racial discrimination in violation of both the equal protection and the due process
provisions of the Fourteenth Amendment.[58]

The foregoing, as well as various other cases, demonstrate
the unpredictability of application of the equal protection
clause. An unexpected recent ruling, which will be discussed
in a later chapter, was the conclusion of the Court that this
limitation on the powers of the states requires population-
based apportionment of the members of both houses of state
legislatures.

Guarantees of Rights in State Constitutions

So far, attention has been confined to rights guaranteed by
the Constitution of the United States. Guarantees of rights
are also a feature of the constitutions of the fifty states. Generally speaking, the fundamental laws of the states contain
stipulations concerning rights which closely resemble those
incorporated in the national constitution. Additional rights of
one type or another are often included. An example is the
recently adopted Constitution of Michigan's provision that
all individuals, firms, corporations, and voluntary associations
have the right to fair and just treatment in the course of
legislative and executive investigations and hearings. Exami-

[58] *Loving v. Virginia*, 388 U. S. 1 (1967)

nation of the constitution of every state would be necessary to an exhaustive discussion of this subject. Furthermore, an indispensable requirement would be ascertainment of judicial interpretations of the rights guaranteed in state constitutions. Final determination of the meaning of these rights and their restrictive effect on state officials rests with the court of last resort of each particular state. All rights guaranteed by a state constitution are binding, as such, only on the state government and local units—not on the national government.

The Duties of Individuals

This chapter has emphasized the *constitutional rights* of individuals and the restrictive effect of these rights on government. Many rights unmentioned in either the national or state constitutions are conferred by laws enacted by Congress, state legislatures, and local legislative bodies.

The tendency of inhabitants of the United States has been to talk at length about their rights but to say little or nothing about their duties. However, for every right there is a correlative duty. Obviously, the conferment of a right on some or all persons places an obligation on others to refrain from action which is invasive of this right. A right which no one need respect is meaningless. Moreover, the possessors of rights are duty-bound not to abuse them. Abuses may be prevented by appropriate legislation. Ample evidence in substantiation of this statement has been presented in the preceding pages.

Governmental imposition of duties on individuals is limited only by such individual rights as are guaranteed by constitutional stipulation. Everyone is under obligation to abide by the laws of the land and these laws impose many particular duties on the individual. Examples are compulsory education up to a designated age; compulsory military service; compulsory payment of taxes for the purpose of financing governmental activities; compulsory appearance in court when summoned as a defendant or subpoenaed as a witness; compulsory service in a *posse comitatus* if summoned by a sheriff; and compulsory service on juries, unless excused. In addition to these and many others too numerous to mention are the duty of loyalty to the United States and the duty of an individual to arrest a person committing a crime in his presence. A notable exception to the fact that practically all duties are established by ordinary law rather than by constitutional provision is the stipulation of the Thirteenth Amendment that neither slavery nor involuntary servitude, except as a punishment for crime, shall exist in the United States or any place subject to its jurisdiction. This provision applies to private individuals as well as to governmental authorities, and individuals have been prosecuted and convicted for disregarding it.

Legally binding duties are distinguishable from ethical obligations. An example of the latter type of obligation, insofar as it pertains to government, is participation in elections on the part of qualified voters. Compulsory voting has not been provided for in the United States. The sphere of ethical obligations comprehends the many things that people ought to do as a matter of moral duty, even though not required to do them as a matter of law.

Rights and duties are inseparable. Until rather recently, few constitutions included provisions concerning duties. Perhaps the time has come for the United States to do what a number of countries have done, viz., to incorporate a statement of the basic obligations of citizenship in the supreme law of the land. On many occasions people seem to forget that duties are just as important as the rights upon which so much emphasis is placed.

Elections, Political Parties, and Pressure Groups

C H A P T E R ☆ F O U R

Elections
    Voting Qualifications and Disqualifications
    Registration of Voters
    Absentee Voting
    Election Methods
        Single Choice-Plurality
        Majority Choice
        Limited and Cumulative Voting
        Proportional Representation
        Types of Ballot
        Safeguards Against Fraud and Intimidation
Nominations
    Partisan Direct Primary: Closed and Open Types
    Non-Partisan Primary
    Caucuses and Conventions
    By Petition
    Self-Announcement
Political Parties
    Functions in Democracies
    Major and Minor Parties in the United States
    Two-Party Situation in the United States: Reasons

One-Party and Multi-Party Situations
Organization of the Democratic and Republican
    Parties
    National Organs; State and Local Organs
    Likeness of the Democratic and Republican Parties
Pressure Groups and Pressure Politics
    Private Associations
    Pressure Politics
    Techniques of Pressure Groups
    Unorganized Interest-Groups
    Individual Efforts
    Extent of Pressure Politics
Public Opinion
    Nature of Public Opinion
    Influence of Public Opinion
    Opinion-Creation by Public Officials
Realities of the Governmental Process

☆ ☆ ☆ ☆ ☆ ☆ ☆ ☆ ☆ ☆ ☆ ☆

In democracies of the representative type, the role of the people in the governmental process differs from that of public officials. The latter make policy-decisions and undertake the task of administering whatever policies have been adopted. Generally speaking, the people do not govern; they merely decide who shall do the governing. An exception to this statement is popular voting on proposed laws through resort to the initiative and the referendum. Although neither device is available at the level of national government, both are provided for in numerous municipalities and by about one-third of the states. Even so, state and local officials normally do the governing. The only surviving examples of direct democracy are found in the smaller towns of the New England group of states.

A popular vote on proposed state constitutions and subsequent amendments is mandatory in almost all of the states and in many states city charters are submitted to the voters for approval. No provision is made for direct popular participation in the process of amending the national constitution.

Though the people do not govern, they have ample opportunity to control or influence the course of governmental action by choosing various officials, by organizing political parties and competing for control of the government, by bringing pressure to bear on officeholders, and by making known their views through exercise of such rights as freedom of speech and of the press, freedom of assembly, and petitioning the government for redress of grievances. In these ways the voice of the people makes itself heard and also felt. More accurately, one should speak of the voices of the people, inasmuch as diversity of opinion is normal, unanimity of opinion rare, and general opinion by no means common.

Elections

At the national level, the only elective officers are the President, Vice President, and members of Congress. A considerable variety of state and local officeholders are chosen by popular vote—members of legislative bodies, usually the chief executive and judges, and sundry administrative officials.

Popular election for fixed terms of office enables the qualified voters to determine who shall do the governing. It also permits replacements in the event of dissatisfaction with performance in office. "Refusal to reelect" is one way of holding an official to account for his actions. Although what-has-been-done cannot always be undone, the replacement of a particular official by another person is a means of decreasing the likelihood, at least for the time being, of a continuation of some policy or policies that have given rise to popular disapproval.

1. *Voting Qualifications and Disqualifications*

Subject to restrictive provisions of the Constitution of the United States (express or implied), the states possess authority to prescribe qualifications for voting in national, state, and local elections. Formerly their power to do so was substantial; today it has dwindled into insignificance.

By express constitutional provision, the right of United States citizens to vote may not be denied because of race, color, or previous condition of servitude; sex; failure to pay taxes (election of national officials); or age—if 18 years or older. This last restriction is incorporated in the Twenty-Sixth Amendment—ratified in June, 1971. With one exception these limitations apply to state and local as well as to national elections.

The exception is the Twenty-Fourth Amendment's provision prohibiting failure to pay taxes as a disqualification for voting in Presidential or Congressional elections. However, in 1966 the Supreme Court decided that the equal protection clause of the Fourteenth Amendment is violated by the states whenever the *affluence of the voter* or *payment of any fee* is established as an electoral standard. This ruling in *Harper v. Virginia Board of Elections*[59] clearly barred tax-paying requirements for participation in the choice of elective state and local officials and presumably precluded a property-owning qualification with respect to such election. Moreover, in *Phoenix v. Kolodziejski* (1970),[59a] the Court held that Arizona's constitutional and statutory provisions excluding non-property owners from elections for approval of general obligation bond issues violated the equal protection clause. Previously, in *Cipriana v. City of Houma*,[59b] it had reached the same conclusion with respect to popular voting on the issuance of utility (revenue) bonds. A New York statute barred persons from voting in school district elections (outside cities) unless they owned or leased real estate or had children in the public schools. This law was declared unconstitutional in *Kramer v. Union Free School District, No. 15* (1969)[59c]. A state may require an extraordinary majority vote on tax and indebtedness measures as long as it does not discriminate against or authorize discrimination against any identifiable class of persons.[59d] The Constitution does not require that a simple majority always prevail on every issue.

The discretion of the states in the matter of voting qualifications is also limited by identical provisions of Article I and the Seventeenth Amendment. These stipulate that individuals eligible to vote for members of the most numerous branch of the state legislature are qualified to participate in the election of members of Congress. Despite the greatly

[59] 383 U. S. 663 (1966)
[59a] 26 L Ed 2d 523 (1970)
[59b] 23 L Ed 2d 647 (1969)
[59c] 395 U. S. 621
[59d] *Gordon v. Lance*, 29 L Ed 2d 273 (1971)

curtailed discretion of the states with respect to voting qualifications, these provisions remain significant.

(a) CITIZENSHIP, AGE, RESIDENCE QUALIFICATIONS
During the 19th and 20th centuries all of the states prescribed citizenship, age, and residence requirements for voting. Now, however, their desires in regard to age qualifications have been superseded by the Twenty-Sixth Amendment and a Supreme Court decision in early 1972 has greatly restricted their authority concerning residence requirements. So did the 1970 Voting Rights Act of Congress which reduced the required length of residence for voting in presidential elections to thirty days—upheld by the Supreme Court in *Oregon v. Mitchell.*[59e]

Since 1926 the privilege of voting has been confined to United States citizens. Before that year various states had permitted aliens to vote if they had declared their intention of becoming citizens.

The Twenty-Sixth Amendment prohibits states from denying the right of United States citizens to vote, if eighteen years old or over, because of age. All but a minority of the states had established twenty-one years as the minimum voting age. In the minority group the age was lowered to eighteen, e.g., Georgia, Kentucky; to nineteen, e.g., Alaska; and to twenty, e.g., Hawaii. Prior to proposal and ratification of the Twenty-Sixth Amendment, the Voting Rights Act of 1970 granted eighteen-year-olds and persons above that age the right to vote in national elections.

Residence within a state is a universal requirement. As recently as 1971, the required period of residence varied from thirty days in one state, to ninety days in five, to six

[59e] 27 L Ed 2d 272 (1970)

months in twenty, and to one year in twenty-four. In addition, residence in the county and/or election district was a requisite in all states, with the required length of residence varying from a minimum of ten days in five states to a maximum of one year in one. Fifteen states fixed the period at six months and most of the others at thirty to ninety days.

The Voting Rights Act of 1970 and a 1972 decision of the Supreme Court in *Dunn v. Blumstein*[59f] have altered the situation with respect to residence requirements. Unfortunately, various questions relative to residence requirements remain unanswered—for reasons that will become apparent upon consideration of the *Dunn* case. Definitely, however, the maximum period of residence required for Presidential elections is thirty days, as prescribed by Congress in the Voting Rights Act of 1970 and subsequently upheld by the Supreme Court.

In *Dunn v. Blumstein* the Supreme Court declared Tennessee's requirement of one year residence in the state and three months in the county unconstitutional in violation of the equal protection clause of the Fourteenth Amendment. The Court asserted that Tennessee had failed to establish a *compelling interest* in justification of its fixed durational residence requirements. In its opinion the Court remarked that a period of thirty days appears ample to prevent fraud and to ensure the purity of the ballot box. It was unimpressed by the argument that long residence requirements are essential to informed voting in state and local elections. The eventual outcome of the Court's ruling is uncertain.

Perhaps thirty days will become the universal state residence requirement for state and local elections, as provided by Congress for Presidential elections. Maybe some state

[59f] 40 Law Week 269

will be able to convince the Court of a sufficient compelling interest to warrant a residence period longer than thirty days, such as thirty-five, forty-five, or sixty. As for county and district requirements, the Court condemned Tennessee's three months county residence stipulation. Local residence requirements equal to or lower than a sanctioned state period of residence probably will meet with Court approval. Seemingly, the most practicable solution for the states is to require thirty days in the state and the same or a shorter period for the county and/or the election district.[60]

(b) LITERACY TESTS Fifteen states provide for some type of literacy test. The requirement commonly amounts to a demonstration of ability to read or to read and write, but

---

[60] Prior to the Voting Rights Act of 1970 and the *Dunn* case, many states had responded to the contention that *interstate* movers should not be disqualified from participation in the choice of presidential electors and that *intrastate* movers should not be denied the privilege of voting for officials chosen on a state-wide basis. About three-fifths of the states had adopted "return to vote" clauses which permitted *intrastate* movers who had registered and then moved before an election to cast ballots in their former election districts—pending fulfillment of residence requirements in their new places of residence. Fifteen states had waived their *state residence* requirement as a requisite for voting in presidential elections and a few applied a return-to-vote clause to *interstate* movers with respect to the same elections.

An issue unrelated to the former plight of interstate and intrastate movers is whether individuals who work in a particular city and pay taxes therein should be permitted to vote in its elections, even though their dwelling places are located outside the municipality's boundaries.

Another question concerning residence and voting pertains to college students. Should residence while attending a college or university be sufficient to qualify for voting in the place where the college or university is located, even though a student is classified by the institution of higher learning as a resident of some other part of the state or of another state? As of 1972 the solution of this problem apparently rests with state and local authorities.

in a few states a person is required to read and understand. This last-mentioned stipulation opened the door to discrimination in the administration of the "understanding" part of the test, with the result that Negroes in some states were denied the voting privilege on the ground of inability to read *and understand*. Because of the discriminatory use of literacy, knowledge, and character tests, the Voting Rights Act of 1965 suspended such tests for determining the qualifications of voters in any state or county wherein less than fifty percent of the voting-age population was registered on November 1, 1964, or voted in the Presidential election of that year. The 1970 Voting Rights Act suspends literacy tests for five years in *all* states.

(c) DISQUALIFICATIONS Disqualifications for voting are established in all of the states. Among the more common are insanity, mental defectiveness, and conviction of such offenses as treason, murder, larceny, forgery, bribery of voters, ballot-box stuffing, and other fraudulent election practices. A pardon may restore the former political privileges of individuals convicted of crimes which entail disqualification for voting.

2. Registration of Voters

In nearly all of the states persons possessing the prescribed qualifications for voting are permitted to vote only if registered. The purpose of *registration* is to prevent denial of the suffrage to qualified individuals, to forestall voting by those unqualified, and to preclude qualified individuals from voting more than once.

A registration system may be *personal* or *official*. If personal, each individual desirous of voting must take the initiative in getting his name placed on the voting list and appear personally before designated registration officials. If official, appropriate officers are charged with the responsibility of preparing a list of all eligible voters.

Registration may be *permanent*, as in most of the states, or *periodic*, as in a small minority. Under the permanent plan, a voter, once registered, need reregister only if he changes his place of residence to another election district. Periodic systems require registration at prescribed intervals of time. The stipulated frequence in one state is every ten years; in three, four years; in two, annually; before every election in one; and prior to every general election in another.

3. *Absentee Voting*

All of the states make provision for absentee voting by persons in the armed forces and most of them extend the privilege to other categories of persons. The purpose of absentee voting laws is to prevent qualified voters from being disqualified merely because of unavoidable absence from their polling places on election day.

Typical procedure involves application for an absentee ballot prior to a specified time in advance of a pending election in which the applicant desires to vote, marking the received ballot in secret, and returning it in a sealed official envelope to the proper election board within the time limit prescribed by law. Among safeguards designed to prevent abuse of the privilege is the requirement that an oath be taken in connection with both the application and the return of the marked absentee ballot.

4. *Election Methods*

(a) SINGLE CHOICE-PLURALITY PLAN The mode of election most extensively used in the United States is the single choice-plurality plan. Each voter may cast his ballot for one of the candidates competing for a particular position and the candidate obtaining more votes than any of his competitors, i.e., a *plurality*, is declared elected. This type of election is favored for the selection of presidential electors, state governors, members of legislatures, judges, various state administrative officials, and numerous local officers chosen by the voters in counties, townships, and cities.

(b) MAJORITY CHOICE METHODS Under the plurality rule, if more than two candidates are running for the same office, the winner's total vote may fall short of a majority (more than half). To prevent the election of a candidate supported by only a minority of the voters, *majority choice* techniques have been adopted in a comparatively small number of jurisdictions—chiefly local. Among the majority choice methods are the second ballot, the Bucklin system, and the alternative vote. Of these, only the last-mentioned is satisfactory. It involves expression of each voter's preferences among the competing candidates; elimination of the lowest candidate at successive stages of the count; and transfer of the latter's ballots according to the next available preference indicated on each ballot. This procedure is followed only if no candidate obtains a "first choice" majority and only until one of the surviving candidates acquires majority support.

(c) LIMITED AND CUMULATIVE VOTING If all or some members of an assembly, e.g., a city council, are elected at-large rather than by single-member districts, both the plurality and majority rules, in combination with one vote for each seat, enable the strongest party or group of like-minded voters to win all of the seats filled in this way. Consequently, some jurisdictions have resorted to either limited or cumulative voting to prevent this result. *Limited voting* prohibits the casting of a ballot for each seat to be filled. Each voter is allowed to vote only for a smaller number, e.g., if three are to be elected, a ballot may be cast for no more than two candidates. *Cumulative voting* retains the standard policy of one vote per seat to be filled, but permits a voter to give all of his votes to one candidate or to distribute them as he sees fit. Thus, if three are to be elected, the voter may cast three votes for one candidate, or two for one and one for another, or one for each of three.

Cumulative voting is provided for in Illinois for the choice of members of the lower house of the state legislature. Otherwise, its infrequent use occurs in the field of local government. Limited voting is encountered more often, but again, not frequently. It is another device which is confined for the most part to the local government level.

(d) PROPORTIONAL REPRESENTATION Cumulative and limited voting ordinarily prevent a clean sweep by the strongest group of like-minded voters, but fall short of insuring proportional representation for the different groups or parties participating in an election for the choice of representatives. To achieve this result, either the *list* or the *single transferable vote* methods of proportional representation may be utilized. The list system has never gained a foothold in the United States and the single transferable vote plan has been adopted by only a small number of local units of government.

The list system is featured by party lists of candidates, by voting for a party list, and by the distribution of seats among parties according to the percentage of the total vote obtained by each. Usually, the voter may indicate his preference among the candidates included within the list for which he casts his ballot. Variations in the details of the list system are too numerous for coverage in this text.

The single transferable vote method involves a single listing of candidates rather than a number of party lists; a preferential ballot which permits each voter to rate all of the candidates in the order of his preference; establishment of the quota of votes required for election (e.g., number of ballots divided by number of representatives to be chosen); and the transfer of ballots, if necessary, until all seats are filled. First choices are counted and candidates obtaining the established quota are declared elected. If seats remain unfilled, the surplus ballots, if any, of elected candidates are transferred to voter-designated nominees lacking the required quota of votes, and if the number of elected candidates still falls short of the number of representatives to be chosen, the lowest competitor is eliminated and the ballots he has so far received are transferred to the surviving candidates in accordance with the expressed preferences of the voters who supported him. This process of eliminating the lowest candidate at successive stages of the count continues until all seats have been filled. The transferring of surplus ballots and those of defeated candidates is always based on the indicated preferences of the voters.

Proportional representation modes of election (P. R.) are unlikely to become more popular in the United States than they have been in the past. Much of the opposition is due to the complexity of these methods as compared with the simplicity of single choice-plurality elections. Inability to understand these systems, especially the single transferable vote plan, and the intense opposition of various vested political interests have defeated most drives to establish P. R. or, if adopted, to retain it.

5. *Types of Ballot*

Two principal forms of ballot are used in the United States. One is the "party column" type; the other is referred to as the "office block" or "office column" variety.

The distinguishing feature of the *party column* ballot is the vertical listing of the candidates of each party for all of the offices to be filled at a particular election. A vertical list of positions is paralleled by as many columns of party candidates as there are parties in competition for placement of their members in office. Usually, party column ballots permit the voting of a straight ticket by simply placing a cross in a space provided for that purpose at the top of the party column on a paper ballot or by moving a designated indicator if voting machines are used.

The *office block* or *office column* ballot differs in that no party columns of candidates are provided. Instead, all candidates for each office are grouped together or listed under the title of the position to be filled. Unless special arrangements are made for voting a straight party ticket, the voter is forced to ascertain his party's candidate for each position and then mark his ballot for that person if he desires to support him.

This procedure is supposed to decrease straight ticket voting because the voter is more likely to split his ticket when his attention is directed to candidates of parties other than his own. Office block or column ballots may be non-partisan in character, i.e., contain the names of candidates without indication of their party affiliation.

6. *Safeguards Against Fraud and Intimidation*

Whatever the methods of election and the forms of ballot, the safeguarding of elections against fraudulent practices and the intimidation of voters is essential. The *registration of voters*, previously considered, serves as a deterrent to such frauds as impersonation, colonizing, repeating, and the casting of ballots for fictitious or dead individuals. Another way of discouraging fraudulent and corrupt practices is to provide punishment for such acts in relation to elections as are placed in the *criminal* category. Among designated "election crimes" are bribery, ballot-box stuffing, tampering with ballots or voting machines, falsification of returns, intimidation of voters, and interference with the functioning of election officials. An additional policy directed against practices detracting from the purity of elections is limiting the *nature and amount of campaign expenditures* and *restricting the sources* from which candidates and parties may obtain money for election purposes.

Provision for *secrecy in voting* is another means of safeguarding elections. Although a preventive of certain types of fraud, its principal value is to furnish some degree of protection against the intimidation of voters. Among the ways of achieving both objectives are the preparation of uniform ballots by governmental officials at public expense, the distribution of ballots only at the polling place by election officials, the banning of assistance in voting except under special circumstances, the prohibition of distinguishing marks on a ballot, and adequate arrangements for voting in seclusion. Some of these features of what is known as the Australian ballot system pertain only to paper ballots which are still used in many jurisdictions. Others are equally pertinent if voting machines are in use.

Additional ways of curtailing intimidation of voters are the maintenance of order at the polls and the prohibition of electioneering within the polling place or within a specified distance therefrom. Some intimidating practices are difficult to prevent. An example is forcible prevention of appearance at the polls. Another is the threat of dire consequences, such as loss of employment, if a particular party or candidate should emerge as winner of an election. A variety of subtle modes of intimidation may be resorted to by persons who seek an election victory and believe that the desired objective justifies any and all means of attaining it.

Nominations

Methods of nominating candidates for elective offices are just as important as modes of election. The quality of the persons elected to office depends on the calibre of the nominees, since the choice available to voters on election day is ordinarily confined to the candidates who have been nominated by whatever methods are established by law.

The Partisan Direct Primary

The most widely used method of nomination is the partisan direct primary. Qualified members of each party, voting separately but usually on the same day and at the same official polling places, select their party's candidates for public office. Ordinarily, a partisan desirous of becoming his party's candidate for an elective office is required to file a petition to have his name placed on the primary ballot, but some jurisdictions permit self-announcement of candidacy, sometimes with the support of a few sponsors, and in a few states names are placeable on the primary ballot by action of pre-primary party conventions. The plurality rule is usually followed in determining the winner among those seeking nomination.

1. CLOSED AND OPEN TYPES   Partisan direct primaries are either *closed* or *open*. The closed type is the more common of the two. Its distinguishing feature is application of a test of party affiliation—either registration as a party member prior to the primary election or the taking of an oath that the voter is a party member if his claim to be such is challenged on the occasion of his appearance at the polls.

The open primary is so called because the voter is free to participate in the primary of whatever party he chooses. No evidence of party membership is required. Of course, no one is supposed to take part in the nomination of a particular party's candidates unless he really belongs to that party, but practice is frequently in conflict with supposition.

A variation of the typical open primary is found in the state of Washington. A voter may cast his ballot for one of the aspirants for nomination by a particular party to one office and then vote for some competitor for nomination by some other party for another office. This arrangement enables a voter to shift from party to party, if he so desires, with respect to each office for which nominations are being made. It amounts to the holding of a separate open primary for every office.

2. PRINCIPAL ADVANTAGE OF PARTISAN DIRECT PRIMARY The principal advantage claimed for nomination by some type of partisan direct primary, rather than by party caucus or convention, is that nominees are selected directly by the rank and file of party members rather than by a small number of influential and powerful partisans. Aspirants for nomination by a party may win the primary election despite the opposition of these leaders. Such is occasionally the case, but as a rule individuals backed by the party organization emerge as winners of the primary election.

Non-Partisan Primaries

Non-partisan primaries are used to nominate candidates for various local offices, for judgeships in about one-third of the states, and for membership in state legislatures in two states (Minnesota and Nebraska). Their purpose is to discourage the drawing of national party lines in state and local elections and also, in the case of judges, to eliminate partisan considerations from the choice of officials whose duties should be discharged without bias and without reference to controversial questions of governmental policy. These efforts to promote non-partisanship in the sense indicated have been successful to some extent but have not entirely eliminated partisan thinking and voting along national party lines on the part of many voters.

Competition in a non-partisan primary is confined to persons who have filed the petitions requisite for having their names placed on the primary ballot. No party designations appear on this ballot. The two competitors who poll the highest total of votes qualify as the candidates whose names will appear on the ballot at the subsequent regular election. In some bodies politic, a competitor in the primary who receives the support of more than half of the voters is forthwith declared elected to the office for which he and his rivals were seeking nomination.

Caucuses and Conventions

The first mandatory state-wide partisan direct primary laws were enacted shortly after commencement of the twentieth century. Prior to that time, with some minor exceptions, party nominations were made by *caucuses* (meetings of partisans) and by *delegate conventions*. Partisan caucuses of various types were commonly relied upon until approximately the beginning of the second quarter of the nineteenth century but lost ground rapidly to the delegate convention which prevailed until replaced by the partisan direct primary.

Delegates to conventions are chosen in various ways—by the rank and file of party members; by local conventions for participation in a convention serving a wider area, e.g., choice of national convention delegates by a state convention; and by party committees, as exemplified by such delegates to a national convention as are selected by state central committees.

As everyone presumably knows, Presidential and Vice

Presidential candidates continue to be nominated by national conventions. A few states still use the convention method for naming candidates for state-wide offices and for seats in the House of Representatives and/or the Senate. This mode of nomination also survives to a limited extent at the local government level.

The merits of nomination by caucuses or conventions were overshadowed by the serious abuses which developed in connection with use of these devices. Generally speaking, unscrupulous politicians gained control of caucuses and conventions and used them to advance their own selfish interests. This development produced the widespread dissatisfaction which led to the introduction and subsequent extensive employment of the direct primary for nominating purposes. None of these three methods of nomination is entirely satisfactory or wholly undesirable, but neither is the petition plan about to be described.

Nomination by Petition

Nomination by petition is mostly used in the field of local government but also to a limited extent at the state level. It is frequently an alternative to nomination by some other method, such as the direct primary.

A person desirous of becoming a candidate for an elective office is required to file a petition signed by whatever minimum number of qualified voters is prescribed by law. This number may be large or small and may be expressed as a definite figure or as a percentage of the total vote cast at the last election for the candidates competing for a designated office. The larger the number of required signatures, the more difficult the process of nomination. To discourage frivolous candidacies, the deposit of a forfeitable fee is some-times required, but not as frequently as it probably ought to be. Forfeiture occurs if a nominee fails to poll a specified minimum vote.[60a]

The chief merit of the petition plan is that it permits nominations to be made by independents as well as by party members. However, the greater freedom in securing nomina-tion by this method may result in an unduly large number of nominees, some of them largely for publicity purposes. Pro-ponents of government by parties claim that the petition plan tends to weaken the responsibility of parties for the way in which public business is conducted.

Self-Announcement

Nomination by petition and/or by non-partisan primary are devices for preventing political parties from monopoliz-ing the selection of nominees for elective offices. Another method serving the same purpose is self-announcement of candidacy. This mode of nomination is exceptional in the United States. Its use is confined for the most part to a comparatively small number of municipalities.

[60a] In *Bullock v. Van Phillip Carter*, 31 L Ed 2d 92 (1972), a state statutory filing-fee scheme requiring candidates in party primary elections to pay large filing fees was declared unconstitutional. Large fees have a substantial impact on exercise of the elective franchise by limiting voters in their choice of candidates, by falling more heavily on the less affluent segments of a community, and by being related to the resources of potential candidates and the voters sup-porting them. Equal protection is denied by such statutes unless reasonably necessary to the accomplishment of legitimate state ob-jectives.

Political Parties

The desires of the people are most effectively expressed through political parties which endeavor to gain control of the government *by placing their members in office*. This immediate aim distinguishes parties from other associations which attempt to influence the course of governmental action. An avowed purpose of all parties is to bring about the adoption of policies to which their leaders and, presumably, their members subscribe. A party in command of the government is able to achieve this objective, if given sufficient time, but even a majority party cannot ordinarily operate in complete disregard of the contentions of minority groups. If two or more parties share control, government by coalition necessarily occurs and no particular party can have its way or be held solely responsible for what is done or left undone.

Functions of Parties in Democracies

One function of political parties, already mentioned, is controlling the government. Another is the furnishing of critical opposition by the parties which have been unable to gain control but have sufficient strength to offer serious competition to the party or parties which, for the time being, are in power. Other important functions are the nomination of candidates; the conducting of election campaigns; persuading persons to register and vote; defining the issues at stake in particular elections; providing the public with information concerning issues and candidates; and enabling voters to act collectively rather than individually in shaping, or striving to shape, governmental policies. Each individual acting alone is unable to accomplish what many persons, acting in organized collaboration, stand a good chance of achieving.

Major and Minor Parties in the United States

Generally speaking, a *two-party situation* prevails in the United States. Although various parties are functioning, only two, the Democratic and Republican, are strong enough to capture control, regularly, of the national, state, and local governments. Minor parties frequently gain seats in legislative assemblies, sometimes place their members in other offices, and occasionally win control of a state or local government, but as a rule the major parties dominate the political scene.

Among the many minor parties which at one time or another have been active in the political life of the United States or of some locality are the Populist Party, the Greenbackers, the Progressive Party, the Farmer-Laborites, the Prohibitionists, the Dixiecrats, the Socialist and Socialist Labor Parties, and the Communist Party. Although minor parties are consistent election losers, their presence has affected the functioning of the major parties and their policy-programs have influenced the course of governmental action.[61]

Reasons for the Two-Party Situation in the United States

A two-party situation has existed in the United States throughout the greater part of its history. A probable con-

[61] For a credible explanation of the place of the minor party in the two-party system see V. O. Key, *Politics, Parties, and Pressure Groups*, 4th ed. (New York, Thomas Y. Crowell Company, 1958), pp. 308–309.

tributing factor has been *consensus* with respect to various political fundamentals, such as the preferability of democracy to authoritarianism, the desirability of separation of church and state, and the maintenance of an essentially private enterprise economy rather than one of a highly socialized variety. Another has been *habit*. Voters have become accustomed to supporting one or the other of the two major parties and question the advisability of "wasting their votes" on minor party candidates. A third factor, unquestionably of major importance, is that no party can gain *control of the national government* unless its voter support is sufficiently widespread, territorially, to win an electoral college majority for its presidential candidate and also to elect its candidates to a majority of the seats in the House of Representatives and the Senate. Parties with voting strength concentrated in a few states can hope for no more than securing representation in Congress or obtaining a limited number of electoral college votes. Awareness of this fact has led to the compromising of differences among groups of voters to the extent necessary for collaboration in support of a presidential candidate. The platforms of both parties are designed to appeal to voters in all sections of the country and usually avoid commitments which are likely to alienate substantial segments of the voting population. A final factor contributing to the dominance of two parties and working to the disadvantage of third parties is the *single choice-plurality type of election*. This election method, in conjunction with the use of single-member districts for the choice of Representatives and the election-at-large of Senators and Presidential Electors by state electorates, constitutes a serious obstacle to minor party efforts to compete successfully against the two major parties in national elections.

One-Party and Multi-Party Situations

A nominal two-party situation exists in all of the states because both the Republican and Democratic parties nominate candidates and campaign for their election. However, in various states one of the two is so strong that it wins election after election and in many states one of the parties is sufficiently stronger than the other to be victorious most of the time. Under such circumstances, what amounts to a *one-party* rather than a two-party situation prevails. Consequently, instead of significant conflict between two parties, the most meaningful competition occurs among the various factions within the dominant party. Factional battles become more important than inter-party contests in state and local politics.

A condition resembling a *multi-party situation* has developed in some legislatures, including Congress. The reason for this statement is that various blocs, such as a farm bloc and a labor bloc, are identifiable within the membership of various legislative chambers, and voting by blocs frequently occurs. Members of both major parties are commonly included within such blocs and as a consequence voting on proposed legislation often fails to correspond to the major party affiliations of particular legislators. Since blocs lack the distinguishing characteristics of parties, the situation referred to is more accurately describable as a multiplicity of blocs rather than of parties.

Organization of the Democratic and Republican Parties

The Democratic and Republican parties, unlike the Conservative and Labor parties of Great Britain, are neither centralized nor well-disciplined. They are loose coalitions of state and local organizations which compose their differences and work together under either the Democratic or Republican banners, primarily on the occasion of a national election.

1. *National Organs*

Both parties hold a *national convention* of locally selected delegates every four years for the primary purpose of nominating candidates for the Presidency and Vice Presidency and at the same time adopting a party platform. This convention nominally selects the members of a *national committee* and also a *national chairman*. The latter is actually named by the presidential nominee and the committee members are nominated by the state delegations to the convention in conformity with state legislation, if any, stipulating the mode of choice, or in accordance with instructions of the state party organization. National committeemen are usually selected by direct primary, by the state central committee, or by a state convention.

Permanent headquarters are maintained by the national committee of each party, but this committee is most active in the years when a President is elected. It meets infrequently and plays a comparatively minor role in developing party organization and discipline. The chairman manages the presidential campaign but thereafter his significance ordinarily declines unless his party wins the Presidency. In that case he usually becomes the chief dispenser of patronage at the disposal of the President. Two other committees at the national level are maintained by the members of each party in the Senate and the House of Representatives. These are the Senatorial and Congressional campaign committees.

2. *State and Local Organs of the Parties*

(a) STATE ORGANS Greatly overshadowing the national agencies in importance are the state and local organs of the parties. Each party maintains a state central committee, a state chairman, and various subcommittees and officers. Practice varies in regard to the method of selecting the central committee members. The unit of representation may be the congressional district, the county, or the state senatorial district. Among the methods of selection are the direct primary, county conventions, the committees of congressional districts or counties, and the state party convention. Sometimes the state committee consists of the chairmen of county committees. The central committee usually selects the state chairman. State conventions no longer possess the significance they once had. In a few states they nominate candidates for various state offices, but their principal function in most jurisdictions is to prepare the state party platform and to select certain party officials.

(b) LOCAL ORGANS Party committees are established in virtually all minor political subdivisions and electoral districts. The most important are usually the county committees and the central committees of the larger cities. Members of the county committees are commonly chosen by a primary election and sometimes by a county convention. A city central committee is likely to be composed of the chairmen of ward committees or include within its membership all ward or precinct committeemen. Each of these committees has a chairman whose political responsibilities and influence are likely to be great. Local conventions are held in some jurisdictions but their functions are of minor significance except in the comparatively few instances in which they name candidates for certain elective offices. Cities are usually divided into wards. Ward committees and their chairmen play an important role in election campaigns and in building up party strength in the intervals between elections.

At the base of the party organization is the *precinct leader, captain,* or *committeeman,* as he is variously known. Sometimes there is a precinct committee. The success of a party at the polls depends in large measure on the proficiency of its precinct leaders. Good ones are on the job every day doing whatever can be done to win support for their parties in their districts. A precinct leader's rating is determined by his ability to deliver the vote on election day, particularly in primary elections.

3. *Relations Between National, State, and Local Organs*

The organization of the Democratic and Republican parties lacks integration from the standpoint of control relationships between the different levels in the hierarchy of committees, chairmen, and other party agencies. Each set of organs functions with a substantial degree of autonomy except insofar as the national and state agencies are depended on for financial assistance, for general guidance in the conducting of national or state election campaigns, and for a sharing of patronage following an electoral victory. No line of authoritative control runs downward from the national party officials, through the state committees, and to the numerous local committees and precinct leaders. Nor do authoritative controls run upwards from the lower to the higher levels.

Both the state and local organizations are powerful and on the whole self-controlling and self-sufficient. The weakest agencies are found at the top, i.e., at the peak of the national party structure. Up to now, at least, the centralizing tendencies which have vastly increased the role of the national government in the fields of regulation and service have not been duplicated in the organization and functioning of the two major parties.

Likeness of the Democratic and Republican Parties

It has often been remarked that the Republican and Democratic parties closely resemble each other, not only in their structure but also in their programs. Both subscribe to the same general objectives and differ principally with respect to the ways and means of achieving them. Even on occasions when opposite positions have been taken in regard to specific issues, the two parties have never been as far apart in their over-all policy pronouncements as have partisans of the extreme right and the radical left. Neither party has strayed far from the middle-of-the-road line of travel.

One reason for the likeness of the Republican and Democratic parties is that most inhabitants of the United States still seem to have an aversion to extremist programs. Another is the fact that any party, if it hopes to gain control of the national government, must stand on a platform which appeals to the electorate in all or most parts of the country. Geographically widespread support is necessary to obtain a majority of electoral votes and to win more than half of the seats in both houses of Congress. This circumstance, even if the established parties were to be replaced by two diametrically opposed partisan organizations, would probably, in the course of time, produce a degree of likeness in the latter comparable to that which is evident in the case of the former.

As in many countries, parties play a significant role in the process of government in the United States. Without parties, governmental agencies would operate differently than they do and the relations between government and the public would be transformed in many respects.

Pressure Groups and Pressure Politics

Private Associations

In modern societies, private associations, i.e., organized interest-groups of many varieties, are commonly found in large numbers. Among them are labor unions, consumers' and producers' cooperatives, business enterprises, manufacturers' associations, chambers of commerce, farm bureaus, religious sects, organizations of veterans, and associations of teachers, lawyers, doctors, engineers, and other professional people.

The principal objectives and functions of groups of the foregoing type are to promote the special interests of their members. These interests may be economic, educational, religious, philanthropic, scientific, or of some other character. The political activities of these groups, insofar as they engage in them, are incidental to the primary reasons for their existence.

Other associations, which like the former are characterized by common interests and shared attitudes, are organized principally or solely for the purpose of dealing with governmental affairs. Examples are better government leagues, taxpayers' associations, governmental research bureaus (privately sponsored), civil liberties unions, and associations advocating civil service reform, equal rights for women, free trade, or prohibition. As these examples indicate, some groups are interested in all problems of government, whereas others are only concerned with particular issues of public policy.

Many associations are permanent in the sense that their members anticipate a continuous associational existence. Some are created on a particular occasion to deal with a specific problem of momentary significance and disband as soon as circumstances make their survival pointless.

Pressure Groups and Pressure Politics

Any association, whatever the purpose of its origin, qualifies as a *pressure group* if it strives in one way or another to influence the determination and/or administration of governmental policy. The engagement in such activity constitutes what is known as *pressure politics*.

Legislatures, chief executives, other agencies of government, and political parties are responsive in some degree to the pressures which private associations exert. Public policy is seldom formulated in complete disregard of their representations and the content of much of the legislation incorporated in the statute books is traceable to their efforts. Pressure may be brought to bear directly on public officials or indirectly through political parties or other channels.

Techniques of Pressure Groups

Many pressure groups, especially the more powerful with ample financial resources, employ paid agents and maintain permanent headquarters at the seat of government in Washington. At the state and local levels, the headquarters, if any, are usually temporary. The agents of pressure groups, paid or unpaid, strive to promote the interests of the groups for which they act by keeping a watchful eye on governmental operations and by utilizing whatever means may seem expedient for the purpose of securing desired governmental action or preventing the adoption of objectionable policies. Origin of the term "lobbying" is attributable to the appearance of pressure-group spokesmen in the lobby of a legislature to urge representatives to support or to oppose the enactment of particular laws.

Various techniques are used by pressure groups in their efforts to influence the functioning of public officials. Many are both legally and morally beyond censure, whereas others are clearly reprehensible.

1. PRESENTATION OF INFORMATION   A widely employed procedure is the presentation of information to public officials. The desires of the group are explained by appearances before legislative committees, by conferences with legislators and administrators, and by providing officials with printed material. Private associations may draft bills and persuade legislators to introduce them.

2. PROPAGANDA   A related technique is the spreading of propaganda to build up public support for a particular pressure-group and its objectives. Among the ways of doing this are the sponsorship of radio and television programs of an educational character, the distribution of pamphlets by mail, the publication of books as well as articles in periodicals and newspapers, astute advertising, and the staging of conferences to which influential persons are invited. The culti-

vation of good public relations sometimes proves helpful in persuading government officials to exercise their powers in a manner beneficial to the pressure-group's interests.

3. POLITICAL MANEUVERS Private associations also engage in pressure activities of a more strictly political type. They may contribute money to candidates and to parties for campaigning purposes, work for the nomination of "safe" candidates, and even campaign actively for the election of favored nominees. Sometimes they endeavor to influence the selection of legislative committee chairmen and members and also the appointment of administrators and judicial officers.

4. MISCELLANEOUS ACTIVITIES Among other techniques designed to influence the conduct of public officials and leading partisans are lavish entertainment; invitations to important social events; gifts; financial assistance; the prompting of people to write, telephone, or send telegrams to representatives; bribery; and threats of reprisal at the polls. Some groups investigate the backgrounds and records of candidates, officials, and party leaders. The information obtained enables a pressure-group to identify "approachable" persons and to resort to methods of approach which may prove effective. Pressure-groups work through whatever channels seem most promising and often devise ingenious ways of attaining their objectives.

Pressure-groups of different kinds often collaborate if they have the same interest in persuading the government to do or not do something. However, rivalry among pressure-groups frequently occurs. If so, they endeavor to discredit each other's contentions, as in the case, for example, of laborers and employers taking opposite sides in regard to the desirability of proposed legislation in the area of management-labor relations. Thus the power of a particular group may be checked by that of another.

Unorganized Interest-Groups

Many interest-groups remain unorganized even though the persons comprising them have identifiable common interests, such as engagement in the same activity or the sharing of an opinion concerning some phase of human relations. Examples are bus riders in a particular community, opponents of Sunday movies, home owners in general, and advocates of withdrawal of the United States from Vietnam. Of course, any such groups may become organized, but failure to do so does not mean that they lack influence over the course of governmental action. Their likely reaction to contemplated policies ordinarily is given consideration by officials, by party leaders, and even by organized groups. The position taken by legislators, administrators, and politicians on questions of policy is often attributable to estimates of the probable effect of particular policy-decisions on the behavior of members of these groups. Reactions to established policies also receive attention and may lead to changes in laws that have been enacted or in the abandonment of previously chosen objectives. The tendency is to pursue policies which are likely to command wide support. Consequently, the more varied the opinions within a group, the less its influence on the course of political events.

Individual Efforts

Particular individuals frequently endeavor to exert pressure on officials. They may send telegrams or write letters urging representatives to support or oppose some policy, transmit letters for publication to newspapar editors, or publish articles and books presenting their views on issues of the day. An aroused citizen may obtain interviews with officials or party leaders for the purpose of stating his case or he may attempt to persuade large numbers of persons to sign a petition requesting the government to do this or that. More spectacular tactics, such as instigation of a march on the seat of government or picketing a public office building, sometimes are resorted to by particular persons. If an individual is successful in enlisting the support of others, his action results in a group movement. As a means of influencing governmental policy, the efforts of persons who go it alone are unproductive as compared to the accomplishments of organized interest-groups.

Extent of Pressure Politics

The number of groups striving to shape the course of governmental action in the United States runs into the thousands. National, state, and local officials cannot avoid hearing whatever it is that these groups desire. Whether what is heard accounts for what is done is another matter. That official behavior is frequently affected by the representations of groups is undoubtedly true, but it is also true that the demands of groups often fail to produce desired results.

Public Opinion

In many discussions of governmental problems or of governmental operations, consideration is given to "public opinion" and to its effects on the conduct of officials, party leaders, and others who are involved in the business of government. Public opinion is generally recognized as a social force which enters into the calculations of active participants in the governmental process.

Nature of Public Opinion

The phrase "public opinion" has acquired a variety of meanings. Disagreement prevails regarding the nature of an "opinion" and the proper signification of the adjective "public." Some scholars have excluded mere hunches or impressions from the "opinion" category and have included only such views as are based on reasonably adequate information, whereas others have taken the position that any belief, conviction, or impression, regardless of its foundation, qualifies as an "opinion." As for the meaning of "public," according to one point of view a "public" consists only of the persons who are interested in or are aware of a specific matter and consequently develop opinions concerning it; another is that an opinion, to be "public," must be held by a substantial number of persons, not merely by a few; and a third maintains that only a community opinion constitutes "real" public opinion. Various other definitions of public opinion have been devised, e.g., public opinion signifies those opinions held by private persons which governments find it prudent to heed.

In the discussion which follows, "public opinion" is broadly conceived as including all opinions identifiable in a community, irrespective of their basis, of the number of persons by whom held, and of whether a government finds it prudent to heed them. Any belief, conviction, or judgment qualifies as an opinion. It may be based on knowledge and deliberation concerning a specific problem, or it may be founded on superstition, prejudice, acceptance of the judgment of a leader or of one's close associates, or on various considerations other than the thoughtful weighing of evidence in regard to the relative merits of different policies.

An individual's political behavior is affected by his opinions—whatever their basis or quality. Defining public opinion as the aggregate of opinions within a community does not mean that all opinions are pertinent to governmental affairs or that all which are carry equal weight.

Influence of Public Opinion

The influence of opinions of the public on the actions of officials depends on a variety of factors. One is the number of persons who share a particular conviction about some question. Another is whether the sharers of an opinion are organized for action and prepared to act. The beliefs of a well-organized and determined minority are more likely to be heeded by public officials than those of an unorganized and comparatively passive majority. Still another factor is the intensity with which an opinion is held. Intensity of belief usually accounts for organization, persistence, and aggressiveness in the advancement of a particular point of view. The financial resources of an opinion-group also have a bearing on its success in gaining consideration for its views. So do such matters as the calibre of its leadership, the prestige of its members, and the probable quality of its contentions. An opinion that is recognized as being based on special knowledge and experience is more likely to carry weight with policy-makers than one which is maintained by groups that are known to be inadequately informed.

From the standpoint of government officials the significance of opinions of the public lies in their likely effect on the political behavior of individuals and groups. How will they vote? Will they abide by a policy which in their judgment is undesirable? How much tension will develop in a community if opinions subscribed to by a sizable segment of the people are ignored? These and other questions arise in the minds of policy-makers and administrators.

The process of government in the United States is characterized by discussion and the interaction of competing opinions, but policy-decisions are ultimately made by public officials. Democracy involves "bargaining" among interest-groups both inside and outside the government. The policies finally adopted are products of interacting opinions—the opinions of officials and the convictions of interest-groups within the community.

In all probability, most opinions merely have minority support. It is doubtful that general opinion often exists concerning the proper solution of particular problems. The apathy of numerous people, the complexity of many social situations, and the uncertainty of large numbers of persons as to what constitutes a satisfactory policy are factors which reduce the likelihood that a particular opinion is held by a sufficiently large proportion of the population to justify the conclusion that it is a generally-held opinion. Even if a general opinion develops with respect to some particular issue, the policy pursued by the government may nevertheless represent the point of view of only a minority.

Opinion-Creation by Public Officials

A clear indication that officials attach importance to opinions of the public is their effort to win popular support for contemplated or adopted policies. Effective techniques for manipulating opinion have been developed and utilized by governmental agencies as well as by private associations. Thus the problem of determining the extent to which opinions of the public influence the behavior of officials has its counterpart, viz., the question of opinion-creation by those who do the governing. Governmental shaping of opinion may be accomplished in various ways, including resort to all the methods of thought-control that have been developed by private interests. Factors contributing to successful manipulation are the prestige of many officials, such as the chief executive and experienced members of the legislature, and the advantageous position enjoyed by officials because of possession of information which may not be available to outsiders. This situation exists in various areas of governmental activity, especially in the field of foreign affairs.

Realities of The Governmental Process

The desires of the people have a bearing on the governmental process—a process which involves far more than the functioning of formal organs of government in conformity with procedures established by law. Popular participation occurs through elections, political parties, pressure groups, and expressions of opinion. Although the people do not govern, they decide who shall do the governing and have substantial opportunity to influence the course of governmental action. The legally established governmental structure constitutes a framework within which the interplay of a multiplicity of social forces occurs.

A superficial account of governmental developments is exemplified by the kind of news item which reports that various agencies of government have taken specific action in the fields of domestic and foreign affairs. Such reports are accurate insofar as they designate correctly the official channels through which particular acts are performed, but they cast no light on the process of decision-making and are not intended to do so.

What considerations led to the reaching of a certain decision? What pressures, if any, were exerted on the officials nominally responsible for the exercise of discretionary powers? Whose will prevailed—that of the officeholders or that of individuals or groups outside the government? Inasmuch as the governmental process is inseparable from the social process in general, the tracing of official action backward to its inception often leads an investigator far afield into the various phases of community life. An official act commonly represents the culmination of a certain sequence of events and of various transactions involving the activities of numerous individuals and groups.

The governmental process in all of its aspects cannot be understood apart from the social environment in which it occurs or in disregard of the many factors which account for the political behavior of men. Realists stress this fact and some of them are inclined to minimize the importance of the formally established machinery of government. But that machinery is as real as political parties, interest-groups, and pressure politics. It, too, has a bearing on the outcome of the governmental process.

The National
Government: Unique
Features

C H A P T E R ☆ F I V E

Separation of Powers
  The Legislative, Executive, and Judicial Branches
  Coordinate Status of the Three Branches
Checks and Balances
  Congressional Checks on the Executive and Judicial
    Branches
  Presidential Checks on Congress and the Judiciary
  Judicial Checks on Congress and the President
The National Government in Action
  Trend Toward Presidential Leadership
    Causative Factors
  Fluctuations in Presidential Influence
Selecting a President
  Nomination of Candidates
    Composition of National Conventions
    Number of Votes per Delegate
    Selection of Delegates
    Functions of National Conventions
  Choice of Presidential Electors
  Minority Presidents

Criticism of Method of Selecting a President
Proposals for Change
Selection of Members of Congress
Choice of Senators
Choice of Representatives
Selection of Other National Officials and Employees
Appraisal of the Presidential-Congressional Plan
Claimed Merits and Defects

☆ ☆ ☆ ☆ ☆ ☆ ☆ ☆ ☆ ☆ ☆ ☆

The national government is organized in accordance with two doctrines (separation of powers and checks and balances). Fear of the concentration of all power in one man or in a group of men led the framers of the Constitution to create three branches of government largely but not entirely independent of one another. As stated by Madison in the *Federalist Papers*,[62] "the accumulation of all powers, legislative, executive, and judiciary, in the same hands, whether of one, a few, or many, and whether hereditary, self-appointed, or elective, may justly be pronounced the very definition of tyranny." Each branch was to be controlled by a different personnel and each was made primarily responsible for the discharge of a major governmental function. However, the several branches were endowed with checks upon one another. To quote Madison again, "the great security against a gradual concentration of the several

[62] No. 47.

powers in the same department [branch] consists in giving to those who administer each department [branch] the necessary constitutional means and personal motives to resist encroachment by the others. . . . Ambition must be made to counteract ambition." [63]

The Separation of Powers

Two aspects of the separation-of-powers doctrine require consideration in describing the organization of the national government. One concerns *structural features* designed to prevent the subservience of any of the component branches of government to any of the others. This end is achieved, principally, by appropriate arrangements for selecting the members of each branch and guaranteeing their tenure of office. The other aspect pertains to the *allocation of powers* among the several branches in such a way as to avoid the concentration of two or more major functions, such as the legislative, the executive, and the judicial, in the same branch. This objective was attained by the framers of the Constitution without excluding any branch from participating in some way and to some extent in the performance of functions primarily assigned to the others. A restricted sharing of functions as a matter of constitutional theory and a more extensive sharing in practice is a feature of national government in the United States.

The Legislative Branch

The first statement of Article I of the Constitution is that all legislative powers herein granted shall be vested in a Con-

[63] *Federalist Papers*, No. 51.

gress consisting of a Senate and a House of Representatives. For reasons to be presented later, Congress is not the sole possessor of "legislative power." However, its enactments, if constitutional, supersede conflicting rules and regulations issued by other organs of the national government.

Members of both houses of Congress are chosen by direct popular vote, but until 1913 Senators were selected by the legislatures of the states. Representatives are elected for a two-year term and Senators for six years. No limit is placed on the number of terms a person may serve. Each house is judge of the elections, returns, and qualifications of its members. Once elected and seated, Senators and Representatives may be removed from office prior to expiration of their terms only if expelled by the house of which they are members. A two-thirds vote is necessary for expulsion.

Neither the President nor the courts are authorized by law to play a part in the selection and/or removal of members of Congress. The President may urge voters to support candidates he favors and he might even suggest that one of the houses expel a member who has incurred his dislike. That is all he can do. Obviously, he is unable to determine who shall or shall not hold a seat in Congress. The same observation holds for the courts. Judges are excluded from both the selective and removal processes.

The Executive Branch

The executive power, as the Constitution specifies, is vested in a President. He is nominally selected by a majority of the electoral college but for all practical purposes by popular vote. Although Presidential electors are now chosen by the electorate in all of the states, the Constitution merely provides that each state shall appoint, in such manner as the legislature thereof may direct, a number of electors equal to its representation in Congress. The discretion of the legislatures is subject to one restriction, viz., that no member of Congress or person holding an office of trust or profit under the national government shall be appointed an elector. At one time various state legislatures chose Presidential electors, but the last ones that did were those of Florida in 1868 and Colorado in 1876. Congress prescribes the manner in which electoral college members are to be appointed by the District of Columbia.

Congress participates in the selection of a President and Vice President only when the electoral college fails to do so. If no Presidential candidate obtains a majority electoral vote, the House of Representatives chooses a President from the three highest competitors. Each state has one vote which is cast by its representation in the House and the support of a majority of the states is required for election. If no candidate for the Vice Presidency polls an electoral majority, the Senate selects a Vice President from the two highest. In this case a majority of the whole number of Senators is necessary for selection of one of the two. One other occasion for Congressional participation in the choice of a Vice President is provided for in the Twenty-Fifth Amendment. Whenever a vacancy occurs in the Vice Presidential office, the President shall nominate a Vice President who shall take office on confirmation by a majority vote of both houses of Congress.

Members of Congress may participate as delegates to the nominating conventions of their parties and campaign for the election of any of the nominated candidates for the Presidency and the Vice Presidency. As voters, too, they may cast ballots for members of the electoral college. Their political influence may be substantial but their political activities are not the equivalent of choice of a President by the legislative branch of the government.

The President and Vice President are chosen for four-year terms. During that period the only way of removing them from office is through impeachment by the House of Representatives and subsequent trial and conviction by the Senate. Use of the impeachment procedure is limited to charges of treason, bribery, or other high crimes and misdemeanors. When the President is tried by the Senate, the Chief Justice of the Supreme Court presides. A two-thirds vote of the Senators present is essential to conviction and removal from office.

The impeachment process may not be invoked for the purpose of removing a President merely because of dislike of his policies or lack of confidence in his judgment. As often stated, a law-abiding President need only remain alive to complete the term for which he was elected. Congress may disregard his recommendations, criticize him severely, and harass him in various ways, but it cannot get rid of him unless he is found guilty of criminal behavior.

The Constitution contains another provision designed to promote Presidential independence. It stipulates that the President shall, at stated times, receive a compensation which shall neither be increased nor diminished during the period for which he was elected. For the four years of a particular term he is guaranteed whatever compensation had been established by act of Congress at the time he takes office.

The Judicial Branch

The judicial power is vested in one Supreme Court and such inferior courts as Congress may from time to time establish. Safeguards against domination of the judicial branch by the President and Congress were provided by the framers of the Constitution. Although judges are appointed by the President with the advice and consent of the Senate, this arrangement is offset by another in regard to tenure. Article III provides that judges shall hold office during good behavior. This stipulation, which has amounted to service "for life," applies to all judges of courts organized under the provisions of the third article.

Judges, like other civil officers of the United States, may be impeached on grounds of treason, bribery, or other high crimes and misdemeanors. If trial by the Senate results in conviction, removal from office necessarily follows. No other mode of removal is available. The virtual guarantee of life tenure, unless criminal behavior occurs, enables judges to decide cases without bowing to the dictates of either the legislative or executive branches.

An additional constitutional provision contributing to judicial independence is the requirement that judges be compensated for their services and that this compensation shall not be diminished during their continuance in office. It may, however, be increased.

Coordinate Status of the Three Branches

The foregoing arrangements pertaining to the selection, tenure, and removability of the President, Vice President, members of Congress, and federal judges account for the mutual independence or coordinate status of the major branches of the national government. A further precaution, designed to insure a different personnel for each branch, is the constitutional provision that no person holding any office under the United States may serve as a member of either house of Congress during his continuance in office. Nor may Senators or Representatives be appointed, during the time for which they were elected, to any civil office under the authority of the United States which was created, or the emolument whereof was increased, during such time.

Checks and Balances

The mutual independence of the legislative, executive, and judicial branches falls short of being absolute. A check and balance system enables each branch to exercise limited control over the others and thereby to protect itself against encroachments on its authority or attempts to place it in a position of subordination. The checks are in some instances associated with grants of power to aid or to influence another branch in the discharge of its primary function.

Congressional Checks on the Executive Branch

One Congressional check on the executive branch has been mentioned, viz., the power to impeach, try, and convict the President and other civil officers of criminal conduct, with the minimum consequence of removal from office. Another, available only to the Senate, is the requirement of its advice and consent to Presidential appointment of superior officers and to the making of treaties by the President.

Of even greater importance are Congressional control of the purse strings, of the organization and procedure of the executive branch, and of the regulatory and service policies of the national government. Both the raising of revenue and the authorization of expenditures are exclusive powers of Congress. The various departments, bureaus, and commissions of the executive branch owe their existence, directly or indirectly, to acts of Congress; the procedures to be followed in the administration of policies are prescribable by Congress; and, subject to exceptions in the field of foreign relations, Congressional approval is essential to the activity programs of the national government.

Another major check on the President and executive agencies is the power of Congress as a whole or of either of its chambers to conduct investigations into the functioning of administrative officials. The investigatory powers of Congress will be discussed in a subsequent chapter.

Congressional Checks on the Judicial Branch

Congress possesses several powers involving some degree of control over the judicial branch. It is authorized to create inferior courts and also, by implication, to fix the size of the Supreme Court. The jurisdiction of the inferior courts is prescribed by Congress within the limits of the federal judicial power as set forth in Article III and the extent of the Supreme Court's appellate jurisdiction is subject to Congressional limitation.

The Senate's approval of Presidential appointments to the bench is requisite and judges are removable through resort to the impeachment process in the event of conduct falling in the criminal category. Amnesties may be declared by act of Congress, with the result that the classes of persons to whom amnesty is extended no longer are subject to prosecution and trial for designated offenses. Finally, the courts are dependent on Congress for provision of the funds needed for carrying on judicial operations.

Presidential Checks on Congress

The Constitution provides that the President shall give Congress information concerning the state of the Union and also authorizes him to recommend measures for Congressional consideration. These are aids to Congress rather than checks upon its action, except that a recommendation may have the effect of preventing Congress from doing what it otherwise would have done. The President may also call special sessions of both houses, or either of them, and adjourn them if they are unable to agree on a time of adjournment.

A major check is the President's suspensive veto power over bills, orders, resolutions, or votes to which the concurrence of the Senate and the House of Representatives may be necessary (except on a question of adjournment). Congress may override a Presidential veto, but a two-thirds vote of each house, a quorum being assembled, is required.

A different type of check occurs when the President, despite his duty to "take care that the laws be faithfully executed," refrains from doing so for whatever reasons seem sufficient to him. He may, for instance, disregard an act of Congress because, in his judgment, it conflicts with the Constitution. No judicial remedy is available for the purpose of compelling him to abide by or enforce the laws. Congress may resort to the impeachment process on the ground that he is guilty of criminal misconduct, but it might be difficult, in view of the two-thirds rule, to obtain his conviction.

Presidential Checks on the Judiciary

The President's principal check on the judicial branch is his power to grant pardons, issue proclamations of amnesty, grant reprieves, and commute sentences which the courts have imposed on convicted defendants in criminal cases. Furthermore, the effective enforcement of judicial decisions depends on his support.

As previously noted, the President, with the advice and consent of the Senate, appoints judges. This power gives him the opportunity to place on the bench individuals whose social, economic, and political outlook corresponds to his own, provided that vacancies occur during his term of office. Once appointed, however, a judge, since he holds office for life, need pay no heed to Presidential desires. Many judges have failed to live up to the expectations of the President who appointed them.

Judicial Checks on Congress and the President

The judicial branch is considered the weakest of the three. Its most important control over Congress, the President, and administrative agencies is the implied right of the courts to decide on the constitutionality of governmental acts if the issue of constitutionality is raised in cases brought before them. Whether governmental action is constitutional or unconstitutional is a question that remains unanswered until such time as a case requiring an answer rises. Possession of the right to declare governmental acts unconstitutional has had the consequence of making the Supreme Court the final interpreter of the documentary constitution.

The judicial branch is unable to force Congress or the

President to comply with its rulings, but voluntary compliance has become traditional. Other officials may be compelled to abide by the law of the land as prescribed by the Constitution, laws in pursuance thereof, and treaties.

The National Government in Action

As the preceding discussion of the separation of powers and check-and-balance features of the national government has shown, the framers of the Constitution were successful in producing a rather complicated type of organization which requires teamwork among its component parts to function satisfactorily at all times. Unless the legislative and executive branches cooperate, effective and expeditious government is unattainable.

Deadlocks are likely with combinations such as a Democratic President and a Republican Congress, or a Republican Senate and a Democratic House of Representatives. Moreover, even if one party is nominally in control of both the executive and legislative branches, the existence of factions within this party, the absence of effective party discipline, and the development of conflicts between the President and the leading partisans of Congress may result in sufficient friction to prevent the collaboration necessary to the successful functioning of a separation-of-powers type of government.

The two following chapters deal in some detail with the Presidency and Congress. For the moment attention will be confined to a general view of the national government in action. From a strictly structural standpoint, a separation-of-powers organization enables each major branch of government to exercise its constitutionally delegated powers as it deems advisable. No branch has sufficient legal control over the others to compel them to submit to its will in matters beyond the scope of its prescribed authority. Such is the theory of a separation of powers. But practice does not always conform to theory.

Legal arrangements often work out differently than intended or anticipated because offices are held by men, and men in general tend to respond to pressures brought to bear on them and to take advantage of particular situations that arise. Since the responsiveness of individuals to pressures and to circumstances varies and inasmuch as the nature and intensity of pressures undergo change, a governmental structure which remains unaltered throughout the years may function differently from time to time during the period of its existence. Such has been the case with the national government.

Trend Toward Presidential Leadership

Despite fluctuations in the relative importance of the several coordinate branches of this government, there has been a definite trend toward potent Presidential leadership in the legislative as well as in the administrative field. The marked growth in the influence of the President, even though his constitutional powers are the same today as in 1789, is attributable to a number of causative factors.

Causative Factors

(1) COMPETITION BETWEEN POLITICAL PARTIES One of the most important causes has been competition be-

tween political parties for control of the government. Each party presents a program to the public and nominates a Presidential candidate who becomes its nominal leader and standard bearer. During the election campaign the Presidential nominees present their views concerning the issues of the day and indicate, although not always too clearly, the general policies they favor and expect to pursue if elected. The major emphasis is on policies rather than on administration, even though the lawmaking authority is vested in Congress instead of in the President. But the party which wins the Presidency, if it also gains control of Congress, runs the political risk of losing the next election if it fails to furnish Congressional support for the policies advocated by the President. Presidential leadership is likely to be followed unless the President proves to be an ineffective leader or unless bitter factional fights develop within the party.

(2) PRESIDENT CHOSEN BY NATION-WIDE ELECTOR-ATE Another factor conducive to the expansion of Presidential influence is the fact that he is the only officer of the national government, other than the Vice President, who is elected by a nation-wide constituency. Senators and Representatives are placed in office by comparatively small bodies of voters.

A nationally-elected President is favorably situated in the event of Congressional opposition to his program. He can appeal to the people for support and the pressure of public opinion may bring about the capitulation of his opponents in Congress. The people expect the President to manage Congress. Not all Presidents possess the qualities required for general popularity and for the winning of confidence in their judgment, but those who do are in a position to become powerful popular and political leaders. The President is a symbol of national unity and the attention of the people as a whole is concentrated on the occupant of the Presidential office. This fact strengthens the hand of all Presidents, even of those who lack a forceful personality.

(3) COERCIVE TACTICS OF PRESIDENTS   A third way in which Presidents are able to gain Congressional backing of their policies is through practices involving the use or threatened use of their legal powers in a manner that is objectionable from the standpoint of members of Congress. For the purposes of this chapter a few illustrations will be sufficient.

Since the appointive power is vested in the President, members of Congress cannot afford to antagonize him unduly unless willing to forego their share in the distribution of patronage. A President can turn a deaf ear to the recommendations of Senators and Representatives who persist in opposing policies he favors.

Another recourse of Presidents is to drive bargains with individual legislators in regard to proposed legislation. A President may indicate that he will oppose a legislator's pet bill unless the latter votes for measures bearing the Presidential stamp of approval.

An additional strategy, among various others, is the threat of a veto. If it seems likely that Congress intends to pass a bill which the President considers objectionable, he may let it be known that the measure will be vetoed. This threat may prove sufficient to forestall the contemplated Congressional action.

(4) RESORT OF PRESIDENTS TO PERSUASION Instead of resorting to coercive tactics, a President may gain his objectives in the legislative field by reliance on persuasion. Apart from the effective use of messages to Congress, the President may win the support of individual members of this body through the device of personal interviews, by invitations to White House breakfasts at which questions of policy are discussed, by conferences with the chairmen of standing committees, and by an exchange of written communications concerning some issue of the day.

(5) INCREASING COMPLEXITY OF GOVERNMENT Another major cause of the President's growing influence in lawmaking is the increasing complexity of government. Generally speaking, members of Congress are neither as closely in touch with social and economic conditions calling for governmental action, nor as well informed concerning the feasibility of proposed policies, as are the various experts serving in the administrative departments and agencies.

The legislature is largely dependent on the specialized personnel of the administrative services for information and guidance in formulating the content of legislation. Many of the major bills eventually enacted into law are drafted in the first instance by administrative officials. Since the President is the general manager of the administrative organization, his hand in policy-determination is greatly strengthened by the inability of Congress to solve complicated problems satisfactorily without the assistance of expert administrative functionaries.

(6) NEED FOR UNIFIED LEADERSHIP Finally, the achievement of effective government is promoted by unified leadership, especially in this day of huge populations, great diversity of interests, and extremely complex living conditions. Although each house of Congress has its own leaders, neither set is able to furnish the kind of over-all leadership that means the difference between uncoordinated action on the part of several branches of government and the type of teamwork among the parts of a whole that is conducive to satisfactory operation. The President is in a better position to provide unified leadership than any other official or group of officials of the national government and to satisfy the public's desire for a government which exhibits unity of purpose rather than haphazard movement in one direction or another.

Fluctuations in Presidential Influence

Presidential influence reaches its peak in times of domestic or international crisis and on those occasions when the President's party has a safe working majority in both houses of Congress, provided that the holder of the office is a man of forceful personality with an aptitude for leadership and with an ample supply of "political know-how." However, since the separation of powers and check and balance structure of the national government is a constant factor in the governmental equation, there is no guarantee of harmonious relationships between the executive and the legislature under the leadership of the former.

If the opposition party controls either or both houses of Congress, as happens now and then, or if factions within the President's party oppose him, even a President of marked ability finds the going rather rough. The predicament of a mediocrity in the White House under the same circumstances obviously is serious. Thus Presidential leadership within a separation of powers framework is a variable factor in the governmental process even though the trend for over a century and a half has been in the direction of Congressional subservience to the President.

Selecting a President

The major steps in the selection of a President are the nomination of candidates, the campaigning for election, the choice of presidential electors, and the casting and counting of electoral votes. Political parties undertake the tasks of nomination and campaigning; the qualified voters of the several states select the presidential electors; the latter cast the electoral votes; and these votes are counted by Congress. The Constitution specifies that a majority vote of the electoral college is necessary for the choice of a President and sets forth the procedure to be followed if no person obtains a majority. It also indicates the number of electoral votes to which each state and the District of Columbia are entitled and authorizes the legislature of each state to prescribe the manner in which its electors are to be appointed, with Congress designating the mode of appointment for the District of Columbia.

The framers expected the electoral college to function as a nominating agency, since they supposed that majority support for one individual seldom would materialize. This supposition was reasonable inasmuch as, originally, presidential electors merely voted for two persons and did not cast distinct ballots for President and Vice President, as subsequently required by the Twelfth Amendment. The House of Representatives, if no person obtained a majority, was to select a President from the five highest, with each state having one vote and support of a majority of the states being required. Since adoption of the Twelfth Amendment in 1804, the House chooses from the three highest, provided no candidate secures an electoral majority. Another reason why the framers believed that the electoral college ordinarily would nominate rather than elect was apparent failure to anticipate the effect of competition among political parties on the selective process.

Nomination of Candidates

Neither the nomination of candidates nor political parties are mentioned in the Constitution. As a matter of practice rather than of constitutional law, candidates for the Presidency and Vice Presidency are nominated by conventions of party delegates. This mode of nomination has been adhered to for more than a century and a quarter. Each political party determines the composition of its own convention and, in the absence of state legislation on the subject, the method of selecting convention delegates.

(1) COMPOSITION OF NATIONAL CONVENTIONS
From time to time both the Democratic and Republican parties alter their rules concerning the make-up of their national conventions. For many years each party allowed every state twice as many delegates (one vote per delegate) as it had seats in Congress. Under this policy a state's delegation consisted of four delegates-at-large (two per senator), two additional at-large delegates for any representative elected

at-large, and two delegates for each congressional district.

In recent times departures from this plan have occurred in consideration of the fact that a party's support at the polls is considerably stronger in some states and districts than in others. Greater representation is granted those states and districts in which the party has made a reasonably good showing.

The Republican party, more so than the Democratic, has considered it expedient to resort to a bonus policy. Additional delegate votes are granted to states in which the party was successful in winning the state's electoral vote; or in electing some designated official, e.g., a United States Senator or a state governor; or in obtaining not fewer than a specified number of votes in a congressional district for presidential electors or for a nominee for a seat in Congress, e.g., an additional delegate for each district casting 10,000 Republican votes at the last election. The purpose of "bonuses" is to give states in which the party is strong a greater voice in the functioning of the convention than is accorded states wherein the party is weak, as in the case of the Republican party in many states of the South.

Measured by the total of votes that could be cast in nominating Presidential and Vice Presidential candidates, the 1968 Democratic convention was larger than any prior convention. Because of adoption of a "bonus" policy, additional delegate votes were assigned to the 44 states won by the Democratic party in the 1964 Presidential election. The 1972 convention was larger.

Both parties award delegates to territories. These may some day become states, as have Alaska and Hawaii. In addition to the District of Columbia, delegates are allotted to Puerto Rico, the Virgin Islands, the Canal Zone, and Guam.

(2) NUMBER OF VOTES PER DELEGATE   The number of delegates to a convention may differ from the number of votes that may be cast. Any discrepancy between numbers and votes is due to the practice of granting fractional votes to delegates. For example, if a state sends twice as many delegates as the number of votes to which it is entitled, each delegate may cast only half a vote.

The Republicans have adhered to the policy of one vote per delegate. Not so the Democrats. In 1960 the number of delegates attending the Democratic convention was 3,042, whereas the authorized total of votes was 1,521; in 1964 the number of delegates was 2,944 but the voting total was 2,316; and in 1968, although the total of votes was 2,622, the delegate strength amounted to 2,989. For 1972 the total of votes was 3,016. The Republican convention of 1964 consisted of 1,308 delegates with a total vote of 1,308. In the 1968 convention the delegate and voting totals were slightly higher, *viz.*, 1,333; in 1972, 1,346.

(3) SELECTION OF DELEGATES   Over two-fifths of the states have provided by law for presidential primaries at which convention delegates are chosen. Many of these states have also arranged for presidential preference primaries in addition to or in combination with the delegate primary. A preference primary enables partisan voters to express a preference among aspirants for the party's nomination to the Presidency. In some states the elected delegates are required to cast their convention ballots, at least for a time, for the aspirant winning the preference primary.

In most states delegates are chosen by district or state conventions; sometimes by state party committees. Since each party is free, except in the "primary" states, to decide on the method of selecting delegates, practice among the several states varies considerably. Generally speaking, whatever the particular mode of choice, state and local party leaders are usually successful in determining the personnel of a state's delegation to the national convention.

(4) FUNCTION OF NATIONAL CONVENTIONS The two most important functions of a national party convention are the adoption of a party platform and the nomination of candidates for the Presidency and Vice Presidency. Conventions are noisy and colorful affairs characterized by music, cheer leaders, nominating speeches, demonstrations for nominees, and, eventually, voting by roll call. Final decisions on issues and candidates are usually the result of pre-convention campaigns, evidence of a popular preference, maneuvering, bargaining, private conferences, and various behind-the-scenes activities.

Both parties now nominate their candidates by a simple majority of the total vote cast. The aim of the professional politicians who dominate the conventions is to draft a platform that will please many and offend few and, above all, to nominate a combination of candidates for the Presidency and Vice Presidency that will have great voter appeal. Consideration is given in some measure to the competence of possible nominees for the Presidential position, but the primary concern of the conventions is to pick a winner. Whether the Republican convention of 1964 exhibited indifference to this consideration, as sometimes has been claimed, is a debatable matter.

Choice of Presidential Electors

The conventions are held in July or August (August in 1968) and shortly after their work has been completed, campaigning begins, slowly at first, but gaining more and more momentum as election day, the Tuesday following the first Monday in November, approaches. On that day voters cast their ballots for the persons who have been nominated as presidential electors by party conventions, committees, or primaries, depending on the mode of nomination prescribed by state law.

In most of the states the names of these nominees are no longer printed on the ballot, with the result that many voters labor under the mistaken impression that they are voting directly for a President and Vice President. This impression is strengthened by the appearance on the ballot of the names of the Presidential and Vice Presidential candidates of the various parties competing for control of the national government.

Presidential electors are chosen from each state at-large rather than by districts. Consequently, since the plurality rule is followed in determining the winners, the party polling the most votes secures a state's entire electoral vote, regardless of the closeness of the election. All that a party needs is one more vote than any of its competitors. For this reason the winner of a Presidential election may receive an overwhelming electoral vote even though the nationwide popular vote is extremely close.

"Minority" Presidents

A "minority" President is one who obtained an electoral college majority but failed to poll a majority (more than half) of the total popular vote. If more than two candidates compete for the Presidency, the combined popular vote of the losers may exceed that of the victor. Even if only two candidates have been nominated, the winner's popular vote may be smaller than that of the loser. This possibility is due to combination of the plurality rule with at-large election of presidential electors in every state.

There have been about a dozen "minority" Presidents. On two occasions, the Hayes-Tilden contest in 1876 and the Harrison-Cleveland competition in 1888, the popular vote of the loser was larger than that of the winner.[64]

Criticism of the Method of Selecting a President

The method of selecting a President has been criticized on several grounds. Chief among them is the charge of unfairness attributable to the plurality rule in association with the at-large choice of presidential electors. No matter how large the popular vote a party polls in a particular state, it obtains none of that state's electoral votes if another party receives only slightly greater voter support. A related criticism, also based on the plurality rule in conjunction with election at-large, is that the distribution of partisan strength among the states is more important than the nation-wide vote polled by the competing parties. Consequently, doubtful states enjoy an advantageous position in determining the outcome of an election, especially if their electoral vote is large. Another criticism is that the electoral college no longer serves the purpose intended by the framers of the Constitution. With occasional exceptions, its individual members,

---

[64] In 1824 John Quincy Adams was elected by the House of Representatives because no candidate obtained a majority electoral vote. Andrew Jackson's popular vote was considerably larger than that of Adams.

having been chosen on a partisan basis, merely record the results of popular voting in the states.

Proposals for Change

A few proposals for change will be summarized briefly without considering the arguments for and against them. The simplest suggestion is abolition of the useless electoral college but retention of the present system of state electoral votes. These would be recorded automatically in accordance with the results of popular voting for Presidential candidates. Another plan is to do away with state electoral votes and to select a President in accordance with the outcome of a nation-wide popular vote, using either the plurality or the majority rule for determining the winner. In 1970 the House of Representatives adopted a direct-election amendment to the Constitution providing that the highest candidate obtaining *forty* percent or more of the popular vote would become President and that a run-off would be held between the two highest if there were no *forty* percent or more winner. The Senate has not acted favorably on this proposed amendment. A third plan calls for distribution of each state's electoral vote on a proportional basis, i.e., every candidate would receive a proportion of the electoral vote corresponding to his proportion of the popular vote. Still another proposal is to provide for the selection of presidential electors by congressional districts, one per district, in combination with the at-large election of two electors, one for each of the two Senators to which every state is entitled. State legislatures can provide for the selection of presidential electors by districts, as some of them have in the distant past, but a constitutional amendment would be necessary to compel use of the district plan in every state.

All of the summarized plans have their advocates and opponents. In view of the diversity of opinion that exists even among the groups which favor alteration of the established method of selecting a President, the proposal and ratification of some type of amendment to the Constitution concerning the choice of a President seems improbable.

Selection of Members of Congress

Since the adoption of the Seventeenth Amendment in 1913, both Senators and Representatives are chosen by popular vote. The qualifications for voting are prescribed by the states, subject to the extensive constitutional restrictions mentioned in a preceding chapter.

Choice of Senators

Each state chooses two Senators. These officials are elected from the state at-large by the single choice—plurality mode of election. Nominations are usually made by the partisan direct primary.

Choice of Representatives

Representatives are apportioned among the states according to population, but each state is guaranteed at least one representative. The single-member district plan for the selection of Representatives has been made mandatory by act of Congress. In 1964 the Supreme Court held that the Constitution requires Congressional districts to be substantially equal in population. Its ruling will be discussed in the following chapter.

At least one exception to the compulsory single-member district arrangement has been authorized. A December, 1967, act of Congress provides that a state entitled to more than one representative, *which in all previous elections has chosen its representatives at-large,* may elect them at-large to the Ninety-First Congress. This exception pertains only to New Mexico and Hawaii. Both states have "previously" elected their representatives (at present, two in each case) at-large.

In the past election at-large was *temporarily* permissible if a *state legislature failed to agree on a district layout* following a reapportionment of representatives among the states. Until agreement was reached, a state gaining seats elected its additional representatives at-large; a state losing seats chose all of its representatives in an at-large election. Whether this procedure remains permissible (under the special circumstances indicated) is uncertain. The 1967 act of Congress requires clarification on this point. However, the situation may not arise because of probable "court imposition" of a districting plan in the event of prolonged legislative inaction.

The few states entitled to but one representative necessarily elect them at-large. Prior to the 1842 action of Congress imposing the single-member district plan on all states, representatives were chosen by districts in some and at-large in others.

As in the case of Senators, the single choice-plurality method of election is used in choosing Representatives. The partisan direct primary is the favored mode for the nomination of candidates.

Selection of Other National Officials and Employees

National officials and employees other than the President, Vice President, and members of Congress are appointed to their positions. Selection by the President with the advice and consent of the Senate is required by the Constitution for "ambassadors, other public ministers and consuls, judges of the Supreme Court, and all other officers . . . , whose appointments are not herein otherwise provided for, and which shall be established by law." Immediately following this provision is another, viz., "but the Congress may by law vest the appointment of such inferior officers, as they think proper, in the President alone, in the courts of law, or in the heads of departments."

Department heads are appointed by the President with the advice and consent of the Senate, as are the members of such agencies as the Interstate Commerce and Federal Trade Commissions as well as many other high and even low officials (federal marshals) of the executive branch. Some important officers are appointed by the President alone, e.g., the Director of the Office of Management and Budget and officials of the President's own immediate staff. The House and the Senate select their respective officers and also the members of their staff services. Although judges are chosen by the President and Senate, the courts appoint their various assistants, such as clerks, court reporters, stenographers, bailiffs, and probation officers.

By far the largest proportion of national officials and employees are appointed by the department and agency heads. Upwards of four-fifths of the civilian officeholders and employees of the national government are selected by these heads. An important limitation on their discretion consists of the requirements of the merit system which dates back to the Civil Service Act of 1883. This act was restricted in its application, but subsequent extensions of the merit principle by statute and by executive order have resulted in nearly complete coverage of the personnel of the administrative services. A more detailed consideration of the personnel policies of the national government will be presented in the chapter dealing with its administrative agencies.

Appraisal of The Presidential-Congressional Plan

Persons dissatisfied with the presidential-congressional pattern of government usually favor substitution of a cabinet-parliamentary type of organization, especially along the lines of the system operative in Great Britain. The distinctive feature of cabinet-parliamentary government is the responsibility of the cabinet, a plural executive with a prime minister as its leading member, to the legislature in the sense that the cabinet is under obligation to resign if it is unable to command the support of a legislative majority. Usually, members of the cabinet are leaders of the majority party in the legislature and hold seats in that body at the same time that they function collectively as the chief executive agency and individually as the political heads of administrative departments.

Claimed Merits

(1) SAFEGUARD AGAINST ARBITRARY GOVERNMENT
The major merit claimed for presidential-congressional government is that its separation of powers feature in association with appropriate checks and balances is an effective safeguard against arbitrary, capricious, and oppressive government. The dangers to individual liberty inherent in an or-

ganization that concentrates ultimate governmental authority in one place presumably are avoided or at least minimized.

(2) GOVERNMENTAL STABILITY   A second contention is that the presidential-congressional plan guarantees governmental stability for a period of years. Since the chief executive and the members of the legislature are chosen for fixed terms, changes in the top governing personnel occur only at regular and predetermined intervals. The chief executive cannot be forced out of office whenever the legislature refuses to follow his leadership or disapproves of the manner in which he exercises his discretionary powers. Nor can the chief executive dissolve the legislature and order a new election if the majority of its members oppose his policies.

A derivative advantage is that the chief executive and highest administrative officials are able to discharge their administrative responsibilities without constant fear of alienating the legislature and consequently losing their positions. Comparative security of tenure for these administrators is likely to result in higher standards of administrative performance.[65]

(3) DEPARTMENT HEADS FREE TO CONCENTRATE ON ADMINISTRATION   Another asserted merit of presidential-congressional government is that department heads, not being members of the legislature (as is commonly the case under the cabinet-parliamentary plan) are free to devote more time and attention of administrative affairs. Although they have

[65] Department and agency heads may be removed by the chief executive.

time-consuming dealings with the legislature, inasmuch as they may find it necessary to provide that body with information, appear before its committees, and press in various ways for the enactment of desired laws, they bear none of the responsibilities associated with regular membership in the legislature.

(4) TOP ADMINISTRATORS LIKELY TO BE EXPERTS Top administrators are likely to be expert in the field of administration to which they are assigned. The principal reason is that the chief executive appoints department heads and other high level administrative officials. In making his selections he may, if he so desires, canvass the personnel market for individuals who are particularly well-qualified to deal with the special problems of particular administrative services. Under the cabinet-parliamentary plan, the highest administrative officials are partisan members of the legislature. Ordinarily, however, a subordinate but permanent professional administrator is provided for in each department.

(5) SINGLE EXECUTIVE One of the claimed commendable features of presidental-congressional government is its single rather than plural executive. An organization, like that of the national government, which makes a single chief executive responsible for general management of the administrative services is more likely to function efficiently and effectively than a system under which the ultimate direction and control of administrative activity is the task of a group of individuals. With a plural executive, the responsibility for administration is shared by members of a group instead of being concentrated in a single person.

(6) CHIEF EXECUTIVE DIRECTLY RESPONSIBLE TO ELECTORATE Advocates of the presidential-congressional plan also maintain that its provision for direct voter control over an extremely powerful and influential official is a highly desirable arrangement. In view of the need for unified leadership in the governmental field and in consideration of the fact that such leadership tends to be furnished by the person or persons heading the executive branch, choice of the chief executive by the electorate increases the likelihood that governmental powers will be wielded for the benefit of the general public rather than primarily for the advantage of powerful minorities. Popular election of the chief executive also is supposed to stimulate citizen interest in public affairs.

(7) VOTING FREEDOM OF LEGISLATORS Finally, the presidential-congressional system is favored by many persons on the ground that it permits independent voting on proposed policies by individual members of the legislature. Under the cabinet-parliamentary plan, the survival of a cabinet depends on continuous majority support in the legislature. Consequently, party lines need to be drawn sharply. A representative under this system lacks the voting freedom which may be exercised without serious political consequences by individual legislators under the presidential-congressional plan. If the latter vote according to their personal convictions instead of hewing to the party line, their action in no way affects the tenure of the president or his principal advisers. The net result of this feature of presidential-congressional government is to curtail the influence of party leaders, to increase the significance of the individual representative, and to strengthen the role of the legislature in policy-determination.

Claimed Defects

(1) NO GUARANTEE OF COOPERATION BETWEEN LEGISLATIVE AND EXECUTIVE BRANCHES One of the principal weaknesses of a separation of powers organization is its failure to insure cooperation between lawmakers and administrators. Inasmuch as no branch enjoys supremacy with respect to the others, reliance must be placed on voluntary cooperation rather than on compulsion.

If the personnel of one branch distrusts the persons controlling the other branches, no immediate remedy is available under a separation of powers government. The legislature cannot discharge the chief executive and his subordinates because of dissatisfaction with their performance and want of confidence in their judgment. Nor can the executive terminate the services of obstructive legislators. In the event of serious disagreement, friction, and ill-feeling between the two major branches of government, deadlocks often occur and inaction becomes the order of the day despite the need for expeditious solution of various social and economic problems. The sole remedy for this type of situation is through action by the voters at elections that are held only when the fixed terms of office of the executive and members of the legislature expire.

(2) CURTAILED RESPONSIVENESS TO PUBLIC OPINION The fixed terms of service associated with presidential-congressional government also curtail responsiveness to public opinion. There is no *continuous* accountability of the executive to the representatives of the people in the legislature, as under the cabinet-parliamentary system, or of the executive and the legislature to the electorate. Even if it becomes ap-

parent that the voters have lost confidence in the legislative majority or in the chief executive, no change in personnel can be brought about until arrival of the regularly scheduled time for conducting an election. The *calendar* rather than the political situation determines the occasions on which the electorate has the opportunity to transfer control of the government from one political party to another. Moreover, even this opportunity is limited in the case of the national government because of the different terms of office of the President (four years), Representatives (two years), and Senators (six, one-third retiring every two years).

The foregoing situation has led to the suggestion that the Constitution be amended to provide a four-year term for members of Congress as well as the President, all to be chosen at the same time, with the probable result that the party winning the Presidency also would secure a majority of the seats in both houses of Congress. This plan would ordinarily prevent one party from controlling Congress and the other the Presidency, but it would greatly strengthen the role of the President in the national governmental process and confine the voters' opportunity of expressing an opinion at the polls to one every four years, instead of every two years, as under the present arrangement.

(3) NO RESPONSIBLE OPPOSITION   The fact that prescribed terms of service preclude immediate changes in the governing personnel accounts for another defect of the presidential-congressional plan, viz., its failure to bring about the development of a responsible opposition under unified leadership. Criticism of the party in power is usually carried on in an uncoordinated, irresponsible, and sporadic manner by individual members of an opposition party or parties to which control of the government cannot be transferred at a moment's notice. Since the opposition need not be prepared to take over the reins of government at any time, it muddles along without an established leader and without a well-conceived program from the standpoint of which the party in power may be subjected to a systematic, sustained, and competently led attack.

(4) DIVIDED RESPONSIBILITY An additional serious shortcoming of presidential-congressional government is division of responsibility for the total governmental result. This defect has two undesirable consequences.

(a) EVASION OF RESPONSIBILITY In the first place, since no single branch of government possesses supreme authority, it is difficult to determine who deserves credit if things go well or whom to blame if public affairs are badly handled. Whenever misgovernment occurs, the executive is likely to shift responsibility to the legislature, and the latter to the former, whereas if the record be satisfactory both branches usually claim that theirs was the good judgment which prevailed. An organization which divides responsibility and thereby promotes its evasion contributes to the difficulty of achieving effective popular control of the governing personnel.

(b) NO SINGLE ORGAN ACCOUNTABLE FOR THE ENTIRE GOVERNMENTAL PROCESS The dispersion of responsibility has another undesirable aspect—no single branch bears the obligation of seeing to it that governmental operations *as a whole* are carried on efficiently and effectively. Each independent branch of the government tends to concentrate on its own tasks and to view the governmental process from the standpoint of its particular interests. Limited power and responsibility often produce a correspondingly limited vision.

(5) AN OVER-BURDENED CHIEF EXECUTIVE Presidential-congressional government, as it has been developing in the United States, is open to the criticism that too great a burden of work and too heavy a responsibility are placed on the President. This point is essentially an argument in favor of a plural executive—which could be provided for under a separation of powers type of government.

(6) POPULAR ELECTION OF CHIEF EXECUTIVE UNDESIRABLE Popular election of the President is another asserted defect of the national governmental structure. This feature is considered objectionable for several reasons.

(a) RESULTS IN MEDIOCRE PRESIDENTS Choice by the voters is said to result, more often than not, in the election of a good politician rather than a well-qualified chief executive. The man seeks the job and the candidate most likely to be successful is one who is adept at "vote-gathering." Demagoguery, willingness to make promises in return for voting support, and success in gaining the backing of powerful political and financial interests are greater assets in winning contests for nomination and election than competence to hold the position to be filled. Many able men are unwilling to undergo the indignities and the uncertainties of an election campaign or to engage in the strenuous activity that campaigning requires.

(b) PROMOTES MIXING OF POLITICS AND ADMINIS-
TRATION   Popular election of the chief executive often
results in a mixing of politics and administration which is
detrimental to the latter. The desire to remain in office for
more than one term is usually so strong that the elected executive is tempted to do what is politically expedient rather
than administratively sound. He is reluctant to take action
which might offend sizable blocks of voters or antagonize
powerful pressure groups. His appointments to office frequently are based on questionable political considerations and
his various other legal powers, including the recommendation
of legislation, are likely to be exercised in a politically advantageous manner without sufficient concern for the requirements of sound government.

(c) PERIODIC ELECTION A CAUSE OF DISTURBANCE
Periodic election of a president who plays an active and
important role in the governmental process is a cause of
disturbance, unrest, and uncertainty at regular intervals,
viz., every four years. During the year in which an election
occurs, and even long before, attention is concentrated on
the nomination of candidates and on campaign plans and
strategies. The effective conduct of public business is hampered by such activities and private interests become uncertain as to what the future holds for them. There is a tendency
to mark time until the outcome of the election indicates the
nature of the policies which the government probably will
pursue. Moreover, some elections are fought so bitterly that
the ill-feeling which is generated fails to subside with the
closing of the polls and has an adverse effect on the subsequent functioning of both the government and political
parties.

The Significance of Claimed Merits and Defects

All of the claimed merits and defects of presidential-congressional government have some basis in fact. Some are more impressive than others, but whether the asserted advantages outweigh the contended disadvantages is a controversial question. The subjective factor looms large in appraisals of forms of government. In the judgment of some persons, more importance should be attached to the results of the functioning of a particular pattern of government than to arguments concerning its apparent good and bad features. Unfortunately, disagreement on the question of results is likely, and even if there were agreement, opinion probably would be divided in regard to the quality of results. Furthermore, whatever the results of governmental action, an important question, difficult to answer, is to what extent the form of government was a causative factor. The structure of government is merely one of many factors accounting for governmental achievements and/or failures.

The framers of the Constitution undoubtedly established a rather complicated machinery of government. Nevertheless, it has functioned reasonably well despite its various shortcomings. The growth of Presidential leadership and the unifying effects of party government have contributed to its fairly successful operation. These developments have tended to offset inherent structural weaknesses. The danger now, according to some commentators, is that the present trend will result in an over-powerful President and a rather impotent Congress, in spite of formal constitutional provision for a separation of powers and check and balance type of government.

Congress

CHAPTER ☆ SIX

Composition of the Senate and the House of Representatives

    The Senate

        Required Qualifications

        Personal Characteristics of Senators

        Size: Equal Representation for States

        Performance as a Representative Body

    The House of Representatives

        Required Qualifications

        Size and Apportionment

        Reapportionment Procedure

        Single-Member Districts

            Required Standards

            The *Wesberry* Case

        Partisan Composition of the House

Compensation of Members of Congress

Privileges of Members of Congress

Powers of Congress

      Constituent; Electoral; Executive; Judicial; Investigatory; and Legislative

      Functions of Congress as a Representative Body

Delegation of Powers

      Permissible and Non-Permissible Delegations

The Investigatory Power of Congress: Its Scope

Congressional Organization and Procedure

Formal Organization of the House and the Senate
Speaker of the House
Vice President: Presiding Officer of the Senate
Standing Committees: House and Senate Sub-
committees
Special Committees
Joint Committees
House Committee on Rules
Senate Committee on Rules and Administration
Committee of the Whole
Conference Committees
Informal Organization: Party Agencies
Caucuses or Conferences
Floor Leaders; Whips
Committees on Committees
Policy Committees
Congress in Action
The Passage of Bills
House Procedure
Senate Procedure
Conferences

☆ ☆ ☆ ☆ ☆ ☆ ☆ ☆ ☆ ☆ ☆ ☆ ☆

The creation of a bicameral national legislature was partly due to the check and balance idea to which most of the delegates to the Philadelphia Convention subscribed. Another reason was the conflicting interests of the large and the small states. The establishment of a two chambered legislature permitted equal representation of the states in one house and representation according to population in the other. Another factor was aversion of the convention delegates to arrangements under which the people would possess direct control over the government. By providing a Senate composed of members chosen by the state legislatures and a President selected by an electoral college, the danger of mass domination of the national government was presumably averted or at least reduced to a minimum. However, Senators, like members of the House from the time of its creation, are now chosen by popular vote, and the President, although still nominally selected by the electoral college, is really placed in office by the voters of the several states.

Composition of The Senate and The House of Representatives

The Senate

(1) REQUIRED QUALIFICATIONS The constitutionally prescribed qualifications for service in the Senate are a minimum age of thirty, United States citizenship for not fewer than nine years, and inhabitancy of the state represented. Determination of the fulfillment of these requirements is a responsibility of the Senate, inasmuch as each house of Congress, by Constitutional stipulation, is judge of the elections, returns, and qualifications of its members. The practice of the Senate has been to seat any properly elected person who possesses the constitutionally specified qualifications.

(2) PERSONAL CHARACTERISTICS OF SENATORS AND REPRESENTATIVES   Most Senators have had a college or professional school training; a majority are lawyers; and a substantial proportion have held state or local offices of some type. The same observation is relevant to members of the House of Representatives. With respect to average age, that of Senators is nearly sixty, that of Representatives slightly above fifty. At any given time the Senate as a whole is composed of experienced legislators. Since the six-year terms of only one-third of the Senators expire at the same time, two-thirds have served at least two or four years. Moreover, many of those most recently elected have completed previous terms as Senators. Only a minority fall in the "rookie" category.

(3) SIZE; EQUAL REPRESENTATION FOR STATES   Inasmuch as each state is entitled to two Senators, the size of the Senate depends on the number of states. The first Senate consisted of twenty-six Senators, the present of one hundred. An increase in the immediate future seems unlikely, but the time may come when Puerto Rico and the Virgin Islands will gain admission to the Union as states.

Equal representation of the states in the Senate, regardless of population differences, is criticized by persons who believe that apportionment according to numbers is a requisite of any truly representative body in countries that subscribe to the principles of democratic government. The two-Senators-per-state arrangement enables states containing a minority of the country's population to select a majority of the Senators. Another feature of the Senate, also said to conflict with democratic doctrine, is the staggered terms of its members. The fact that the terms of only one-third of the

Senators expire at the same time often prevents the political complexion of the Senate from changing promptly in response to a shift in nation-wide support from one party to another.

(4) SENATE'S PERFORMANCE AS A REPRESENTATIVE BODY Despite the foregoing features, the Senate's performance as a representative body compares favorably with that of the House. As a rule, it has responded to the needs of the nation and given fair consideration to the desires and problems of the numerous interest-groups of which the national population is composed.

Senators are chosen by the entire electorate of a state. A senatorial candidate, to be elected and later reelected, has to keep in mind a far greater diversity of interests than members of the House (nearly all) who owe their election to comparatively small district constituencies in which particular interest-groups may be predominant. The equal representation of equal numbers of people is insufficient in itself to justify the claim that a legislative chamber, so constituted, will be adequately representative of the numerous and diverse interests of the general public. Various other factors have a bearing on the complexion of particular legislative bodies and on the way in which they function. Examples of such factors are the size of an assembly, its rules of procedure, the methods of electing its members, the geographical distribution of voting strength, and the prevailing conception of a legislator's responsibilities.

The House of Representatives

(1) REQUIRED QUALIFICATIONS To be constitutionally eligible for membership in the House of Representatives,

an individual must have attained the age of twenty-five, been a citizen of the United States for at least seven years, and be an inhabitant of the state by which he is chosen. Custom has added another requirement, viz., residence within the congressional district. Legally, any inhabitant of a state may compete for election in any of its congressional districts, but his chances of being nominated and elected are slight. Occasionally, usually in a metropolitan area, the voters of a district have chosen a non-resident to represent them in the House.

The House, as judge of the qualifications of its members, has exercised this power differently than the Senate. It has denied seats to duly elected persons who met the constitutional requirements for eligibility. Such action was taken in 1900 in the case of Brigham H. Roberts of Utah (a Mormon) on the ground that he was a polygamist. Nineteen years later Victor Berger of Wisconsin was denied a seat because he had been convicted of seditious conduct during World War I. Berger was a Socialist. In 1966 the House refused to seat Adam Clayton Powell of New York's Harlem district on charges of misappropriation of funds and other misconduct. The constitutional issue concerning necessary qualifications has been settled. In *Powell v. McCormack*[65a] the Supreme Court held that Congress, in judging the qualifications of its members, is limited to the qualifications prescribed in the Constitution—thus endorsing the past practice of the Senate and overruling that of the House. Powell should have been seated.

The Constitution expressly authorizes each house of Congress to expel its members. No mention is made of the reasons

[65a] 395 U. S. 486 (1969)

justifying such action. Expulsion requires a two-thirds vote, whereas denial of a seat, as in Powell's case, can be accomplished by an ordinary majority. Each house also is empowered to punish its members for disorderly behavior.

(2) SIZE   The size of the House is determined by Congress. Whatever the size, representatives must be apportioned among the states on a population basis, subject to the guarantee that each state is entitled to at least one representative, regardless of the number of its inhabitants.

The first House contained sixty-five members. Since 1912 the number has been 435, except for a temporary increase to 437 after the admission of Alaska (1958) and Hawaii (1959) as states. In 1961 the present figure of 435 was re-established. As long as Congress adheres to the policy of leaving the size of the House unaltered, substantial changes in the comparative populations of the several states necessarily result in decreased representation for some states and an increase for others. The only way to avoid decreases is by continuously enlarging the membership of the House.

(3) REAPPORTIONMENT PROCEDURE   Following each decennial census, the issue of reapportionment arises. Under present legislation, its settlement is based on the following procedure: (a) the Bureau of the Census calculates the number of representatives per state in accordance with the method of equal proportions,   (b) the results of its figuring are transmitted to the President and by him to Congress, and   (c) the Bureau's apportionment calculations become effective unless Congress, within fifteen days, devises and adopts a different plan.

(4) SINGLE-MEMBER DISTRICTS: REQUIRED STANDARDS   Except under the special circumstances noted in the preceding chapter, members of the House are elected by single-member congressional districts. Congress first prescribed the district plan in 1842.[66] At that time and subsequently, it established certain standards to be observed by state legislatures in laying out Congressional districts, e.g., the 1911 requirement that districts be of compact and contiguous territory and, as nearly as practicable, of equal population. In 1929 Congress eliminated these restrictive standards. It has not restored them (1972) but may revert to its earlier policy as a consequence of the Supreme Court's 1964 decision in *Wesberry v. Sanders.*[67]

(a) THE WESBERRY CASE In the *Wesberry* case the Court held that congressional districts must be substantially equal in population. It based its ruling on a decidedly broad and loose interpretation of the stipulation in Article I that representatives are to be chosen by the people of the several states and apportioned among the states on a population basis. A majority of the Court maintained that the framers of the Constitution subscribed to the one-man-one-vote idea. The majority opinion discounted the significance of the constitutional provision that the times, places, and manner of holding elections for Representatives and Senators shall be prescribed in each state by the legislature thereof, and that Congress may at any time by law make or alter such regulations, except as to the places of choosing Senators.

Prior to its 1964 ruling the Court had held, as recently as 1946 in *Colegrove v. Green,*[68] that the Constitution conferred on Congress *exclusive* authority to secure fair repre-

[66] The single-member district stipulation was abandoned in 1852 but restored in 1862.
[67] 376 U. S. 1.
[68] 328 U. S. 549.

sentation by the states in the House and had placed on that House the responsibility for determining whether states had fulfilled their obligation. It took the position that the question of fairness is political and that no judicial remedy is available. However, in *Baker v. Carr*,[69] a 1962 case, it reversed itself and decided that the issue of malapportionment in districting is justiciable. By so doing it gave itself the power to dictate standards of fairness. The *Baker* ruling paved the way for the *Wesberry* case.

Despite impressive grounds for questioning the correctness of the Supreme Court's interpretation of the Constitution in *Wesberry v. Sanders*, the fact is that legislative acts creating congressional districts must henceforth conform to the standard set by the Court, or be rejected as unconstitutional. The judicial branch is now the final arbiter with respect to the extent of permissible population disparities among congressional districts. Whether the Court will also put an end to gerrymandering remains to be seen.[70]

(5) PARTISAN COMPOSITION OF THE HOUSE   The partisan composition of the House of Representatives responds more quickly than that of the Senate to changes in political sentiment throughout the country. Such is the case for two reasons. Representatives serve for two years instead of for six as Senators do and the terms of all Representatives expire at the same time. The only holdover members, of whom there are usually many, are Representatives who meet with success in seeking reelection. However, there

[69] 369 U. S. 186.

[70] Gerrymandering is the practice of drawing district boundaries in such a way as to give a political advantage to the party in control of the state legislature at the time a districting plan is devised. This can be accomplished without disregarding the Supreme Court's ruling that the populations of districts must be substantially the same.

is no legal barrier to drastic changes in the personnel of the House on the occasion of a scheduled election.

Compensation of Members of Congress

In 1969 the salary of Representatives and Senators was raised from $30,000 to $42,500 per annum; that of the Speaker and the Vice-President is $62,500 plus a $10,000 expense allowance (all taxable). The majority and minority leaders of both houses receive $49,500. Members of Congress also enjoy a free first-class mailing privilege, an allowance for stationery, postage (airmail and special delivery stamps), long-distance telephone calls, telegrams, and travel, as well as such fringe benefits as pensions and group life insurance. Office space is furnished them and they are provided with a substantial allowance for staff hire. Congress decides on the compensation and other monetary grants to its members.

Privileges of Members of Congress

The Constitution stipulates that Senators and Representatives shall, in all cases except treason, felony, and breach of the peace, be privileged from arrest during their attendance at the sessions of their respective houses, and in going to and returning from the same; and for any speech or debate in either house they shall not be questioned in any other place.

The last clause of this provision is of major importance. No member of Congress may be proceeded against because of any statements he may have made in the course of transaction of Congressional business, including participation in debate, committee hearings, or other legislative proceedings. Thus a member enjoys immunity from suits for libel or slander for remarks, written or oral, made in connection with the discharge of his official responsibilities. He may, however, be censured by his colleagues.

The first part of this guarantee merely confers immunity from arrest on civil process and from compulsory jury service or appearance in court to testify. No exemption from the processes of criminal law is provided.

The Powers of Congress

Lawmaking is the primary function of Congress but some of its powers or those of one of its chambers fall outside the legislative category. Its non-legislative powers are commonly classified as constituent, electoral, executive, judicial, and investigatory. In addition, Congress performs functions that are attributable to its representative role rather than to specific powers that have been conferred on it.

Constituent Powers

Congress participates in the process of constitutional amendment. It may propose amendments by a two-thirds vote of each house and is under obligation to call a constitutional convention on application of the legislatures of two-thirds of the states. The Constitution requires Congress to designate which of two constitutionally prescribed modes of ratification is to be used by the states when proposed amendments are submitted to them. These powers of Congress are constituent in character.

Electoral Powers

Certain electoral powers are assigned to Congress, either to one or to both houses. The counting of electoral votes for President and Vice President is undertaken by Congress in a joint session presided over by the President of the Senate; the House of Representatives chooses a President from the three highest candidates if none obtains a majority electoral vote; and the Senate selects a Vice President from the two highest under the same circumstances. Furthermore, both houses appoint their own officers.

Executive Powers

The Senate possesses two important executive powers, viz., approval of Presidential appointments and giving or withholding consent to treaties made by the President with foreign countries. The House possesses the sole power of impeachment. When it impeaches and prosecutes civil officers of the United States it performs a function comparable to that of prosecuting attorneys in connection with the enforcement of criminal law. This power is executive in character, although often classified as judicial.

Congress exercises control over administration in several ways, usually by the enactment of laws or adoption of resolutions. It creates departments and other administrative agencies, possesses authority to prescribe administrative procedures, and authorizes expenditures for administrative purposes. When controlling administration in these and other ways it is discharging a function that is assignable to the executive category.

Judicial Powers

The clearly judicial powers of Congress include the Senate's sole power to try impeachments and the authority of each house to be judge of the elections, qualifications, and returns of its members. In addition, Congress may compel persons to testify before it and its committees. If they refuse to do so it may impose punishment for contempt. Each house may compel the attendance of its absent members under such penalties as the house prescribes and may authorize a number of members smaller than a quorum to take such action. Also, each house is empowered to punish its members for disorderly behavior.

Investigatory Power

An important subsidiary to the various substantive powers of Congress is its authority to conduct investigations. Without this implied power, Congress would be unable to obtain all of the information required for the proper discharge of its many responsibilities, including the enactment of laws and the exercise of such controls over the executive and judicial branches of the national government as are consistent with the separation of powers and check and balance features of the Constitution. Each house possesses this investigatory power.

Legislative Powers

The legislative powers of Congress overshadow all of its other powers. Except for its lawmaking authority, the role of Congress in the governmental process would be insignificant. Although the President is a powerful and influential chief executive, he is unable to achieve his objectives unless Congress is willing to follow his leadership. The enactment of laws requires an affirmative vote by both the House of Representatives and the Senate. No President, however great his prestige, can afford to antagonize a Congress which controls the purse strings and possesses the ultimate legal power, within the limits established by the Constitution, to prescribe the domestic policies of the national government and also to determine, indirectly for the most part but to some extent, its foreign policy. Congressional support is essential to fulfillment of most of the President's desires.

The Constitution expressly grants all legislative power to Congress. However, for reasons to be considered later, all law is not the product of Congressional action. Article I enumerates the legislative powers of Congress. Most important among them are the power to lay and collect taxes, to borrow money, to regulate foreign and interstate commerce, to raise and support the armed forces of the United States, to declare war, and to make all laws necessary and proper for carrying into execution all powers vested in the national government or in any department or officer thereof.

As pointed out in the second chapter, a listing of the powers specifically granted to the national government is an unreliable way of indicating the extent of its authority. Broad interpretation of expressly delegated powers, including the necessary and proper clause, has enabled the national government to render many services and to regulate individual and group behavior in numerous fields of activity far beyond the apparent jurisdiction of the national authorities as defined by the written provisions of the Constitution.

Congress, as the primary national lawmaking agency, bears

the major legal responsibility for whatever policies the national government pursues. Of course, Presidential recommendations carry great weight and the endorsement of the
Supreme Court is eventually necessary to sustain liberal
interpretations placed by Congress on the powers expressly
granted it. Consequently, all of the principal branches of the
national government share responsibility for its numerous
activities and sundry policies.

Both houses of Congress possess the same lawmaking authority. No bill can become law, with or without Presidential approval, unless it has passed both houses in identical
form. A majority vote in each house, provided a quorum has
assembled, is essential to initial passage and a two-thirds majority is required to override a Presidential veto.

An exception to the general principle that the House and
the Senate possess equal lawmaking power is due to the part
assigned the Senate in the matter of treaties with other countries. Since treaties, like the Constitution and laws made in
pursuance of it, are part of the supreme law of the land, the
Senate possesses a special lawmaking power which is denied
the House. However, unless a particular treaty is self-executing, such laws as may be required to give effect to its
provisions must be passed by the House as well as by the
Senate.

The Constitution stipulates that all bills for raising revenue
shall originate in the House. This proviso means little inasmuch as the Senate may propose amendments to such bills.

Functions of Congress as a Representative Body

One function of Congress ascribable to its representative
character is that of acting as an organ for the expression of

public opinion. Its members give vocal expression to their own views and also to those of their constituents. A related function is responding to the requests of private persons for information and assistance in their dealings with the national government. Much of the time of members of Congress is spent in serving their constituents in various ways. A third function is educating the public. The publicity commonly given to the debates and discussions taking place in Congress or at meetings of its committees provides the public with information which becomes a factor in shaping the views of many persons and groups in regard to current policy. Legislators provide leadership in the development of public support for some policies and in stimulating opposition to others. Thus Congress and its members not only serve as mediums for the expression of public opinion but also contribute to its molding.

The Delegation of Powers

As a consequence of the separation-of-powers feature of the national government, powers vested in one branch may not be delegated or transferred by it to the others. If such action were permissible, the form of government could be altered without resort to the process of constitutional amendment. The chief executive may not transfer his appointive power to the legislature; the judicial branch may not delegate its power of deciding cases to the chief executive; and the legislature may not shift its lawmaking power to the chief executive or the courts.

Although the rule prohibiting a delegation of powers is an established principle of constitutional law, application of this rule to particular situations involves complications. The question to be decided is just when an unconstitutional delegation of powers occurs. Many acts of Congress have delegated rule-making authority to the President and other agencies of the executive branch. If the constitutionality of such a delegation is challenged in a proper case, the Supreme Court eventually decides the issue that has been raised.

Permissible and Non-Permissible Delegations

Various decisions and opinions of the Court have resulted in the drawing of a rather vague line of demarcation between permissible and non-permissible delegations. The Court has taken the position that the *essence* of legislative power may not be delegated and that this rule remains unviolated as long as Congress establishes a general policy and prescribes standards limiting the discretion of the governmental agency to which rule-making authority is delegated. Unfettered lawmaking discretion may not be granted to the President and other administrative functionaries.[71]

Although the Court still recognizes limitations on the delegation of legislative power in the field of domestic affairs, it has refused to apply the same restrictions in the sphere of international relations. In *United States v. Curtiss-Wright Export Corporation et al.*,[72] the Court stated: ". . . if, in the maintenance of our international relations, embarrassment . . . is to be avoided and success for our aims achieved, congressional legislation which is to be made effective through negotiation and inquiry within the international field

---

[71] See *Schechter Poultry Corporation et al. v. United States,* 295 U. S. 495 (1935).
[72] 299 U. S. 304 (1936).

must often accord to the President a degree of discretion and freedom from statutory restriction which would not be admissible were domestic affairs alone involved."

The Supreme Court has been extremely liberal in upholding delegations of power by Congress and seldom has ruled that Congress has gone so far as to abdicate its essential legislative function. Its generosity is attributable to practical considerations in an era of highly complicated government. Congress is unable to do more than establish basic policies and procedures. Detailed rules and regulations are necessarily formulated by the chief executive and various administrative agencies engaged in executing the general policies which Congress is capable of prescribing. These rules, regulations, and ordinances, commonly referred to as "administrative legislation," constitute a body of subsidiary law which is great in volume.

The Administrative Procedure Act of 1946 requires publication of this type of law in the *Federal Register* which is issued five times a week. A casual examination of issues of the *Register* is sufficient to reveal the magnitude of administrative legislation.

The judicial branch also performs a lawmaking function, apart from the Supreme Court's power, delegated by Congress, to establish procedural rules to be observed by the lower national courts. In deciding cases, courts are confronted with the necessity of ascertaining what the law is and interpreting acts of Congress and administrative rules and regulations. A body of case law is developed in the process of adjudication and supplements the written law of the land. For the parties to a particular controversy, the court's decision amounts to an authoritative determination of what "the law" is.

The Investigatory Power of Congress

In 1792 the House of Representatives adopted a resolution providing "that a committee be appointed to inquire into the cause of the failure of the expeditions under General St. Clair and that the committee be empowered to call for such persons, papers, and records as may be necessary to assist their inquiries." The Senate first created a select committee with compulsory power of investigation in 1818. This action resulted from reports that General Jackson had assumed extraordinary powers in waging the Seminole War. In 1859 the Senate appointed a committee to determine the facts concerning John Brown's raid at Harper's Ferry. In so doing, the Senate, for the first time in its history, exercised its power of compulsion for the purpose of collecting information to aid it in the performance of a legislative function.

The inquiries that have been mentioned represent merely a few of the frequent occasions since 1792 on which the House and the Senate have conducted compulsory investigations as a means of gaining objectives within the scope of their constitutionally delegated authority. Both houses always have taken a broad view of their inquisitorial power and have utilized compulsory processes to procure information needed for the effective exercise of the various express and implied powers which they possess.

These powers are assignable to several broad categories, viz., (1) powers relating to the membership of the houses, to the safeguarding of their constitutionally conferred privileges, and to the prevention of interference with their functioning; (2) powers enabling Congress to exercise control over the organization and operation of administrative agencies; (3) the power to remove civil officers by resorting to the impeachment process; (4) powers pertaining to governmental expenditures and the raising of revenue; (5) the power to determine the policies of the national government; and (6) the power to protect and preserve the Constitution against overthrow by foreign or domestic enemies.

Scope of the Power of Investigation

The power to investigate is coupled with the power to compel appearance before either house of Congress or its committees, to require the answering of questions, to order the production of papers and documents, and to impose penalties for contempt. This power is not absolute.

In *Kilbourn v. Thompson*[73] and *McGrain v. Daugherty*,[74] the Supreme Court stated that the power of inquiry is limited and that neither house possesses general power to inquire into private affairs and compel disclosures. These and other cases have cast light on the scope of the investigatory power and on the rights of private persons appearing before investigating committees.

The legal situation in regard to the investigatory power of Congress and the rights of witnesses may be summarized as follows:

1. Congress possesses the implied power to conduct compulsory investigations into any and all matters relevant to exercise of the various powers delegated to it by the Constitution.

2. In conducting investigations, neither Congress nor

[73] 103 U. S. 168 (1881).
[74] 273 U. S. 135 (1927).

either house is bound by the procedural safeguards or the strict rules of evidence which apply to trials by courts. The manner in which inquiries are conducted is a matter of legislative discretion.

3. The power to punish for contempt enables either house to order imprisonment for a period not extending beyond the date of adjournment. Congress also may provide by statute, as it has, for the judicial trial and punishment of persons who fail to respond to a summons or refuse to testify.

4. The courts presume that Congress, in providing for an inquiry, is seeking information which will aid it in discharging its various responsibilities. A statement to that effect in the authorizing statute or resolution is accepted at its face value, and even in the absence of such a statement, an investigation will be upheld as valid if the subject matter of the inquiry falls within the scope of powers delegated to Congress. To be valid, an investigation does not require a declaration of what Congress intends to do when its inquiry is completed. Nor will the courts inquire into the motives of legislators.

5. The fact that the power of inquiry may be exercised abusively or oppressively does not warrant denial of the power. Legislative self-restraint and the ballot box, rather than resort to the courts, are the ultimate remedies for bias as well as for dishonest and vindictive motives.

6. The giving of testimony, when properly summoned, is a public duty to which there are few exceptions.

7. The guarantee of freedom of speech in the First Amendment does not preclude investigation into propaganda activities.

8. A witness may rightfully refuse to answer questions on the following grounds, viz., the Congress, or one of its com-

mittees, lacks authority to conduct a specific investigation; that a particular question is not pertinent to the subject matter of the inquiry; and that he relies on the right against self-incrimination guaranteed in the Fifth Amendment. The witness must assert this last mentioned right if he desires protection and may remain silent with impunity unless complete immunity from prosecution is offered.

9. A witness need not testify or produce papers in the absence of a committee quorum.

Congressional investigations have been criticized on various grounds. Committee procedures have been condemned as unfair in many respects, including the charge that witnesses are not permitted to face their accusers, to cross-examine other witnesses, or to be assisted by counsel. Another criticism is that occasional committees have seemed more desirous of smearing and discrediting particular persons than of securing information. These and other specific complaints amount to the general accusation that Congress and its committees are too indifferent to the rights of such individuals as are summoned to appear and testify. Since the courts have been reluctant to interfere with and restrict the investigatory power of Congress, the remedy for misuse of this important power lies with the legislature itself.

Congressional Organization and Procedure

Collective action by any body of individuals, especially one of large size, requires satisfactory organization and suitable procedures if its responsibilities are to be discharged efficiently and effectively. Subject to a few constitutional stipulations, the House of Representatives and the Senate are free to organize themselves as they see fit and to adopt whatever rules of procedure they consider appropriate.

The presence of political parties in Congress has a major bearing on the way in which the House and the Senate, as formally organized, function. An understanding of party organization and procedures is essential to a comprehension of Congress in action. The realities of Congressional proceedings differ in various respects from the formalities.

Constitutional Stipulations

The Constitution provides that the House of Representatives is to choose its Speaker and other officers and that the Vice President of the United States shall be the presiding officer of the Senate. The Senate is authorized to select its other officers, including a president *pro tempore* who is to preside in the absence of the Vice President.

Although the power to prescribe rules of procedure is granted both chambers of Congress, their discretion in doing so is limited in several ways. The Constitution states that a majority of each house is the required quorum for transacting business, but a smaller number may adjourn from day to day and be authorized to compel the attendance of absentees. Neither house, while Congress is in session, shall adjourn, without the consent of the other, for more than three days or to any place other than the one in which the houses are sitting.

Each house must keep and publish a journal of its proceedings, except for such parts as may require secrecy. Furthermore, the yeas and nays of members on any question shall, if desired by one-fifth of those present, be recorded in the journal. Such recording is mandatory if the houses are voting on the overriding of a Presidential veto.

The remaining constitutional stipulations are as follows: every order, resolution, or vote to which the concurrence of both houses may be necessary must be presented to the President for approval; a two-thirds vote of each house is required to override a Presidential veto; bills for raising revenue shall originate in the House of Representatives; and Congress shall assemble at least once a year, beginning on January 3 unless a different date is prescribed by law.

Formal Organization of the House and the Senate

The principal officers of the House of Representatives are the speaker, the parliamentarian, the clerk, the legislative counsel, the sergeant-at-arms, the doorkeeper, the postmaster, and the chaplain. In the case of the Senate, the president *pro tempore* serves as presiding officer when the Vice President is absent. The secretary of the Senate is the equivalent of the clerk of the House. Like the House, the Senate has a number of other officers, among them a secretary for the majority, a secretary for the minority, a chief clerk, a legislative counsel, and a chaplain.

The formal organization of both houses includes standing committees and special or select committees. In addition the rules of each house provide for membership on a few joint committees and on conference committees which are appointed to iron out differences between the House and the Senate when the two houses disagree concerning the content of particular bills. Committees of this type include both

Senators and Representatives. With these exceptions, each house confines service on its committees to its own members. Congress has been unwilling to substitute a joint committee system for the traditional dual committee arrangement.

By far the most important of the formal agencies of the two houses are the Speaker of the House of Representatives, the standing committees and their chairmen, and the conference committees. They play a major role in the functioning of Congress as a lawmaking body.

Nominally, each house selects its officers and standing committee members, but the actual process of selection, which is dominated by partisan considerations, involves the functioning of various party agencies in accordance with well-established practices of the Democratic and Republican parties. As for special and conference committees, their members are appointed by the presiding officers of the House and the Senate.

(1) SPEAKER OF THE HOUSE The Speaker of the House of Representatives is elected by the House but the actual choice is made by the majority party which decides on its candidate in a meeting or conference of its House membership. Although the minority party also chooses a candidate in the same way, the outcome of the formal election by the House is almost always predictable with certainty inasmuch as the representatives vote on a partisan basis.

The Speaker is the most powerful individual member of the House. Its rules confer important powers upon him and he exercises these to promote the interests of his party. Speakers never function as impartial presiding officers in the way that speakers of the British House of Commons do. Under House rules now in effect, the Speaker possesses many powers which, in combination with his position as leader of his party in the House, enable him to exert great influence on the transaction of legislative business. Even so, his powers are more restricted than those of speakers prior to 1911.

a. POWERS OF THE SPEAKER Among the powers of the Speaker are the following: (1) the preservation of order and decorum; (2) interpretation of the rules and deciding points of order; (3) recognizing representatives, if he so desires, who wish to address the House or offer motions; (4) deciding when bills will be brought to the floor; (5) putting questions to a vote and determining the outcome of unrecorded voting; (6) refusing to entertain dilatory motions; (7) determination of the presence of a quorum; (8) appointing members of special committees and conference committees; (9) selecting a speaker *pro tempore* to serve during his absence; (10) naming the chairman of the Committee of the Whole when the House sits as a committee; and (11) referring introduced bills to standing committees—a power which is important only if a bill deals with matters falling within the jurisdiction of more than one committee as defined by House rules.

The Speaker, being an elected member of the House, is entitled to vote and may, if he wishes, participate in debate. Although the formal powers of the Speaker are substantial, the fact that he is the leader of his party accounts in large measure for his dominant role in the functioning of the House.

(2) THE VICE PRESIDENT The Vice President of the United States, as presiding officer of the Senate, lacks the power and influence of the Speaker. He exercises the powers

of his office far more impartially than the latter and his position corresponds rather closely to that of the typical moderator of an assembly. Not being a Senator, he may cast a vote only in the event of a tie.

(3) STANDING COMMITTEES Standing committees and especially their *chairmen* play a particularly important role in the functioning of Congress. Each house has its own set of committees. There are twenty-one standing committees in the House and seventeen in the Senate.

All bills, following introduction, are referred to a standing committee by the presiding officers of the two houses and the fate of a bill thereafter usually depends on what the committee, particularly its chairman, decides to do with it. Most bills die in committee. If the chairman is opposed to a bill, it fails to receive consideration; if he brings it before his committee, its fate depends on what the committee, functioning under his leadership, decides to do.

A bill which survives committee consideration is reported on favorably to the house of which the committee is an agent. However, a favorable report is by no means indicative of a bill's future. Most reported bills make no further progress and those which do may meet with defeat when considered and voted on by the House and/or the Senate.

Without standing committees, Congress would be unable to give proper consideration to the thousands of bills which its members introduce. The committee system, which is based on the principle of division of labor, increases the likelihood that proposed measures will receive sufficient preliminary examination to provide at least some justification for their ultimate fate. Committees perform the first step in a sifting process which is essential to the adequate functioning of a legislative assembly—but this initial sifting function need not be assigned to standing committees as in the case of the House and the Senate.

(a) HOUSE STANDING COMMITTEES The twenty-one standing committees of the House vary in size from a minimum of nine to a maximum of fifty-five (1972). Most of them have from twenty-five to thirty-seven members. The titles of the committees indicate the type of bills to which their jurisdiction extends, such as Agriculture, Appropriations, Armed Services, Education and Labor, Judiciary, Interstate and Foreign Commerce, Rules, and Ways and Means (revenue). As will become apparent later, the Committee on Rules is an extremely powerful agency of the House. Other important committees, to mention a few, are the Committees on Appropriations, Ways and Means, Armed Services, and Public Works.

(b) SENATE STANDING COMMITTEES The smaller number of Senate standing committees (17) average about seventeen members in size, with seven the minimum and twenty-four the maximum (1972). Among them are the Committees on Appropriations, Finance, Armed Services, Commerce, Judiciary, Foreign Relations, and Aeronautical and Space Sciences.

(c) SUB-COMMITTEES Although the number of standing committees in Congress is comparatively small, the total of committees of all types is large, principally because of the creation of numerous subcommittees by most, but not all, of the standing committees. In 1972, for example, there were 123 subcommittees in the House and

121 in the Senate. Usually, subcommittees are established by the chairmen of standing committees. Their membership is determined in a variety of ways, including designation by the chairmen along or in consultation with the ranking minority members of the standing committees. Among the reasons for large-scale resort to subcommittees are the growing need for specialization and the opportunity which these subcommittees provide for a more effective role in the legislative process on the part of junior members of standing committees as distinguished from their seniors who dominate the functioning of the full committees. With rare exceptions, the reports of subcommittees are submitted to the standing committees by which they have been created.[75]

(4) SPECIAL COMMITTEES In addition to standing committees and their subcommittees, both houses of Congress create special or select committees. Committees of this type are usually established for investigatory purposes. Examples are the Special Committee on Aging and the Select Committee on Small Business of the Senate and the Select Committee on Astronautics and Space of the House.

(5) JOINT COMMITTEES Joint committees, too, are usually investigative in nature, as are the Joint Committees on Defense Production and on Internal Revenue Taxation. Like the special committees, they are established for a particular purpose and usually for a limited time, rather than permanently, as in the case of standing committees. Occasion-

[75] George Goodwin, Jr., "Subcommittees: The Miniature Legislatures of Congress," *American Political Science Review*, Vol. LVI, No. 3, September, 1962, pp. 596–604.

ally, joint committees are given standing committee status. Present examples are the Joint Committee on Atomic Energy and the Joint Economic Committee.

(6) THE HOUSE COMMITTEE ON RULES The Committee on Rules of the House of Representatives (a standing committee) deserves special consideration because of its dominant role in the transaction of House business. Proposed changes in the standing rules of procedure are referred to this committee, once a newly elected House has become organized, and the fate of proposed changes depends on the action which the committee takes.

Of great importance is the power of this committee to make decisions about the handling of a particular bill by the House. Its authority includes determination of the standing rule under which a bill is to be considered and also the right to provide a special rule in the form of a resolution which, if adopted by the House as it is likely to be, controls consideration of the particular bill that is the subject matter of the special rule. Special rules may and do go so far as to limit the time for debate, waive points of order against certain provisions of the bill or proposed amendments, and even forbid any amendments or all amendments other than those proposed by the standing committee which reported the bill to the House. The extensive power of the Rules Committee is attributable to a combination of the formal rules of the House and the fact of majority party domination of this all-important committee.

(7) THE SENATE COMMITTEE ON RULES AND ADMINISTRATION The Senate Committee on Rules and Administration lacks the authority of the House committee. Its

comparative weakness is due to the fact that rules of procedure of the Senate confer greater freedom on Senators as
individuals, and consequently on minorities, than the rules
of the House grant to individual Representatives. Senators
may speak on any subject as long as they please, whereas
Representatives are bound by a one-hour time limit and
debate is restrictable in other ways, among them by adoption
of special rules devised by the Committee on Rules and by
moving the previous question—a motion which, if adopted,
ends debate.

The unlimited freedom of debate accorded Senators permits filibustering, which is difficult to stop because the
closure rule of the Senate requires a two-thirds vote (of
those present and voting) for adoption of a motion for
closure. The greater liberality of Senate rules is attributable
primarily to the smaller size of the Senate. Other factors
contributing to Senatorial freedom are the long terms of
Senators, the large constituencies by which they are chosen,
and the fact that most Senators are important party leaders
in their home states.

(8) COMMITTEE OF THE WHOLE The device of
"committee of the whole" is resorted to by the House but
not, as at one time, by the Senate—except in considering
treaties.

For the purpose of dealing with "money bills," the House
may resolve itself into *The Committee of the Whole House
on the State of the Union.* When the House sits as a committee, one hundred members are sufficient to constitute a
quorum; a member named by the Speaker presides; debate
occurs under the "five minute" rule; and no recorded votes
are taken. After completing its business, this committee of

the whole arises and reports to the House which then functions under its formal rules of procedure in considering the committee's report.

The "committee of the whole" procedure also is used in handling "private" bills. In this case the formal title is *Committee of the Whole House.*

(9) CONFERENCE COMMITTEES No bills can become laws unless adopted by both houses in identical form. Any differences between the House and Senate versions of a bill dealing with a particular problem must be resolved by agreement. Unless one house is willing to accept changes made by the other, *conference committees* are resorted to for the purpose of overcoming disagreement.

The presiding officers of the House and the Senate name the conference members (known as "managers"). If agreement is reached, the conference committee members report to their houses and the latter act on the report. Ordinarily, conference reports are voted on favorably by the members of both houses, with the result that the measure agreed upon is transmitted to the President as required by the Constitution.

Informal Organization: Party Agencies

With one exception, the Senate Republican and Democratic Policy Committees, the rules of the House and the Senate make no provision for organization of the political parties represented in Congress. Each party is free to organize itself in whatever way it chooses. Both the Republican and Democratic parties have developed essentially the same type of organization. The several agencies of these parties include a conference or caucus, floor leaders, whips and assistant whips, committees on committees, and steering or policy committees.

(1) CONFERENCES OR CAUCUSES A conference (caucus) is a meeting of the entire membership of a particular party in the House or the Senate. All Republicans in the House, for instance, are members of the Republican Conference and all Democrats in the Senate constitute the Democratic Conference of that chamber. In recent years, these partisan conferences, particularly those of the Democratic party, have lost most of their former power.

Conferences are designed to promote united action by the party membership in the process of decision-making by a legislative chamber. Today, the chief function of the conferences of both parties in Congress is the selection of floor leaders and the nomination of candidates for the speakership in the House, the president *pro tempore* of the Senate, and other House and Senate officers. The conferences also ratify the standing committee assignments of the party committees on committees, but this is ordinarily a meaningless formality.

Other examples of conference action are the choice of party whips by the Republican conferences, selection of the chairman of the Republican Policy Committee by the Senate Republican conference, and choice of the Democratic members of the House Committee on Ways and Means by the Democratic conference.

Conference decisions are binding on party members when the House and Senate choose their officers and the personnel of their standing committees. A Republican is duty-bound to vote for the individuals nominated by his party and a Democrat for the Democratic party's list of nominees. This obligation is political rather than legal, i.e., imposed by the parties and not by the rules of the House and the Senate.

Generally speaking, party members are free to vote as they please on bills under consideration by Congress, but at times in the past conference decisions on questions of legislative policy, with certain exceptions, were considered binding on party members, e.g., in the case of the Democratic party during the administration of former President Wilson. The circumstances under which members of Congress are under obligation to abide by conference decisions is strictly a matter of party policy which each party in each house decides for itself.

(2) FLOOR LEADERS   Floor leaders lead their parties in the maneuvering which occurs in the conduct of legislative business. They are the strategists or tacticians who are supposed to take advantage of every opportunity under the formal rules of procedure to further the interests of their parties in the course of legislative proceedings.

In addition to providing leadership in debate, floor leaders usually decide which partisans are to be recognized by the presiding officer in the discussion of proposed policies and endeavor to persuade members of their parties to support measures favored by the party leaders. Obviously, the majority floor leader is a more potent factor in the legislative process than his minority party counterpart. Floor leaders, whether of the majority or minority party, commonly function as spokesmen for the President, provided, of course, that the floor leader and the President belong to the same party.

The power of a floor leader depends on such considerations as the personality of the man, his political know-how, the party complexion of the legislative chamber, and the other partisan positions which the practices of his party permit him to hold, e.g., chairman of the committee on committees, with the right to select all or most of its members. Generally speaking, the partisan members of both houses find it inexpedient to antagonize the floor leaders of their parties.

(3) WHIPS Party whips perform several functions. Perhaps the most important of these is seeing to it that party members are in attendance on occasions when crucial voting occurs in the legislature. Whips serve as contact men between the leaders of their parties and the rank and file of party members. By conducting polls they acquire information concerning how the members intend to vote on pending legislation. This knowledge proves helpful to the leaders in planning legislative strategy.

(4) COMMITTEES ON COMMITTEES The partisan committees on committees control the assignment of party members to the standing committees of the House and the Senate. Each party is represented on the latter committees in approximate proportion to the ratio of representation of the majority and minority parties in each chamber of Congress.

(a) THE SENIORITY RULE: PAST AND PRESENT STATUS For nearly two generations the seniority rule was followed automatically in the naming of committee chairmen. The committee member of longest consecutive service belonging to the majority party became the chairman of that committee and the minority party member of longest consecutive service was recognized as the "ranking member"—which meant that he would become chairman if and when his party attained majority status. In making committee assignments other than the chairmanship, committees on committees considered (and still do) various factors in addition to seniority, including the desirability of maintaining some geographical balance on a committee, previous political experience, professional qualifications, the preferences of individual members of Congress, and the recommendations of party leaders.

The seniority rule with respect to chairmen and ranking minority-party members has been sharply criticized because it precludes consideration of such factors as intelligence, ability, and party regularity. Defenders of the rule maintain that seniority is a guarantee of knowledge of the subject matter over which a committee has jurisdiction and also ensures acquaintance with the intricacies of legislative proceedings. Adherence to some other rule or rules probably would reveal unanticipated shortcomings.

The principal consequence of strict adherence to the seniority rule in the assignment of committee chairmanships was that the chairmen of most standing committees in both houses came from states and congressional districts in which a "one party" situation prevailed. States or districts in which the parties were about evenly matched rarely had Senators or Representatives with sufficiently long periods of consecutive service to qualify for chairmanships under the seniority rule. When the Democratic party was in the majority, most of the important standing committee chairmen were Southerners, whereas committee chairmanships were held by Senators and Representatives from safe Republican states and districts when the Republican party was in power.

In 1971 both major parties in the House and the Senate

made minor changes affecting absolute adherence to the seniority rule—without abandoning it. The House Democrats terminated *automatic* operation of the seniority rule by permitting ten or more Democratic members to demand a caucus vote on assignments to chairmanships and committee membership recommended by the Democratic committee on committees. The Democrats also limited committee chairmen and other senior members to the chairmanship of one subcommittee. As for the Republican party in the House, it also ended the necessity of abiding *automatically* by the seniority rule and provided for a secret caucus vote on the nomination of *ranking* committee members, i.e., those destined to become chairmen when the Republicans are in the majority.

The Senate, after hearings, rejected a proposal to abandon the seniority rule. However, the Democrats required caucus approval of its committee on committee's recommended appointments of chairmen and committee members, but required acceptance or rejection of the recommendations as a whole without a vote on individual assignments. The Republicans created a study committee and merely provided that no Republican could be a "ranking member" of more than one standing committee.

The eventual result of the changes summarized in the preceding paragraphs remains to be seen. In all likelihood the seniority rule will usually continue to be determinative of committee assignments, particularly chairmanships and ranking minority members.

(b) COMPOSITION OF COMMITTEES ON COMMITTEES

The composition of the party committees on committees lacks uniformity. In the House of Representatives the Democratic members of the Committee on Ways and Means constitute that party's committee on committees, whereas in the Senate the Democratic floor leader, as chairman, selects all the committee members except two who serve *ex officio*, viz., the secretary of the Democratic conference and the Democratic whip. The Republican committee on committees in the House is composed of one member from each state having Republican representation (chosen by the state's Republican delegation), with each member being given a number of votes equal to the number of Republican representatives from his state. This committee's chairman is the party's leader in the House. In the Senate, the chairman of the Republican conference designates the usual five to seven members of the Republican committee on committees.

(5) POLICY COMMITTEES Both parties have policy or steering committees in the House and the Senate. The Democratic steering committee in the House is composed of six *ex officio* members (the Speaker, majority floor leader, whip, chairman of the conference, secretary of the conference, and chairman of the Democratic Congressional Campaign Committee) and eighteen members elected by Democratic representatives of the states as grouped in geographical zones. This committee exists but apparently does not function.

The Republican policy committee in the House has thirty-three members, ten of them *ex officio* (floor leader, whip, chairman of the conference, secretary of the conference, chairman of the Republican campaign committee, and five Republican members of the House Committee on Rules), eighteen elected from nine geographical zones, and five non-voting members chosen by each of five classes of Republicans most recently elected to the House. This committee meets frequently (weekly) and votes on legislative issues. Although not binding, its votes influence the voting of Republican representatives.

In the Senate, the policy committee of the majority party determines when legislation should be brought to the floor of the Senate. The Democratic policy committee consists of the majority floor leader (its chairman), twelve members appointed by him, and two *ex officio* members, viz., the whip and the secretary of the Democratic conference. As for the Republicans, their policy committee is chaired by a Republican elected by the conference, six members appointed by this chairman, and seven *ex officio* members, among them the floor leader, the whip, the chairman of the conference, and the chairman of the committee on committees. When the Republicans are in power this committee, like its Democratic counterpart, schedules legislation. In power or not, it occasionally issues a policy statement and also undertakes policy studies for the party.

Congress in Action

Congress in action involves the functioning of both the formal and the partisan agencies of the House and the Senate. Political parties necessarily carry on their activities within the framework of the formal organization and in accordance with the rules of procedure established by the two houses, but partisan considerations determine the official personnel of each house, the composition of standing and other committees, and the use made of the procedural rules of the two chambers.

Party lines are commonly disregarded in voting on proposed measures. Combinations of Democratic and Republican members often vote together in supporting or opposing the adoption of specific policy proposals. This occurrence is attributable to the decentralized and undisciplined character of the parties, to the existence of factions and blocs within the parties and Congress, and to the fact that voting along party lines is unnecessary to the continuance in office of the President and members of Congress. Despite deviations from the party line, policies favored by the majority party ordinarily prevail, unless it lacks a safe working majority in both houses of Congress and unless the President happens to be a member of the minority party in the legislature.

In the preceding pages many details of organization and procedure, both formal and informal (partisan), have been described. It would have been simpler to state that both houses of Congress, especially the House of Representatives, function under the domination, or near domination, of a comparatively small number of individuals, viz., the Speaker of the House, the Committee on Rules of that chamber, the chairmen of the standing committees of both houses, the majority and minority floor leaders of the parties, the party whips, and the chairmen and secretaries of the party conferences. Representatives and Senators of long experience, plus considerable political astuteness, occupy these positions and provide the leadership which almost always develops in assemblies of substantial size.

Whether the dominant figures of the House and the Senate collaborate or oppose each other depends on such factors as the political complexion of the houses, the potency of Presidential leadership, and the nature of the controversial issues confronting the country. The lawmaking process is characterized by bargaining and compromising among the established leaders of groups of legislators functioning under the pressures brought to bear on them by the President, administrative agencies, privately organized interest-groups, the press, and the voters of the states and congressional districts.

The Passage of Bills

To become a law, a proposed measure must be adopted in identical form by both houses of Congress and survive consideration by the President. A bill submitted to the President may be signed by him; become law without his signature if he fails to exercise his veto power during the ten days allowed him for its consideration while Congress remains in session; and, if vetoed, be enacted as law if passed thereafter by a two-thirds vote of each house of Congress.

In the following description of the passing of a bill, it will be assumed that the bill originates in the House and that Senate action occurs after the bill's passage by the House. However, the place of origin may be the Senate and in that event consideration by the House constitutes the second major stage in the lawmaking process.

(1) HOUSE PROCEDURE: (a) INTRODUCTION OF BILLS A member of the House of Representatives introduces a bill by handing it to the Clerk of the House or by placing it in a box known as the hopper. The bill is numbered, referred to the proper standing committee, printed, distributed among the House members, and recorded by number and title in the Journal. This step constitutes the "first reading" of the bill. All bills survive this stage.

(b) COMMITTEE CONSIDERATION The next step is

consideration of a bill by the standing committee to which it was referred. In the case of public bills, i.e., those dealing with general matters and of general applicability, each bill is referred automatically (by the House Parliamentarian on order of the Speaker) to the committee which under the rules of the House has jurisdiction over the bill's subject matter. In case of doubt concerning the proper committee, the Speaker makes the assignment. Private bills are referred to the committee designated by the bill's sponsor. A private bill is one that applies to a particular person or place rather than to the general public. All bills are referred to a committee but the vast majority make no further progress.

Standing committees examine bills and decide on their merits. This process may involve no more than a cursory examination by committee chairmen who determine the advisability of full committee consideration. Bills scrutinized by a committee are evaluated on the basis of information obtained from various sources, including *public hearings* on bills believed sufficiently important to resort to this technique. Practically all bills disapproved by a standing committee "die" at this stage, unless the House compels the committee to discharge a bill. Compulsory discharge rarely occurs because the rules of the House make such action extremely difficult.

(c) REPORTING OF BILLS Bills favored by a standing committee majority are "reported" to the House, either as introduced or with a recommendation for amendments. Sometimes a substitute measure is submitted. The report contains the committee's reasons for supporting the bill. Committee members opposed to the bill may present a dissenting minority report. Occasionally, a standing committee reports unfavorably on a bill, but most bills to which a committee objects are "killed" without bothering to explain the action taken.

(d) CALENDARS Reported bills are placed on one of three regular calendars in an order which depends solely on the timing of committee reports. One of the calendars is the *Calendar of the Committee of the Whole House on the State of the Union.* Public money bills, i.e., those directly or indirectly raising revenue, authorizing expenditures, or pertaining to public property, are placed on this calendar. All other public bills are assigned to the *House Calendar.* A *Private Calendar* is provided for bills of the private variety. The House has two special calendars of lesser importance, viz., the *Unanimous Consent Calendar* to which non-controversial bills are assigned and the *Discharge Calendar* which lists motions to discharge committees which refuse to report a bill.

(e) ORDER OF CONSIDERATION OF BILLS In principle, the place of a bill on a calendar determines the order in which it will be considered by the House, but in practice this order is commonly disregarded. Moreover, many bills appearing on the calendars never receive consideration by the House and consequently perish at this stage of the proceedings.

The usual way of departing from the schedule of bills on the calendars is by the adoption of a special rule reported by the House Committee on Rules. Some bills, by reason of their subject matter, fall in the category of "privileged business." For instance, appropriation and revenue bills can be taken up at almost any time because of the priority accorded them under the rules of the House. Other devices for securing immediate consideration of a bill, regardless of its calendar position, are suspension of the rules by a two-thirds vote or the obtainment of unanimous consent. In addition, definite days are assigned for certain categories of bills, e.g., District of Columbia business on the second and fourth Mondays and private bills on the first and third Tuesdays of each month. On "Calendar Wednesday," standing committees whose business is "unprivileged" have the opportunity to call up bills for consideration, but this arrangement is chiefly beneficial to committees with titles beginning with letters near the top of the alphabet, inasmuch as the alphabetical order is followed in inviting committees to "bring up" bills.

The formal procedures for departing from the order of bills on the House calendars are necessarily utilized in the lawmaking process, but control over the scheduling of legislation is actually exercised by the House leadership. Among those who decide which bills will be considered, and when, are the Speaker, the Committee on Rules, the majority floor leader, standing committee chairmen, and the chairman of the majority party conference. Since partisan desires prevail, the leaders of the majority party dominate the process by which bills are selected for consideration by the House.

(f) SECOND READING Bills reaching the floor of the House are usually read in full at this stage (the second reading) which is the crucial one in the career of a bill. At this time debate occurs and amendments may be proposed, provided that consideration does not take place under a special rule which restricts the opportunity for both discussion and the proposal of changes. The floor leaders of the majority and minority parties, together with the Speaker, decide on the Representatives who will be permitted to speak for or against a bill. Among the usual participants in debate are the chairman and ranking minority member of the standing committee which reported the bill, the majority and minority floor leaders, and other Representatives whom the Speaker chooses to recognize.

Bills on the Union Calendar are considered by the Committee of the Whole House on the State of the Union. The chairman of this committee is named by the Speaker and it functions in the manner previously described, reporting to the House which then acts on the committee's report. Bills on the House Calendar receive direct consideration by the House as such, but private bills also are handled through the "committee of the whole" procedure. At the conclusion of discussion and voting on proposed amendments, if any, which occur on the occasion of second reading, the House votes on the following question: "Shall the bill be engrossed and read a third time?" [76]

(g) THIRD READING   If the foregoing question is voted on favorably, the bill proceeds to its third reading which almost without exception is by title only. An engrossed bill adopted at this stage is signed by the Speaker and the Clerk and then transmitted to the Senate.

(2) SENATE PROCEDURE   Senate procedure generally resembles that of the House but differs in several respects. Senators gain recognition by the presiding officer in order to announce the introduction of a bill. Introduced bills are numbered, printed, recorded in the Journal, and referred to the appropriate standing committee. A bill which has been passed by the House is assigned to a committee and, like other bills, receives such committee consideration, if any, as

[76] An engrossed bill is a bill in the form in which finally adopted by the House.

the committee chairman deems desirable. After due investigation and deliberation, bills that the committee majority favors are reported to the Senate and placed on the single legislative calendar which the Senate maintains. The only other calendar is an executive calendar for treaties and for Presidential nominations to offices requiring Senate approval. As in the House, standing committees of the Senate have the power to kill bills by refusing to report them.

The scheduling of legislation in the Senate is determined by the policy committee of the majority party and the majority floor leader. Since bills are commonly taken from the calendar and brought to the floor of the Senate by unanimous consent, the policy committee finds it expedient to consult the leader of the minority party. In lieu of this procedure, the majority leader, ordinarily, or any Senator may move that a designated bill be given consideration. The rules committee of the Senate is unable to prevent action on bills which the majority party decides to bring before the Senate for a vote.

Debate in the Senate may be prolonged because Senators are permitted to speak at length on any subject. That is why filibusters may be undertaken by Senators opposed to a particular measure. Cloture may be brought about only when proceedings are initiated by a petition filed by sixteen Senators and a two-thirds vote favoring cloture is obtained two days after filing of the petition. Ordinarily, debate is *voluntarily* limited by advance agreement concerning the ending of discussion and the beginning of voting.

If a House bill is adopted without change by the Senate, the next step is transmission to the President. When changes are made, the House is notified, and if it accepts the changes, Presidential consideration follows. Unwillingness on the part of either house to approve changes made by the other normally results in a request for a conference.

(3) CONFERENCES The members of a conference committee customarily include the chairmen and ranking majority and minority members of the standing committees which were in charge of the bills during their progress through the House and the Senate. Additional conferees may be appointed, usually members of the standing committees recommended by their chairmen.

In theory, conference committees are supposed to deal only with the points of disagreement between the two houses, but in practice they often rewrite provisions which both houses had approved. Conference committees function in secrecy; no minutes or other formal records of their proceedings are kept.

Conference reports to the houses fall in the category of "privileged business" and are almost always endorsed by the House and the Senate. The power and influence of conference committees is so great that they have been said to constitute a "third house" of Congress.

The leaders of the Senate and the House of Representatives, most of whom have been identified above, are primarily responsible for the way in which the legislative branch of the national government exercises its powers. Relations between Congress and the President will receive attention in the following chapter. Presidents play an important role in the lawmaking process, partly by reason of the constitutional powers of the Presidency but largely because of political factors of various kinds.

The Presidency

CHAPTER ☆ SEVEN

Qualifications
Compensation
Succession to the Presidency
Presidential Disability
The President and Lawmaking
    Legal Basis of the President's Role in Lawmaking
    Political Sources of Presidential Influence over Lawmaking
The President as Chief Executive
    Direction and Control of Administration
    Preparation of the Budget and Control over its Execution
    Power of Appointment
        Its Scope
        Limitations on Presidential Discretion
    Power of Removal
        Myers, Humphrey, and *Wiener* Cases
    Commander-in-Chief of the Armed Forces
        War-Time Powers of the President
    Determination of Foreign Policy
    The Pardoning Power
The Rating of Presidents

☆ ☆ ☆ ☆ ☆ ☆ ☆ ☆ ☆ ☆ ☆ ☆ ☆

The President of the United States is an extremely powerful official whose preeminent role in the governmental process is attributable to a combination of legal authority and various extra-legal factors. Among the latter are the need for leadership, partisan politics, and the disposition of the general public to support the only official at the national level, other than the Vice President, who is chosen by the country as a whole.

Qualifications

To be legally eligible for the Presidency, an individual must be a natural-born citizen of the United States, at least thirty-five years old, and a resident of the United States for fourteen or more years. The term of office is four years and no person may be elected more than twice. Nor may a person succeeding to the office and holding it for more than two years of a term to which someone else had been elected be selected more than once. The foregoing provisions concerning permissible terms of service are incorporated in the Twenty-Second Amendment adopted in 1951. Prior to the election of Franklin D. Roosevelt for four successive terms, a two-term tradition had prevailed from Washington's time onward.

Compensation

The compensation of the President is fixed by act of Congress and may neither be increased nor decreased during the four-year period for which a particular incumbent was elected. At present (1972), the President's salary is $200,000 per annum and his annual expense allowance is $50,000. Both of these items are taxable. In addition he may expend $40,000 per year (non-taxable) for official entertainment and travel expenses. The President is provided with an executive mansion, a suite of offices, a secretariat, and such facilities as a fleet of automobiles and an airplane. Former Presidents receive a life-time pension of $25,000 per annum plus a $65,000 yearly allowance for an office staff. Widows of Presidents are granted a $10,000 annual pension.

Succession to The Presidency

Succession to the Presidency when a vacancy occurs is regulated by provisions of Article II of the Constitution, the Twentieth and Twenty-Fifth Amendments, and a 1947 act of Congress.[76a] The Vice President becomes President in the event of a vacancy, but if there be no Vice President the line of succession, as prescribed by Congress, is the Speaker of the House of Representatives, the President *pro tempore* of the Senate, the Secretary of State, the Secretary of the Treasury, the Secretary of Defense, Attorney General, and thereafter the Secretaries of the executive departments in the order of their creation.

[76a] amended in 1965 and 1966.

A prolonged vacancy in the office of Vice President is unlikely because the Twenty-Fifth Amendment authorizes the
President to nominate a Vice President who shall take office
upon confirmation by a majority vote of both houses of
Congress. The Twentieth Amendment provides that the
Vice President is to become President if a President-elect dies
before taking office. If no President shall have been chosen
or if a President-elect fails to qualify, the Vice President shall
act as President until a President qualifies. Congress is authorized to deal with a situation in which neither a President-
elect nor a Vice President shall have qualified. In such a case
Congress provides by law for the person who is to act as
President until a President or Vice President qualifies.

Presidential Disability

The Twenty-Fifth Amendment is concerned primarily
with cases of Presidential disability. If a President informs
the Speaker of the House and the President *pro tempore* of
the Senate, in writing, that he is unable to discharge his
official responsibilities, the Vice President shall act as President until the President transmits a written declaration
stating that he is able to resume his duties. The Vice President also is to act as President if he and a majority of the
principal executive officers or of some other body provided
for by law transmit a written declaration to the Speaker and
the Senate's President *pro tempore* that the President is unable to discharge his responsibilities. Thereafter, if the President declares in writing that no disability exists, he shall
resume his duties unless the Vice President and those col-

laborating with him disagree. In the latter event Congress, by a two-thirds vote, decides whether the Vice President shall continue to act as President or whether the President is capable of exercising the powers of his office.

The President and Lawmaking

The Constitution vests "the executive power" in a President of the United States. It specifically lists some of his powers, a number of which pertain to lawmaking, but this enumeration fails to indicate, clearly and indisputably, the scope of his constitutional authority.[77] Acts of Congress are another source of Presidential powers.

Of importance equal to or greater than the legal authority of Presidents is the *political power or influence* which particular incumbents of the Presidency have been successful in wielding. A combination of powers in the legal sense and power that is political in character accounts for the part played by Presidents in the functioning of the national government. The President has become a far more important official, particularly in the field of policy-determination, than apparently anticipated by the framers of the Constitution.

[77] Two schools of thought are identifiable. Former President Theodore Roosevelt believed that a President has the right to do whatever the needs of the nation demand unless such action is forbidden by the Constitution or the laws. Another ex-President, Taft, rejected the idea of an undefined residuum of power. Taft maintained that no power can be exercised unless reasonably and fairly traceable to some specific or implied grant of authority in the Constitution or acts of Congress.

Legal Basis of the President's Role in Lawmaking

Of the constitutional provisions sanctioning Presidential participation in lawmaking, the two most important are (a) his power and responsibility of providing information concerning the "state of the union" and recommending measures for consideration by Congress and (b) his power to veto every order, resolution, or vote to which the concurrence of both the House and the Senate is necessary. The power to recommend is positive; the veto power negative in regard to policy-determination.

(1) MESSAGES TO CONGRESS At the opening of each Congressional session, the President delivers his state of the union message, customarily in person, before a joint meeting of the two houses. In this message, which nowadays is televised and broadcast by radio, the President presents his general views concerning the legislative needs of the country and also comments on international problems and the foreign policy he intends to pursue. Subsequent messages, such as the one dealing with the budget or a special message urging the adoption of a specific policy, are more detailed in character and often are accompanied by reports and sometimes by drafts of bills designed to accomplish what the President has in mind. Although bills may be introduced in Congress only by its members, those drafted by the executive branch, as many are, invariably find sponsors among the many holders of seats in the House and the Senate. Most messages are delivered in writing and read to the houses by their clerks.

Presidential messages are influential to an extent which is difficult to determine. So much depends on variables like the astuteness of a President, the political composition of Congress, a President's popularity, the character of the problems confronting the country, and the need for prompt solutions. Messages of a President focus attention on particular issues and the fact that a President favors certain policies and is opposed to others decreases the likelihood that Congress will pursue policies that conflict in every respect with the position taken by the chief executive.

(2) THE VETO POWER A President cannot *compel* Congress to abide by his wishes on questions of policy, but he can ordinarily prevent the adoption of policies to which he is opposed. His *veto power* is the reason. This power is merely suspensive while Congress remains in session. It becomes absolute if Congress adjourns before expiration of the ten days, not counting Sundays, allowed him for taking action on acts of Congress.

Measures passed by Congress, excluding proposed constitutional amendments and concurrent resolutions, must be transmitted to the President for approval or disapproval. During the ten days granted him for passing judgment on what Congress has done, provided it remains in session, the President may sign a bill, in which case it becomes law; permit it to become law without his signature; or veto it and return it to the house in which it originated, with the reasons for his disapproval. Congress, by a two-thirds vote of those present in each house, provided a quorum has assembled, may override his veto.

If Congress adjourns prior to expiration of the ten days accorded the President, his failure to sign a bill prevents it from becoming law. What is known as a "pocket veto" occurs. The President need not give reasons for his refusal to sign and Congress, at a subsequent session, may *not* override this type of veto. A pocket veto is absolute.

The frequency with which the veto power is employed varies from administration to administration. At first used sparingly, the frequency of its use has tended to increase, but not to so great an extent that Presidential vetoes are the rule rather than the exception. Most bills enacted by Congress survive Presidential consideration. When vetoes occur, the chances of repassage by a two-thirds vote of Congress are poor.

Vetoes probably would increase in number if the President could veto parts of a bill, e.g., items in an appropriation act. An item or sectional veto is denied him. He must approve or disapprove of a bill in its entirety and lacks the power to endorse one part and reject another. Consequently, Congress may attach "riders" [78] to bills, knowing that the President, although opposed to a rider, is unlikely to veto a measure which in general meets with his approval.

The veto power enables the President to influence the content of legislation prior to enactment of a law by Congress. If, while a measure is under consideration by the House and the Senate, it becomes known that a Presidential veto will be forthcoming unless certain features of the bill are altered, the changes desired by the President are apt to be made. Not only that, but the threat of a veto may be sufficient to cause the defeat in Congress of a measure that otherwise might receive majority support.

(3) CALLING OF SPECIAL SESSIONS Another power of the President in relation to Congress is his authority to call

[78] A rider deals with an issue that is unrelated to the general subject matter of a bill.

special sessions of either or both houses. When the President decides to convoke a special session, his reasons for doing so are publicized and the attention of the general public is directed to the situation which has given rise to the call. For this reason Congress may take action which it has evaded during a regular session. Once assembled, however, Congress may do whatever it likes and need not confine its deliberations to the matter which led the President to bring about a resumption of its functioning. The outcome of a special session could prove embarrassing to a President. Since the regular sessions of Congress begin in January and extend throughout the greater part of a year, the necessity for calling special sessions occurs infrequently.

(4) ADJOURNMENT OF CONGRESS The Constitution authorizes the President to adjourn Congress only if the two houses are unable to agree on a time for adjournment. In view of this limitation, his power to adjourn is one of minor importance.

(5) POWER OF SUBSIDIARY LEGISLATION The President possesses powers of subsidiary legislation which are traceable to two sources, viz., acts of Congress and the Constitution. As pointed out in the preceding chapter, Congress may delegate rule-making authority to the President and other administrative agencies, provided it establishes a general policy and prescribes standards limiting the discretion of the officials to whom the power of auxiliary legislation is granted. The essence of legislative power is not delegable.

Apart from delegations of authority by Congress, the power of the President to issue rules, regulations, and ordinances is derivable by implication, if at all, from the constitutional stipulation that the executive power is granted to the President, that he "shall take care that the laws be faithfully executed," and that he shall be commander-in-chief of the armed forces of the United States. However, uncertainty prevails concerning the extent to which and the circumstances under which the President, solely on the basis of his constitutional position, may prescribe rules of an obligatory type directly or indirectly affecting private rights.

(a) *The Korematsu Case.* In time of war Presidents have done many things of debatable legality which, because of crisis conditions, have subsequently been ratified by Congress and survived scrutiny by the judicial branch. An example is former President Roosevelt's executive order, during World War II, authorizing the creation of military areas from which any or all persons might be excluded. Individuals of Japanese ancestry, even though United States citizens, were evacuated from such an area along the West Coast and, eventually, placed in "war relocation centers," actually concentration camps. Penalties for violation of the military orders and regulations were subsequently established by Congress. This drastic action of the President and Congress was upheld as constitutional in *Korematsu v. United States.*[79]

(b) *The Youngstown Sheet and Tube Co. Case.* A different example with a different result is afforded by President Truman's executive order of 1952 which authorized the Secretary of Commerce to seize and continue operation of the steel mills. This action was taken a few hours before a strike deadline set by the United Steel Workers of America. Congress had not authorized such seizure, but the President based his action on his constitutional power as chief executive and commander-in-chief of the armed forces. In *Youngs-*

[79] 323 U. S. 214 (1945).

town Sheet and Tube Co. et al. v. Sawyer,[80] the Supreme Court declared this Presidential action invalid. Its decision was based on two grounds—a lack of statutory authorization and the conclusion that the executive power of the President, including his law enforcement responsibility, was insufficient in itself to provide constitutional justification for the Presidential order. In the words of the Court, "the President's power to see that the laws are faithfully executed refutes the idea that he is a lawmaker."

A Congressional grant of authority provides the safest legal foundation for Presidential rule-making. In its absence, the President necessarily relies on such power as the Constitution confers on him, but this is a matter of implication rather than express stipulation. Whatever the legal source of the President's power of subsidiary legislation, that power is probably subject at all times to the overriding authority of a Congress in which, as stated in the Constitution, "all legislative power herein granted shall be vested."

Political Sources of Presidential Control over Lawmaking

The role of the President in lawmaking is considerably greater and far more effective than it would be if based solely on his legal power of participation in the legislative process. Presidential influence over Congress has political aspects which are fully as important as his power to recommend legislation or to veto measures that both the House and the Senate have passed.

Some Presidents are more successful than others in securing Congressional endorsement of their policy programs. Many

[80] 343 U. S. 579 (1952).

variable factors account for disparities in the degree of influence of successive Presidents. Among them are the personal qualities and talents of particular Presidents, their convictions concerning the proper way for the chief executive to function, the partisan complexion of the House and/or the Senate, and the comparative popularity of the President and Congress.

(1) POPULAR SUPPORT AND POLITICAL LEADERSHIP
When choosing a President, the voting public is primarily interested in the policies advocated by the competing candidates and their parties. Comparatively few voters give thought to the capabilities of the competitors as administrators. A President who has defeated his opponent by a substantial margin can usually count on extensive popular support for his policy program. Unless the opposition party is in control of one or both houses of Congress, that body is likely to act favorably on his major proposals. When the President's party dominates Congress, his recognition as party leader is ordinarily sufficient to discourage significant opposition to his leadership.

(2) PRESTIGE OF THE PRESIDENCY In addition to his influence as a party and/or popular leader, the prestige of his office lends weight to a President's proposals. A positive stand for or against a particular policy, even in the case of a President who is rather unpopular and at odds with his own party members, or faced by a Congress controlled by the opposition party, may enable a President to obtain legislative results not entirely in conflict with his desires. The prestige of the Presidency discourages indifference to Presidential recommendations.

(3) PERSONAL CONFERENCES Personal conferences with members of Congress, especially its leaders, constitute another means by which a President may affect the course of legislative proceedings. Face-to-face contacts provide an opportunity to convince members of Congress that Presidential policies are sound. A persuasive President may accomplish much by resort to this technique. Personal telephone calls and letters also may prove helpful.

(4) PRESSURE-GROUP SUPPORT If backed by powerful interest-groups of the organized variety, the President may invoke their support for the purpose of securing legislation which he advocates. Pressures exerted by these groups are seldom ignored by Congress.

The President also relies on the influential efforts of his department heads and other administrative subordinates. The "administrative lobbying" that occurs in Washington is a major factor in the outcome of the legislative process.

(5) COERCIVE TACTICS To overcome opposition in the legislative branch, a President may resort, as many have done, to tactics of the coercive or arm-twisting variety.

One type of punitive measure is disregard of a legislator's recommendations for appointments to federal offices. Another arm-twisting device is discrimination in the allocation of federal funds among the states and congressional districts. Furthermore, bills in which a particular Representative or Senator is interested may be opposed unless support for Presidential proposals is forthcoming. Also, the services which administrative agencies are usually willing to render members of Congress, as a means of currying their favor, may be denied. To mention but one more technique of the coercive variety, the leaders of Congress, working to advance the interests of the chief executive, may resort to the disciplinary measure of denying choice standing committee assignments to Congressmen who are unwilling to follow the President's leadership.

The legislative-liaison staffs of the White House and the departments gather information concerning the needs, interests, and voting records of Congress's members. This knowledge is used in whatever ways seem promising as a means of winning Congressional support.

(6) MAGNITUDE OF PRESIDENTIAL INFLUENCE   The magnitude of Presidential influence over Congress varies with the man and the times. It is rarely insignificant and ordinarily considerable, but it has never, so far, reached the point of Presidential dictatorship in the field of policy determination. Nor is it likely to in the foreseeable future. In a recent study of the legislative process at the national level, Daniel M. Berman concludes a discussion of the President and Congress with the following comment: "For all the time and effort expended by the Executive Branch on congressional relations, the results are often skimpy, in terms of promoting the basic legislative program of an activist administration." [81]

The President as Chief Executive

Apart from his role in the legislative process, the President is the chief administrator of the national government, the principal determiner of its foreign policy, and the civilian

[81] *In Congress Assembled* (New York, The Macmillan Company, 1964), p. 94.

commander-in-chief of its armed forces. He is charged with the duty of enforcing national laws, possesses important powers of appointment and removal, shares the treaty-making power with the Senate, and is authorized to grant pardons and issue reprieves. His executive powers are derived from constitutional provisions, either by express stipulations or by implication, and also from acts of Congress.

Direction and Control of Administration

The President is the directing head or general manager of the administrative branch of the national government. He is held responsible for the performance records of its many officials and employees who are engaged in the task of law enforcement and rendition of the many services undertaken for the benefit of the general public. However, he shares control over administration with Congress, inasmuch as the legislative branch has the power, which it exercises, to determine the number and nature of executive departments and other administrative agencies, to prescribe administrative procedures, to deal with many phases of the personnel policy of the national government, and to provide the funds necessary for administrative operations. The President is general manager of whatever facilities are placed at his disposal for the purpose of executing the policies of the national government and the quality of his leadership definitely influences the behavior of his numerous subordinates.

(1) AIDS TO GENERAL MANAGEMENT To function effectively as chief administrator, the President needs adequate assistance and certain important powers, such as the appointment of high ranking administrative officials, the power of removal, authority to issue rules and directives, and control over departmental spending. Even with the help now available, a President is faced with a monumental task in managing a huge organization composed of departments, bureaus, divisions, and other administrative agencies. He necessarily relies to a great extent on subordinates who are accountable to him but do not share his political responsibility to the general public.

Among the major aides to the President in the administrative field are the department and agency heads, whom he has a free hand in selecting, and various components of the Executive Office of the President which, as constituted in 1972 but always subject to change, included such units as the following: the White House Office comprised of assistants to the President (both special and administrative) as well as counsellors, advisers, personal secretaries, and press secretaries; the Office of Management and Budget; the Council of Economic Advisers; the Office of Economic Opportunity; the Office of Emergency Preparedness; the Office of Science and Technology; the National Aeronautics and Space Council; the National Security Council;[82] the Office of the Special Representative for Trade Negotiations; the Office of Consumer Affairs; the Council on International Economic Policy; the Council on Environmental Quality; the Domestic Council; the Office of Intergovernmental Relations; the Office of Telecommunications Policy; and the Special Action Office for Drug Abuse Prevention.

The Office of Management and Budget and some of the

[82] The Central Intelligence Agency (CIA) is established under the National Security Council.

Presidential assistants, especially the former, have more to do with problems of general administrative management than the Executive Office's other components. The latter provide assistance pertaining largely to the recommendation of policies to Congress or to special problems in the field of foreign affairs.

Under authority granted by the Reorganization Act of 1939, President Roosevelt undertook organization of the Executive Office of the President for the purpose of providing the chief executive with adequate machinery for the administrative management of the executive branch. Succeeding Presidents have reorganized the Office in various ways, as future Presidents probably will do. Consequently, any description of its component units is unlikely to hold true for more than a limited period of time.

(2) INSTITUTIONALIZATION OF THE PRESIDENCY Existence of the Executive Office of the President is evidence of an important twentieth century development, viz., institutionalization of the Presidency, attributable to the fact that the executive power can no longer be exercised by a single individual. "It requires a staff of loyal, devoted, and competent aides to enable a President or governor today to meet the political, policy, and administrative load of his job." The "institutionalized executive is with us to stay." [83]

(3) THE PRESIDENT'S CABINET The President's cabinet has no significance in regard to the function of administrative management. It is a purely advisory body which exists as a matter of custom and tradition rather than by legal

[83] John D. Millet, *Government and Public Administration* (New York, McGraw-Hill Book Co., Inc., 1959), p. 291.

provision. Although most of its members are department heads who, in that capacity, discharge a managerial function, the cabinet itself has no collective responsibility for administrative direction and control. Its principal purpose is discussion of whatever matters the President decides to bring to its attention. Except for its title, it has nothing in common with the cabinets of countries having a cabinet-parliamentary form of government. Its importance depends entirely on what a particular President chooses to make of it —very little as a rule.

Heads of the major administrative departments enjoy Cabinet status. Its well-established members include the Attorney-General (Department of Justice) and the Secretaries of State; Treasury; Defense; Interior, Agriculture; Commerce; Labor; Health, Education and Welfare; Housing and Urban Development; and Transportation. The Vice-President has become a regular participant in Cabinet meetings. Heads of other agencies attend when invited.

Preparation of the Budget and Control over Its Execution

(1) PREPARATION Since enactment of the Budget and Accounting Act of 1921, the President has been responsible for preparation of the budget, which is a financial program dealing with both expenditures and revenues. This Act created the Bureau of the Budget, at first located in the Treasury Department but subsequently transferred to the Executive Office of the President and *now* replaced therein by the Office of Management and Budget.

The Office of Management and Budget, directly responsible to the President, discharges the function of budget preparation. It has authority to assemble, correlate, revise, reduce, or increase the estimates of the several departments and establishments of the administrative branch with respect to the funds needed to carry on their work programs. Final decision concerning the items to be included in the budget rests with the President who presents it to Congress for approval. Congress, although free to do as it pleases, ordinarily acts favorably on most of the budgetary proposals of the chief executive. Inasmuch as administrative agencies are required to present requests for funds through the President, rather than directly to Congress, he is able to control their work programs, subject, however, to the power of Congress to prescribe the regulatory and service policies of the national government.

(2) EXECUTION OF THE BUDGET   Presidential control over departmental spending is exercisable in various ways in connection with execution of the financial program finally legalized by Congress. The Office of Management and Budget plays an important part in the process of execution. Its Director apportions the money expendable by an administrative agency during the different quarters of the fiscal year, i.e., reviews and approves of the quarterly work program prepared by a department. He may require the setting aside of reserves which cannot be spent without approval of the management and budget office. The combination of Presidential preparation of the budget and such controls as the President possesses over its execution greatly strengthens his position as general manager of the administrative branch.

The Power of Appointment

(1) ITS SCOPE   The offices filled by Presidential appointment constitute a very small percentage of the total of nearly three million civilian officers and employees of the national government. Most appointments are made by department and agency heads in conformity with the requirements of a merit system administered by the Civil Service Commission.

The President selects the highest ranking officials, such as the heads of the administrative departments, the personnel of the independent regulatory commissions, ambassadors, and judges. He also fills many positions in the lower levels of the administrative hierarchy, e.g., collectors of customs, district attorneys, and marshals. Of the many thousands of Presidential appointees,[83a] practically all are chosen by the President with the advice and consent of the Senate. The others, several hundred in number, are appointed by the President alone, as a consequence of Congressional power to vest the appointment of inferior officers in the President alone, in the courts, or in the heads of departments. For example, Presidential assistants and the Director of the Office of Management and Budget are selected in this way.

(2) LIMITATIONS ON PRESIDENTIAL DISCRETION Apart from the restrictive effects of the need for Senatorial confirmation, the President is free to appoint whatever persons he desires, subject, however, to their possession of such qualifications, if any, as may be established by act of Congress. In view of the vast number of positions to be filled by Presidential appointment, it is obvious that the chief executive necessarily relies on recommendations com-

[83a] About sixteen thousand

ing from a variety of sources, including members of Congress, political leaders, pressure groups, and various persons desirous of influencing the choice of personnel.

No President has adequate personal knowledge of a sufficiently large number of individuals to fill all of the positions at his disposal without help. Even if he had, a President finds it politically expedient to heed the suggestions of others and to use his appointive power to advance the interests of his party. Such is the prevailing practice.

(a) ADVICE AND CONSENT OF THE SENATE   In the case of positions filled by the President with the advice and consent of the Senate, the Senate is able to block the appointment of persons to whom it is opposed. If the President is unsuccessful in obtaining Senate confirmation of a particular nominee, he may await recess of the Senate and then appoint his man to the vacant position, but the commission granted his appointee expires at the end of the next Senate session. The usual procedure, if the Senate rejects a nominee, is Presidential nomination of someone else for the office to be filled.

Confirmation by the Senate is almost always forthcoming when the President selects his department heads, diplomatic representatives, and other top-ranking administrative officials upon whose cooperation and loyalty the President necessarily depends. Considerations of fairness have given rise to customary Senate approval of Presidential choices for positions which play an important part in determining the success or failure of a particular President's administration. The Senate has rarely, for example, refused to approve a President's selection for the headship of a department with cabinet status.

(b) SENATORIAL COURTESY The situation differs in regard to the filling of positions of the national government located in the states. Among offices of this type are judges of the inferior federal courts, district attorneys, marshals, and collectors of internal revenue. A custom known as "senatorial courtesy" prevails in the selection of individuals for such positions.

This practice is characterized by courtesy to Senators and discourtesy to the President. What it amounts to is Senate refusal to confirm a Presidential nominee for a particular post if the Senator or Senators from the state in which the position is located object to the appointment, provided the Senators are members of the President's party. For this reason the President commonly consults these Senators about a contemplated appointee or nominates a person suggested by them. If there are no Senators of the President's party from a particular state, the usual practice is to rely on recommendations made by the party's organizations, state and local, in that state. Although the House of Representatives, unlike the Senate, lacks a formal voice in the appointive process, its members are secondary beneficiaries of the custom of senatorial courtesy, inasmuch as Representatives who belong to the Presidential party are permitted, as a matter of practice, to exercise a controlling influence over appointments to federal offices of the patronage variety located in their districts.

For the most part, senatorial courtesy is observed only with respect to national offices having a state location. Occasionally, the Senate may withhold consent to appointments to other offices, e.g., those situated in Washington, D. C., if the President has nominated a person from a particular state to whom the Senator from that state, a member of the President's party, strenuously objects.

The Power of Removal

The President's power of removal, like his appointive authority, is an essential legal ingredient of his role as chief administrator. Without this power, he would be unable to deal effectively with cases of incompetence, uncooperativeness, and insubordination on the part of his administrative subordinates. Such removal power as the President possesses is derived by implication from the Constitution or conferred by act of Congress. The Constitution's only express provisions concerning removals pertain to the expulsion of their members by each house of Congress and to the impeachment process which results in the removal of civil officers of the United States when convicted by the Senate of charges of treason, bribery, or other high crimes and misdemeanors.

(1) LEGAL BASIS AND EXTENT OF THE REMOVAL POWER   The legal basis and extent of the removal power of the President has been indicated by three important decisions of the Supreme Court rendered during the period from 1926 to 1958. Of these cases, the first, *Myers v. United States*,[84] endorsed a broad conception of the Presidential removal power, but the later cases, *Humphrey's Executor (Rathun) v. United States*[85] and *Wiener v. United States*,[86] resulted in modification of the position taken by the Court in the *Myers* case.

(a) THE MYERS CASE   The *Myers* controversy resulted from the removal of Myers, postmaster of Portland,

[84] 272 U. S. 52 (1926).
[85] 295 U. S. 602 (1935).
[86] 357 U. S. 349 (1958).

Oregon, by executive order of President Wilson in disregard of an act of Congress of 1876 which stipulated that postmasters of the first, second, and third classes could only be removed with the approval of the Senate. Chief Justice Taft, a former President, wrote the opinion of the Court.

The Court held (1) that the removal power of the President was inferable from his position as chief executive and possessor of the executive power, his duty to see to the faithful execution of the laws, and his power of appointment and (2) that Congress lacked authority to place limitations on the President's power to remove executive officers appointed by him with the advice and consent of the Senate. The requirement of Senate approval of the removal of postmasters, as established by the 1876 statute, was declared unconstitutional.

Because of general observations in the Court's opinion, the *Myers* case was believed to prevent Congress from limiting the removal power of the President even in the case of officials discharging quasi-legislative or quasi-judicial functions, if appointed by the President with the advice and consent of the Senate. However, nine years after the *Myers* decision, the Supreme Court narrowed the scope of the *Myers* ruling and reasoning.

(b) THE HUMPHREY CASE   The *Humphrey* case arose because of President Roosevelt's removal of Humphrey from the Federal Trade Commission after Humphrey refused to resign at the President's request. Roosevelt's reason for the request and subsequent removal was that his views and Humphrey's differed on questions of policy and administration—no reflection was cast on the service record of Humphrey. The act of Congress creating the Federal

Trade Commission authorized Presidential removal of a commissioner for inefficiency, neglect of duty, or malfeasance in office. In deciding that the President had exceeded his authority in removing Humphrey, the Supreme Court maintained that Congress may place limitations on the removal power with respect to officials performing quasi-legislative or quasi-judicial functions as distinguished from functions of a purely executive character, such as those of a postmaster.

(c) THE WIENER CASE In the more recent *Wiener* case, President Eisenhower had removed Wiener from a War Claims Commission established by Congress in 1948. His reason was the desire to replace an appointee of his predecessor in office with a man of his own choice. The act of Congress creating the Commission included no provision for the removal of a commissioner. Pointing out that the Commission was established as an *adjudicating* body, the Supreme Court concluded that the failure of Congress to deal with the question of removal indicated its intention to place commissioners beyond the dismissal power of the President.

On the basis of the *Wiener* and *Humphrey* cases, the Court's position seems to be that the power of the President to remove officials performing functions that are primarily *quasi-legislative* or *quasi-judicial* in character depends on conferment of such power by Congress, either expressly or by implication. As for officials discharging essentially *executive* functions, the ruling of the *Myers* case still holds, viz., Congress may neither take away nor impose limitations on the constitutionally derived power of the President to remove officials of this type who are appointed by him with the advice and consent of the Senate.[87]

(d) UNSETTLED QUESTIONS Several constitutional aspects of the general problem of removal remain unsettled. For instance, may Congress make removals without resorting to the impeachment process? If so, with respect to what kinds of positions and under what circumstances? By act of Congress, the Comptroller General, appointed by the President with the advice and consent of the Senate, may be removed only by impeachment or by joint address of the House and the Senate. Since no attempt has been made, by either the President or Congress, to remove a Comptroller General, the opportunity to obtain a judicial ruling has not arisen. Until it does, and the Supreme Court decides, pronouncements concerning the issue remain in the realm of speculation.

Commander-in-Chief of the Armed Forces

"The President shall be commander-in-chief of the army and navy of the United States, and of the militia of the several States when called into the actual service of the United States." So reads the Constitution. If reworded today mention probably would be made of the air force and the phrase "national guard" substituted for the word "militia."

As civilian head of the armed forces, the President issues rules and regulations for their governance, subject to the overriding authority of Congress to do the same, and directs

[87] Neither the *Humphrey* nor the *Wiener* case affords ground for concluding that Congress may require Senate confirmation of removals from quasi-legislative or quasi-judicial commissions.

their distribution and use, both inside and outside the country, again subject to such restrictions as the legislative branch may have power to impose, indirectly if not directly. The constitutional powers of Congress seem sufficiently great to prevent the President from doing *whatever he pleases* with the military forces of the nation. Nor may the President, in his capacity as commander-in-chief, disregard provisions of the Constitution.

(1) CONGRESSIONAL AUTHORITY REGARDING MILITARY MATTERS The extensiveness of Congressional authority in regard to military matters is indicated by its expressly granted powers, viz., to declare war, grant letters of marque and reprisal, and make rules concerning captures on land and water; to raise and support armies; to provide and maintain a navy; to make rules for the government and regulation of the land and naval forces; to provide for calling forth the militia to execute the laws of the Union, suppress insurrections, and repel invasions; to provide for organizing, arming, and disciplining the militia, and for governing such part of them as may be employed in the service of the United States, reserving to the states the appointment of the officers and the authority of training the militia according to the discipline prescribed by Congress. These powers are supplemented by Congressional control of the purse strings and by the general power to make all laws necessary and proper for carrying into execution the foregoing powers and all other powers vested by the Constitution in the national government or in any department or officer thereof.

(2) THE PRESIDENT'S MILITARY POWERS What Congress may do and what it actually does are obviously distinguishable. Its delegations of authority to the President, together with his post as commander-in-chief, enable him to do many things with the armed forces of the country that affect its vital interests both at home and abroad. An aggressive President may take action, perhaps in excess of his legal authority, which Congress, even though unwillingly, deems it expedient to endorse or ratify.

The President lacks authority to create armed forces at his pleasure. He may only use such forces as Congress provides and spend such money as Congress makes available. The President may resort to military power to enforce the laws of the national government, to suppress insurrections and rebellions, and to resist invasions. His use of the armed forces abroad, presumably to protect the vital interests of the United States and its citizens, may plunge the country into war. Examples are involvement of the United States in the Korean war and in the present armed conflict in Vietnam. Congress may complain and criticize, but after the President has taken the initiative, about all it can do is support what has been done.

(3) WAR-TIME POWERS OF THE PRESIDENT When the United States is at war or confronted with insurrection or rebellion, e.g., the effort of the South to secede from the Union, the President, as chief executive and commander-in-chief, may take action in the "theater of war" which is distinguishable from his control over the movement of the armed forces. For instance, he may establish a military government (declare martial law) superseding civil authorities in any area in which the latter, including the courts, are unable to function. Again, in the case of occupied territory, the President may provide for its government until such time as Congress makes arrangements for a civilian regime.

The wartime powers of a President, like those of Congress, are extensive. Congress usually grants him many powers, both as chief executive and commander-in-chief, for the purpose of bringing the war efforts of the country to a successful conclusion. The need for unified leadership results in the creation of what is appropriately denominated "a constitutional dictatorship." Such Presidents as Lincoln, Wilson, and Roosevelt did not hesitate to act on their conception of Presidential powers and responsibilities in the prosecution of war and neither Congress nor the courts were disposed toward interference with their actions during emergency situations.

In commenting on the "war powers" of the national government, former Associate Justice Jackson had this to say: "No one will question that this power is the most dangerous one to free government in the whole catalogue of powers. It usually is invoked in haste and excitement when calm legislative consideration of constitutional limitations is difficult. It is executed in a time of patriotic fervor that makes moderation unpopular. And, worst of all, it is interpreted by judges under the influence of the same passions and pressures. Always, . . . the Government urges hasty decision to forestall some emergency or serve some purpose and pleads that paralysis will result if its claims to power are denied or the confirmation delayed." [88]

Determination of Foreign Policy

A traditional function of chief executives throughout the world has been the maintenance of relations with foreign

[88] *Woods v. Miller*, 333 U. S. 138 (1948), concurring opinion of Mr. Justice Jackson.

countries and determination of the policies to be pursued. The framers of the Constitution expected the President to speak for the United States in its dealings with other countries and granted him a few specific powers which, in conjunction with the general grant of "executive power," provide the constitutional basis for the President's role as the principal determiner of the foreign policy of the national government. These specific powers are the appointment of ambassadors, other public ministers, and consuls (subject to Senate confirmation); the receiving of ambassadors and other public ministers accredited to the United States by foreign countries; and the power to make treaties with the advice and consent of the Senate, two-thirds of the Senators present concurring.

Although the President's control of foreign relations falls short of being absolute, his role in the determination of foreign policy is so great that for all practical purposes the standing of the United States in the international community depends on what he does. Congress alone has the power to make a formal declaration of war, but the President, as several have, may maneuver the country into a situation which makes war inevitable. His attitude toward particular countries, evidenced in various ways; his use of the armed forces; and his willingness, or lack of it, to collaborate with other nations in seeking a solution to problems threatening world peace, are primary factors in determining the part played by "Uncle Sam" in shaping the trend of world events.

Since the Constitution provides for a chief executive agency of the single rather than plural variety, the function of foreign policy determination is chiefly, although not entirely, the responsibility of one person. The President may be greatly influenced by the views of his Secretary of State and other administrative subordinates, but these officials, whom he chooses, are directly accountable to him—not to either Congress or the general public. As for the part of Congress in the foreign policy field, it is too restricted to constitute a major road-block to Presidential pursuit of the policies he favors in dealing with other countries.

Strange as it may seem, what virtually amounts to one-man rule in matters that frequently result in international warfare is accepted without serious objection in the United States. A like arrangement for the solution of problems of domestic concern would be strenuously opposed.

(1) THE DEPARTMENT OF STATE   The Department of State is headed by a Secretary directly responsible to the President. Through this department and the diplomatic representatives of the United States accredited to foreign countries, and the public ministers of these countries stationed in Washington, contact with other states is maintained and business with them transacted. However, the President may utilize special agents of one type or another and communicate directly, if he chooses, with the heads of foreign governments. In other ways, too, such as through speeches and messages to Congress, the President makes known the policy of the United States with respect to problems of international concern.

(2) RECOGNITION OF STATES AND GOVERNMENTS An important responsibility of the President is the recognition of new states and of the new governments of existing states. President Eisenhower recognized the Castro government of Cuba in 1959 following the fall of the Batista dic-

tatorship and Franklin D. Roosevelt accorded recognition
to the Soviet government of Russia in 1933. So far no President has been willing to recognize Red China's government,
even though the power to do so clearly belongs to the chief
executive. The President, too, may break diplomatic relations with any country, as President Kennedy did with the
Castro regime in 1961.

Contrary to a common impression, recognition merely
indicates willingness to transact business with a new state
or a newly established government through regular diplomatic channels. It does not signify endorsement of policy
programs pursued by a foreign country. Recognition may
be accomplished through any of several procedures, among
them receiving a diplomatic representative from a particular
government, appointing a public minister to deal with its
official head, or negotiating a treaty with it.

(3) TREATY-MAKING The treaty-making power is
shared by the President and the Senate, but the role of the
latter is secondary to that of the former, inasmuch as the
initiative lies with the President and final decision on the
question of exchanging ratifications, after the Senate has
approved a treaty, also rests with the chief executive.

Treaties are negotiated only if the President is willing to
do so; his views determine the provisions to which the
United States is willing to agree; and after a treaty has been
drafted and signed by the parties to it, the President decides
whether to submit it to the Senate. If he withholds it from
Senate consideration, the prospective treaty is dead; if he
presents it to the Senate, without subsequently withdrawing
it, its approval by a two-thirds vote of those present is
requisite to the eventual exchange of ratifications. Should

the Senate insist on alterations, the President may or may not reopen negotiations with other parties to the tentative treaty.

If the Senate approves a treaty as submitted, the President is still free to stop further proceedings. His is the final act of ratification that is essential to an exchange of ratifications with the other countries involved.

An astute President generally keeps in close touch with the Committee on Foreign Relations of the Senate, especially its chairman, during the several stages of the treaty-making process. By so doing, his chances of obtaining Senate approval are greatly enhanced. Support from the House of Representatives also is sought, even though the House is not a direct participant in the making of treaties. Many treaties require supplementary legislation in order to carry out their provisions, including the authorization of expenditures, and, in the matter of lawmaking and financing the activities of the national government, favorable action by both the House and the Senate is a constitutional essential.

(4) EXECUTIVE AGREEMENTS The President may reach understandings with foreign governments in various ways. One technique is the negotiation of an "executive agreement." Such agreements do not require Senatorial approval. Although sometimes authorized by Congress, the President has sufficient power in the field of foreign affairs to enter into them without prior Congressional permission or subsequent approval.

Whatever the legal status of executive agreements in the United States, some of which have received judicial recognition as "law," the national government is placed under obligation to abide by such commitments as it makes to the foreign country or countries that are parties to an agreement. The President, by negotiating executive agreements, may achieve objectives to which the Senate might not subscribe if incorporated in a treaty. As might be expected, however, short-circuiting the Senate by this device has met with opposition, with the result that Presidents proceed more cautiously in resorting to executive agreements than has been the case on various occasions in the past.

The Pardoning Power

The President possesses power to grant pardons and reprieves for offenses against the United States, except in cases of impeachment. By offenses against the United States are meant violations of national law. The granting of pardons for offenses against state law is a power exercisable only by the states.

(1) AMNESTY   A pardon may be granted to an individual or to a group. A group or blanket pardon is known as "amnesty." Issuance of a Presidential proclamation of amnesty is the usual means of accomplishing a group pardon. Congress, too, may pass an act granting amnesty to designated classes of persons. A grant of amnesty relieves its beneficiaries from prosecution for acts, such as engaging in rebellion, which otherwise might result in trial, conviction, and punishment.

(2) UNCONDITIONAL AND CONDITIONAL PARDONS Pardons granted to individuals may be unconditional or conditional. The effect of the former type is to free the recipient from such disabilities as may have been incurred by him as a consequence of criminal behavior. Conditional pardons differ in that the President may limit the effects of his acts of clemency to whatever extent he deems advisable.

An individual who is granted a pardon need not accept it. He cannot be compelled to do so—as decided by the Supreme Court as long ago as 1833. Although the Court still adheres to this ruling, acceptance by the grantee is not required if the President commutes a sentence or grants a reprieve.

A commutation of sentence occurs if a less severe punishment is substituted for the one initially imposed by a court, e.g., replacing a death penalty with life imprisonment. The issuance of a reprieve amounts to no more than postponing the execution of the sentence resulting from conviction of a criminal act.

(3) SCOPE OF THE PARDONING POWER The pardoning power extends not only to statutory crimes, i.e., those defined by legislative act, but also to criminal, as distinguished from civil, contempt of court. In the Grossman case,[89] decided in 1925, the Supreme Court upheld the power of the President to pardon an individual found guilty of violating an injunction issued by a federal district court under the provisions of the Volstead Act which was passed to implement the Eighteenth Amendment establishing prohibition.

A question that has not been ruled on by the Court is whether the pardoning power of the President extends to an individual cited for contempt of Congress. A pardon was issued in one such instance by President Roosevelt in 1938, but his action was not challenged in a court case.

[89] *Ex Parte Grossman*, 267 U. S. 87.

(4) PURPOSE OF THE PARDONING POWER   The pardoning power of the President provides a means of remedy-
ing mistakes of the courts and miscarriages of justice. It is a
check on the judicial branch of the government. Like other
powers it may be abused, but so far Presidents have escaped
criticism on this ground. Pardons may be granted for offenses, "either before trial, during trial, or after trial, . . .
conditionally or absolutely," without modification or regulation by Congress, whether committed by individuals or
classes.[90]

The Rating of Presidents

The rating of Presidents as strong, weak, or somewhere
in between is a self-assumed task undertaken by historians,
political scientists, journalists, and a variety of individuals
who appraise the performance records of particular incumbents of the Presidency. Judgment is based primarily on a
President's accomplishments as a leader—on the vigor with
which he exercises his official powers and on his success in
securing Congressional and popular approval of the policies
he favors. His policy program may be good for the country, or otherwise. On that matter the raters are likely to
disagree, even if all or most of them assign a President to
the "strong" category. For example, both enthusiastic supporters of Franklin D. Roosevelt's New Deal and its most
extreme opponents agree that he was a strong President.
Among some of the Presidents usually rated as "weak" are
Grant and Harding. During their administrations, the lead-

[90] *Ibid.*

ers of Congress and other powerful political figures were more important as determiners of policy than the chief executive.

The strength or weakness of particular Presidents (in the sense indicated) depends in large measure on their leadership capabilities, intelligence, integrity, decisiveness, diligence, tact, popularity, and political know-how. However, some Presidents subscribe to a conception of the Presidency which causes them to refrain from attempting to dominate the political scene, despite apparent possession of the ability to do so.

Even an able and aggressive President may be handicapped by circumstances that *happen* to prevail during his administration. If Congress, or one of its houses, is controlled by the opposition party, he experiences difficulties which need not be surmounted by a President dealing with a friendly legislature. Some Presidents, of course, are more successful than others in coping with a situation of the foregoing type.

A particularly important factor bearing on the performance records of Presidents is the presence or absence of crisis conditions. In times of crisis, such as war or a serious economic depression, Congress is ordinarily reluctant to resist Presidential leadership. If no emergency situations exist either at home or abroad, opposition to a President's policy program may become formidable. Presidential recommendations are unlikely to escape censure when Congressional refusal to collaborate with the President seems unlikely to prove harmful to the country. Crisis conditions may make a President look stronger than he actually is; they may also reveal the ineptness of a particular incumbent of the Presidency.

All Presidents, strong or weak, share responsibility with Congress for the policies pursued by the national government. In the field of international relations, Presidential responsibility is considerably greater than that of the legislative branch; in regard to domestic affairs, both branches bear about the same degree of responsibility. A potent President may lead Congress, but Congress is accountable for following his leadership, and a weak President may be severely criticized for his failure to persuade Congress to adopt the policies he recommends. The sharing of accountability is a concomitant of the divided responsibility which features a separation of powers and check and balance type of government. This fact remains unchanged whatever the calibre of a particular President and the personnel of the Congresses that function during his stay in office.

Administrative
Agencies

CHAPTER ☆ EIGHT

Importance of Administration

Control of Administration by Congress, the President, and
    the Judiciary

Structure of the Administrative Branch
    Reorganization Acts
    Types of Administrative Agency
    Departments: State; Treasury; Justice; Defense; In-
        terior; Agriculture; Commerce; Labor; Health,
        Education, and Welfare; Housing and Urban De-
        velopment; Transportation
    Independent Establishments: Interstate Commerce
        Commission; Federal Maritime Commission;
        Civil Aeronautics Board; Federal Trade Com-
        mission; Federal Communications Commission;
        Federal Power Commission; Securities and Ex-
        change Commission; National Labor Relations
        Board; General Services Administration; Veterans
        Administration; Tennessee Valley Authority; Na-
        tional Aeronautics and Space Administration;
        Atomic Energy Commission; United States Postal
        Service

Appraisals of National Administrative Organization
    Major Studies

        Criticisms
        Results of the Studies and Reports
    Personnel Policies of the National Government
        Problems Requiring Solution
        Civil Service Reform
        Civil Service Commission and Departmental Personnel
            Offices
        Entrance Appointments
        Promotions
        Dismissals from the Service
        Compensation and Fringe Benefits
    Administrative Legislation and Adjudication
    Securing Compliance with Governmental Policies: Non-
        Coercive and Coercive Methods.

☆ ☆ ☆ ☆ ☆ ☆ ☆ ☆ ☆ ☆ ☆ ☆ ☆ ☆

The administrative agencies of the national government execute the policies of regulation and service that Congress adopts. These agencies also are involved in policy determination, inasmuch as supplementary rule-making authority is usually delegated to them and their recommendations carry weight with the chief executive and members of the legislature.

Importance of Administration

Too much emphasis cannot be laid on the importance of administration. In the first place, the administrative functionaries of any government are largely responsible for the quality of service rendered to the public. The beneficial effects of many a policy have been lost because of poor administration.

Secondly, the administrative branch spends practically all of the money raised for public purposes. It costs comparatively little to finance the activities of the legislative and judicial branches. If the taxpayer is to receive a maximum return for his tax dollar and if governmental expenditures are to be kept at a minimum without curtailing necessary services, every effort must be made to raise the standards of administrative performance.

Third, the way in which administrative officers and employees perform their functions has a major bearing on the treatment received by individuals at the hands of government. Administrators apply general policies to specific situations and the opportunities for arbitrary, unreasonable, and inconsiderate action are numerous. Although legal remedies usually are available for infringements of rights, many individuals have neither the money nor the time to resort to the courts for relief.

Fourth, the attitude of the individual towards government is determined to a large extent by the impression created by the administrative personnel with whom he comes into direct contact. An insolent clerk in a postoffice, an uncooperative employee of the Internal Revenue Service, or an arrogant Selective Service official can destroy or prevent the development of that good will and respect which are essential to cooperation between the government and the individual.

Finally, the administrative branch exercises so substantial an influence on the determination of policy that in large measure it constitutes "the government." In a democracy, popular control of the legislature and the chief executive is no longer sufficient to insure government in the interest of the people. Keeping administrative agencies under effective control is a problem requiring continuous attention in this day of large-scale bureaucracy.

Control of Administration by Congress, the President, and the Judiciary

Control by Congress

As previously pointed out, Congress possesses power to determine the organization of the administrative services, to prescribe procedures, to conduct investigations, to authorize expenditures, and, among other direct or indirect means of control, to establish many features of the personnel policies of the national government.[91]

Control by the President

The President, in his capacity as chief administrator, is responsible for the direction and supervision of administration in general,[92] but some administrative agencies, such as independent regulatory bodies like the Interstate Commerce Commission, are not controllable by him in the way that the major executive departments are, e.g., the Departments of State, Defense, and Agriculture. Presidential authority in regard to organization of the administrative branch exists only to the extent that Congress is willing to delegate it.

[91] *Supra*, pp. 159–160, 201–202, 208–209.
[92] *Supra*, pp. 251–255.

Other powers of the President in relation to administration have been discussed in the preceding chapter, among them his powers of appointment, removal, and budget preparation.

Judicial Control

Unlike the controls over administration exercisable by Congress and the President, judicial control is confined to the legality of administrative action. Courts lack authority to deal with questions of administrative wisdom, efficiency, and effectiveness. If the action of administrative agencies is challenged in a proper case, all that the courts can do is decide on the legality or illegality of the administrative acts that have given rise to litigation.

Structure of the Administrative Branch

The structure of the administrative branch is determinable by Congress. Such authority as the President possesses with respect to administrative organization depends on Congressional delegation of organizing power to him. With an exception to be noted later, all of the major administrative departments and independent regulatory commissions have been created by act of Congress, as have many minor administrative agencies.

Reorganization Acts

The efforts of Presidents to obtain a more satisfactory organization of the administrative services date back to the beginning of the twentieth century, but the first Reorganization Act granting the President power to prescribe organizational arrangements was passed in 1918. Numerous "reorganization acts" have been enacted since that time—1932, 1933, 1945, 1949, 1953, 1955, 1957, 1961, 1964, 1966, 1969, and 1970. The reason for the passage of so many acts is the reluctance of Congress to delegate reorganizing power to the President for a period longer than about two years. Many of these acts merely extended the duration of the 1949 act with some modifications.

All of the acts placed limitations on the power delegated to the President and all required that Presidential plans to reorganize administrative agencies be submitted to Congress for approval or disapproval.[92a] Every recent Reorganization Act stipulates that a plan submitted by the President is to take effect automatically within sixty days, unless disapproved by a simple majority vote of either house of Congress. In some previous acts, disapproval required the concurrence of both chambers (acts of 1939 and 1945) or a majority vote of the entire membership of either house (act of 1949).

Under the 1953 Reorganization Act, President Eisenhower created the Department of Health, Education, and Welfare without experiencing Congressional disapproval of his action, but all acts from 1914 on prohibit the creation of new executive departments by Presidential submission of a reorganization plan. On the basis of the enabling acts referred to above, Presidents have prepared a substantial number of reorganization plans. Only a small proportion of them have been rejected by Congress.

[92a] amendments of 1970 and 1971 provide that plans must be submitted to Congress before April 1, 1973 and that a provision contained in a reorganization plan may take effect only if transmitted to Congress prior to the same date.

Types of Administrative Agency

The administrative branch of the national government includes a vast number of agencies of various types. These are classified in the *United States Government Organization Manual* (published annually) under the following headings: (1) executive departments, (2) independent agencies, and (3) boards, committees, and commissions.

There are eleven executive departments directly responsible to the President. One of them, the Department of Defense, includes three component departments, viz., the Department of the Army, the Department of the Navy, and the Department of the Air Force.

The number of independent agencies is about fifty. An independent agency is an organizational unit which exists outside the executive departments. Some of them, such as the Veterans Administration and the General Services Administration, are primarily administrative bodies bearing close resemblance in their functional nature to the executive departments; others discharge important regulatory functions, e.g., the Interstate Commerce Commission, and are "independent" not only in the sense of being located outside the executive departments but also because they are partially independent of Presidential control.

Boards, committees, and commissions that are not included in either of the foregoing categories are engaged in various activities. For the most part, their functions are of minor importance and in many instances strictly advisory in character.

The following condensed description of the functions of the executive departments and the most important independent establishments is designed to indicate the character of the

Administrative Agencies

service and regulatory policies of the national government. Limitations of space prevent a more thorough and adequate account of this government's numerous activities.

Departments (as of 1972)

Each of the executive departments has a single head, rather than a board or commission, appointed by the President with the advice and consent of the Senate. Lines of authority run downward from this head (in most cases entitled "Secretary" of the department) through an under- or deputy-secretary, assistant secretaries, and the heads of component bureaus, divisions, or offices to the lowest ranking officers and employees of the department. Lines of responsibility run upward through the same channels. Since nomenclature varies, the major subdivisions of some departments are known as divisions and of others as bureaus, services, or offices. The particular title is unimportant as compared to the fact of the establishment of major and minor components within each department.

(1) THE DEPARTMENT OF STATE   The Department of State, through its Secretary, is usually chief adviser to the President in the field of foreign affairs. It is primarily responsible, subject to Presidential direction and control, for initiating and implementing foreign policies and communicating with the diplomatic and consular representatives of the United States abroad and also with the spokesmen of foreign countries accredited to the United States.

The Department includes numerous regional bureaus specializing in such areas as the following: African Affairs,

Inter-American Affairs, European Affairs, Far Eastern Affairs, Near Eastern and South Asian Affairs, and International Organization Affairs. Among other bureaus are the Bureau of Educational and Cultural Affairs and the Bureau of Security and Consular Affairs. The Peace Corps and the United States mission to the United Nations are associated with this department.

(2) DEPARTMENT OF THE TREASURY The Department of the Treasury superintends and manages the finances of the national government. It includes the Internal Revenue Service, well-known to persons required to fill out an income tax return; the Bureau of Customs which collects duties, taxes, and fees due on imported merchandise; the bureaus concerned with the coinage and printing of money; the United States Savings Bond Division; the Office of the Comptroller of the Currency, an integral part of the National Banking system, which is responsible for executing the laws pertaining to national banks; and the Office of the Treasurer of the United States which is charged with the custody and disbursement of public funds.

The Secret Service and the Bureau of Narcotics are subdivisions of the Treasury Department. Each renders an important service. The Secret Service bears the responsibility of protecting the President (also his immediate family) and the Vice President. In addition it is charged with the task of detecting offenses against the laws pertaining to coins, currency, and securities of both the United States and foreign countries. The Bureau of Narcotics administers national laws concerning narcotics; investigates, detects, and prevents violations of these laws; and issues narcotic import and export permits.

(3) THE DEPARTMENT OF DEFENSE   The Department of Defense was established in 1949. Prior to that time two departments, War and Navy, created in 1789 and 1798 respectively, functioned as major administrative units headed by Secretaries who were members of the President's Cabinet and directly responsible to the chief executive. Both departments survive as subdivisions of the Department of Defense along with the recently created Department of the Air Force.

The Defense Department is charged with the heavy responsibility of insuring the security of the United States in times of peace and war, insofar as that can be accomplished through the maintenance and use of adequate military forces. These forces may be utilized by the President for law enforcement purposes in those unusual situations in which the customary civilian enforcement agencies prove unequal to the task. Congress provides the armed forces, the President is their civilian commander-in-chief, and the Defense Department endeavors to achieve maximum results with the facilities placed at its disposal.

(4) THE DEPARTMENT OF JUSTICE   The Department of Justice functions under the direction of the Attorney General of the United States. It is a law enforcement agency which includes such divisions as Anti-Trust, Civil Rights, and Internal Security, among others, as well as the Federal Bureau of Investigation and the Immigration and Naturalization Service.

The Department supervises and directs United States attorneys and marshals. It furnishes legal counsel in Federal cases, conducts all suits in the Supreme Court in which the national government is concerned, and gives advice and renders opinions on legal questions at the request of the President and department heads. Another responsibility is the supervision of Federal penal institutions.

(5) DEPARTMENT OF THE INTERIOR　The Department of the Interior, custodian of the natural resources of the United States, formulates and administers programs for the management, development, and conservation of these resources. Within it are located the Geological Survey; the Bureaus of Mines, Land Management, Reclamation, and Outdoor Recreation; the Fish and Wild Life Service; and the National Park Service.

The Department includes three Power Administrations, viz., Bonneville, Southeastern, and Southwestern. In each of these regions it markets electric power generated at various Federal hydroelectric power projects. Other responsibilities of the Department are the handling of Indian affairs and promotion of the welfare of non-contiguous territorial possessions of the United States.

(6) DEPARTMENT OF AGRICULTURE　The national government has adopted many policies pertaining to agriculture. Most of them are administered by the Department of Agriculture. Many of its activities are of a research, educational, and informative type, but it administers various regulatory laws designed to protect the farmer and the consumer, e.g., meat and poultry inspection, animal and plant quarantine, and provision for the safe and effective use of pesticidal chemicals by regulating their composition and labeling.

Research is conducted with respect to many matters, such as ways of controlling animal and poultry diseases, nutrition and consumer-use, improvement of methods of soil and water management, and finding new and expanded uses for agricultural products. The Department aids farmers in planning and installing erosion-control and other soil and conservation measures; administers the acreage allotment, marketing quotas, and price support programs of the national government; and makes loans to farmers and farmer cooperatives.

The Forest Service is located in this Department. So are the Office of Rural Areas Development, the Rural Electrification Administration, and the Farmers Home Administration.

(7) THE DEPARTMENT OF COMMERCE   The Department of Commerce bears the responsibility of fostering, promoting, and developing foreign and domestic commerce and the manufacturing and shipping industries. It collects and disseminates information through the Bureau of the Census and the Office of Business Economics; conducts coast and geodetic surveys; establishes commodity weights, measures, and standards; issues patents and registers trademarks; administers a Federal aid program for economic "redevelopment areas"; and, through its Bureau of International Commerce, promotes foreign trade and assists United States business in its operations abroad.

Among other activities too numerous to mention are those of the United States Travel Service and the Maritime Administration. The former is concerned with the development of a program designed to encourage the travel of foreigners to the United States, whereas the latter's purpose is to aid the development and operation of the United States merchant marine by subsidizing shipbuilders and steamship lines and providing other governmental aids to merchant shipping.

The Department also issues weather forecasts. Its Weather Bureau operates a national network of field offices and forecast centers that provide weather predictions for shipping on the high seas and for domestic and international aviation.

(8) THE DEPARTMENT OF LABOR   The Department of Labor is charged with administering and enforcing statutes intended to promote the welfare of wage earners, improve their working conditions, and enhance their opportunities for profitable employment. It collects and publishes statistics of various kinds, undertakes research projects, and disseminates information about labor problems. Labor standards, labor-management relations, and manpower are the principal fields to which the Department's many activities are assignable. The following paragraph refers to merely a few of its component units.

An Office of Manpower Policy, Evaluation, and Research develops and recommends plans for a comprehensive manpower program. The Department's Bureau of Employment Security is concerned with the administration of a nationwide public employment service, state unemployment insurance programs, and Federal unemployment compensation plans; also with special programs designed to relieve the effects of unemployment and to promote maximum utilization of the country's manpower. Wage and Hours and Public Contracts Divisions enforce (a) the Fair Labor Standards Act which establishes minimum wage, overtime compensation, and child labor standards for employees engaged in interstate or foreign commerce or in the production of goods for commerce and (b) legislative acts establishing labor standards to be met by parties to public supply and service contracts.

(9) THE DEPARTMENT OF HEALTH, EDUCATION, AND WELFARE The Department of Health, Education, and Welfare was established to improve the functioning of such agencies of the national government as are primarily responsible for promoting the welfare of the public in the fields of health, education and social security.

An Office of Education carries on research and administers grant-in-aid programs; a Welfare Administration is concerned with assistance to needy individuals and families, with providing welfare and medical assistance and services for children, the aging, and other groups, and with maternal and child health services—largely through grants-in-aid to state and local governments which are required to conform to federally prescribed standards; and the Social Security Administration administers the retirement, survivors, and disability programs and also the policy of health insurance for the aged (hospital and supplementary medical insurance —Medicare).

Other subdivisions of the Department are the Public Health Service, the Food and Drug Administration, a Vocational Rehabilitation Administration, and an Administration on the Aging.

(10) THE DEPARTMENT OF HOUSING AND URBAN DEVELOPMENT The tenth executive department is the Department of Housing and Urban Development. Its objective is to encourage solution of problems of housing, urban development, and mass transportation through state, local, and private action. The functions, powers, and duties of the

Housing and Home Finance Agency, Federal Housing Administration, Public Housing Administration, and Federal National Mortgage Association were transferred to this department. It provides technical assistance and information to state and local governments and controls the allocation of millions of dollars for urban renewal and rehabilitation, for public housing, for urban mass transportation projects, and for basic water and sewerage facilities. The granting of rent supplements to low-income families is an additional activity of this department.

(11) THE DEPARTMENT OF TRANSPORTATION The eleventh department was created in late 1966, viz., the Department of Transportation. Its purpose is to develop a broad program for solution of the country's transportation problems, but Congress failed to endow it with sufficient power for the discharge of this responsibility. A number of existing administrative agencies were placed in the new department, viz., the Bureau of Public Roads, the Federal Aviation Agency,[93] the Coast Guard,[94] the St. Lawrence Seaway Corporation, the Great Lakes Pilotage Association, and the Alaska Railroad. The Department is responsible for the establishment of safety standards for automobiles, the beautification of highways, development of a supersonic transport plane and fast passenger trains for short runs, and

[93] The Federal Aviation Agency regulates air commerce, assigns use of the navigable airspace of the United States, controls both civil and military operations in that space, promulgates safety regulations of various types, and operates air navigation facilities.

[94] The Coast Guard is charged with the saving and protection of life and property on the high seas and on waters subject to the jurisdiction of the national government, the enforcement of maritime law, and, among other responsibilities, the provision of navigational aids to maritime and trans-oceanic air commerce.

the prescription of standards for highway projects, airports, and the like, subject to approval of these standards by Congress.

The Department's powers over transportation are severely restricted inasmuch as control over rates remains in the hands of agencies like the Interstate Commerce Commission (rail, truck, and barge rates), the Federal Maritime Commission (rates of waterborne foreign and domestic offshore commerce), and the Civil Aeronautics Board (airline fares). The spending powers of the Department are also limited, e.g., subsidies for commuter railroads and transit systems remain under control of the Department of Housing and Urban Development and the Maritime Administration of the Department of Commerce retains its power to grant subsidies to shipbuilders and steamship lines.

Independent Establishments

Many independent establishments are of minor importance but a substantial number administer major policies of the national government. Among the latter are the independent regulatory commissions and administrative agencies like the Veterans Administration, the Farm Credit Administration, the Atomic Energy Commission, the National Aeronautics and Space Administration, and the Selective Service System. A brief account of the powers and duties of most of the independent regulatory commissions and a few other independent establishments is all that will be undertaken in this text.

(1) THE INTERSTATE COMMERCE COMMISSION The Interstate Commerce Commission is the oldest of the independent regulatory bodies. It consists of eleven members appointed by the President with the advice and consent of the Senate. The Commission's jurisdiction extends to common carriers, by land or water, engaged in interstate or foreign commerce within the United States—railroads, motor carriers, ships (coastwise, intercoastal, and inland), express companies, pipe lines (excluding water and gas), and sleeping car companies; also to freight forwarders, i.e., persons other than carriers who employ the services of rail, water, and other carriers to transport property for the general public.

The Commission was created to promote safe, adequate, economical, and efficient service and to foster sound economic conditions in transportation. To this end it was granted power to regulate rates, schedules, and service standards; to approve or disapprove of proposed consolidations and mergers; to prohibit discriminatory practices; and, among other powers, to establish regulations concerning safety appliances and safety measures.

(2) THE FEDERAL MARITIME COMMISSION AND THE CIVIL AERONAUTICS BOARD The Federal Maritime Commission possesses powers and responsibilities similar to those of the Interstate Commerce Commission in regard to common carriers by water and other persons engaged in the foreign commerce and domestic offshore trade of the United States.

In the field of aviation, the Civil Aeronautics Board authorizes carriers to engage in interstate and foreign air transportation and has jurisdiction over rates and fares. It also investigates accidents involving civil aircraft.

(3) THE FEDERAL TRADE COMMISSION The Federal

Trade Commission is composed of five members appointed by the President and Senate. It administers acts of Congress designed to promote free and fair competition in interstate commerce, to safeguard the consuming public against fraudulent and deceptive practices, to prevent price discriminations and monopolistic arrangements, and, broadly speaking, to preserve a free enterprise system by protecting it against activities that menace its survival.

For the purpose of realizing these objectives the Commission has power to deal with such matters as boycotts, deceptive advertising, untruthful labeling of textile and fur products, and price-fixing agreements. The Commission commonly relies on voluntary and cooperative procedures but has authority to issue cease and desist orders and secure conformity to its rulings through formal litigation.

(4) THE FEDERAL COMMUNICATIONS COMMISSION
A Federal Communications Commission is charged with regulation of communication by wire, radio, and television. Companies engaged in interstate or foreign communication by wire or radio fall in the category of common carriers. As such, they are controllable by the Commission with respect to such matters as the reasonableness of their rates, the adequacy of their services, and the fairness of their practices.

The Commission issues and may modify or revoke licenses, assigns radio and television frequencies, and prescribes the nature of permissible service. Its jurisdiction extends to telegraph, telephone, and cable companies; also to radio broadcasting and television. The latter two are not considered common carriers. A Safety and Special Radio Services Bureau is responsible for the licensing and regulation of a considerable variety of radio stations not in the broadcasting or common carrier categories, e.g., aviation, public safety (e.g., police and fire), land transportation, and amateur.

(5) THE FEDERAL POWER COMMISSION   The Federal Power Commission has jurisdiction over the transmission and sale of both electrical energy and natural gas in interstate commerce. Public utilities engaged in such commerce are subject to control by the Commission. It regulates rates, charges, and services; prescribes a uniform system of accounts; and passes on applications of privately-owned utilities to issue securities, to dispose of, merge, or consolidate facilities, or to acquire securities of other public utilities. Among other activities, it is responsible for the licensing of hydroelectric projects on government lands or on navigable waters of the United States.

(6) THE SECURITIES AND EXCHANGE COMMISSION To protect the interests of the public and investors against malpractices in the securities and financial markets, Congress has enacted various laws establishing standards to be met by enterprises engaged in the sale of securities in interstate commerce or through the mails. Administration of these laws is entrusted to the Securities and Exchange Commission.

Securities offered for sale must be registered with the Commission, as must securities exchanges, brokers, investment companies, investment advisers, and public utility holding companies. In all instances of registration, financial and other information must be provided to enable the Commission to determine compliance with standards prescribed by statutes and by supplementary rules and regulations of the Commission.

The Commission possesses power to deal with cases of misrepresentation, manipulation, and other fraudulent practices in connection with the purchase and sale of securities. It may, for example, revoke the registration of a broker-dealer firm, suspend or expel it from membership in a national securities exchange, or suspend or withdraw the listing and registering of a security upon an exchange.

(7) THE NATIONAL LABOR RELATIONS BOARD The National Labor Relations Board administers legislation which recognizes the right of employees to self-organization and to bargain collectively through their chosen representatives with the enterprises employing them. The Board is authorized to designate appropriate units for collective bargaining, to conduct secret ballots for the choice of bargaining representatives, and to prevent such unfair labor practices by employers or unions as are specified by law.

(8) MEDIATION BOARDS Two other agencies dealing with labor-management problems are the National Mediation Board which has the primary function of mediating disputes between the railroads, express and Pullman companies, and airlines, on the one hand, and their employees, on the other; and the Federal Mediation and Conciliation Service which offers its facilities for the settlement of labor-management disputes in any industry affecting interstate commerce. Both of these agencies may mediate and conciliate, but not compel. There is also a President's Advisory Committee on Labor-Management Policy.

(9) OTHER IMPORTANT INDEPENDENT ESTABLISH-MENTS Of many other administrative agencies located outside the executive departments, only seven more, the General Services Administration, the Veterans Administration, the Tennessee Valley Authority, the National Aeronautics and Space Administration, the Atomic Energy Commission, the United States Postal Service, and the Civil Service Commissions will be given special consideration. The activities and responsibilities of the Civil Service Commission are discussed in the section of this chapter dealing with the personnel policies of the national government.

(a) THE GENERAL SERVICES ADMINISTRATION The General Services Administration, established in 1949, was created to provide an economical and efficient system for management of the national government's property and records. Among its subdivisions are the Federal Supply Service which purchases and distributes common-use items of supply to all federal agencies; the Public Building Service —responsible for the construction, maintenance, and operation of buildings owned or leased by the national government; the Transportation and Communications Service which develops and administers programs for the procurement and utilization of communication, transportation, and public utility services; the Utilization and Disposal Service, responsible for the use and disposal of the national government's real estate and related personal property; and the National Archives and Records Service which is concerned with the preservation and disposal of records and with the publication of laws, amendments to the Constitution, Presidential documents, and administrative regulations.

(b) THE VETERANS ADMINISTRATION The Veterans Administration administers laws providing a variety of

benefits for former members of the armed forces, their de-
pendents, and other beneficiaries of deceased members.
Among such benefits are medical and hospital care, compensation for service-connected disability or death, vocational rehabilitation, life insurance policies, and special housing for seriously disabled veterans.

(c) THE TENNESSEE VALLEY AUTHORITY   The Tennessee Valley Authority is one of a number of government
corporations created to operate public enterprises which
have business functions. These corporations are administrative agencies of the national government. Examples of such
corporations, other than the TVA, are the Federal Deposit
Insurance Corporation and the Export-Import Bank of
Washington.

The TVA constructs and maintains dams for navigation
and flood control in the Tennessee river valley; operates
electric power generating plants and sells electric power to
industries, municipalities, and cooperatives; and develops,
produces, and distributes fertilizers, primarily for research
and educational programs. A Presidentially appointed Board
of Directors is the controlling authority of this government
corporation. Its principal administrative officer is a General
Manager responsible to the Board.

(d) NATIONAL AERONAUTICS AND SPACE ADMINIS-
TRATION   The National Aeronautics and Space Administra-
tration was created to promote the devotion of space activities to peaceful purposes. Its functions are to conduct
research for solution of problems of flight within and outside the earth's atmosphere; to construct and operate space
vehicles, manned and unmanned, for space exploration; to

cooperate with other nations in space activities; and to disseminate information concerning its activities and results.

(e) ATOMIC ENERGY COMMISSION   The Atomic Energy Commission is concerned with the development, use, and control of atomic energy with the objective of contributing to the general welfare, to the common defense and security, and to the promotion of world peace. It provides programs for research, production of atomic energy and special nuclear materials, and disseminates scientific and technical information. One of its duties is to encourage private participation in these programs. Another is protection of the health and safety of the public by regulating the use of nuclear materials.

(f)   UNITED STATES POSTAL SERVICE   The United States Postal Service was created in 1970 and became operative in 1971. It is headed by a Board of Governors composed of nine members appointed by the President with the advice and consent of the Senate plus the Postmaster General and the Deputy Postmaster General. This board directs the functioning of the postal service, reviews practices and policies, and controls expenditures. The Postmaster General is the chief executive officer of the service. He is appointed by and removable by the Board. The Deputy Postmaster General, the chief operating officer, is selected by the Postmaster General and the Board, subject to removal by them. In addition to the above, Congress created a Postal Rate Commission of five members independent of the Postal Service and appointed by the President and Senate. Its function is to hold hearings on postal rate requests and to grant or deny approval, i.e., determine charges for mail service.

Appraisals of National Administrative Organization

The task of devising a satisfactory organization of the administrative services is both endless and monumental in the case of any government that carries on an expanding multiplicity of activities in a dynamic society. At the national level the movement for reorganization extends back many decades and various studies of the organization and operation of the administrative branch have been made and probably will continue to be undertaken in the future.

Major Studies

Among the most comprehensive investigations and reports of the past are those of the President's Committee on Administrative Management (1937), the first Hoover Commission (1947), and a second Commission also headed by Herbert Hoover (1953). The reports of these investigatory bodies deal with questions of personnel and administrative procedures as well as with problems of organization.

Criticisms of the Administrative Branch

Among the criticisms of the national administrative organization included in these reports were (a) its cumbersomeness and unmanageability, (b) the grouping of unrelated activities in the same administrative unit, (c) the division of responsibility for the administration of policies within a given field of governmental activity; (d) various undesirable restrictions on the authority of the President to direct and control administration; (e) the excessive use of boards or commissions for administrative purposes, and (f) the inadequacy of the managerial agencies of the government and of the staff services available to the President and department heads for assistance in discharging their managerial responsibilities.

Results of the Reports

Many of the proposals of these investigating groups have been carried out. Examples are the granting of reorganizing authority to the President, the strengthening of the Executive Office of the President, and the creation of a Department of Defense and a General Services Administration as recommended by the first Hoover Commission.

Various recommendations have been disregarded, maybe wisely and perhaps not, depending on one's point of view concerning the desirability of particular arrangements. For instance, the President's Committee on Administrative Management criticized the functions of the General Accounting Office, headed by the Comptroller General of the United States. It recommended restoration to the Executive of complete responsibility for accounts and current financial transactions and establishment of accountability of the Executive to Congress by providing a genuine independent post-audit of all fiscal transactions. This proposal has not borne fruit. The question is controversial and will be discussed later in a chapter dealing with governmental expenditures.

Although the major executive departments are few enough in number to be manageable, the existence of an unduly large number of independent establishments still makes the organization as a whole unmanageable. Apart from this consideration, Presidential control over the independent regulatory agencies continues to be restricted. The regulatory commissions were referred to as a headless fourth branch of the government by President Roosevelt's Committee on Administrative Management. It conceded that these commissions should be wholly independent of executive control in discharging their judicial functions, but favored their subjection to Presidential supervision with respect to their policy-determining and administrative responsibilities. The desirability of this recommendation remains controversial.

With the exception of the Department of Health, Education, and Welfare, the major executive departments are essentially of the unifunctional type. Although the grouping of unrelated activities in the same administrative unit is no longer as common as it once was, this undesirable organizational arrangement has not been entirely eliminated. Past examples were placement of the Public Health Service in the Treasury Department and inclusion of the Bureau of Public Roads in the Department of Agriculture. The Health Service is now a component unit of the Department of Health, Education, and Welfare and the Bureau of Public Roads, after being transferred several times to other agencies, is presently located in the recently created Department of Transportation.

The administrative organization continues to be marked by a division of responsibility for the administration of policies, within a given field of governmental activity, among two or more separate administrative agencies. Examples are the Federal Aviation Agency (placed in the Department of Transportation) and the Civil Aeronautics Board, both concerned with aviation but functioning independently of each other; the Federal Maritime Commission, an independent establishment, and the Maritime Administration of the Department of Commerce; the administration of policies pertaining to farmers by the Department of Agriculture and the Farm Credit Administration; and the existence of several agencies engaged in activities pertaining to labor, viz., the Department of Labor, the National Labor Relations Board, the Federal Mediation and Conciliation Service, and the National Mediation Board.

Many administrative agencies, including the major executive departments, have single heads. However, boards or commissions are still used to head agencies that perform strictly administrative rather than quasi-legislative or quasi-judicial functions.

What has been said above scarcely does justice to the reports of the investigating bodies—their criticisms, their recommendations, and the fate of their proposals for change. The problem of administrative organization and procedure will continue to plague the President and Congress in the future as in the past. A permanent solution is out of the question, not only because of conflicting views concerning the most advisable arrangements but also because of the changing functions and activities of the national government. As new services are undertaken and old ones modified or sometimes abandoned, adjustments in organization necessarily occur.

The Personnel Policies of the National Government

Proper administrative organization is but one of several factors contributing to the achievement of high standards of administration. Others are a competent personnel and the use of effective procedures and methods. Unless officials and employees are well-qualified to perform the tasks assigned them, mediocre service is the best that can be expected.

Problems Requiring Solution

Many problems require solution in developing a sound personnel policy. The most important are (1) the selection of qualified persons for entrance into government service, (2) establishment of ways and means of basing promotions, demotions, and dismissals from the service on merit, (3) providing training for recruits and for officers and employees who have been in the service for some time, (4) installing an adequate compensation plan based on the principle of equal pay for equal work, (5) devising an appropriate retirement and pension system, (6) regulating such matters as hours of work, vacations, and sick leave, (7) providing proper working conditions to insure the safety and welfare of employees, and (8) developing a fair policy in regard to employee organizations.

The Spoils System

One of the most undesirable personnel policies is the "spoils system." Its distinguishing feature is that appointments, promotions, and dismissals from public service are based primarily on party affiliation, party loyalty, and the degree of service rendered a party in its efforts to gain control of the government. Ability to discharge official responsibilities is given secondary, if any, consideration.

The political party that wins an election throws out the

rascals connected with the unsuccessful opposition and replaces them with its loyal supporters. Such a personnel policy makes public service uncertain, develops a strong distaste for governmental service on the part of numerous capable citizens, lowers quality and morale, and causes public servants to think more about getting and retaining voter support than about doing satisfactory work—to the victor belong the spoils.

A Career Service

As governmental operations become more complicated and technical in character, the need for establishment of public service on a career basis grows rapidly. Such a service provides for entrance on a merit basis, furnishes ample opportunity for advancements in pay and promotions in rank to able persons, and adequately protects officers and employees from demotion and dismissal for reasons other than incompetence. A career service enables loyal and competent individuals to serve government for the duration of their working lives with excellent prospects of bettering their positions as the years go by.

Government in the United States at all levels has suffered for a long time, and still suffers to an appreciable extent, from adherence to the spoils system. Fortunately, considerable progress toward personnel policies based on merit and career ideas has been made, especially so in the case of the national government and many of the larger cities.

Civil Service Reform

Following the triumph of Jacksonian democracy in 1828, the spoils system, which had originated in the states and local units, became firmly established at the national level of government. Agitation for civil service reform gained momentum after the Civil War, but the first major legislation intended to curb the spoilsman was the Pendleton Act of 1883, passed by Congress after the assassination of President Garfield by a disgruntled office-seeker. This act created a classified service and provided that appointments thereto be based on the results of open competitive examinations. In 1883 the "classified service" included only about ten percent of the total number of positions in the executive civil service.

To some extent by acts of Congress, but for the most part by executive orders of successive Presidents under authority delegated by Congress, the classified service has been expanded until it covers approximately 2,500,000 of the officers and employees comprising the executive civil service, i.e., close to eighty percent. Many positions not included within the "classified" category are nevertheless filled on a merit basis by agencies like the Foreign Service of the State Department and the Federal Bureau of Investigation, which administer their own personnel policies without being subject to the jurisdiction of the Civil Service Commission.

The Civil Service Commission

Administration of the national government's merit system, subject to the exceptions just mentioned, involves the functioning of a central personnel agency, the Civil Service Commission, and the personnel offices of the major executive departments and agencies. Although there is a trend toward greater decentralization by delegating more authority to departmental personnel offices, great emphasis is still placed on centralization. Opinion is divided concerning the most desirable combination of centralized and decentralized administration.

The Civil Service Commission is composed of three members appointed by the President with the advice and consent of the Senate. Presidential discretion is limited by the Congressionally imposed requirement that no more than two members shall be adherents of the same political party. The term of service is six years under a "staggered" arrangement, i.e., the terms of the members do not begin or expire at the same time.

Of the three members, one is designated as chairman by the President and serves as the chief executive and administrative officer of the Commission. An executive director, appointed by the chairman, coordinates the internal management of the Commission and directs its operating and staff activities. Among the component units of the Commission are a Board of Appeals and Reviews, an Office of Career Development, and such Bureaus as Recruiting and Examining, Policies and Standards, and Retirement and Insurance.

In addition to the central office of the Commission, located in Washington, there are ten regional offices situated in such cities as Atlanta, Boston, Philadelphia, New York, and Seattle. The regional offices have jurisdiction over local boards of examiners and conduct examinations, prepare lists of eligibles, and certify eligible persons to appointing officials when vacancies occur in the field services of national administrative agencies.

Departmental Personnel Offices

The Departmental Personnel Offices perform a variety of functions. Their responsibilities have been increased in recent

years and include the classification of individual jobs, the
rating of employees, giving certain examinations and preparing eligible lists, and planning and supervising training
programs. The discharge of these responsibilities is subject
to supervision and inspection by the Civil Service Commission, which also renders advisory and consultative assistance.

Entrance Appointments

Most positions in the classified service are filled on the
basis of performance in competitive examinations of one type
or another. However, veterans enjoy various preferences;
appointments to positions in the central offices in Washington must be apportioned among the states, territories,
and the District of Columbia on a population basis; and
residence in proximity to the area in which a field position is
located has a bearing on priority of certification.

Registers, i.e., eligible lists, are maintained in the central
and regional offices of the Commission. When a vacancy
occurs the usual procedure is certification of the three highest names on the appropriate register to the appointing
authority. The person selected serves for a probationary
period, usually a year, before his appointment becomes absolute.

Promotions

Promotions are handled differently than entrance appointments. Each agency is required to establish a promotion
program which meets standards prescribed by the Civil
Service Commission. The appointing officer selects the employee to be promoted, subject to the requirement that the

person possesses the legal qualifications for holding a particular position and that the principle of merit be respected.

Among the standards established by the Commission with respect to agency promotion policies are (1) that all promotions in the competitive civil service be based on merit, (2) that promotions be made only in accordance with approved agency promotion plans, (3) that each promotion plan use areas of competition as wide as possible and that evaluation methods be reasonable, valid, and applied fairly, and (4) that an agency's employees be fully informed of the policies and procedures governing its promotion plan.

Dismissals from the Service

The power to discharge employees within the classified service is subject to a number of restrictions that are designed to prevent arbitrary removals. First, no person shall be removed except for such cause as will promote the efficiency of the service and for reasons stated in writing. Second, the person to be removed is to be notified, given a copy of the charges preferred against him, and allowed a reasonable time to reply in writing. Third, no removal may be made for withholding any contribution of money or other valuable thing for any political purpose. Fourth, an employee may not be removed for joining a union not involving the obligation to strike against the national government. Fifth, in making removals, no discriminations shall be exercised for political or religious reasons.

Exceptions to the rule prohibiting dismissals for political reasons were established by the Hatch Act of 1939. It imposes the penalty of immediate removal on officers and employees of the executive branch engaging in certain prohibited political activities, such as using their authority to influence an election, or taking an active part in political management or in political campaigning, or belonging to any political party or organization advocating "overthrow of our constitutional form of government in the United States." On the basis of both legislation and executive orders, removals may also be made on "disloyalty" grounds.

The provisions of the Hatch Act apply to both the classified and unclassified service, with the exception of the President, Vice President, department heads and assistant heads, and a few other categories of high officials occupying policy-determining positions. Enforcement of the Hatch Act has proved difficult.

(1) THE CIVIL SERVICE COMMISSION AND REMOVALS. The Civil Service Commission may investigate cases of dismissal upon allegation, with offer of proof, that removal was made for political or religious reasons or in violation of procedure established by civil service rules. Special privileges have been conferred on veterans by the Veterans' Preference Act of 1944. They have the right to appeal to the Civil Service Commission in all serious matters. The 1944 act provided that the Commission "shall submit its findings and recommendations to the proper administrative officer," but did not require compliance with the Commission's recommendations. However, acts of Congress passed in 1947 and 1948 made Civil Service recommendations *binding* on any administrative agency involved in an appeal based on the Veterans' Preference Act of 1944. Since so large a proportion of the employees of the national government are veterans, this policy affects the relations between an operating agency and its employees to a far greater extent than confinement of Commission control to cases involving veterans indicates.

Compensation

The compensation of civilian employees of the executive branch is determinable by Congress. In 1960, 1962, 1964, and 1970 Congress provided pay increases for most civilian employees ("classified" employees, postoffice workers, and a few other specified groups)[94e] by enacting a single, omnibus pay bill. . . . Prior to that time separate bills for different categories of public servants were often passed, e.g., the Postal Field Service Compensation Acts of 1955 and 1958. Other acts of Congress have dealt with the pay rates of a limited number of other employee groups, such as members of the Foreign Service.

Pay for blue-collar workers (trades and crafts) is determined by department and agency wage boards on the basis of prevailing wages in the locality wherein the workers are stationed. In a few instances, an administrative agency fixes the compensation of its own employees within Congressionally prescribed standards. An example is the Tennessee Valley Authority.

Fringe Benefits

Various fringe benefits supplement the salaries or wages which employees receive. Among them are retirement annuities, group life insurance, disability and unemployment benefits, incentive awards, and paid vacations.

[94e] Military pay boost provided in 1971

Administrative Legislation and Adjudication

Administrative Legislation

Administrative legislation occurs whenever administrative agencies issue rules having the force of law that prescribe or affect the rights and duties of individuals. The delegation of such authority to administrators serves the purpose of establishing the details of general policies adopted by the legislature and of controlling the application of policies to particular situations.

(1) ADVANTAGES. Administrative legislation is advantageous in several respects. An expert personnel with special knowledge of subject matter, of the conditions requiring regulation, and of what is administratively practicable is better qualified for detailed rule-making than a legislative body composed of laymen. Comparatively informal procedures expedite the rule-making process and also simplify consultation with interested parties during the preparatory stages. Rules may be altered readily whenever occasion demands.

(2) DISADVANTAGES. A major disadvantage is the tendency to issue a confusing multiplicity of rules and to alter them with discouraging frequency. Another is the risk that rules will be prepared without giving private interests an adequate opportunity to be heard. A third is the hazard of lack of proper publicity. Two other disadvantages are the danger of arbitrary action by administrative agencies and the frequent blindness or indifference of administrators to what is *politically* feasible.

(3) OVERCOMING THE DISADVANTAGES. Congress enacted a Federal Administrative Procedure Act in 1946. Its motive was to meet objections to both administrative legislation and administrative adjudication. This act establishes minimum standards with respect to rule-making, adjudication, sanctions, and judicial review. It also directs each executive agency to publicize its formal procedures.

In regard to administrative legislation, the 1946 act requires notice of intent to make a rule by publication in the Federal Register, the granting of opportunity for interested persons to submit data and arguments in writing and at a public hearing (if the administrative agency decides to hold one), and publication of the rule or rules eventually adopted. The act also confers on interested persons the right to petition for a new rule or for the amendment or repeal of an existing rule. Once a rule has been adopted and applied, persons affected may challenge its validity on various grounds, including its constitutionality, in a proper case falling within the jurisdiction of the national judiciary.

Administrative Adjudication

Administrative adjudication takes place when administrative bodies settle controversies arising in the course of policy execution through a process involving the giving of notice, the holding of a hearing, the presentation of evidence, and the pronouncement of a decision concerning legal rights and duties. If every such settlement had to await recourse to the ordinary courts, governmental operations could not be carried on effectively and with proper dispatch.

Among the occasions giving rise to administrative adjudication are the development of disputes regarding such matters as the value of property of a utility, the reasonableness of rates charged by a common carrier, the fairness of a particular trade practice, the extent of an individual's tax obligation, and the merits of insurance claims of veterans.

Many national administrative agencies exercise quasi-judicial powers. Among the better known are the Interstate Commerce Commission, the Federal Trade Commission, the Federal Power Commission, the Federal Communications Commission, and the Securities and Exchange Commission. Various executive establishments include boards of appeal, e.g., the Department of Commerce, the Civil Service Commission, and the Veterans Administration.

(1) ADVANTAGES. The advantages of adjudication by administrative agencies rather than by the ordinary courts are manifold. Included among them are less delay, more informal procedures, freedom from highly technical and cumbersome rules of evidence, more thorough investigation, and lower costs. Another advantage is the settlement of disputes by officials who possess expert knowledge of particular problems instead of by judges who are learned in the law but fail to qualify as specialists in the various fields of governmental policy.

(2) THE PRINCIPAL DISADVANTAGE AND WAYS OF OVERCOMING IT. The principal objection to administrative adjudication is that controversies are decided by the very agency of government which is charged with the responsibility of rule-making and of executing policies. An impartial settlement of disputes is asserted to be unlikely under these circumstances.

To meet this criticism provision has been made in some jurisdictions for assignment of the investigatory and prosecuting, the hearing, and the final decision functions to different persons. Although all belong to the same administrative agency, the use of different and mutually independent officials for the performance of each of these functions is supposed to reduce the likelihood of unfair adjudication.

To promote fairness in administrative adjudication, the Federal Administrative Procedure Act of 1946 requires (1) notification of proceedings, with information concerning the time, place, and nature of a hearing (if required by law), the legal authority under which the hearing is to be held, and the matters of fact and law asserted, (2) opportunity to submit facts, arguments, proposals of adjustment, proposed findings and conclusions, or exceptions to tentative decisions, (3) hearing officers to make the initial decision, (4) no participation in the making of a decision by investigatory or prosecuting agents, (5) the transcript of testimony, exhibits, and all papers filed in the proceedings to be the exclusive record for decision, (6) the administrative agency, when considering a hearing officer's decision on appeal or review, is to reexamine the issues, (7) the right to be represented by counsel, and (8) any person suffering a legal wrong because of agency action, or adversely affected thereby, is entitled to judicial review.

Administrative legislation and adjudication affect the interests of individuals and groups to so great an extent that every precaution should be taken to prevent arbitrary exercise of these important powers. At the same time, the attainment of efficient and effective government should not be hampered by an undue and unreasonable concern for the interests of individuals. Procedures that simultaneously safeguard the interests of the government and those of private persons are clearly needed.

Securing Compliance with Governmental Policies

Administrative legislation and adjudication are two of many functions involved in the general process of securing compliance with governmental policies. Of additional methods of administrative action having the same objective, some are non-coercive and others coercive.

Non-Coercive Methods

Non-coercive measures include persuasion, educational and informative campaigns, the declaration of a public policy merely as a guide to private action, the setting of an example by government with the hope that private interest-groups will be influenced thereby, the holding of conferences, mediation and conciliation, and conditional grants of money, sometimes referred to as the purchase of consent.

Resort to the foregoing and other non-coercive techniques occurs under a variety of circumstances. Such measures are preferred, for example, if adequate to the objective sought, if the government's legal authority is questionable, or if processes of compulsion are too costly or likely to prove unsuccessful.

Coercive Methods

Coercive methods involve the imposition of penalties of one type or another which ultimately, as a rule, are enforceable through resort to the courts. *Inspection* is undertaken to determine compliance with legally established standards. If it fails to produce voluntary compliance, the eventual remedy is prosecution for non-compliance. *Licensing* is the granting of permission to engage in a particular activity. Its compulsory aspect is that a license may be denied, suspended, or revoked for failure to comply with legally prescribed conditions. *Administrative orders* of individual application serve the purpose of making a general statutory requirement specific. The ultimate remedy, in the event of disregard of such orders, is judicial imposition of such sanctions as are provided by law. *Administrative adjudication* is a dispute-settling function.

Sanctions

Sanctions consist of the penalties that are appliable in case of non-compliance with legally imposed obligations. Usually, action by the courts is necessary for the application of sanctions, but there are exceptions to this general rule. Examples are the refusal or withdrawal of benefits, as in the case of exclusion from use of the mails; the denial, suspension, or revocation of a license; and summary action by administrative officials, such as the sale of a delinquent taxpayer's property, the destruction of condemned meat or meat products, and the seizure of contraband drugs. Generally speaking, judicial enforcement is essential to the imposition of most sanctions, particularly fine and imprisonment.

The execution of governmental policies would be extremely difficult if it were always necessary to compel people to abide by the law of the land. Fortunately, conformity to legal regulations usually occurs as a matter of habit, probably for two principal reasons. One is the realization that governments possess the right and the means of compelling compliance. The other is recognition of the necessity of government as a means of attaining an orderly community life and of promoting the welfare of the general public. Few people subscribe to the doctrines of anarchism, i.e., to the abolition of government and its replacement by a social order featured solely by voluntary rather than involuntary cooperation.

The National Judiciary

CHAPTER ☆ NINE

Jurisdiction of the National Judiciary
    Subject Matter; Character of the Parties
    Exclusive and Concurrent Jurisdiction
    How Cases Reach National Courts
    Congressional Control over Jurisdiction
Organization of the National Judiciary
    Constitutional and Legislative Courts
    Federal District Courts
    United States Courts of Appeals
    The Supreme Court
    Special Courts
    Judicial Conferences
    Administrative Office of the United States Courts
    Federal Judicial Center

The Supreme Court and Rules of Procedure
Selection, Tenure, and Compensation of Judges
Judicial Review
    Marbury v. Madison: Marshall's Reasoning
    Expansion of Judicial Review
    Curbing Judicial Review
    Packing the Court: the Abortive Roosevelt Plan
    Judicial Self-Restraint
    Judicial Activism

    Claimed Advantages and Disadvantages of Judicial Re-
        view
    Improving Judicial Review
    Judicial Lawmaking

☆ ☆ ☆ ☆ ☆ ☆ ☆ ☆ ☆ ☆ ☆ ☆ ☆

A dual system of courts is one of the features of
federalism in the United States. Instead of having a single
hierarchy of tribunals for the settlement of legal controversies, this important function is shared by a national
judiciary and the courts of the several states. From a constitutional standpoint, the status of the fifty state systems is
identical in regard to their power of adjudication and their
relation to the courts of the national government. Consequently, the term "dual" accurately describes the situation
with respect to the all-important matter of jurisdiction.

Jurisdiction of the National Judiciary

Article III of the Constitution sets forth the extent of the
judicial power of the national government. Jurisdiction is
granted in three categories of cases. In one of these the
determining factor is the subject matter of a legal controversy; in another the character of the parties to a case, regardless of subject matter; and in a third, no longer of major
importance, both the character of the parties and subject
matter are the determinants of federal jurisdiction.

The Subject Matter Category

The subject matter class of controversies includes all cases, in law and equity, arising under the Constitution, national laws, and treaties made by the United States and also all cases of admiralty and maritime jurisdiction. In controversies of the foregoing type, the character of the parties to a case is immaterial.

The Character of the Parties Category

Irrespective of subject matter, the jurisdiction of the national judiciary extends to cases which affect ambassadors, other public ministers, and consuls (referring to representatives of foreign governments accredited to the United States); controversies to which the United States is a party; controversies between two or more states of the Union; controversies between one of the states and citizens of another; cases to which a state or its citizens and foreign states or aliens are parties; and suits between citizens of different states.

The states are not suable in the national courts by their own citizens, by the citizens of other states, by aliens, or by foreign countries. Amendment Eleven states explicitly that the judicial power of the United States shall not be construed to extend to any suit . . . commenced or prosecuted against one of the United States by citizens of another state, or by citizens of any foreign state. State immunity from being made a defendant in suits commenced by its own citizens was upheld by the Supreme Court in *Hans v. Louisiana;* [95] by a foreign state, in *Monaco v. Mississippi.* [96]

[95] 134 U. S. 1 (1880).
[96] 292 U. S. 313 (1934).

The Court took the position that the non-suability of the states by plaintiffs of the type involved in these cases was inferrable from the Eleventh Amendment and from evidence of the intent of the Constitution's framers. In the Monaco case the Court also observed that international complications might arise if suits by a foreign country against a state were permitted.

As matters now stand, a state may be sued without its consent in only two types of cases, viz., if action is brought against a state by either the national government or another state. Failure of the defendant state to appear normally results in a judgment against it by default.

The Subject Matter and Character of the Parties Category

The third type of case falling within the jurisdiction of the national judiciary involves a combination of requirements, viz., the character of the parties and the subject matter of the controversy. These requisites are citizens of the same state claiming lands under grants of different states. The right of the national courts to deal with this kind of controversy is probably no longer as important as it once was.

Exclusive and Concurrent Jurisdiction

Congress has authority to provide that cases falling in all three of the categories just described may be decided only by the national courts. It has not done so. However, the national judiciary has exclusive jurisdiction over some controversies, such as suits between two or more states, prosecutions for violation of federal criminal law, actions against representatives of foreign countries accredited to the United States, and all admiralty, maritime, patent-rights, copyright, and bankruptcy cases.

Exclusive jurisdiction has been conferred on state courts, provided the amount in controversy is $10,000 or less, over suits between citizens of different states and civil actions involving a federal question. If the amount exceeds $10,000, suits of this type may be instituted in the national or state courts, as may all other cases included within the judicial power of the national government except those over which Congress has vested exclusive jurisdiction in either the national judiciary or the tribunals of the states. At any time, of course, Congress may alter prevailing arrangements with respect to the spheres of exclusive and concurrent jurisdiction.

How Cases Reach National Courts

Cases reach the national courts in several ways. First, any case falling within the exclusive original jurisdiction of the national judiciary must necessarily be brought before the appropriate national tribunal. Second, if both the national and state courts have original jurisdiction, the plaintiff has a choice. He may institute action in a state court, but if he does, the case may be *removed* to a national court of first instance in accordance with provisions of the national judicial code.

Such removal, usually at the request of the defendant, must occur prior to final judgment by the state court. This circumstance under which a case is brought before a national court does not amount to an appeal from one court to another. It is merely a matter of transferring a case from one jurisdiction to another before a decision is handed down. The primary purpose of this removal procedure is to place the defendant on an equal footing with the plaintiff, who makes the initial choice between a national or a state court if their jurisdiction is concurrent.

The third way in which a case gets into the national courts is by an appeal from the decision of a *state court of last resort* to the Supreme Court of the United States. In some types of cases the parties have a right of appeal but ordinarily review of the ruling of a state court of last resort is left to the Supreme Court's discretion. In either instance, the appellate jurisdiction of the Court is exercisable only in cases involving a federal question, i.e., when some right or immunity is claimed under the national constitution, laws, or treaties. No national court other than the Supreme Court is authorized to review the decisions of state courts. The latter, of course, have exclusive jurisdiction over all legal controversies falling outside the judicial power of the national government as delineated in Article III.

Congressional Control over Jurisdiction

In describing the organization of the national judiciary, the jurisdiction of the different levels of national courts will be summarized briefly. With one exception, Congress has complete control over this matter.

The exception is that Article III specifies the original jurisdiction of the Supreme Court. Cases which may be commenced in that court are those to which a state is party and all controversies affecting ambassadors, other public ministers, and consuls. Although Congress may neither increase nor decrease this original jurisdiction of the highest court, it may determine whether it shall be exclusive. The jurisdiction is exclusive if the parties to a case are two or more states, but the national district courts have concurrent jurisdiction in cases affecting foreign diplomatic and consular representatives and in some cases to which a state is a party, e.g., controversies between the national government and a state.

Organization of the National Judiciary

Constitutional and Legislative Courts

National courts are assignable to two categories, viz., constitutional and legislative. Constitutional courts are those organized by Congress in pursuance of the various provisions of Article III. This article contains safeguards in regard to tenure and compensation intended to promote judicial independence.

Legislative courts are created under the authority of Congress to deal with a variety of matters, such as its power to regulate foreign and interstate commerce, to govern the territories of the United States, to lay and collect taxes, and to make rules for the government and regulation of the military forces. Judges of these courts may be appointed for limited terms rather than for "good behavior," e.g., eight-year terms for judges of territorial courts, and be made removable by methods other than impeachment and subsequent trial. Their salaries may be reduced. Unlike the constitutional courts, they may be required to perform legislative and administrative as well as judicial functions.

At present, the only legislative courts are the territorial

tribunals (Puerto Rico, Guam, Virgin Islands, Canal Zone), the Court of Military Appeals, and the United States Tax Court. Various legislative courts of the past, such as the United States Court of Claims and the United States Court of Customs and Patent Appeals, have been given the status of "constitutional courts" by Congress.

Federal District Courts

The national (federal) district courts are the most numerous of the constitutional courts. Their jurisdiction is original, which means that cases are commenced in these courts without previous consideration and disposition by some other court.[97] The number of district courts and judges varies from time to time, with an increase regularly occurring because of a steady expansion of the amount of judicial business.

As of 1972, the District Courts numbered 89 and the judges 331. The country is divided into districts, with each state having at least one and many containing two or more. There are 88 district courts in the fifty states and one in the District of Columbia. The territorial court of Puerto Rico is called a "court of the United States" because its jurisdiction is the same as that of the district courts located in the states.

District court judges vary from a minimum of one to as many as 23 in the Southern District of New York. Whatever the number in a particular district, most trials are presided over by a single judge, but Congress has provided

[97] The district courts have no appellate jurisdiction in the technical sense of that phrase. However, some actions of United States commissioners and of certain administrative agencies are reviewable by these courts.

that three judges must try certain kinds of cases, e.g., a suit seeking an injunction to prevent enforcement, on the ground of unconstitutionality, of national or state laws.

United States Courts of Appeals

Immediately above the district courts of first instance are the United States Courts of Appeals. The country is divided into ten numbered intermediate appellate court circuits (districts) with a Court of Appeals in each. These numbered circuits include three or more states and, in addition, the territories assigned to some of them. An eleventh circuit, unnumbered, is the District of Columbia. The Courts of Appeals consist of from three to fifteen judges, with a total of 97 (1972). Cases are heard by a least three judges but sometimes by the entire number in those circuits having more than three. The senior judge of a circuit is its chief judge.

United States Courts of Appeals possess only appellate jurisdiction. This jurisdiction extends to cases decided by the district courts, territorial courts, and some special courts; also to the orders of various independent regulatory commissions (such as the Securities and Exchange Commission and the National Labor Relations Board) and of a number of administrative establishments, e.g., the Tax Court of the United States. Except for the few instances in which cases may be carried directly from the Federal District Courts to the Supreme Court, the Courts of Appeals review district court decisions, but only if either of the parties to a case takes advantage of his right of appeal.

Decisions of the Courts of Appeal are final unless the Supreme Court is willing to review them or under obligation to do so because of a right of appeal conferred on litigants by act of Congress. Only a minority of cases move upward from the District Courts to the Courts of Appeals, and even fewer from the latter to the court of last resort, i.e., the Supreme Court. The end of the road for an overwhelming proportion of cases is located in the district courts of original jurisdiction. Most of those which are carried to the intermediate courts of appeal progress no further.

The Supreme Court

The Court of last resort, with respect to controversies included within the jurisdiction of the national judiciary, is the Supreme Court. It has been composed of nine members since 1869. Prior to that year its size varied from six in 1789 to five in 1801, seven in 1807, nine in 1837, ten in 1863, and seven in 1866. Congress determines the size of the court.

(1) ORIGINAL JURISDICTION OF THE COURT The Supreme Court's original jurisdiction is limited. Only a few cases may be commenced there, viz., those to which a state is a party or controversies involving the diplomatic or consular representatives of foreign states accredited to the United States.

(2) APPELLATE JURISDICTION OF THE COURT Although Congress may neither increase nor decrease the Court's original jurisdiction, the situation differs with respect to its appellate jurisdiction. Article III states explicitly that in all cases other than those falling within the Court's original jurisdiction, the Court shall have appellate jurisdiction, both as to law and fact, *with such exceptions and under such regulations as Congress shall make.*

Exercise of the Supreme Court's appellate jurisdiction depends largely on its willingness to do so. Cases ordinarily reach the Court by the granting of a *writ of certiorari* on the petition of a dissatisfied litigant. Grant or denial of this writ rests solely with the discretion of the Court. Most of the applications for this writ are denied even though a favorable vote of four justices is all that is necessary for its issuance. A writ of certiorari directs the lower court to send up the entire record in a case for review.

Another method by which Supreme Court rulings are obtainable is through *certification.* This technique, which is seldom used, involves a lower court request that the Supreme Court answer specified questions of law. The only courts which may certify questions to the Court for review are the United States Courts of Appeals and the United States Court of Claims.

A third method of securing Supreme Court consideration of a case is by a *right of appeal* conferred by law on the parties to a legal controversy. Technically, the Court must review cases brought up on *appeal as a matter of right,* but it does so only if its members believe that a substantial federal question is involved. The right of appeal is limited to certain types of cases designated by Congress, e.g., if a state court of last resort has declared a national law or treaty unconstitutional or upheld a state law which has been challenged as being in conflict with a national law, a treaty, or the Constitution of the United States.

Appellate cases come from the following sources: the United States Courts of Appeals; the Federal District Courts (in a limited number of cases); the United States Court of

Claims; the United States Court of Customs and Patent Appeals; the legislative courts (permissible in some instances); and state courts of last resort in cases involving a federal question.

Special Courts

The national judicial branch includes a number of special courts in addition to the tribunals of general jurisdiction that have been described. Among these courts are those of the District of Columbia, territorial courts, the Court of Military Appeals, the Court of Claims, the Court of Customs and Patent Appeals, the Customs Court, and the United States Tax Court. The last four will be described briefly.

(1) THE COURT OF CUSTOMS AND PATENT APPEALS The Court of Customs and Patent Appeals reviews decisions of the Customs Court, settles legal controversies arising from findings of the Tariff Commission in regard to unfair practices in the import trade, and reviews decisions of the Patent Office concerning patents and trademarks. A chief judge and four associate judges constitute the personnel of this court.

(2) THE COURT OF CLAIMS The Court of Claims consists of seven justices having jurisdiction over suits against the United States in which the plaintiff claims monetary compensation from the national government, e.g., for services rendered, for injuries caused by the negligent or wrongful behavior of government employees, or because of the provisions of a contract. This court passes on the validity of designated claims with respect to which the United States has waived its immunity from suit by individuals.

(3) THE CUSTOMS COURT The United States Customs Court reviews appraisals of imported merchandise and other challenged decisions of collectors of customs. It is composed of nine judges.

(4) THE UNITED STATES TAX COURT The United States Tax Court consists of a chief judge and seventeen associate judges (twelve year terms). It settles controversies concerning deficiencies or overpayments with respect to the following taxes: income, estate, gift, excess profits, and personal holding company surtaxes. The Court has Article I status and is a legislative court.

Judicial Conferences

Several types of judicial conference are held one or more times a year for the general purpose of improving the administration of the national judicial system. These conferences consider ways and means of handling the business of the national courts.

(1) THE JUDICIAL CONFERENCE OF THE UNITED STATES The Judicial Conference of the United States, which meets at least once a year, is chaired by the Chief Justice of the Supreme Court who functions to some extent as a directing and supervising head of the national judiciary. Its other members are the chief judge of each circuit; a district judge per circuit chosen by its district and court of appeals judges; the chief judge of the Court of Claims; and the chief judge of the Court of Customs and Patent Appeals.

Among the functions of the Conference are making surveys of business in the national courts, preparing plans for the assignment and transfer of judges, recommending remedial measures to Congress, and supervising the Administrative Office of the United States Courts.

(2) LOWER LEVEL CONFERENCES Two lower level judicial conferences meet once or twice a year in each circuit to consider the condition of judicial business. One is composed of the judges of the circuit's Court of Appeals. The other, held annually, is a conference of both the appellate and district judges of a particular circuit summoned by the circuit's chief judge.

The Administrative Office of the United States Courts

The Administrative Office of the United States Courts is headed by a Director and Deputy Director appointed by the Supreme Court. It functions under the direction of the Supreme Court and the Judicial Conference of the United States. Both of these bodies carry on their activities under the guidance of the Chief Justice of the Supreme Court.

The Administrative Office performs a variety of tasks. Examples are supervising administrative matters pertaining to the offices of clerks, examining the state of the dockets of the courts, preparing the budgets of the lower courts, auditing accounts, and purchasing and distributing equipment and supplies.

The Federal Judicial Center

The Federal Judicial Center's purpose is to promote the development and establishment of improved judicial administration in the courts of the United States. It is supervised by a Board composed of the Chief Justice of the Supreme Court (permanent chairman), the Director of the Administrative Office of the United States courts, and two judges of the United States Courts of Appeals and three District Court judges—all elected for staggered four-year terms by the Judicial Conference of the United States. The Board appoints the Director of the Center.

The Supreme Court and Rules of Legal Procedure

The rules of legal procedure followed by the national courts in trying cases are traceable to several sources. One is the Constitution, which contains a number of stipulations pertaining for the most part to criminal proceedings. Another is enactments of Congress. A third source is the Supreme Court to which Congress has delegated procedural rule-making authority. The Court has promulgated many rules to be observed by the lower national courts in handling cases of various kinds, e.g., civil and criminal cases, bankruptcy proceedings, and copyright controversies. This policy of delegating control over procedure to the highest court strengthens its position within the structure of the national judiciary.

The Selection, Tenure, and Compensation of Judges

Although provisions of the Constitution concerning the selection tenure, and compensation of judges have received attention in preceding chapters, it seems advisable to repeat briefly what was said and to add other material. The functioning of judicial tribunals is affected considerably by the way in which their members are chosen and by the sense of security associated with the rendition of judicial service.

Selection of Judges

Judges of the national courts are appointed by the President with the advice and consent of the Senate. This mode of selection is mandatory for the Supreme Court, but Congress is authorized to vest the appointment of inferior officers in the President alone, the courts, or the heads of departments. Acting under this grant of power, Congress probably could provide for the selection of lower court judges by the President alone, by the Supreme Court, or by the Attorney General, unless the Supreme Court were to substitute its judgment for that of Congress concerning the line of demarcation between superior and inferior officers.

(1) PARTISAN AND OTHER CONSIDERATIONS Presidential appointments to the national courts are based on partisan considerations. During the period from 1933 to 1963, for example, a total of 799 court appointments was made. Of the persons appointed, 92.4% had the same party

affiliation as the President who made the appointment. The percentages for each of the four Presidents in office during this period were Roosevelt, 93.3%; Truman, 89.9%; Eisenhower, 93.8%; and Kennedy, 91.4%.[98] With respect to appointments to the inferior courts, the practice of Senatorial courtesy prevails.

It is unfortunate that partisan considerations enter into the selection of judges who are supposed to discharge their judicial responsibilities in a strictly non-partisan manner. Most of them probably do. The fact that party affiliation plays so important a part in the selection of judges does not warrant the conclusion that competence is disregarded. Presidents receive advice from a variety of sources. Among them are members of Congress; the Senate Judiciary Committee; the Department of Justice; national, state, and local bar associations; and party organizations (national, state, and local). The recommendations of at least some of these advisers, perhaps of all of them, are based on considerations of merit. Nevertheless, party affiliation is obviously a determining factor.

Other factors taken into account by Presidents in making appointments to the bench, including the Supreme Court, are personal friendship, geographical and sectional considerations, previous judicial experience, age, religious and ethnic affiliations, and the social, economic, and political views of a prospective appointee.

---

[98] *Congress and the Nation, 1945–1964* (Washington, D. C., Congressional Quarterly Service, 1965), pp. 1443–1444.

Tenure

In regard to tenure, the Constitution stipulates that judges shall hold office during good behavior. This provision has been construed as meaning "for life." It does not apply to the personnel of "legislative courts."

The only way of removing judges with life tenure is through impeachment by the House of Representatives followed by trial and conviction by the Senate, but only on charges of treason, bribery, high crimes, and misdemeanors. These provisions concerning tenure are designed to promote judicial independence of the executive and legislative branches in the settlement of legal controversies.

Compensation

An additional constitutional provision contributing to judicial independence prohibits decreases in the compensation of Article III judges during their continuance in office. Increases are permissible. Substantial salaries are now provided for judges of the national courts. As of 1972, the salaries of judges were as follows:

Supreme Court—Chief Justice, $62,500; Associate Judges, $60,000.

Courts of Appeals—$42,500 for every member

Court of Customs and Patent Appeals—$42,500

Customs Court—$40,000

Court of Claims—$42,500

District Courts—$40,000

Tax Court—$40,000

Territorial Courts—$40,000

Full salary is payable for life in the case of judges serving on "constitutional courts." Judges of the Supreme Court, Courts of Appeals, and District Courts may retire on full salary at age sixty-five after fifteen years of continuous service, or at seventy after ten successive years of service. They also receive full salary if retirement occurs because of disability after serving continuously for ten years. For fewer than ten years, half salary is paid for retirement caused by disability.

Judicial Review

One of the most important functions of the national judiciary is final determination of the meaning of the Constitution of the United States. This function, known as "judicial review," is the result of inference from, rather than express provision of, the Constitution.

Judicial review is definable as the power of the courts to pass judgment on the constitutionality of governmental action of any kind, be it classifiable as legislative, executive, administrative, or judicial. It extends to acts of both the national government and the states. This power is exercised only when the issue of constitutionality is raised in a case properly brought before the courts and only if the case cannot be disposed of without a ruling on whatever constitutional questions are involved.

The lower as well as the higher courts wield this power, but the Supreme Court possesses the authority of the final word concerning proper interpretation of the national constitution. Cases in which constitutional questions are necessarily ruled upon by the lower courts eventually find their way to the Supreme Court.

Marbury v. Madison

In the famous case of *Marbury v. Madison*,[99] decided in 1803, Chief Justice Marshall, speaking for the Court, took the position that it had the power to pass judgment on the constitutionality of an act of Congress. His line of reasoning represented an attempt to show that this power was inferable from the Constitution. This early assertion of authority on the part of the judicial branch proved successful and judicial review has become an accepted feature of the governmental system of the United States. In the *Marbury* case the Court held that Congress lacked authority to increase the original jurisdiction of the Supreme Court as defined in Article III. Congress had done so in the Judiciary Act of 1789.

(1) MARSHALL'S REASONING   Marshall advanced various arguments in support of judicial review. He contended that the purpose of a written constitution would be defeated if the legislative branch could ignore its explicit provisions; that the nature of the judicial function is to determine what the law is and that in so doing a court must consider constitutional as well as statutory provisions; that judges are required to take an oath to support the constitution; that the jurisdiction of the national judiciary extends to cases *arising under the constitution;* and that the sixth Article stipulates that this Constitution and the laws *in pursuance thereof* are the supreme law of the land. For all of these reasons Marshall concluded that it was the Court's duty to refuse to enforce any act of Congress in conflict with constitutional provisions.

[99] 1 Cranch 137.

(2) CRITICISM OF MARSHALL'S REASONING The basic criticism of Marshall's reasoning is that he was guilty of begging the question. He failed to show why the judicial rather than either the legislative or executive branches should be the final interpreter of the Constitution. Each of his arguments could be used to justify final interpretation by the President or by Congress.

For example, the President, being charged with the duty of executing the laws, must decide what the law is; he, like all other officers of the national government and the states, is bound by oath or affirmation to support the Constitution; and the law enforcement responsibilities of the President pertain to the Constitution and laws *in pursuance* thereof. Marshall's contention that a constitution is binding on the governmental organs it creates is unquestionably sound, but it fails to prove that one branch of the government rather than another is to have the power of final interpretation.

Criticisms of the foregoing type were included in the dissenting opinion of Justice Gibson of the Pennsylvania Supreme Court in *Eakin v. Raub*.[100] The judge made other points, viz., that the business of the courts is to interpret the law and not to scan the authority of the legislature; that the responsibility of determining what the law is merely justifies inquiry into the form of enactment, i.e., to ascertain whether the law was passed in accordance with the procedure prescribed by the Constitution; and that the several branches of the government were placed on an equal footing by the Constitution's framers, no one of them to enjoy superiority with respect to the others. Gibson maintained that the oath of office was designed as a test of the political

---

[100] 12 Sergeant and Rawle 330 (1825).

principles of the person taking it and also as a safeguard against usurpation by one branch of the powers of the others. He also made the point that correction of abuses in legislation is ultimately the responsibility of the people.

The Marshall point of view has prevailed and it is probably true that the framers of the Constitution anticipated and favored judicial review. Some of them undoubtedly did. For instance, Alexander Hamilton stated the case for judicial review in the *Federalist Papers*[101] in such a way as to create the impression that Chief Justice Marshall's line of reasoning was largely borrowed from Hamilton. Whatever the merits of the constitutional arguments, judicial review seems likely to remain an important factor in the governmental process of the United States. Consideration will be given subsequently to the claimed advantages and disadvantages of judicial supremacy in the matter of constitutional interpretation.

Expansion of Judicial Review

Judicial review has expanded greatly since the *Marbury* decision. In that case the Supreme Court protected itself against part of an act of Congress which extended the Court's original jurisdiction beyond that explicitly set forth in Article III.

Fifty-four years later, a second national law was declared unconstitutional, viz., the Missouri Compromise Act of 1820.[102] In this instance the Court substituted its judgment for that of Congress with respect to the scope of Congress's

[101] No. 78.
[102] *Dred Scott v. Sanford*, 19 Howard 393 (1857).

power to "make all needful rules and regulations respecting the territory . . . belonging to the United States." Since that time approximately eighty acts of Congress have met the same fate on one ground or another—a small proportion of the total of national laws enacted by the legislative branch.

A significant expansion of judicial power occurred after the Civil War period. The Supreme Court did more than protect itself against interference by Congress or pass judgment on whether Congress had been granted a particular power. It began to decide on the constitutionality of *methods* and *motives*. Neither Congress nor the states, in exercising their conceded powers, may validly resort to "arbitrary methods" or seek to achieve "wrongful purposes." [103]

Many state laws have been declared unconstitutional by the Supreme Court, beginning with the case of *Fletcher v. Peck*[104] in 1810 and increasing rapidly in number after adoption of the Fourteenth Amendment which prohibits the states from abridging the privileges or immunities of United States citizens, depriving persons of life, liberty, or property without due process of law, and denying to any person the equal protection of the laws. As previously pointed out, the due process and equal protection guarantees have been construed as prohibiting unreasonable, arbitrary, capricious, and oppressive governmental action.[105]

---

[103] The material incorporated in this and the two preceding paragraphs with respect to the expansion of judicial review was derived from R. E. Cushman, "The Role of the Supreme Court in a Democratic Nation," Lecture at the University of Illinois, March, 1938. This lecture is included in H. M. Bishop & S. Hendel, *Basic Issues of American Democracy* (New York, Appleton-Century-Crofts, Inc., 1948) pp. 171–181.

[104] 6 Cranch 87.

[105] *Supra*, Chapter 3, pp. 100–108.

The issue of constitutionality is by no means confined to laws enacted by Congress, state legislatures, and city councils. It also pertains to action by executive, administrative, and judicial authorities. In a significant number of cases, the Supreme Court has passed judgment on the constitutional validity of acts of governmental agencies of this type. For example, convictions of persons accused of crime have been set aside because of an unfair trial or on the ground that persons arrested by police officials have been denied immediate access to legal counsel.

Curbing Judicial Review

On various occasions judicial interpretations of the Constitution have been severely criticized. Recent examples are the Supreme Court decisions barring segregation in the public schools and requiring both houses of a state legislature to be apportioned on a population basis. Some critics have asserted that the power of judicial review should be curbed. How?

In the first place, the Constitution may be amended to restrict or even to abolish this power of the courts. The amending process is difficult and requires far greater dissatisfaction with the functioning of the courts than has developed up to the present time.

A second means of limitation is by legislative restriction of the jurisdiction of the courts. Congress possesses authority to prescribe the jurisdiction of such inferior courts as it creates and to place limitations on the appellate jurisdiction of the Supreme Court. It also may prohibit state courts from deciding cases in which actions of the national government and the states are claimed to be in conflict with the

Constitution of the United States. This way of curbing the power of judicial review seems impracticable. It probably would give rise to a variety of troublesome complications and prove to be an unsatisfactory solution of the problem of checking the judicial settlement of particular constitutional controversies.

The establishment of limitations on the power of judicial review seems unlikely. However, adverse judicial interpretations of the Constitution may be overruled by the adoption of constitutional amendments. Such action has been taken several times. The Eleventh Amendment was adopted because of dissatisfaction with the Supreme Court's decision in *Chisolm v. Georgia*, the Thirteenth and Fourteenth Amendments superseded rulings of the Court in *Dred Scott v. Sanford* (on the slavery and citizenship issues), and the Sixteenth was added in 1913 after the Court held that an income tax had to be apportioned among the states according to population.[106]

Packing the Court

"Packing" the Supreme Court is a strategy which may be resorted to for the purpose of securing a desired interpretation of the Constitution. By packing is meant appointing judges who are likely to construe constitutional provisions in line with the point of view of the appointing authority. Many Presidents and the Senate have taken into consideration the apparent views of possible appointees concerning political, social, and economic issues or have at least endeavored to ascertain the general attitude, whether liberal

[106] *Pollock v. Farmers' Loan and Trust Co.*, 158 U. S. 601 (1895).

or conservative, of persons whose selection is being contemplated. There is no assurance that the desired results will be obtained and various Presidents have been disappointed with the behavior of the judges they have placed on the bench. Since federal judges serve for life, Presidents have the opportunity to exercise the appointing power only when vacancies occur during their administrations. This fact led to President's Roosevelt's court proposal plan of 1937.

The Roosevelt Plan

The Supreme Court, dominated by "old men" selected by Roosevelt's predecessors, had ruled that several major New Deal policies were unconstitutional. A disturbed Roosevelt recommended that Congress adopt the following plan: authorize the appointment of an additional federal judge for every judge, 70 years old or over and on the bench ten or more years, who failed to retire, subject to the limitation in the case of the Supreme Court that its size could not exceed fifteen. At the time of this recommendation six judges of the highest court were over 70. Consequently, Roosevelt would have been able to appoint six additional members of the Court, if the proposed law had been passed and if none of the six justices 70 or over had voluntarily retired.

The proposal was severely criticized both inside and outside of Congress as a "court-packing" measure. It met with defeat. Under the Constitution Congress possesses authority to fix the size of the Supreme Court and the President has the right to recommend legislation pertaining to the judicial branch, including the highest court. Opponents conceded the legal validity of the proposed plan but maintained that it involved violation of the "spirit" of the Constitution and questioned its advisability on various grounds.

Judicial Self-Restraint

Unless judicial review is abolished or severely restricted by law, the only effective curb on the exercise of this power is judicial self-restraint. What this means is that the Court refrains from substituting its judgment for that of the political branches of the government in all instances in which there is reasonable ground for sustaining the interpretations that these branches have placed on the Constitution. Throughout its history numerous members of the Court have subscribed to this point of view.

Judicial Activism

Many justices have favored an aggressive attitude in the sense that the Court should take advantage of every opportunity to interpret the Constitution so as to achieve results in line with the social, economic, and political thinking of its members. The latter type of judges, referred to as "judicial activists," have controlled the Court from time to time. When the activists are dominant, judicial self-restraint approaches the vanishing point.

The activists, of course, claim that they are guided solely by the Constitution. This pretense is easy to maintain when the constitutional provisions being interpreted are broad and indefinite in character, as in the case of the "due process" stipulations of the Fifth and Fourteenth Amendments and the "equal protection" clause of the Fourteenth. Recently, for example, the Court held that "equal protection" requires both houses of a state legislature to be apportioned on a numbers basis. Up to now, it has approved apportionment according to either population or the number of registered voters.

Claimed Advantages and Disadvantages of Judicial Review

Although judicial review seems destined to survive indefinitely in the United States, its advisability is open to question. As with many other features of a governmental system, much can be said both for and against it. In the paragraphs which follow, claimed advantages and disadvantages will be summarized without reference to the constitutional basis of this power. The constitutional aspect was considered in discussing the *Marbury v. Madison* and *Eakin v. Raub* cases.

(1) CLAIMED ADVANTAGES (a) A standard argument in favor of judicial review is that judges are particularly well-qualified by reason of their legal knowledge and experience to settle controversies concerning the meaning of constitutional provisions. The interpretation of a documentary constitution is in line with the normal judicial function of construing statutes, executive rules and regulations, and various legal instruments.

(b) Another claimed merit of judicial review is that most constitutional restrictions are directed against legislative and executive authorities, rather than the judiciary. Unenforceable restraints are largely, if not entirely, valueless, and consequently an external check on these most potent of all governmental agencies is clearly needed. Of all branches of the government, the judicial is the weakest. The hazards involved in making it the final interpreter of the Constitution are minor compared with the risks associated with adherence to the principle of either legislative or executive supremacy.

(c) A related contention is that courts are more likely than legislatures to be unbiased in the consideration of constitutional issues. A legislative body such as Congress is principally a policy-determining agency and therefore inclined toward constitutional interpretations that broaden its powers, whereas courts play a passive role in the governmental process. Political considerations are uppermost in the minds of legislators because of the nature of their functions and the manner of their selection. Judges are far less likely to be responsive to partisan pressures and considerations.

Essentially the same line of reasoning is followed in opposition to final interpretation of the Constitution by the chief executive.

(d) Judicial review is also favored on the ground that the rights of individuals and of minority groups, as guaranteed by constitutional stipulations, lose their significance if a judicial remedy against infringement by the government is unavailable. Unless courts have the right to declare legislative and executive acts unconstitutional, the will of legislative majorities or of administrative officials necessarily prevails. Petitions to the legislature or to the executive for redress of grievances are inadequate substitutes for the immediate relief which courts may provide if they possess the power to refuse enforcement of governmental acts on grounds of unconstitutionality. Nor is the ultimate political remedy of bringing about a change in the governing personnel by resort to the ballot box an effective means of protecting particular individuals against unconstitutional government action in specific situations.

(e) Still another point emphasized by advocates of judicial review is that it promotes the development of widespread popular and official support for constitutional government and for a regime of law rather than of men. Cases involving constitutional issues attract public attention and the rulings of courts together with their reasoned opinions remind both the people and government officials of the fundamental principles and ideals on which the governmental institutions of the country are based.

An authoritative and impartial settlement of constitutional controversies by the courts is a deterrent to the growth of arbitrary government and to the loss of respect for the documentary constitution. The presence of a restraining power in the hands of the judicial branch tends to stabilize and to rationalize the judgment of the policy-determining and administrative officials of the government.

(2) CLAIMED DISADVANTAGES (a) A major objection to judicial review is that the settlement of constitutional disputes involves much more than the solution of a strictly legal problem. Some disputes are essentially of this type, but many, particularly the most important, are actually controversies in which questions of policy are at stake. Disputes concerning the meaning of a constitution usually arise only because two or more interpretations are justifiable. The making of a choice among several plausible interpretations amounts to the determination of basic policy in regard to questions of governmental organization, authority, and procedure.

Every time one interpretation rather than another is endorsed, or when a particular provision is applied to a given situation in one way, even though it could, with equally good reason, have been given a different application, the Court is performing a function analogous to that of a continuous constitutional convention. Thus racial segregation was upheld as consistent with the equal protection clause in 1896 but condemned as in conflict with the same clause in 1954. Again, minimum wage legislation was declared unconstitutional in 1923 on the ground of a denial of liberty without due process of law, whereas it was found consistent with the requirements of due process in 1937. The equal protection clause of the Fourteenth Amendment dates back to the ratification of this amendment in 1868. Nearly a century later, in 1964, the Supreme Court held that "equal protection" requires both houses of a state legislature to be population-based.

(b) The foregoing illustrations, among others that could be presented, account for the contention of critics of judicial review that the Constitution changes at the pleasure of a majority of the Supreme Court justices. The latter's opinions, of course, are so worded as to create the impression that their rulings are a necessary consequence of the *manifest* meaning of the Constitution. Dissenters from majority opinions occasionally call attention to what is going on and some judges of the Court have frankly asserted that the Constitution is what the judges say it is and that the Supreme Court is the Constitution.

Most opponents of judicial review, stressing the realities of what the Court is doing, contend that only a representative body, such as the legislature, should be entrusted with the responsibility of making basic policy-determining decisions. Inasmuch as the Constitution is supposed to be an

expression of the will of the people, ultimate determination
of its meaning should rest with Congress. Courts are not
intended to be representative of different interest-groups or
of the people in general. Nor is the typical training and
outlook of judges of such a nature as to fit them for the
task of deciding questions of policy and, in effect, re-
writing the Constitution.

(c) Another objection to judicial review stresses the political irresponsibility of judges whose tenure of office is for
life. Their constitutional interpretations have tremendously
important consequences, but there is no effective way of
holding them to account for decisions of questionable merit.
Judges serving for life constitute a ruling oligarchy—provided they have the final say concerning the meaning of
the Constitution and persistently exercise this power for
the purpose of imposing their views in regard to desirable
policies on other agencies of the government. Judicial vetoes of legislative acts on questionable constitutional grounds
are a major cause of opposition to judicial review.

(d) Judicial review, as it operates in the United States,
also is opposed as an obstacle to effective government. It
gives rise to an excessive amount of litigation and causes
uncertainty concerning what the law is. These undesirable
consequences develop because *any person* may challenge the
constitutionality of *any governmental act* before *any court*
and also because court rulings on constitutional issues are
obtainable only *after* the legislature enacts laws and *after*
their enforcement is undertaken by the administrative
branch. Early in its history the Supreme Court refused to
render advisory opinions at the request of other branches of
the government.

The fact that legislation and administration precede litigation has this result: neither the government nor the public knows whether established policies are constitutional or unconstitutional until such time as the constitutionality of a legislative act is questioned in a case brought before the courts and finally disposed of by the tribunal of last resort. Several years, perhaps many, may elapse before the judicial branch is called upon to decide the constitutional issue.[107] Even if a law is challenged shortly after its enactment, it takes a while for a case to reach the Supreme Court and additional time passes before the Court hands down its decision. Guessing what the Court's edict will be has become a feature of the governmental process in the United States.

(e) Opponents of judicial review usually assert that the restraints of public opinion and availability of the political remedy of refusing to re-elect members of the legislature are adequate safeguards against legislative disregard of constitutional limitations. The suspensive veto of the President may also be used if he believes that Congress has taken action of dubious constitutionality. Moreover, persons who dislike judicial review commonly maintain that legislators are as likely as judges to be conscientious about conformity to constitutional provisions. In support of these contentions, attention is directed to the experiences of various countries in which courts are under obligation to enforce all acts of the national legislature.

Improving Judicial Review

Some of the criticisms of judicial review could be met without eliminating this power of the courts. The giving

---

[107] An extreme example is the action of the Supreme Court with respect to the Missouri Compromise of 1820. That act of Congress was declared unconstitutional in 1857.

of advisory opinions would prove helpful. So would restrictions on the nature of the parties allowed to seek a judicial ruling with respect to certain kinds of controversy. For example, the privilege of instituting proceedings for the settlement of disputes concerning their respective powers could be confined to the national government and the states; also, resort to the courts for the purpose of preventing one branch of the government from infringing on the powers of the others could be made an exclusive right of the branches immediately concerned.

The settlement of some constitutional controversies could be expedited by requiring the Supreme Court to pass judgment on the constitutionality of acts of Congress within a specified period of time following their enactment and prior to their administration by the executive branch. Another means of curtailing delay would be to expand the original jurisdiction of the Supreme Court to include cases involving designated types of constitutional controversy. Most of these remedies, certainly the last one, would necessitate a constitutional amendment. None of them is likely to be adopted.

Need for an Ultimate Center of Legal Reference

Constitutional controversies are inevitable under a constitution like that of the United States which divides powers between the national government and the states, sets up a government based on the doctrines of separation of powers and checks and balances, and places numerous substantive and procedural restraints, many of them broadly worded, on governmental authorities.

Some method of settling these controversies is essential. That method, whether judicial review or some alternative, must provide for a single ultimate center of legal reference to insure that the meaning of the Constitution is the same for all governmental authorities throughout the country. In spite of various shortcomings, judicial review, as it has developed in the United States, has worked well enough for nearly two centuries to survive the attacks directed against it from time to time.

Judicial Lawmaking

Even if judicial review were abandoned, courts would continue to engage in lawmaking in the process of construing the provisions of statutes and administrative rules and regulations. An exercise of discretion occurs in choosing one of several plausible interpretations and the choice made determines the law for the particular case and for others as well if the practice of *stare decisis* be followed, i.e., if subsequent cases of like character are decided in conformity with the previous most authoritative decision. Of course, objectionable court interpretations of statutory provisions can be rectified by appropriate legislative action, whereas resort to a constitutional amendment is necessary in the case of a judicial ruling concerning the meaning of the Constitution.

State Constitutions

CHAPTER ☆ TEN

National Constitutional Restrictions on State Governmental Organization.

Requirements of a Satisfactory Constitution

Comparison of First State Constitutions with Those of Today

    Reasons for Increased Length and Incorporation of Non-Fundamental Material

    The Model State Constitution

    Chief Defects of Most State Constitutions

Amendment and Revision of State Constitutions

    The Legislative Proposal Plan

    Amendment by Initiative Petition

    Constitutional Conventions

    Revisory Commissions in Combination with Legislative Proposal

Obstacles to Constitutional Revision

☆ ☆ ☆ ☆ ☆ ☆ ☆ ☆ ☆ ☆ ☆ ☆

The major political subdivisions of the United States are the fifty states. Thirty-seven of them were admitted to the Union at various times after the Constitution became effective in 1789, with Alaska and Hawaii the most recent additions to the family of states comprising the United States. Although the states differ greatly in many respects, such as population, area, climate, and resources, all of them are legally equal in terms of their powers under the national constitution.[108]

Broadly speaking, the states may adopt whatever policies are deemed desirable for promotion of the safety, health, morals, convenience, and general welfare of their inhabitants, subject to the restrictive provisions of the national constitution and the supremacy of the national government within the sphere of its delegated powers. As for the authority of a state's government, that depends on the provisions of the state constitution.

The *residual* (unenumerated) powers of the states extend to many matters. Among them are criminal law; civil rights; control over the acquisition, use, and disposition of property; regulation of agriculture, manufacturing, mining, and intrastate commerce; establishment of standards for the practice of professions, e.g., law, medicine, dentistry, and engineering; labor-management relations; marriage and divorce; social welfare; public health; education; conservation of natural resources; construction of public works, including highways; local government; and traffic regulation.

The national government's powers enable it to establish binding policies pertaining to some of the subjects mentioned in the preceding paragraph, or to influence the exercise of discretionary power by the states, e.g., through conditional grants-in-aid. However, its legislative authority is limited as compared to that of the states and the latter enjoy exclusive

---

[108] *Supra*, Chapter 2. The second chapter of this text deals with the respective powers of the national government and the states.

jurisdiction in various spheres of human relations, such as the inheritance of property, local government, the maintenance of a public school system, and marriage and divorce.

As indicated by the above long but incomplete list of matters subject to the jurisdiction of the states, these major political subdivisions play an important role in the governmental process, both as regulators of individual and group behavior and as furnishers of many beneficial services. Accordingly, each state ought to provide itself with a satisfactory governmental organization and pursue sound practices in lawmaking and administration.

National Constitutional Restrictions on State Governmental Organization

Subject to a few restrictions in the Constitution of the United States, the states are free to organize themselves as they please by adopting constitutions which serve as the foundations of their governmental systems.

An important explicit restriction is the requirement of a republican form of government (Article IV). In addition, amendments to the Constitution prohibit denial of the right of United States citizens to vote because of race, color, previous servitude, sex, or age (eighteen or over).[109]

An implied limitation, asserted by the Supreme Court in 1966, is the banning of voting qualifications based on the affluence of the individual or on the payment of any fee. Two years earlier the Court concluded that the equal protection clause of the Fourteenth Amendment requires the apportionment of members of state legislatures on a popula-

---

[109] See *Supra,* Chapter 4. The Twenty-Fourth Amendment applies only to the election of national officials.

tion basis.[110] Whether the Court will discover other un-suspected organizational restraints remains to be seen.

In the following pages attention will be directed to the quality of state constitutions and to the methods of amend-ing or revising them. Have the states done well or poorly in drafting their constitutions?

Requirements of a Satisfactory Constitution

An appraisal of constitutions involves the establishment of standards with respect to which a particular constitution may be evaluated. Most political scientists agree that a con-stitution, to be given a rating of "satisfactory," ought to meet most of the following requirements.

Content Confined to Fundamentals

The contents of a constitution should be confined to establishment of the fundamental features of a body politic's governmental system. Generally speaking, constitutions should not be used for the purpose of prescribing policies that are most appropriately reserved for legislative deter-mination. If, for example, a constitution contains detailed provisions concerning minimum wages and maximum work-ing hours, prescribes traffic regulations pertaining to travel on highways, or specifies the number of school days per year, changes in these policies require a constitutional amendment. Policies of this type, when incorporated in the constitution, limit the authority of the legislature and pre-

[110] See *Infra,* Chapter 11, for a discussion of the case of *Reynolds v. Sims.*

clude alterations by statutory provision in the light of
changing situations and attitudes.

Elasticity

A second requirement, related to the one just mentioned,
is that a constitution should be sufficiently elastic to meet
the needs of successive generations without constant resort
to formal amendments. Adaptability to changing social and
economic conditions is largely dependent on the exclusion
of provisions that are likely to prove unsuitable after the
lapse of a comparatively short period of time, on the avoidance of excessively detailed arrangements, and on the use of
words and phrases that can be construed broadly without
being so vague as to be meaningless.

An Adequate Grant of Power

A constitution ought to endow the government it creates
with sufficient power to realize the objectives which its
framers have in mind. An adequate grant of authority is
essential to the effective functioning of any government.

Provision for Settlement of Constitutional Controversies

Still another requisite of a satisfactory constitution is
definite provision for the settlement of controversies concerning its meaning. No matter how carefully a constitution
is worded, such controversies are inevitable. The problem
of resolving disputes is soluble in different ways. Whether
one solution is preferable to others is a debatable matter, but

the desirability of making definite arrangements for the final disposition of constitutional disputes is seldom questioned.

A Suitable Mode of Amendment

A constitution should also specify the procedure by which its provisions may be altered. The formal mode of amendment or revision should be neither too easy nor too difficult. Drafting a constitution is a speculative venture. It is necessary to look ahead, to anticipate coming events, and to plan for the future as well as for the present. Unfortunately, not even the wisest and best informed persons can be certain that their handiwork will stand the tests of time and experience. For this reason and to avoid controversy, every constitution ought to make provision for needed alterations through some orderly and practicable procedure.

Comprehensiveness and Brevity

A constitution should be comprehensive in the sense of covering all basic problems of governmental organization, powers, duties, and procedures, but it should deal with these matters as briefly as possible. Unnecessarily long constitutions with complicated and excessively detailed stipulations usually give rise to many more problems than they solve.

Comparison of First State Constitutions with Those of Today

A comparison of state constitutions of the late 18th and early 19th centuries with those of the 20th century reveals

two striking differences. One is the much greater length of
the latter. The other is that most contemporary constitutions no longer meet one of the major requirements of a
satisfactory constitution, viz., that its contents be confined
to fundamental questions of governmental organization,
procedure, and authority.

With some exceptions, the first state constitutions were
shorter than the Constitution of the United States which
now consists of approximately 7,000 words. Their brevity
was due to confinement of their provisions to guarantees of
individual rights, to creation of the principal organs of state
government, and to stipulations concerning voting and
office-holding qualifications.

State constitutions became longer during the first half of
the 19th century and the lengthening trend continued after
the Civil War. More and more limitations were imposed on
legislatures, various policies were prescribed by constitutional provisions; governmental powers and procedures
were specified in greater detail; and governors became elective and were granted additional powers.

Only three of the state constitutions now in effect contain
fewer words than the national constitution. Four have more
than 7,000 but fewer than 10,000 words; twenty between
10,000 and 20,000; nineteen from 20,000 to 50,000; and four
considerably more than 50,000, viz., Louisiana 236,000,
Alabama, 80,000, and California and Oklahoma, 70,000.

Reasons for Increased Length and Incorporation of Non-Fundamental Material

Various reasons account for either or both increased
length and failure to confine the content of state constitu-

tions to basic matters. By far the most important causative factor is lack of faith in the judgment and integrity of the day-to-day agencies of government, particularly the legislature.

Other reasons, some of them attributable to the loss of confidence in legislatures, are the preference for detailed rather than general stipulations; the consequent need for piece-meal amendments; the success of special interest-groups in securing constitutional provisions in furtherance of their aims; the extension of governmental functions in response to the needs of a dynamic society and the resultant tendency of constitution-makers to pay heed to newer fields of governmental activity; the desire to forestall adverse judicial interpretations or the need to overcome particular rulings that the courts have handed down; the retention of obsolete and useless provisions; and lack of comprehension of the proper purpose of a constitution. In some states, a comparatively easy process of amendment has been a factor in the multiplication of constitutional provisions.

(1) CAUSES OF LOSS OF FAITH IN LEGISLATURES The loss of faith in state legislatures resulted from serious abuses of the extensive powers of these bodies, especially during the last half of the 19th century and the early part of the 20th. Extravagant expenditures were authorized; unwarranted indebtedness was incurred; laws were passed conferring privileges on private interests with little or no regard for the public welfare; and undue and detrimental state interference in the field of local government occurred frequently. There was evidence of bribery, grafting, and corruption on a large scale. The parties engaged in exploitation of the public were officeholders, state and local political bosses, and private individuals and groups who sought special privileges within the power of government to grant.

(2) RESORT TO UNFORTUNATE REMEDIES   Instead of reorganizing state legislatures for the purpose of improving the quality of their work, the favorite remedy was to curtail the powers of these bodies and to limit both the frequency and length of legislative sessions. The framers of constitutions often incorporated desired policies in these instruments to prevent the legislature from changing them.

If a constitution is used as a substitute for statutory prescription of particular policies, detailed provisions are necessarily included and the constitution grows in length. Detail breeds further detail as the need for alterations in temporarily satisfactory policies becomes apparent or because original stipulations require clarification. Once the practice of legislating by constitutional provision commences, various interest-groups press for inclusion of their pet projects in the constitution, with the result that the content of this document is no longer confined to basic matters of organization, procedure, and general authority. Rigidity rather than flexibility becomes a constitutional characteristic.

Although the performance records of contemporary state governments are probably superior to those of their predecessors, public lack of faith in these governments survives. A constitutional convention in Michigan drafted a new constitution in 1961–1962. In discussing the product of this convention, James K. Pollock, a delegate and political scientist of the University of Michigan, made the following comment: ". . . the Convention did succeed in eliminating much legislative detail from the Constitution, but unfortunately it did not go far enough in this direction. The trouble here was . . . that the Convention, like the whole state, continues to distrust the Michigan Legislature . . . and . . . the delegates did not want to take any chance, so they said, "Let's put it in the Constitution." [111]

Of the present state constitutions, those of Alaska, Hawaii, New Jersey, and Missouri are usually given the highest ratings from the standpoint of conformity to the requirements of a satisfactory constitution. They are comparatively brief and simple. For the most part their contents are confined to the type of material which belongs in a constitution of the documentary type.

The constitutions of the other states, in varying degrees, are in need of revision to facilitate active and dynamic government, both state and local, and to end the common practice of including specific prohibitions, mandates, or prescriptions in a constitution for the purpose of predetermining decisions with respect to policies and services.[112]

The Model State Constitution

In 1921 the National Municipal League undertook the task of preparing and publishing a *Model State Constitution* designed to be "a practical help to persons interested in improving the constitutions of actual states in the union." The sixth and latest edition of this Model was published in 1963. It contains the following articles: Bill of Rights; Powers of the State; Suffrage and Elections; the Legislature; the Execu-

[111] James K. Pollock, *Making Michigan's New Constitution, 1961–62* (Ann Arbor, The George Wahr Publishing Company, 1962), p. 83.
[112] See J. P. Wheeler, ed., *Salient Issues of Constitutional Revision* (New York, National Municipal League, 1961), pp. 165–172.

tive; the Judiciary; Finance; Local Government; Public Education; Civil Service; Intergovernmental Relations; and Constitutional Revision.

The longest articles are those dealing with the legislature, the executive, the judiciary, and local government. Provisions concerning finance, education, civil service, and intergovernmental relations are brief and limited to the stipulation of a few fundamental principles of policy and procedure. For instance, the article pertaining to education consists of only forty-four words and merely directs the legislature to provide for the maintenance and support of a system of free public schools and to establish such other public educational institutions as may be desirable. In regard to finance, to cite another example, the *Model Constitution's* provisions (slightly over 200 words) are confined to matters of procedure, such as the requirement that no debt shall be contracted unless authorized by law for specified projects or objects; that the budget estimate shall be prepared by the governor for submission to the legislature at a time fixed by law; and that no money shall be withdrawn from the treasury, or any obligation for the payment of money incurred, except as authorized by law.

Unlike the constitutions of many of the states, this Model *does not* specify that the proceeds of certain taxes may be used only for designated purposes, e.g., gasoline taxes for highway construction and maintenance; *does not* place limitations on tax rates and indebtedness; *does not* prohibit borrowing for specified purposes, such as capital improvements, or require a referendum as a condition for the incurrence of debt.

For the purpose of comparison, consideration will be given to the "educational" provisions of the new Michigan constitution and to the "taxation and finance" article of the constitution of Pennsylvania as adopted in 1874 and subsequently amended.

The Michigan constitution's article on education contains approximately 900 words. It directs the legislature to maintain and support a system of free public elementary and secondary schools; to foster and support institutions, programs, and services for the care, treatment, education, or rehabilitation of those inhabitants who are physically, mentally, or otherwise seriously handicapped; and to provide by law for the establishment and support of public libraries. All fines assessed and collected in the several counties, townships, and cities for any breach of the penal laws shall be applied *exclusively* to the support of public libraries provided for by law. In addition to such specific and wordy stipulations as the foregoing, the article deals in considerable detail with the organization and functions of the state board of education, the superintendent of public instruction, and the controlling boards of the state's universities and colleges, including public community and junior colleges. Obviously, if experience indicates the desirability of changing these arrangements, a constitutional amendment will be necessary. Alteration by statutes is precluded.

Pennsylvania's constitution (1968) includes extensive provisions, approximately 3,000 words, concerning taxation and finance. It stipulates that all taxes shall be uniform, upon the same class of subjects, within the territorial limits of the authority levying the tax, and shall be levied and collected under general laws. The legislature is authorized to grant various tax exemptions and also to establish special tax provisions of designated types. Two sections pertain to the taxation of public utilities and corporations. The proceeds from gasoline and other motor fuel excise taxes, motor vehicle registration fees and license taxes, operator's license fees, and other excise taxes imposed on products used in motor transportation may be spent *solely* for the construction and maintenance of public highways, bridges, and air navigation facilities and for the promotion of safety on these facilities.

In addition to provisions concerning budgeting, appropriations, and auditing, the constitution deals with the subject of state and local indebtedness. Certain purposes for which debt may be incurred without limit are specified; subject to *approval by majority popular vote*, unlimited debt is also permitted for purposes specifically enumerated in laws authorizing indebtedness; and indebtedness for capital projects itemized in a capital budget may be incurred *without voter approval*, if such debt will not result in an outstanding net debt, with stated exceptions, exceeding 175% of the average of annual tax revenues over a period of five years. Among other aspects of indebtedness covered by the constitution are the issuance of tax anticipation notes, the permissible debt of local governments, and the incurrence of indebtedness by Philadelphia.

Pennsylvania's constitutional provisions with respect to taxation and finance, even as revised in 1968, afford a good example of the sort of excessively detailed material that ought to be excluded from a constitution. Like the citizens of many other states, Pennsylvanians have been reluctant to endow the state government with sufficient discretionary power to deal properly with many of the problems confronting the commonwealth. Their policy has been to tie the hands of state authorities and to loosen these bonds only on occasions when the need for doing so has become urgent.

Chief Defects of Most State Constitutions

Judged by the requirements of a satisfactory constitution as summarized at the beginning of this chapter, most of the state constitutions have serious shortcomings. Their chief defects are failure to confine their contents to fundamentals, undue rigidity because of the inclusion of highly detailed stipulations concerning matters that ought to be dealt with by statutory provision, far too many restrictions on the authority of the day-to-day agencies of state government, and, as a consequence of the defects mentioned, excessive length.

All of the state constitutions meet the requirement that a procedure for amendment and/or revision be provided, but in some cases the amending process is too difficult and in others too easy. As for definiteness in regard to the settlement of constitutional controversies, the universally accepted arrangement, even though not specified, is final interpretation by the judicial branch.

Amendment and Revision of State Constitutions

The states have been active in substituting new constitutions for old ones, especially during the period from 1870 to 1910, and in resorting to the process of piece-meal amendment. According to the *Book of the States, 1966–1967,* 134 constitutions have been adopted and 3,909 amendments, of a reported total of 6,248 proposals, ratified.

Twenty-two states have had but one constitution, whereas twenty-eight have adopted two or more. The leaders in this respect are Louisiana with 10, Georgia 8, Alabama, New

York, and South Carolina 6, and Arkansas, Florida, Texas, and Virginia 5.

Forty-one of the states are operating under constitutions that became effective prior to 1910. Only nine have constitutions which were drafted and adopted after that year, the most recent being those of Michigan, 1964; Alaska, 1959; Hawaii, 1959; New Jersey, 1947; and Georgia and Missouri, 1945.

The modernization of state constitutions is unquestionably necessary. "Most are lengthy documents, replete with statutory materials and unnecessary and unjustified restrictions on state government, cluttered with obsolete and sometimes inconsistent statements, badly written and illogically arranged." [113] Unfortunately, the obstacles to modernization are numerous and formidable. These will be reviewed after consideration of the formal procedures for revision and/or amendment.

Modes of Amendment and Revision

Methods of amendment and revision ordinarily have two stages, viz., proposal and ratification. Fourteen states provide three different procedures for altering their constitutions; the remainder have two. The modes of alteration utilized are of three different types: (1) legislative proposal and ratification by popular vote, (2) proposal by initiative petition followed by a popular vote, and (3) proposal by a constitutional convention and submission of its proposals to the qualified voters. A few exceptions to the foregoing procedures will be noted below. The third method is the most

[113] *Ibid.*, p. xii.

suitable for drafting a new constitution or for extensive revision of an old one, whereas the first two are chiefly appropriate for making partial alterations.

The details of the processes of constitutional modification differ considerably among the several states. For instance, the legislative proposal plan is easier in some states than in others and the size of the affirmative popular vote required for ratification of proposals, whether originating with legislatures, conventions, or petitioners, varies to some extent.

The most convenient source of information concerning modes of constitutional change in all of the states is *The Book of the States*. It is published biennially by the Council of State Governments. This volume is an authoritative source of information concerning the structures, working methods, financing, and functional activities of state governments. Each issue emphasizes developments during the two years preceding publication.

The Legislative Proposal Plan

Amendment by legislative proposal in combination with ratification by popular vote as the final step is provided for in all of the states except Delaware and South Carolina. In Delaware the action of two consecutive sessions of the legislature is sufficient for the adoption of an amendment. South Carolina provides for initial action by the legislature, then a popular vote, and, if that is favorable, final approval by the legislature. These are the only states in which the legislature possesses the power of final decision with respect to constitutional changes originating with the legislative branch.

(1) PROPOSAL In most of the states, proposal by a single legislative session is sufficient, but in fourteen the action of two successive sessions is necessary. Proposal requires a favorable vote of two-thirds of the membership in each house of a bicameral legislature in nineteen states, three-fifths in seven, three-fifths in the only state with a unicameral legislature (Nebraska), and a simple majority vote in seventeen states. In the six other states, a variety of unusual arrangements are found. For example, Massachusetts requires a majority of the members of its bicameral legislature sitting in two consecutive joint sessions and New Jersey provides for alternative procedures, viz., three-fifths of all members of each house or an ordinary majority of all members of each house in two successive sessions.

(2) RATIFICATION As for the size of the popular vote required for ratification of a legislatively proposed amendment, constitutional arrangements also vary. In most of the states, a majority of those voting on a proposal is sufficient, but in a few states (six), a majority of those voting in the election at which the proposal appears on the ballot is necessary.

Several states have different arrangements: Illinois, a majority of votes cast in the election or a two-thirds majority of those voting on an amendment; Nebraska, a majority on the proposal which must constitute at least 35% of the total vote at the election; New Hampshire, a two-thirds majority of those voting on the amendment; Rhode Island, a three-fifths majority of the votes cast on an amendment; Tennessee, a majority of the total vote polled by gubernatorial candidates; Oklahoma, a majority on the amendment if submitted at a special election but otherwise a majority of the votes cast at the election; and in New Mexico, although a majority of those voting on an amendment is ordinarily sufficient, amendments dealing with specified sections on the elective franchise or education require a three-fourths vote of the electorate and a two-thirds vote in each county after proposal by a three-fourths vote of the legislature.

The stipulations concerning size of the popular vote required for ratification determine the comparative ease or difficulty of the amending process. Of the different requirements mentioned, the simplest is an ordinary majority of those voting on a proposed amendment. If a majority of those voting in a general election is necessary, a proposal may be defeated even though favored by more than half of the voters voting on the proposition. Many persons who cast ballots in a general election fail to vote on proposed constitutional changes.

Amendment by Initiative Petition

Fourteen states permit the proposal of constitutional amendments by initiative petition. A subsequent popular vote determines the fate of proposals. This method opens the door to constitutional changes despite the unwillingness of the state legislature to submit particular proposals or to call a constitutional convention.

(1) PROPOSAL The minimum number of qualified voters necessary for proposal of an amendment by initiative petition varies. Two states require signing of the petition by 15% of the votes cast at the last general election—in one case for candidates for the office of governor and in the other for the office receiving the highest number of votes. Seven states fix the percentage at 10. Four of them specify

10% of the votes cast for gubernatorial candidates, including two which require 5% in each of a designated number of counties; one, 10% of the qualified electors; one, not more than 10% of the legal voters in the last election for justices of the supreme court; and one, 10% of the total vote cast at the last general election in 75% of the counties. Two states require 8% of the vote cast for gubernatorial candidates at the last general election and one 8% of the legal voters for the position of secretary of state. In Massachusetts, 3% of the total vote for governor at the preceding biennial state election, with no more than one-fourth from any one county, is sufficient for proposal of an amendment. The support of a fixed number of voters, 20,000, is required in North Dakota.

(2) RATIFICATION In all but two of the initiative petition states, ratification of a proposed amendment requires an affirmative vote of a majority of those voting on the proposal. An additional requirement in Nebraska and Massachusetts is that the majority must constitute at least a specified percentage of the total vote at the election—35% in the former state and 30% in the latter.

Michigan and Oklahoma stipulate that a majority of those voting in the election is necessary for ratification. In Oklahoma, an ordinary majority of those voting on an amendment is sufficient if the proposal is submitted at a special election.

Constitutional Conventions

All but eleven states provide by constitutional stipulation for revision of their constitutions, or for the drafting of a new constitution, by a constitutional convention followed by a popular vote on the convention's proposals. Of the eleven states in which the existing constitution makes no mention of this mode of alteration, the legislatures of seven have been held to possess authority to provide for calling a convention. In the other four, there appears to be no established procedure with respect to this matter.

(1) CALLING A CONVENTION: PROCEDURE   The initiative in bringing about a constitutional convention rests with the legislature in most of the states. About half of these require an ordinary majority vote and the others a two-thirds vote. In one state a three-fifths vote is specified. Only Kentucky requires action by two consecutive legislative sessions.

The next step in most of the states is submission of the question of calling a convention to the voters. About three-fourths of these states require approval by a majority of those voting on the question, whereas the others provide that a majority of the total vote cast at the election is necessary. In some states, the size of the popular vote needed for holding a convention is determinable by the legislature.

To avoid giving the legislature exclusive control over the calling of a convention, mandatory submission of the question to the voters is required every seven years in one state, ten years in three, sixteen years in one, and twenty years in four. In most of these states, perhaps in all, the legislature may submit the question at other times. Some twenty states provide for the initiative in regard to state legislation and, unless prohibited by their constitutions, the question of holding a convention may be placed before the voters by resort to this procedure. Generally speaking, however, the calling of conventions depends on the willingness of state legislatures to take the initial step.

(2) COMPOSITION AND ORGANIZATION OF CONVEN-TIONS   The constitutions of a few states contain provisions concerning the composition of a constitutional convention, but ordinarily this matter rests with the discretion of the legislature. It prescribes the number of delegates, the manner of their selection, their compensation, if any, and the time and place of meeting.

Delegates are commonly chosen by popular vote from districts or by a combination of election-at-large and by districts. Whether the apportionment of delegates among districts must be in reasonably close proportion to population is a question which the Supreme Court of the United States has not had opportunity to decide. In view of its ruling that the equal protection clause of the Fourteenth Amendment requires such apportionment in the case of state legislatures, a like pronouncement with respect to constitutional conventions may some day be forthcoming.

Conventions are usually free to organize themselves and adopt their rules of procedure. The establishment of committees is a customary practice, with each committee being assigned the task of giving preliminary consideration to designated constitutional problems. Eventually, the entire convention decides on the revisions it will propose.

(3) PREPARATORY GATHERING OF INFORMATION   In recent times information pertaining to constitutional problems has been assembled in advance of the functioning of a convention. This work, sometimes of an extremely comprehensive nature, is commonly undertaken by persons skilled in carrying on research activities. Examples of agencies that gathered materials for the assistance of particular conventions are the Illinois Legislative Reference Bureau (1919), a Constitutional Convention Committee appointed by the governor of New York (1938), and a citizens' committee in conjunction with the University of Missouri (1943).

(4) RATIFICATION   Most of the states require popular ratification of convention proposals. The conventions decide on the manner of submission of their proposals to the voters. Thus the latter may be required to vote for or against a revised constitution as a whole, or may be given the opportunity to vote separately on each of a series of proposed alterations, or may be allowed to vote separately on a few controversial recommendations but be required to approve or disapprove of the remainder of the revised constitution in its entirety. The fate of a convention's proposals may depend on the manner of their submission to the voters. Preference should be given to the method most likely to meet with success, provided that the quality of the constitution finally ratified will not be impaired as a consequence of so doing.

(5) THE AUTHORITY OF CONVENTIONS   Both theory and practice vary in regard to the extent of a convention's authority to propose constitutional changes. A widely supported position is that a constitutional convention is free to make whatever proposals it desires, subject only to restrictions incorporated in the state constitution and to such limitations on the powers of the states as are imposed by the Constitution of the United States. An opposing point of view is that the agency which possesses power to call a convention may limit the scope of its authority. The legislatures of some states have pursued this policy. This issue remains unsettled in those states in which neither the existing constitution nor rulings of the courts have dealt with this problem.

Revisory Commissions in Combination with Legislative Proposal

A number of state legislatures have provided for the appointment of constitutional commissions for the purpose of undertaking the task of recommending changes in the state's constitution, either on a large scale (revision) or by partial amendment. In a few instances the governor of a state has taken the initiative in appointing such a commission. These commissions are supposed to deal objectively with the problem of constitutional change and sometimes proceed by arranging for studies conducted by persons with research experience.

The outcome of their efforts is the presentation of recommendations to the legislature, which is free to reject them or to act favorably on all or some and submit them to the voters for approval. Up to now no state constitution provides for proposal by commissions of this type and direct submission of their recommendations to the voting population. Legislative acceptance and subsequent reference to the electorate continues to be an essential feature of this procedure. An alternative to this mode of action is the calling of a constitutional convention by the legislature and transmission of the commission's proposals to the convention.

(1) ASSERTED ADVANTAGES AND DISADVANTAGES OF COMMISSIONS Commissions are smaller and less expensive than conventions and function more informally. Advocates of these commissions contend that their personnel, being appointive rather than elective, is usually superior to that of constitutional conventions; that they are not as susceptible to political pressures and to log-rolling as a convention; and that the final product of a commission's deliberations is better in quality than that of a convention.

Opponents question the authenticity of these claims. They maintain that commissions are likely to be influenced in their recommendations by estimates of the probable reaction of the legislature; that their members are subject to the same prejudices and political pressures that are brought to bear on legislatures and conventions; that commissions are inexpensive only if their efforts prove successful; and that the performance of commissions often fails to measure up to expectations.

Whatever the merits of these claims and counter-claims, one fact is indisputable, viz., that the legislature or a convention, if one is convoked, finally passes judgment on the proposals which result from the functioning of a commission. In the future, of course, some states may provide for direct presentation of commission recommendations to the electorate. Until that is done, the device of a commission is merely a preliminary step to subsequent action by either the legislature or a convention.[114]

[114] For an appraisal of New Jersey's experience with commissions prior to 1950, see B. M. Rich, "Convention or Commission?", *National Municipal Review*, Vol. XXXVII, No. 3, March 1948, pp. 133-139.

Obstacles to Constitutional Revision

The prevailing authoritative opinion in this country is that most state constitutions are defective in numerous respects and ought to be given a thorough overhauling. Why, then, has comparatively little been accomplished?

Opposition to extensive constitutional change comes from individuals and groups (economic, social, and political) who fear the alteration or abrogation of provisions that have proved of special benefit to them. As pointed out several times, state constitutions deal with many matters that ought to be subject to legislative determination. The pressure-groups which brought about the inclusion of such material oppose any movement that may result in its elimination. All groups having a vested interest in maintenance of the status quo, whatever their particular aversion to change, work together in opposition to reform in general, even though many of them have no objection to alterations unlikely to affect their special interests. Any combination of groups which for one reason or another believe a constitutional revision may work to their disadvantage constitutes a formidable opposition.

Another obstacle to large-scale revision seems to be the popular inclination to revere established ways of doing things. Institutions of long standing, e.g., bicameral legislatures, and practices looked upon with favor by successive generations, such as the popular election of various administrative officials and judges, are presumed to be more desirable than other arrangements which might be incorporated in a new constitution. The inhabitants of the United States are almost always willing to try anything new of a mechanical type, such as an automobile or an airplane, but are extremely conservative, if not reactionary, with respect to experimentation in the field of social and political relations. General revision is viewed with suspicion; piece-meal amendment is considered a safer way of proceeding.

There are legal barriers to the calling of constitutional conventions. In most of the states legislative action is a prerequisite and an extraordinary majority in each of two houses, such as support of two-thirds of the entire membership, is necessary in about half of the states. Although a favorable popular majority of those voting on the question of calling a convention is sufficient in approximately three-fourths of the states, a minority require a majority of those voting in the election at which the question is submitted.

Until recently, rural areas were over-represented in state legislatures. This fact was formerly considered an important cause of the reluctance of legislatures to provide for constitutional conventions, since rural representatives wanted to retain their political dominance. Now that the Supreme Court has ordained representation according to population, urban and suburban communities will gain control of the legislature in various states and be more adequately represented in all of them. It remains to be seen whether these reconstituted legislatures will be more favorably disposed toward the holding of constitutional conventions than their predecessors.

Other obstacles to the extensive overhauling of state constitutions are partisan politics, public apathy, social inertia, divided opinion concerning the need for change or the character of the alterations that ought to be made, lack of popular comprehension of the relationship between constitutional arrangements and the quality of state government, and a continuing distrust of state governments, which causes reluctance to transform a constitution from a bundle of restrictions on governmental action to an instrument which endows a workable governmental machinery with sufficient power to meet the needs of a dynamic society.

Obstacles of the type mentioned play into the hands of the pressure groups that derive special benefits from existing constitutional provisions. Organized minority opposition is probably the most important of all the road-blocks to the modernization of state constitutions.

State Government:
Legislative Branch

CHAPTER ☆ ELEVEN

State Legislatures
  Number of Chambers
    Bicameral versus Unicameral Bodies
  Size
  Apportionment of Legislators
    The *Reynolds* Case
    Prohibited Practices
    Gerrymandering
    Agencies Responsible for Reapportionment
  Qualifications for Legislative Service; Disqualifications
  Election Methods
    Multi-Member and Single-Member Districts
    Prevalence of Partisan Elections
  Terms of Office
  Compensation
Functioning of State Legislatures
  Frequency and Length of Sessions
  Presiding Officers
  Committee Systems
    Dual and Joint Systems
    Selection of Standing Committee Members
    Number of Standing Committees
    Role of Standing Committees

Lawmaking Procedure
     Time Limits on Introduction of Bills
     Committee Consideration
     Passage of Bills
     Governor's Veto Power
Aids to Legislative Action
     Legislative Councils
     Legislative Service Agencies
Realities of the Legislative Process
Performance Records of Legislatures
Direct Legislation
     The Initiative: Direct and Indirect
     The Petition or Protest Referendum
     Desirability of Direct Legislation

☆ ☆ ☆ ☆ ☆ ☆ ☆ ☆ ☆ ☆ ☆ ☆ ☆

The governments of the several states conform to the same general organizational pattern. Provision is made for three major branches of government, viz., the legislative, executive, and judicial, which are so organized as to be substantially independent of one another in the exercise of their constitutionally delineated powers. As in the case of the national government, this separation of powers feature is combined with a check-and-balance arrangement.

Another feature of all state *governments* is their limited powers. Every state constitution places a variety of restrictions on the governmental organs it creates, with the result that state governments necessarily function under two categories of limitations, those imposed on the states by the national constitution and those which each state has placed on its ordinary governmental agencies.

The executive and judicial branches of state governments may exercise only such powers as are granted them, either by constitutional or statutory provision, but a different principle of law applies to state legislatures. These assemblies possess all powers that are not denied them, either expressly or by implication. Distrust of state legislatures has resulted in the imposition of numerous constitutional restraints on their acknowledged plenary powers.

Although the governments of the fifty states exhibit the general features to which attention has been called, diversity in matters of detail is so extensive that there is no adequate substitute for a separate description of each state's governmental system. The best that can be done in a volume of this type is to portray in somewhat greater detail, but still in a general way, the organization and functioning of the principal instrumentalities of state government.

State Legislatures

A discussion of the structure of state legislatures requires consideration of the number of chambers, their size, the apportionment of their members among the component subdivisions of a state, qualifications for membership, the methods of selecting representatives and their terms of office, and, in the case of bicameral bodies, the relationship between the two chambers. The matter of compensation for serving in a legislature, although not a structural feature, has a bearing on the attractiveness of such service and on the quality of the personnel of legislative bodies.

The functioning of legislatures is affected by their structure, by their organization for the transaction of business, and by their formal and informal rules of procedure, including their customary patterns of behavior. Among various subjects pertinent to the way in which a legislature operates are the frequency and length of legislative sessions, the powers of presiding officers, the type of committee system, the arrangements for obtaining needed information, and the influence of political parties and pressure groups. The role of the chief executive, i.e., the governor, is a particularly important factor in the legislative process.

The Number of Chambers

With the exception of Nebraska, all of the states have bicameral legislatures. Georgia and Pennsylvania abandoned their early unicameral bodies in 1789 and 1790 respectively and Vermont replaced its unicameral legislature with a two-chambered assembly in 1836. Nearly one hundred years later, in 1934, Nebraska established the single-chambered legislature which still survives in that state. The continuing adherence of the states to bicameral legislatures is probably attributable to the habit of resisting abandonment of old and familiar political institutions, to the influence of vested interests which benefit from existing arrangements, and to the enduring lack of faith in state legislatures.

(1) ARGUMENTS IN FAVOR OF BICAMERAL BODIES
One of the traditional arguments in favor of bicameralism

is no longer pertinent to this issue at the level of state and local government in the United States. The reason is the Supreme Court's decision that the members of both houses of state legislatures must be apportioned among the constituent parts of a state in reasonably close proportion to their population. Consequently, bicameralists can no longer argue that the bicameral plan permits establishment of houses based on different principles of representation and plans of apportionment, such as equality of representation for political subdivisions in one house and representation according to population in the other.

A contention which remains relevant is that a two-chambered arrangement permits the creation of houses that differ in such respects as size, qualifications for membership, terms of office, and the methods of selecting representatives, e.g., the use of multi-member districts for one house and single-member districts for the other. Differences of this type, according to the Court, remain constitutionally permissible.

A major argument in support of bicameralism is that consideration of proposed laws by two chambers is likely to result in a better quality of legislation. Errors committed by one house probably will be detected by the other. Two separate appraisals of proposed bills also provide a double check on the expediency of specific policies and on the merits of detailed provisions of particular laws.

A related claim is that the existence of two chambers is a safeguard against impetuous and emotional action. Double consideration involves delay. The longer the lapse of time between the proposal of a law and its final approval, the less the likelihood that some policy will be adopted because of a momentary demand by an aroused public which may have been swayed by appeals to its emotions and prejudices. The existence of a second chamber provides opportunity for sober second thought.

Some persons favor a bicameral legislature as a means of protection against capricious, oppressive, and unreasonable legislation. The danger of arbitrary exercises of lawmaking authority is believed to be greatly reduced if the affirmative action of two different bodies is required for the enactment of laws. This point is made despite the fact that the combination of constitutional guarantees like due process and equal protection with judicial review constitutes a safeguard against arbitrary legislative action. However, the judicial remedy is available only after a law has been passed and its enforcement undertaken. Bicameralism, presumably, tends to prevent the passage of such laws.

Another contention in behalf of a two-chambered legislature is that it discourages attempts to obtain desired legislation through resort to corrupt practices. The general idea is that it is more difficult to corrupt two houses than one.

Finally, a bicameral legislature is sometimes advocated as a means of preventing the executive from becoming too powerful. A chief executive is less likely to gain ascendancy over a two-chambered legislature than over a unicameral body. The chances are good that one or the other of two houses will be able to offer effective resistance to such pressures as a chief executive is able to exert on members of legislative assemblies.

(2) ARGUMENTS IN FAVOR OF UNICAMERAL LEGIS-LATURES The case for a unicameral legislature is based on several considerations. Some contentions arise from the conviction that a bicameral body is an obstacle to the attainment of genuinely democratic government. Others are attributable to the belief that unicameralism is a means of achieving efficiency in the lawmaking process. A number of additional arguments have been inspired by the claims of proponents of bicameralism. Unicameralists maintain that these claims are discredited by the performance records of two-chambered state legislatures.

A bicameral legislature is considered detrimental to the proper functioning of democracy for three principal reasons. One is that the division of responsibility for lawmaking between two houses adds to the difficulty of holding representatives to account for their actions. Voters need to watch both chambers to keep track of bills and to place the blame for unsatisfactory results where it properly belongs. Under a unicameral structure responsibility is definitely located in one house and consequently its members cannot confuse the public by blaming a second chamber for legislation of poor quality or for failure to adopt policies which most people favor.

Another point made by persons who consider a two-chambered legislature less responsive to the desires of the people than a unicameral body is that the former often involves resort to conference or conciliation committees as a means of ironing out differences between the two houses on questions of policy. The evil of conference committees is that their members are very likely to submit to the demands of minority groups and alter a bill by inserting provisions that would stand little chance of acceptance by a legislative majority if submitted at earlier stages of the lawmaking process. Conference committee reports seldom are rejected by the houses because almost any sort of agreement apparently seems preferable to a deadlock. The conference committee evil has been especially noticeable in the United

States, both nationally and at the state level. One way of eliminating it is to establish a unicameral legislature.

A third objection to bicameralism from a democratic standpoint is that one house may be so constituted as to be representative of a minority rather than a majority of the people. However, since the ruling of the Supreme Court in the *Reynolds* case, this argument is no longer pertinent to state legislatures—the apportionment of members of both houses must be population-based.

Efficiency in lawmaking is claimed to be greater under the unicameral system. The needless delays inherent in the bicameral plan are eliminated; duplication of effort in conducting investigations and in the appearance of interested persons before committees is avoided; and deadlocks between rival chambers dominated by different interest-groups or political parties cannot arise. Moreover, a single legislative leadership replaces the dual leadership which almost invariably develops within a bicameral legislature.

Unicameralists assert that the performance records of bicameral state legislatures refute the claims that action by two houses produces better laws and serves as a preventive of either hasty and emotional or arbitrary legislation. The legislatures in which the people of the several states lost faith were bicameral bodies. Proponents of unicameral legislatures maintain that the quality of legislation depends primarily on the procedures observed and the techniques used in lawmaking; that undue haste in the passage of laws can be checked through appropriate procedural rules; and that there are means other than the establishment of bicameral legislatures for curtailment of the risks of arbitrary action, such as the suspensive veto of governors and constitutionally guaranteed rights in combination with judicial review.

Another argument of the sponsors of single-chambered legislatures is that the quality of legislators is improved. The greater importance of a unicameral body adds to the prestige of participation in its deliberations and has the effect of attracting better men to legislative service.

Finally, the advocates of unicameral legislatures contend that such assemblies are more effective as a deterrent to the growth of power of chief executives than two-house bodies. A strong unicameral legislature is a better counterbalance to the executive than a legislature composed of two comparatively weak chambers. The deficiencies of bicameral bodies have been a factor in the growth of executive power and prestige. As previously noted, the supporters of two-chambered assemblies disagree with this diagnosis and maintain that bicameralism is a safeguard against the development of an overpowerful executive.

(3) NEBRASKA'S EXPERIENCE   Nebraska is the only state having a unicameral legislature. The pessimistic predictions of those who opposed its creation have been proved unwarranted. Nor has this legislature lived up to all of the expectations of its sponsors. However, appraisals of its performance to date are generally favorable.

As stated by one observer, "the people of Nebraska have accepted completely the non-partisan one-house legislature. The abortive attempts to alter it by petition, the favor with which it is viewed by those who have served in it, and the lack of popular criticism of the system itself bear out this statement." "It is certain . . . that the unicameral principle is here to stay in Nebraska." [115]

[115] J. W. Rodgers, "One House for 20 Years," *National Municipal Review*, Vol. XLVI, No. 7, July 1957, pp. 341, 347.

Unicameral city councils have become an established and successful feature of urban government in the United States and single-chambered assemblies have functioned satisfactorily in the major political subdivisions of Canada (provinces) and Switzerland (cantons). The *Model State Constitution* of the National Municipal League provides for a unicameral legislature.

The risks involved in substituting unicameral for bicameral bodies at the state level seem negligible. Nevertheless, the prospect for the immediate future in the United States is that two-chambered legislatures will be retained by most of the states.

Size of State Legislatures

The size of state legislatures varies considerably from state to state. Some state constitutions specify the number of members of one or both houses; others establish maximum and minimum limits within which legislative determination of size is permissible; and still others leave the matter of size entirely to the judgment of the legislature. In all the bicameral states the upper chamber is smaller than the lower— as a rule about either one-third or one-half as large.

As a result of judicial ordainment that the apportionment of seats in state legislatures must be in approximate proportion to population, changes in size are currently occurring in various states. For many years the largest upper chamber was that of Minnesota—67 members. However, in 1972 a federal district court ordered a reduction in size to 35.[115a] Assuming that the district court order remains effec-

[115a] *National Civic Review*, Vol. 61, No. 5, May 1972, pp. 249, 250

tive, the largest upper chambers, as of 1971–1972, were those of New York (60), Illinois (59), Georgia (56), and Mississippi (52). Most of the other states had upper chambers ranging from 29 to as high as 50 members (six states).

The largest lower houses existed in New Hampshire (400), Massachusetts (240), Pennsylvania (203), and Georgia (180); the smallest in Alaska and Nevada (40), Delaware (41), and Hawaii (51). Most of the other states had from 80 to 177 lower house members.[115b]

The Apportionment of Legislators and Members of Local Bodies

Until 1964 the structure of state legislatures was thought to be a matter falling solely within the discretion of the states, subject only to the provision of Article IV of the national constitution which guarantees a republican form of government to the several states. But in the year mentioned, in *Reynolds v. Sims*,[116] the Supreme Court declared that the equal protection clause of the Fourteenth Amendment requires the apportionment of state legislators, among the component subdivisions of a state, in proportion to their populations—unless all are elected at-large. A year later, in *Burns v. Richardson*,[117] the Court approved an apportionment plan for Hawaii based on the number of registered voters rather than on population. Other apportionment bases, such as "citizen population" or "the num-

---

[115b] The figures with respect to the size of state legislatures were obtained from *The Book of the States, 1972–1973.*
[116] 377 U. S. 533
[117] 384 U. S. 73 (1965)

ber of votes cast at a designated preceding election," also may be subjected to judicial scrutiny.

As for local bodies, in *Avery v. Midland County* (1968),[117a] the Supreme Court ruled that disproportionate representation in local policy-determining bodies also conflicts with the equal protection clause of the Fourteenth Amendment. In 1970 the one-man, one-vote rule was applied to school boards in the case of *Hadley v. Junior College District of Metropolitan Kansas City*.[117b] The Court declared that when members of an elected local body performing governmental functions are chosen from separate districts, each district must be so established that, as far as is practicable, equal numbers of voters can vote for proportionately equal numbers of officials.

(1) THE REYNOLDS CASE In the Reynolds case, the Supreme Court recognized the impracticability of exactly proportionate apportionment, but explicitly stated that neither history alone, nor economic or other sorts of group interests, nor considerations of area alone are permissible factors in attempting to justify disparities from population-based representation. Chief Justice Warren's opinion, endorsed by a court majority, contains such profound statements as the following: "legislators represent people, not trees or acres"; "legislators are elected by voters, not farms, or cities, or economic interests"; and "the fact that an individual lives here or there is not a legitimate reason for overweighting or diluting the efficacy of his vote."

[117a] 390 U. S. 474
[117b] 397 U. S. 50

In a dissenting opinion, Justice Harlan conceded that people vote but asserted "it is surely equally obvious, and, in the context of elections, more meaningful to note that people are not ciphers and that legislators can represent their electors only by speaking for their interests—economic, social, political—many of which do reflect the place where the electors live." The foregoing quotations indicate the controversial character of the issues involved in solving the apportionment problem.

As matters stand, apportionment schemes must survive judicial scrutiny. After considerable delay and litigation, all the states have established population-based apportionments for both houses of their legislatures. Since judges now possess the final word concerning the apportionment of members of state legislatures, continuous litigation on one ground or another appears probable, especially so because action necessarily precedes an appeal to the courts under the system of judicial review prevailing in the United States.

(2) PROHIBITED PRACTICES The Supreme Court's edicts have closed the door to a continuance of traditional disproportionate representation. Rural areas have been over-represented and urban communities under-represented in many of the states.

In some cases this situation resulted from the failure of state legislatures to reapportion seats following each decennial census, even though required to do so by state constitutional provisions. Constitutional stipulations in various states either disregarded population differences entirely or accorded them only limited recognition. Examples were the New Jersey plan of equal representation of counties in the

upper chamber, the Vermont policy of equal representation
for towns in the lower house, and the placement of a maximum limitation on the number of representatives per designated type of political subdivision, regardless of population,
as in New York and Pennsylvania. Another kind of constitutional provision which resulted in disproportionate representation was the guarantee of at least one representative per
county or other specified political unit, no matter how sparse
its population. Sometimes a guarantee of this type was combined with a limitation on the maximum number of seats
allocable to particular component parts of a state.

All arrangements of the foregoing variety, *even if approved by the voters of a state*,[118] are no longer permissible
as a consequence of the Supreme Court's precedent-breaking
interpretation of the equal protection clause of the Fourteenth Amendment.

(3) GERRYMANDERING   Although   population-based
representation has become mandatory at the state and local
government levels, gerrymandering has not been ruled unconstitutional by the country's highest tribunal. Prevention
of the common practice of drawing election district boundaries in such a way as to work to the advantage of a
particular party still depends on the provisions of state
constitutions and laws.

A constitutional command that districts must be composed
of compact and contiguous territory, if properly enforced,
affords some degree of protection against gerrymandering,
but its effective enforcement requires specific standards
against which the items of compactness and contiguity can

---

[118] *Lucas v. Colorado General Assembly*, 377 U. S. 713 (1964).

be measured. Such standards remain to be devised. There appears to be no simple solution of this problem.

(4) AGENCIES RESPONSIBLE FOR REAPPORTION-MENT The task of reapportioning seats in state assemblies after each decennial census is a legislative responsibility in most of the states. A few have different arrangements. Examples are assignment of this function to the governor in conjunction with an advisory board in Alaska; to the governor, auditor, secretary of state, and one representative from each major political party (selected by their respective legislative leaders) in Ohio; and, as in Arkansas, to a State Board of Apportionment composed of the governor, secretary of state, and attorney general. Several states provide for reapportionment by similar non-legislative commissions *if the legislature fails to act* within a specified period of time.

(5) CHANGED COMPLEXION OF LEGISLATURES Since population-based apportionment has become compulsory, state legislatures will be controlled by the representatives of urban areas in every state in which the urban population outnumbers the rural. In other states urbanites will receive the representation to which their numbers entitle them. It will be interesting to compare the performance records of these reconstituted legislatures with those of their predecessors in which rural populations were, generally speaking, over-represented.

Qualifications for Legislative Service

The qualifications for service in state legislatures are commonplace. United States citizenship is a universal requirement, as are residence within the state and the electoral district. Usually a longer period of residence within the state than in the election district is necessary, e.g., two years in the state and sixty days in the district. Sometimes, too, residence requirements for service in the upper chamber are longer than for membership in the lower house.

Minimum age qualifications are invariably established. The age for holding a seat in the upper chamber is usually higher than for the lower house. In most cases twenty-one is sufficient for membership in the latter chamber, whereas the range for service in the former is from twenty-one to thirty. Obviously, qualifications of the type required have little or no bearing on competence for the discharge of legislative responsibilities.

Disqualifications

Disqualifications for membership in state legislatures vary with the state, but practically all states prohibit service by officials of the national government or by the executive, administrative, and judicial officers of state governments during their continuance in office. The occupants of local offices are disqualified in some states. Conviction of designated crimes is a disqualification in various states. Examples are bribery, perjury, embezzlement, and crimes of an "infamous" type.

Generally speaking, the chambers of state legislatures are judges of the qualifications of their members. However, in 1966 the Supreme Court of the United States invalidated the refusal of the lower house of the Georgia legislature to seat a legislator because of his comments on Vietnam and the draft. The Court held that the freedom of speech guarantee of the national constitution requires that legislators be given the widest latitude in expressing their views on issues of policy.[119]

Occupations of State Legislators

Analysis of the occupational groups represented in state assemblies reveals that lawyers and farmers greatly outnumber legislators assignable to such categories as bankers, contractors, manufacturers, engineers, and salesmen. Lawyers are more numerous than farmers. These two groups combined include nearly half of the membership of state legislatures. The current reapportionment of seats in legislatures on a population basis may result in a decrease in the contingent of farmers and an increase in the number of lawyers and members of miscellaneous occupational groups. Of the lawyer group, more may come from heavily populated urban and suburban areas than from the smaller county-seat municipalities.

Election Methods

The prevailing method of election is the single choice–plurality plan. A notable exception is the use of cumulative voting in the selection of members of the lower house in Illinois.

(1) MULTI-MEMBER AND SINGLE-MEMBER DISTRICTS Multi-member and single-member district plans

[119] *Bond v. Floyd*, 385 U. S. 116.

are used in the selection of both the upper and lower chambers of state legislatures. The proportion of states using either or both varies from time to time, especially since the one man-one vote ruling of the Supreme Court in 1964. Recently the situation was as follows: *lower houses*—a combination of multi- and single-member districts in thirty states, single-member districts in sixteen, multi-member only, in three;[119a] *upper houses*—both multi- and single-member districts in twenty-two states, single-member districts in twenty-seven, and multi-member only, in one.

Single-member districts must be substantially equal in population. Presumably, too, the ratio of representatives to population in the multi-member districts of a particular state will have to be approximately the same in each and also in comparison with single-member districts if a "mixed" system is used. With respect to multi-member electoral district systems the Supreme Court has declared[119b] that these are subject to challenge whenever the circumstances of a particular plan may operate to minimize or to cancel out the voting strength of racial or political elements of the voting population. What the eventual results of the above pronouncement will be is unpredictable.

(2) PREVALENCE OF PARTISAN ELECTIONS In all but two states the party affiliations of candidates for legislative seats appear on the ballot. Nominations are made by partisan direct primary in most of the states and by party

---

[119a] The unicameral legislature of Nebraska was classified as an upper rather than a lower house.

[119b] *Fortson v. Dorsey*, 379 U. S. 433 (1965); *Whitcomb v. Chaves*, 29 L Ed 2d 363 (1971)

conventions in a few. Non-partisan elections for members of the state legislature are confined to Minnesota and Nebraska.

Terms of Office

Terms of office are either two or four years. All except four of the bicameral states prescribe two-year terms for lower house members; the others provide a term of four years, as does Nebraska for its unicameral legislature.

Three-fourths of the states have four-year terms for senators and the remainder two. Staggered or overlapping terms are provided for in many of the states in which the upper chamber members are elected for four years.

Compensation (1970–71)

State practice with respect to the compensation of legislators is characterized by the usual diversity of policy in the field of state government. In about one-third of the states the basic compensation is fixed by constitutional provision; elsewhere by statute or by a special commission.

As of 1970-71, the *annual salary* distribution was as follows: $10,000 to $20,000—ten states; $5,000 to under $10,000—eleven states; under $5,000—fifteen states. Most of the remaining states provided compensation on a *per diem* basis, i.e., a specified dollar remuneration for each day of a legislative session or for a fixed number of session days. One state paid on a weekly basis and a few monthly. The range of per diem compensation was from $5 to $50.

The highest *annual salary* in 1971 was $19,200 in California; the lowest compensation was $200 per biennium in

New Hampshire. However, all of the states pay limited traveling costs, most of them make provision for additional expense allowances, and more than half have retirement plans. The extras are by no means insignificant. For example, annual salary plus expense and mileage allowances in California are reported to have totalled $48,950 per legislator for the 1970-71 two-year period.

The Functioning of State Legislatures

Of the many matters that ought to be discussed in regard to the functioning of state legislatures, only those having a major bearing on the lawmaking process will be given consideration. These include the frequency and length of legislative sessions, the role of presiding officers, the committee systems, the principal procedural steps in the enactment of laws, and the arrangements for providing legislators with needed guidance and information.

Frequency and Length of Sessions

About three-fourths of the states have constitutional provisions either permitting or not prohibiting annual regular sessions. In the others regular sessions are scheduled every other year, i.e., biennially. Since the amount of business confronting legislatures is expanding, special sessions are being called more and more frequently in various states. Eventually, the traditional biennial session in the states where it survives probably will be replaced by regular annual sessions. This movement continues to gain momentum.

All state governors are empowered to call special sessions. In one-fourth of the states the legislature may do so, but only, in about half of these states, on petition of an extraordinary majority of their members, usually two-thirds.

As for the business that may be transacted in special sessions, that is restricted, in approximately half of the states, to such matters as the governor submits for consideration. In the other states, the legislature determines the subject matter with which it will deal.

(1) LIMITATIONS ON LENGTH OF SESSIONS Limitations on the permissible length of sessions, either regular or special, are imposed in a substantial number of states. In the thirty-three states which restrict the length of regular sessions (either in terms of legislative or calendar days), about half prescribe 60 days and the range in the others is from as low as 30, 36, and 40 to as high as 120, 140, 160, and 195. The trend is toward easing or eliminating limitations.

Although no limitations on the length of special sessions are imposed in slightly more than half of the states, indefinite duration is unlikely in those states wherein the legislature may consider only such matters as the governor designates in his call for a special session. In the group of states limiting the length of special sessions, the allowable time varies from 15 to 60 days, with most of these states providing for a session of about one month. Some states resort to an indirect way of discouraging lengthy sessions, whether regular or special. They limit the number of days for which a per diem compensation will be paid.

Restrictions on the frequency and length of legislative sessions are undesirable. The workload of legislatures is increasing steadily and problems should be dealt with as they arise, instead of being laid aside until such time as sessions of limited duration are held, either annually or biennially. Annual sessions of unrestricted length not only permit prompt consideration of policy proposals but also tend to eliminate or curtail some of the most objectionable developments in the functioning of many legislatures, e.g., inadequate deliberation and the end of the session rush which accounts for the passage of numerous laws without proper scrutiny.

(2) THE MODEL CONSTITUTION PROVISIONS The *Model Constitution* of the National Municipal League provides for a legislature which "shall be a continuous body" and meet annually in regular sessions as provided by law. Special sessions are callable by the governor or, at the written request of a majority of the legislative membership, by the presiding officer of a unicameral legislature or by the presiding officers of a bicameral assembly.

Presiding Officers of State Legislatures

State legislatures have the customary line of officials and employees, such as presiding officers, secretaries and clerks (both major and minor), sergeants-at-arms, chaplains, doorkeepers, postmasters, messengers, pages, and custodians. The most important are the presiding officers.

(1) LOWER HOUSES Lower houses are presided over by a speaker who is chosen by the house membership in an election dominated either by partisan considerations or by a division between supporters of the governor and his opponents. This means that the actual selection is made by the majority party, or by a majority composed of members who subscribe to the leadership of the governor, or by a majority consisting of legislators opposed to the chief executive.

Most speakers use their customary powers as presiding officers to promote the interests of the group that placed them in office. With few exceptions, they appoint the members of standing committees (subject to various restrictions on their discretion) and also refer bills to these committees for consideration. Their freedom of choice in the assignment of bills is formally limited to the extent that house rules clearly indicate the subject matter over which particular committees have jurisdiction. Possession of the important powers of appointment and reference accounts for the fact that speakers of the lower houses of state legislatures are sometimes more powerful than the speaker of the national house of representatives.

(2) UPPER HOUSES Popularly elected lieutenant governors are the presiding officers of state senates in thirty-six of the thirty-eight bicameral states which provide for this office. In thirteen states, including two having a lieutenant governor, the presiding officers are *presidents* chosen by the upper house membership.[120] Their powers include the appointment of standing committees, except in Alaska, and the reference of bills to these committees.

Lieutenant governors, not being members of the upper chambers, are less influential than these senate-elected presidents and the speakers of lower houses. Of the thirty-six who preside only fourteen appoint members of standing

[120] Nebraska's unicameral legislature elects its presiding officer. The lieutenant governor does not serve in that capacity.

committees. In the other states of this group, committee appointments are made by the president *pro tempore* (6 states), a committee on committees (9 states), the committee on rules (2 states), and by senate election (5 states).

Twenty-nine of the presiding lieutenant governors possess the power of referring bills to committees. Of the seven states that deny them this power, each has an arrangement which differs from that of the others. The seven distinctive agencies which assign bills to committees are the rules committee, a bills committee, a committee on committees, the president *pro tempore*, the clerk, the majority leader, and the senator who introduces a bill.

Committee Systems

(1) DUAL AND JOINT SYSTEMS Most of the states have *dual committee systems*, i.e., each house of a bicameral legislature has its own set of committees. The use of joint committees in these states is exceptional.

Only three states, Connecticut, Maine, and Massachusetts, utilize a *joint committee system*. All or nearly all of their standing committees are composed of members of both houses. Bills introduced in either house are referred to the appropriate joint committee, with the result that members of both houses work together at the earliest major stage of the legislative process.

Under the dual system, the service of members of both houses on the same committee normally occurs solely for the purpose of resolving differences between bills dealing with the same subject that each house, acting separately, has passed. Conference committees are brought into operation *after* rather than before each house has taken a definite stand on a question of policy.

(a) MERITS OF A JOINT SYSTEM   Establishment of a joint committee system is a means of overcoming some of the shortcomings of bicameral legislatures. Duplication of effort is curtailed because investigations and hearings are conducted by a single committee instead of by two; responsibility is more definitely located since the same joint committee report is presented to both houses for subsequent action; and differences between the two houses are likely to be adjusted before bills are passed, with the consequence that the occasions for resorting to conference committees are considerably reduced in number.

The joint system reduces the number of committees on which legislators are required to serve. Another advantage is that this system promotes better relations and understanding between the lower and upper legislative chambers. Their members work together to a greater extent than is the case with bicameral bodies having a dual set of committees.

(2) SELECTION OF STANDING COMMITTEE MEMBERS   The legal procedures for appointing standing committee members were delineated in discussing the powers of presiding officers. However, formal arrangements in the states are affected by practices resembling those of Congress.

Thus different political parties and factions within parties are represented on these committees and the influence of political leaders on the making of assignments is substantial. Some state legislatures adhere to the seniority rule with respect to chairmanships and the allocation of members to the more important committees, but the rule is seldom observed in the states to the same extent as in Congress. Other factors affecting appointments are geographical and personal considerations, the demands of powerful pressure groups,

and the desire to avoid antagonizing influential members of
the legislature.

(3) NUMBER OF STANDING COMMITTEES A criti-
cism directed against most state legislatures has been too
many standing committees and an excessive number of committee assignments per individual member. During the last
twenty years substantial reductions have been made. In
1946 three-fourths of the states had from 31 to 70 committees in their lower houses and half of them from 31 to
70 in their upper chambers. By 1967 the range in number of
committees was from 11 to 46 in forty-one lower houses
and from 11 to 40 in forty-one senates. The maximum number was 46, the minimum, 10 or under in eight upper and
seven lower chambers.

(4) ROLE OF STANDING COMMITTEES The standing
committees of state legislatures play a significant role in the
legislative process, but in many states their recommendations
carry less weight than those of like committees in Congress.
Their most potent weapon is the power to prevent bills
from receiving consideration. Refusal to report a bill is the
equivalent of an absolute veto. Although rules of procedure
usually enable a chamber to compel a report, the requirements for such action in many states are too difficult to
overcome committee opposition.

About one-fourth of the states require committees to
report on all bills that have been referred to them. In a few
states, as a matter of practice rather than because of a
procedural rule, committees report on all previously unre-
ported bills, but without recommendation, on the final day

of a legislative session. This practice is largely a gesture of slight importance.

Lawmaking Procedure

The principal steps in the enactment of laws are the same in state legislatures as in Congress, viz., (1) the introduction of bills by individual members or committees, (2) the reference of each bill to a standing committee, (3) committee consideration, (4) the reporting of bills by committees to the houses, (5) action of the houses on such committee reports as are called up for consideration, (6) passage of a bill by both houses in identical form, (7) submission of adopted bills to the governor, and (8) subsequent consideration of bills that the governor vetoes. Since there are fifty states, the details of this general procedure vary from state to state.

(1) TIME LIMITS ON INTRODUCTION Most of the states have established time limits on the introduction of bills—largely because of limitations on the length of legislative sessions. These limits vary from the 18th, 20th, 21st, 25th, and 30th days to the 60th, 70th, and 90th days. A few states stipulate weeks rather than days, e.g., fifth week or seventh week. Only about one-fifth of the states have no time limits on the introduction of bills.

Exceptions to established limits are provided for in many states, usually by virtue of an extraordinary majority vote of the house membership. Unanimous consent is required in a few states. In a number of states exceptions are also made for committee bills, revenue and appropriation bills, or at the request of the governor.

The time limit arrangement in Massachusetts differs from that of other states in that bills must be introduced one month before the beginning of the legislative session. Later introduction is permissible only at the request of the governor or by a four-fifths vote of the members present and voting.

(2) COMMITTEE CONSIDERATION Attention has been called to the reference of bills to committees by the presiding officers of most houses but by different agencies in a few. Mention also was made of the fact that in most states committees are not compelled to report on bills referred to them.

Committee consideration of a bill may involve the holding of a hearing. In a minority of the states, a hearing, if held, must be open to the public, but in a majority, committees are free to conduct hearings on either an open or closed basis.

(3) PASSAGE OF BILLS Bills reported by committees are scheduled for subsequent consideration by being placed on a house calendar. Many of them die there. Bills taken from the calendar are discussed and subject to amendment at this time, which is the crucial stage of the legislative process. The second of the three readings of a bill, required in most states, usually occurs on this occasion, but in some states this is the third rather than the second reading. A common constitutional stipulation is that the three readings must take place on separate days.

Passage of a bill requires a majority vote of the membership in two-thirds of the states, whereas in the remainder a majority of those present and voting, or of those present, is sufficient if a quorum is in attendance. A bill passed by one house is transmitted to the other and if the latter approves it without alteration, it is submitted to the governor in all but one of the states. When the houses disagree on some of the provisions of a bill, the next step is establishment of a conference committee. Thereafter, if agreement is reached by the conferees and both houses approve of their report, the bill is sent to the governor.

(4) THE GOVERNOR'S VETO POWER The governor of every state except North Carolina possesses a veto power. This veto, being suspensive rather than absolute, may be overridden by the legislature. The vote required to override is an extraordinary majority in most states—usually two-thirds of the elected membership of each house or two-thirds of those present, but three-fifths in a few states and three-fourths in one. A majority vote of the members is sufficient in six states.

In all but eight states the governor may veto items in appropriation bills. Other measures, except in Washington and emergency measures in Oregon, must be accepted or rejected as a whole. The time permitted the governor for the exercise of his veto power, while the legislature is in session, varies from three days in nine states and five days in twenty-one to ten in twelve states, fourteen in one, and fifteen in two. Unless vetoed during this time, a bill becomes law, with or without the governor's signature.

Variations among the states exist in regard to the fate of bills when the legislature adjourns prior to expiration of the time allowed the governor during the continuance of the legislative session. In nearly three-fifths of the states a bill becomes law under these circumstances *unless vetoed* within such different time limits as five, ten, twenty, or forty-five days. Approximately one-fifth of the states provide that a bill dies *unless signed* within a specified number of days, e.g., three, ten, twenty, or thirty. Two states allow no gubernatorial action after adjournment—bills unsigned at the end of a session do not become law. In three states, bills passed in one session become law unless returned within a few days, e.g., three, after the legislature reconvenes.

The veto power is a negative control over legislation. However, the possibility or probability of its exercise may affect the content of bills during the formative stages of the lawmaking process. As will be pointed out in a subsequent discussion of the gubernatorial office, governors possess other "legislative" powers and also extra-legal ways of influencing the policy-decisions of legislatures.

Aids to Legislative Action

Legislative bodies, like most groups, function more satisfactorily if properly led and furnished with reliable information and appropriate technical services. Generally speaking, the leadership of governors has proved more effective than that which has developed within the legislatures themselves.

A dispersion of leadership is characteristic of the chambers of state legislatures. Although the leadership structure varies considerably among the states and frequently lacks clarity, the most influential members are likely to be the speakers of lower houses; spokesmen for the governor; committee chairmen; majority, minority, and factional leaders; and the more experienced and politically astute individuals among the totality of representatives and senators.

(1) LEGISLATIVE COUNCILS To promote some degree of coordinated leadership and program planning, a large majority of the states have created *legislative councils* or council-type agencies. These councils discharge such functions as ascertaining the problems requiring legislative consideration, directing research projects, submitting the results of their studies to the legislature, and recommending programs for legislative action. The councils have operated more satisfactorily in some states than in others. All are bipartisan bodies which, with a few exceptions, are composed exclusively of members of the legislature.[121] In many states both houses are granted equal representation; in others, the lower house members outnumber those of the upper chamber.

Most persons serving on legislative councils are appointed, usually by the presiding officers of the upper and lower houses,[122] but nearly all councils include a number of *ex officio* members, almost always the presiding officers and in some cases the senate president *pro tempore*, or the majority and minority floor leaders, or the chairmen of designated standing committees. In three states, the entire membership is *ex officio*, but these members, with one exception, are holders of legislative seats.

The size of legislative councils ranges from lows of 5, 7, and 8 members to highs of 110, 147, and 260. Most councils consist of from 10 to 27 members.

[121] Two states, New Hampshire and Utah, provide for the inclusion of three non-legislator citizens. One, South Carolina, makes its secretary of state an *ex officio* member.

[122] Examples of appointment other than by the presiding officers are two members, one from each house, by the governor (Arkansas); by the president *pro tempore* of the upper chamber; and by a senate committee on committees.

(2) LEGISLATIVE SERVICE AGENCIES   All states have
established one or more permanent legislative service agencies for the purpose of improving the quality of legislation.
Among them are reference libraries, research bureaus, bill
drafting specialists, legal counseling for legislators, statutory
revision commissions, and fiscal review and budget analysis
agencies that are intended to aid legislatures in passing judgment on the merits of executive budgets. Another development designed to improve the performance of legislators is
the provision of adequate staffs for standing committees and
the establishment of advisory councils for some committees.

Realities of the Legislative Process

The principal formalities of the legislative process have
been reviewed briefly. Among the realities which rules of
procedure fail to reveal are (1) the leadership and influence of the governor, (2) the leadership situation within
the legislative chambers, (3) the role of party leaders
both inside and outside the legislature, (4) the degree of
influence exerted by standing committees, their chairmen,
and conference committees, (5) the potency of pressures
exerted on legislators by interest-groups of various types,
especially those that are well-organized and persistent in
their advocacy of particular policies or opposition to others,
(6) the effect of public opinion and the desires of constituencies on the behavior of individual legislators, (7)
the fact that many bills introduced by legislators originate
with administrative agencies and pressure groups, (8) the
extent to which log rolling and bargaining determine the
outcome of the legislative process, and (9) the consequences of the end of the session rush attributable to various

factors, such as limitations on the frequency and length of legislative sessions and intentional delays for the purpose of enhancing the chances of passage of particular bills.

Performance Records of Legislatures

The performance records of most state legislatures remain sufficiently mediocre to justify the demands for reform emanating from various sources. In large measure, the shortcomings of these assemblies are due to poor organization and the fact that most of them are poorly equipped to do what is expected of them. "They do not meet often enough or long enough; they lack space, clerical staffing, professional assistance; they are poorly paid and overworked; they are prey to special interests, sometimes their own; their procedures and committee systems are outmoded; they devote inordinate time to local interests that distract them from general public policy; they sometimes cannot even get copies of bills on which they must vote. They work, in short, under a host of conditions that dampen their incentive and limit their ability to function effectively." [123] The need for reform is obvious and so are some of the remedial measures, but whether or when the necessary steps will be taken are unanswerable questions.

Direct Legislation

Direct legislation signifies lawmaking by the people, usually by means of either the initiative or the petition refer-

[123] A. Heard, ed., *State Legislatures in American Politics* (Englewood Cliffs, Prentice-Hall, Inc., 1966), pp. 1–2.

endum. Popular voting on laws also occurs under other circumstances. A legislature may voluntarily submit one of its acts to the voters for approval or disapproval, or the constitution of a state may require that certain types of measures, e.g., proposed bond issues, be voted on by the people. In neither of these instances is the filing of a petition by the voters a procedural requirement, as it is in the case of the initiative and the petition or protest referendum.

The Initiative

Twenty states, by constitutional provision, authorize the enactment of laws by resort to the initiative. This procedure enables a designated minimum number of voters to propose a law which will become effective if approved by a majority of those voting on the proposition at a subsequent election. Specified types of law are excluded from the scope of the initiative, e.g., acts authorizing expenditures or levying taxes.

(1) THE DIRECT INITIATIVE Two varieties of the initiative are distinguishable, viz., the direct and the indirect. Under the direct variety, a proposed law, after being filed with a designated state official (commonly the secretary of state), is placed on the ballot for voter approval or disapproval without any intervening steps.

(2) THE INDIRECT INITIATIVE In the case of the indirect type, the proposed measure is first transmitted to the legislature for acceptance or rejection. If enacted by the legislature without alteration, the proceedings are terminated; if rejected, the proposal is submitted to the voters and their reaction determines its fate. The direct initiative is provided for in ten states, the indirect in four, and both types are available in six.

(3) REQUIRED NUMBER OF SIGNATURES   The minimum number of signatures of qualified voters in support of an initiative petition may be stated by a definite figure, such as 10,000 in North Dakota, or in terms of a percentage of the total vote cast at a designated election, which is the policy in the other states wherein this device is available to the people. Such percentages as 3, 5, 7, 8, and 10 are provided for in one or more states.

The election usually designated is the most recent one for governor. Some states prescribe another percentage base, such as the number of qualified voters or the vote cast for candidates for the office of secretary of state.

The Petition or Protest Referendum

The petition or protest referendum is established in twenty-three states. It may be invoked against laws *which have been enacted by the state legislature*, subject to such stipulated exceptions as appropriation and revenue measures or legislation which the legislature, usually by an extraordinary majority vote, has declared to be of an emergency type.

The purpose of the petition referendum is to give voters an opportunity to veto legislative acts. This type of referendum is mandatory in the sense that the legislature is powerless to prevent a popular vote if a valid petition is filed.

(1) REQUIRED NUMBER OF SIGNATURES As in the case of the initiative, the required minimum support of qualified voters for a petition referendum varies among the states. In North Dakota, 7,000 signatures are needed, but in the other states the minimum is a prescribed percentage of some designated base. The percentages vary from 2 to 10, with 5% the most common requirement.

As for the base, the one most widely used is the total vote cast for gubernatorial candidates at the last general election. Among others are the number of qualified voters or the votes cast at the last election for some office other than that of governor.

(2) POPULAR VOTE REQUIRED The size of the popular vote necessary for approval of a legislative act submitted to the voters as a consequence of the filing of a valid petition is a majority of those voting on the measure. An additional requirement in Massachusetts is that the majority must constitute at least 30% of the vote cast at the election. The same proviso applies to popular voting on measures proposed by the initiative.

The Desirability of Direct Legislation

The desirability of direct legislation by means of the initiative or the referendum is a controversial subject. Both its proponents and opponents have advanced a variety of claims. Lack of faith in legislative bodies is the chief reason for favoring direct legislation and lack of confidence in the judgment of the people is the principal ground of opposition.

The supporters of direct legislation do not advocate

abandonment of lawmaking by legislatures. They merely believe in providing a remedy for situations in which legislatures prove unresponsive to the desires of the public.

Opponents doubt that direct legislation will be resorted to only under such circumstances. They contend that special interest-groups will appeal frequently to the electorate when dissatisfied with the action of the legislature. If so, the initiative and the referendum will tend to become a substitute for the superior process of lawmaking by a deliberative assemblage of elected representatives.

Experience with direct legislation in the United States for nearly three-fourths of a century, at both the state and local levels, has neither sustained nor refuted all of the various contentions of either its sponsors or its antagonists. Like other devices in the governmental field, its results have been satisfactory in some respects and unsatisfactory in others.

State Government: Executive and Judicial Branches

CHAPTER ☆ TWELVE

The Executive Branch
    The Governor
        Selection and Term of Office
        Removal from Office
        Qualifications
        Compensation
        The Governor and Legislation
        The Governor and Administration
            Appointive Power
            Removal Power
            Responsibility for Law Enforcement
            Management of the Administrative Services: Limitations
            Administrative Reorganization: Its Importance
            Personnel Policies of the States
        The Governor and Pardons
        Excerpts from the Model State Constitution
The Judicial Branch
    Organization
        Courts of Original Jurisdiction

Intermediate Appellate Courts
Courts of Last Resort
Disintegrated Judicial Administration
A Unified Judicial System
Judicial Councils
Judicial Conferences
Selection of Judges
    Objections to Popular Election
    Merits of Executive Appointment
    Executive Appointment and Popular Endorsement
    Missouri Plan; California and Other Plans
    Model State Constitution's Provisions
Removal of Judges
    Impeachment and Trial
    By the Legislature
    Miscellaneous Modes of Removal
Functions of the Judiciary
Administration of Justice; Factors Determining Its Quality

☆ ☆ ☆ ☆ ☆ ☆ ☆ ☆ ☆ ☆ ☆ ☆ ☆

The policies of a state are ultimately established by legislative action, except insofar as some of them are incorporated in the state's constitution. Among the participants in the policy-determining process (which terminates in the passage of laws by the legislature) are the governor, administrative officials, party leaders, and pressure groups. After laws have been enacted, their enforcement involves the functioning of the executive and judicial branches of government.

Policies prescribed by the legislature are executed by the governor and numerous administrative agencies, e.g., the construction and maintenance of highways, the issuance of driver's licenses, and the regulation of public utilities. The role of the judicial branch in law enforcement is primarily that of settling controversies which arise under the law and result in litigation.

The Executive Branch

The Governor

(1) SELECTION The chief executive in every state is an *elected* governor. Ordinarily a plurality vote is sufficient for election, but a few states require a majority of the votes cast for all gubernatorial candidates. One of these is Georgia and in the 1966 election no candidate obtained a majority.

Georgia's constitution provides for selection of the governor by the legislature under such circumstances—its choice to be made from the two highest candidates. Court action was instituted to prevent the legislature from doing so, on the ground that legislative selection conflicted with the "one person, one vote" holding of the Supreme Court in the apportionment cases. In a five to four decision, the nation's highest tribunal ruled that nothing in the Constitution of the United States prohibits a state from providing for legislative selection of its governor either in the first instance or as a consequence of the failure of some other method to result in the choice of a governor.[124]

(2) TERM OF OFFICE Forty-three states provide a four-year term for the governor and the others two years. Nine prohibit service for successive terms and sixteen permit two consecutive terms—without limiting the number of times a person may be chosen; two allow no more than two consecutive terms; and twenty-three place no restriction on the number of terms that may be served.

(3) REMOVAL FROM OFFICE Removal from office before expiration of a governor's term usually requires impeachment by one house of the legislature followed by trial and conviction by the other on such charges as malfeasance, maladministration, and criminal conduct. Few governors have been impeached and removed from office.

A minority of the states, about one-fourth, permit recall of the governor by popular vote after the filing of a recall petition signed by a designated minimum of qualified voters.

(4) QUALIFICATIONS The usual qualifications for holding the gubernatorial office are United States citizenship, a minimum age, and a minimum period of residence within the state. Age requirements vary from twenty-five to thirty-five, with thirty the most commonly prescribed minimum. At least five years residence is most frequently stipulated, but the range is from two to ten years.

(5) COMPENSATION The compensation of governors is prescribed by constitutional provision in some states but

[124] *Forston v. Morris*, 385 U. S. 231 (1966).

by statute in most. In 1971 the established highest pay was $85,000 in New York, $55,000 in Texas, and $50,000 in New Jersey. The salaries in ten states ranged from $40,000 to under $50,000; in twenty from $30,000 to under $40,000; and in fourteen from $20,000 to under $30,000. Three states paid the least, *viz.*, Arkansas ($10,000), North Dakota and South Dakota ($18,000). Provision of an executive mansion is a common practice, as is the granting of expense allowances.

(6) THE GOVERNOR AND LEGISLATION Governors are the most prominent state officials and also the most powerful, but their powers, as a whole, are more limited than those of the President of the United States. For reasons to be mentioned shortly, governors are more effective as legislative leaders than as chief administrators.

The legislative powers of the governor include the recommendation of policies to the legislature, a suspensive veto (no veto in North Carolina), and the calling of special sessions. Governors also possess such ordinance-making or auxiliary rule-making powers as are conferred by constitutional or statutory provision, usually the latter.

(a) THE POWER TO RECOMMEND The power to recommend policies is the same as that of the President. Its effectiveness depends on such variable factors as the skill and prestige of particular governors, their potency as political leaders, the partisan complexion of the legislature, and the support forthcoming from pressure groups for the policies a governor favors. The recommending power is far different from a power to compel, but it enables the governor to concentrate attention on problems calling for legislative action and constitutes a weapon of persuasion in the hands of an astute leader.

(b) CALLING OF SPECIAL SESSIONS The power of governors to call special sessions of the legislature is stronger in some respects than the corresponding power of the national chief executive. In many states, the legislature in special session may consider only such matters as fall within the scope of the purposes of the session as declared by the governor, whereas Congress, if assembled in special session by the President, is free to transact whatever business it pleases.

Gubernatorial power to call special sessions is especially important because of the limitations commonly placed on the frequency and length of the regular sessions of state legislatures.

(c) THE VETO POWER The veto power of governors was discussed in the preceding chapter.[125] Suffice it to point out again that most governors possess an item veto with respect to appropriation acts and that in some states they may reduce as well as eliminate items. The President lacks such a veto. He must approve or disapprove Congressional enactments as a whole, including appropriation acts, despite his reaction to particular provisions of a specific act.

(7) THE GOVERNOR AND ADMINISTRATION Compared with the President and many local executives, governors possess limited powers in the field of administration. The restrictions imposed on them are considerably greater in some jurisdictions than in others.

[125] For details concerning the veto power of governors and their power to call special legislative sessions, see Chapter 11. These powers of the President are discussed in Chapter 7.

(a) RESTRICTIONS SUMMARIZED Practically all governors share executive power with officials over whom they have no control; their powers of appointment and removal are subject to a variety of limitations; their law enforcement responsibility is great but they are unable to control numerous officials upon whom reliance is placed for executing certain subdivisions of the body of state law, e.g., criminal law; and in many states they are handicapped to an even greater degree than the President by the necessity of directing and supervising an unmanageable administrative organization. Governors also lack needed tools of management. Another handicap is the typical state constitutional provision declaring that the *chief* executive power is vested in the governor. This stipulation gives rise to a stricter judicial interpretation of gubernatorial power than would be the case if "executive power" were granted the governor without the modifying adjective "chief." The national constitution provides that "the executive power" shall be vested in a President.

The trend in recent times has been toward a strengthening of the governor's position in relation to administration, as in New Jersey, Hawaii, and Alaska. Much remains to be done in most of the states. Progress is slow because of the usual opposition to departure from traditional arrangements and also because of the necessity for constitutional revision.

(b) ELECTIVE AND LEGISLATIVELY SELECTED ADMINISTRATIVE OFFICIALS The number of elective administrative officials in addition to the governor varies from none in four states (Hawaii, Maine, New Hampshire, New Jersey), and one in two (Alaska, Tennessee), to as many as eight, nine, and ten in Louisiana, Mississippi, North Dakota, and Oklahoma. Most of the states have four or five and a few six or seven.

The officials most frequently chosen by popular vote are the attorney general (42 states), the treasurer (40), the secretary of state (39), the auditor general (29), and the superintendent of public instruction (21). Controllers are elected in ten states. Other elected top-rank administrators are provided for in such functional fields as agriculture (12 states), insurance (9), public utility regulation (8), land (7), labor (5), mining (4), revenue and taxation (3), highways (1), and corrections (1). These officials are chosen for definite terms and the governor has no effective control over them if they prove uncooperative.

In various states, too, some of the above-mentioned officials are selected by the legislature. Such is the case with the secretary of state in three states, the auditor in eight, the treasurer in four, the controller and public utility commissioners in two, and the attorney general and superintendent of public instruction in one.

(c) APPOINTIVE POWER OF THE GOVERNOR   The appointive power of governors is more limited in scope than that of the President who selects department heads, the members of commissions, many other administrative officials, and even the judges of the national courts. In most of the states judges are chosen by popular vote. So are a considerable number of officials engaged in the execution of state laws, including not only those mentioned above but also others, e.g., locally elected prosecuting attorneys. Some state positions, too, in addition to the few previously identified, are filled by the method of legislative selection.

Even in instances in which the governor appoints, a

particular incumbent of the gubernatorial office may be unable to select the holders of certain positions. This situation arises when the term of an official is longer than that of the governor and does not expire while the latter is in office. Commissions with long and staggered terms are established in many states and even if the terms of some of the commissioners terminate during a governor's tenure, the number of retiring commissioners may constitute only a minority of the entire membership.

A restriction on the appointive power of governors is the common requirement of approval by the upper chamber of the state legislature, or, in a few states, by an executive council. In an occasional state, the consent of both chambers is required. At the national level, senatorial confirmation of presidential appointments to superior offices is also essential, so in this respect the governors of most states are no worse off than the President.

(d) REMOVAL POWER OF THE GOVERNOR The removal powers of governors are restricted in various ways. In many instances, fixed terms of service preclude gubernatorial removal. Officials who are elected by the voters or appointed by some agency other than the governor may not be removed from office by the latter, although the governor in some states may suspend them temporarily for cause and sometimes remove them as a consequence of proceedings initiated by the legislature. Various states, too, subject the removal power of the governor to approval by the legislature, usually only one of the two houses of a bicameral assembly.

Because of restrictions of the foregoing type, governors are handicapped as chief administrators by the necessity of dealing with nominal subordinates who need not fear loss of their positions even if incompetent or uncooperative. The President, unlike governors in general, may remove executive officers at his pleasure. Congress may restrict his removal power only with respect to agencies discharging quasi-legislative or quasi-judicial functions.

(e) RESPONSIBILITY FOR LAW ENFORCEMENT A typical provision of state constitutions charges the governor with the duty of law enforcement. Although a substantial number of officials engaged in the administration of state policies are controllable by the governor, many are not, e.g., officials elected by the voters or chosen by the legislature.

The fact that the governor's responsibilities exceed his powers is especially noticeable in enforcement of the criminal laws of a state. This task is largely performed by the attorney general (popularly elected in most of the states) and by such local officials as county or district prosecuting attorneys, sheriffs, and municipal police forces over whom the governor is unable to exercise meaningful control.

All of the states have police forces or highway patrols accountable to the governor, but these agencies are too limited in size to assume the entire task of dealing with the crime problem and highway patrols lack the powers which police officers ordinarily possess. Frequently, too, state police are restricted in jurisdiction to areas outside incorporated municipalities. Governors have command of the state militia or national guard. However, the use of these forces is commonly confined to emergency situations. The frequent observation that governors in general lack powers commensurate with their responsibilities is particularly well-founded in regard to the enforcement of criminal law.

(f) GUBERNATORIAL MANAGEMENT OF THE ADMINISTRATIVE SERVICES—OBSTACLES The obstacles confronting governors in the field of administration usually include an unmanageable administrative organization. In many states the number of administrative agencies nominally subject to general management by the governor is too large for satisfactory direction and supervision by anyone, no matter how competent or conscientious.

The managerial function of governors is also made more difficult by the frequent division of responsibility for the administration of particular policies among several departments; by the grouping of unrelated activities in the same administrative unit; and by the fairly common use of boards or commissions to head administrative agencies. Single heads directly responsible to the governor are preferable to boards unless the functions of an administrative establishment are primarily quasi-legislative or quasi-judicial in character.

Many governors are unable to operate properly as general managers of the administrative services because of inadequate staff assistance and failure to equip them with needed tools of management. Examples of the latter are control over accounting, record-keeping, and departmental spending during the course of the fiscal year. Although more than four-fifths of the governors possess the budget-preparing authority and most of these an item veto over appropriation bills, several governors are denied the power to prepare the state budget. In Arkansas this power is vested in the legislative council and in Florida and West Virginia the budget-making authority is a commission composed of the governor, as chairman, and six elected officers, viz., the secretary of state, comptroller or auditor, treasurer, attorney-general, commissioner of agriculture, and superintendent of public instruction. In Indiana, Mississippi, and South Carolina, the budget-making agency consists of a combination of administrators and legislators.

(g) ADMINISTRATIVE REORGANIZATION The first major departure from a mishmash of disconnected offices, departments, boards, and commissions occurred in Illinois in 1917. Over one hundred agencies of various types were abolished and their functions transferred to a small number of departments, originally nine and subsequently thirteen and fifteen. In 1927 New York consolidated some one hundred eighty agencies into eighteen departments. Other states have undertaken reorganization for the purpose of developing a more manageable and efficient administrative apparatus, so that approximately three-fifths of the states are no longer operating with an unplanned accumulation of disintegrated administrative agencies.

A recent example is the new Michigan constitution's provision for a maximum of twenty departments to replace an administrative structure which included about one hundred twenty-six different establishments. Previously, a few states, including Alaska, Hawaii, Massachusetts, New Jersey, and New York, had limited the permissible number of departments to twenty. However, there is no optimum maximum number of departments, such as twenty, since the proper number of major administrative units depends on various considerations, such as the extent and variety of a state's governmental activities and the desirability of creating unifunctional rather than multifunctional administrative units.

Fewer than twenty departments are probably sufficient for most states, whereas a larger number may be justifiable in some cases. Even so, the manageability of an administrative organization becomes increasingly questionable as the number of departments rises beyond some figure in the vicinity of twenty.

The administrative organization of a state is the product of both constitutional and statutory provisions. In a few states, the governor possesses reorganizing authority, subject to subsequent legislative approval, and in two of these this power is conferred by the constitution, viz., in Alaska and Michigan. Michigan's constitution authorizes the governor, by executive order, to make changes in the organization of the executive branch or in the assignment of functions among its units; requires submission of these orders to the legislature; and grants the legislature 60 calendar days of a regular session to disapprove each order. Unless disapproved by a majority of the elected membership of each house, an order shall become effective at a date thereafter designated by the governor. A similar provision is included in the *Model State Constitution* of the National Municipal League. Such grants of reorganizing authority to a governor do not extend to features of administrative organization incorporated in the state constitution.

(h) PERSONNEL POLICIES OF THE STATES   The quality of state administration depends not only on organization but also on personnel. Many of the states still adhere to personnel policies of an undesirable type, e.g., the spoils system, which lower the standards and increase the cost of public service.

The extent to which merit systems were operative in the several states in 1966 was as follows: [126] general coverage—

[126] See *The Book of the States,* 1966–67 (Chicago, The Council of State Governments, 1966), pp. 158–161.

32 states; partial coverage—18 states. The partial coverage group consisted for the most part of states which installed a merit system to qualify for federally-aided programs in such fields as public assistance, unemployment compensation, child welfare, public health, and vocational rehabilitation. It also included states in which the merit principle is applied to particular service departments, e.g., state police or highway patrol and health.

Coverage is seldom complete even in the "general coverage" group. Although the extent of coverage is a fact of some significance, it casts no light on the quality of the personnel system in operation. Nor does it indicate whether legal requirements are adhered to in practice. There are many ways of circumventing standards prescribed by law.

(8) THE GOVERNOR AND PARDONS A traditional power of chief executives is the granting of pardons, the commutation of sentences, and the issuance of reprieves. About three-fourths of the states vest the pardoning power in the governor. Most of these provide an advisory board or commission to assist him in the discharge of this important function and some require the concurrence of an executive council, the senate, or a pardon board. In a minority of the states the granting of pardons rests with the discretion of a board of pardons, but the governor is usually a member of this board.

The *Model Constitution* provides that the governor shall have power to grant reprieves, commutations, and pardons, after conviction, for all offenses. It authorizes him to delegate these powers subject to such procedures as may be prescribed by law. This type of provision is recommended because the granting of pardons involves complex judgments of a correctional and behavioral nature which chief executives are neither trained to exercise nor have any special interest in exercising.

(9) EXCERPTS FROM THE MODEL STATE CONSTITUTION The position of governors in relation to administration requires strengthening in most of the states. Provisions of the type incorporated in the *Model State Constitution* are designed to achieve this end. Pertinent excerpts from this Model include the following:

1. The executive power of the state shall be vested in a governor.
2. The governor shall appoint and remove the heads of all administrative departments. All other officers in the administrative service shall be appointed and may be removed as provided by law.

   The legislature shall provide for the establishment and administration of a system of personnel administration in the civil service of the state and its civil divisions. Appointments and promotions shall be based on merit and fitness.
3. The governor shall commission all officers of the state. He may require information, in writing or otherwise, from the officers of any administrative department, office, or agency upon any subject relating to their respective offices.
4. The governor shall be commander-in-chief of the armed forces of the state and may call them out to execute the laws, to preserve order, to suppress insurrection, or to repel invasions.
5. The governor shall be responsible for execution of the

laws. He may, by appropriate action or proceeding brought in the name of the state, enforce compliance with any constitutional or legislative mandate, or restrain violation of any constitutional or legislative power, duty, or right by any officer, department, or agency of the state or of any of its civil divisions.

6. The governor shall submit to the legislature a budget estimate for the next fiscal year setting forth all proposed expenditures and anticipated income of all departments and agencies of the state, as well as a general appropriation bill to authorize the proposed expenditures and a bill or bills covering recommendations in the budget for new or additional revenues.

7. All executive and administrative offices, agencies, and instrumentalities of the state government, and their respective functions, powers, and duties, shall be allocated by law among and within not more than twenty principal departments, so as to group them as far as practicable according to major purpose. Regulatory, quasi-judicial, and temporary agencies established by law may, but need not be, allocated within a principal department.

The governor may make such changes in the allocation of offices, agencies, and instrumentalities, and in the allocation of functions, powers, and duties, as he considers necessary for efficient administration. If such changes affect existing law, they shall be set forth in executive orders, which shall be submitted to the legislature while in session and become effective sixty days after submission, or at the close of the session, whichever is sooner, unless specifically modified or disapproved by a resolution concurred in by a majority

of all members (unicameral body) or of all members
of each house (bicameral body).

The *Model Constitution* provides for only one elected
administrative official, viz., the governor. Consequently, the
administrative organization is one of the integrated type
with the governor at its head. Each department is placed
under the direction and supervision of heads appointed and
removable by the governor. Subject to the restriction that
the number of major departments may not exceed twenty,
the legislature is free to determine the details of the administrative structure. However, the governor may make
changes that become effective unless disapproved by the
legislature within a designated period of time. Unlike the
constitutions of most of the states, flexibility in the matter
of administrative organization is provided for within the
framework of a few basic guide lines.

The Judicial Branch

Every state has its own system of courts. The variations
from state to state are so numerous that it is extremely difficult to present a general description without innumerable
qualifications of one type or another. For example, the title
of a court is by no means a certain indicator of its jurisdiction and position in the judicial hierarchy of a particular
state. In New York, to cite a specific case, the title "Supreme Court" is borne by trial courts at a lower rung of the
judicial ladder, whereas the court of last resort bears the
title "Court of Appeals." Again, in some states a "superior
court" is an intermediate appellate tribunal but in others this

label is applied to major trial courts which are primarily courts of first instance.

A hierarchy of tribunals is provided for in every state, but the number of tiers of courts varies—three in nearly twenty states, four in slightly over half, and five in a few. The variation is due to the establishment of two levels of courts with limited original jurisdiction in a substantial number of states and to the existence of an intermediate appellate court in about one-third of the states. All states have at least one tier of courts with limited original jurisdiction; major trial courts of first instance having practically unlimited jurisdiction; and a court of last resort at the peak of the judicial hierarchy.

Courts of Original Jurisdiction

(1) JUSTICES OF THE PEACE Courts with original jurisdiction confined to minor civil and/or criminal cases constitute the lowest level of tribunals in all of the states. Except in a minority group, these courts are conducted by justices of the peace, squires, magistrates, or aldermen (depending on the title in use) and their jurisdiction in civil actions is limited to controversies involving comparatively small sums of money, such as $100, $200, or $500, and in criminal cases to offenses falling in the minor misdemeanor category, e.g., traffic violations, breaches of the peace, or infractions of local ordinances.

In addition to settling controversies of the foregoing type, justices of the peace issue warrants of arrest and function as committing magistrates, i.e., they hold preliminary hearings to determine whether persons accused of serious crimes should be released or whether the evidence against them is sufficient to warrant detention in jail or release under bail pending subsequent proceedings by other authorities, viz., prosecuting attorneys or grand juries. Other tasks are commonly discharged by justices of the peace, among them the issuance of search warrants, the performance of marriage ceremonies, and the attestation of documents.

No special qualifications for serving as justices of the peace are required. Few, if any, have had legal training. Popular election of these officials is the prevailing practice, but in about one-fourth of the states they are appointed, e.g., by the board of county commissioners in Idaho, by the governor and executive council in Massachusetts, and by the senior circuit judge of the circuit in which a county is located in South Dakota. Their term of office is two or four years and in many states their compensation is based on a fee system.

Generally speaking, justice of the peace courts have proved unsatisfactory and should be replaced, as they have been in Missouri, New Jersey, Connecticut, and a few other states, by tribunals of a far more adequate type. Although the jurisdiction of justices of the peace is confined to cases categorized as "petty" in legal parlance, most individuals who become involved in litigation are parties to controversies of this "minor" type. Of the various defects of state judicial systems, and there are many, the survival of outmoded justice of the peace tribunals is one of the worst.

(2) COUNTY AND OTHER COURTS Courts of limited original jurisdiction, other than those of justices of the peace, include county courts, municipal courts, police courts, and such specialized tribunals as probate, juvenile, traffic, domestic relations, and small claims courts. One or more courts of this type are found in most of the states and their personnel is usually chosen by popular vote.

County courts of restricted original jurisdiction constitute a second tier of tribunals in about two-fifths of the states. The cases which may be commenced in them involve more money and somewhat more serious crimes than those decidable by justices of the peace, but the cases are nevertheless of the "petty" variety. Ordinarily, these courts are authorized to consider appeals from the rulings of justices of the peace. An appealed case is usually considered on all of its merits, just as if it had been brought to the county court in the first place, as it might have been in most states.

(3) MAJOR TRIAL COURTS From a legal standpoint, the most important courts of first instance in all of the states are the major trial courts with practically unlimited jurisdiction. Their appellate jurisdiction is restricted to cases commenced in the courts of limited jurisdiction described in the preceding paragraphs. Among the titles of these major trial courts are "circuit court," "district court," "superior court," and, in New York, "supreme court." Their jurisdiction extends to civil actions, regardless of the amount in controversy, and to crimes of all types, including those classified as felonies and those falling in the misdemeanor category.

In most of the states judges of the major trial courts are chosen by the voters, with terms varying from four and six years to as high as ten, fourteen, and fifteen. Six-year terms are the most common. In Massachusetts and Rhode Island the judges are appointed by the governor with the consent of the Council in the former state and the consent of the Senate in the latter. These judges serve for life. Life tenure is provided in New Jersey if a major trial court judge is reappointed by the governor and senate after serving an initial seven-year term. In New Hampshire the judges appointed by the governor and council serve to the age of seventy.

Judges of major trial courts are salaried. As of 1970, the salary range was from $10,500 to $39,100, with compensation over $20,000 in approximately three-fifths of the states.

Intermediate Appellate Courts

Intermediate appellate courts have been established in a minority of the states to lighten the work load of the court of last resort. In some states, as in Pennsylvania, a single court of this variety possesses state-wide jurisdiction, whereas in others several such tribunals are organized on a district basis. As usual, the titles of these courts vary, e.g., superior court or court of appeals, as do the number of judges, three or more.

The judges of intermediate courts are chosen by popular vote in most of the states for terms that range from four and six years to ten and twelve. They receive salaries varying from a minimum of $15,000 in 1970 to a maximum of $42,000. Many of them are paid over $30,000.

Although the jurisdiction of these intermediate courts is primarily appellate, some states have conferred a strictly limited original jurisdiction upon them. Most of their work is the handling of appeals from the decisions of major trial courts.

Courts of Last Resort

Every state has a court of last resort which almost always bears the title "supreme court." Other titles are "court of appeals" (Kentucky, Maryland, New York); "supreme judicial court" (Maine, Massachusetts); and "supreme court of appeals" (Virginia, West Virginia).

In nearly two-thirds of the states judges of the court of last resort are chosen by popular vote, in five by the legislature, in six by the governor with the consent of the senate or an executive council, and in seven by a combination of gubernatorial appointment and popular election—a method that will be explained subsequently. Terms of office vary from as low as two years in Vermont, six to twelve years in four-fifths of the states, fourteen in two, fifteen in one, twenty-one in one, life in three, and to age seventy in one.

The variations in size of courts of last resort are from three to nine, with five and seven the figures for four-fifths of the states. Judges of these courts receive salaries of $40,000 and over in three states, $30,000 to under $40,000 in eleven, $20,000 to under $30,000 in thirty-six. The minimum is $20,000 and the maximum $45,000.

Although some courts of last resort have original jurisdiction in certain types of action, practically all cases reach them on appeal from major trial courts or from intermediate appellate courts in the minority of states having tribunals of the latter variety. On questions of state law, the rulings of these courts of last resort are final. In controversies involving federal questions, however, a case may be carried from a state court of last resort to the Supreme Court of the

United States. Unlike the situation at the national level, the highest courts in a few states render advisory opinions at the request of the governor or the legislature.

Disintegrated Judicial Administration

The establishment of different levels of courts along the lines described in preceding paragraphs indicates that judicial proceedings are integrated in the sense of a progression of cases from courts of first instance to tribunals having appellate jurisdiction—provided that parties to a case take advantage of the opportunity to have a higher court review the decisions of a lower court.

However, this feature of the process of adjudication does not mean that a court system is also integrated for the purpose of achieving a maximum degree of operational efficiency in the transaction of judicial business. In most of the states each of the many courts established by constitutional and/or statutory provision functions without direction and supervision from above in dealing with such matters as the maintenance of property like court houses and law libraries; the furnishing of needed equipment and supplies; the solution of auxiliary personnel problems, including the employment of clerks, stenographers, and bailiffs; the keeping of records, accounts, and files; fixing the time and length of court sessions; and determining the order in which cases shall be tried.

Generally speaking, the management of judicial business in all of its many aspects is conducted haphazardly and inefficiently in a substantial proportion of the states. This situation is one of the causes of delay, congested calendars, and a dearth of reliable information concerning the condition of judicial affairs. The judicial systems of many states function without management, supervision, operating statistics, administrative rules, and recurrent conferences of their key personnel.[127]

A Unified Judicial System

A recommended remedy for these and other defects in judicial administration, such as a multiplicity of courts with overlapping jurisdiction and an unfair division of work among judges, is the establishment of a unified judicial system. The distinguishing feature of this type of organization is the existence of a general court of justice with appropriate branches, divisions, and subdivisions for the exercise of original and appellate jurisdiction and with an administrative head authorized to direct and supervise the property, employees, record-keeping, and reporting practices of the component courts; to assign judges to the divisions of each level of courts; to transfer them temporarily from one court level to another in consideration of the work-load in terms of pending cases; and to establish rules for expediting the transaction of judicial business. The chief justice of the highest appellate branch, assisted by a subordinate administrative director and by an adequate staff, would serve as the chief administrator of this unified judiciary.

The *Model State Constitution* provides for a unified system including a supreme court, an appellate court, a general trial court, and such inferior courts of limited jurisdiction as may be established by law. An important power of the supreme court is the formulation and promulgation of rules

[127] A. T. Vanderbilt, "The Essentials of a Sound Judicial System," *Northwestern University Law Review*, March–April, 1953.

governing the administration of all courts, including rules covering practice and procedure in civil and criminal cases. The latter rules are subject to change by the legislature by a two-thirds vote of its membership. In most states these rules are ~stablished by both constitutional and statutory provisions.

A few states, e.g., New Jersey, Alaska, Hawaii, and Michigan, have installed a unified judicial system. A number of other states have taken substantial steps in this direction, but in most jurisdictions a disintegrated judicial organization survives.

Judicial Councils

About three-fourths of the states have created judicial councils presided over by the chief justice of the court of last resort and composed of other judges, attorneys, and sometimes members of the legislature and laymen. The composition of these councils varies. Their usual function is to investigate the court system and recommend changes in organization and procedure that will improve the operation of the judicial branch.

Judicial Conferences

About three-fifths of the states have provided for judicial conferences participated in by all or some of the judges of the different levels of courts. Their purpose is to consider ways of raising the standards of judicial performance.

Administrative Offices

Another indication that the states are becoming increasingly aware of the need for judicial reform is that more than half of them have created an administrative office headed by a director selected in several ways, viz., by the court of last resort, by its chief justice, or by the judicial council. This office collects statistics, suggests ways of achieving efficiency and economy, and performs a variety of routine functions.

While progress toward an improved judicial branch has been made in many states, much remains to be done in most of them. The road-blocks to reform are numerous. Apart from opposition emanating from different sources, a major obstacle is the necessity of constitutional revision, something which is not easily achieved in most of the states.

Selection of Judges

One of the requisites of a satisfactory judicial branch is the quality of its personnel. Competent judges are as necessary to the proper functioning of the courts as sound organization and appropriate procedures. A question to be decided is the method of selection most likely to result in the choice of capable jurists.

Judges are chosen by popular vote in most of the states, by the legislature in five, by the governor with the consent of the senate or an executive council in six, and by a combination of gubernatorial appointment and popular endorsement in a minority group of seven. In some states the mode of selection is not the same for all courts. Thus in Illinois magistrates are appointed by circuit judges, whereas other judges are chosen by popular vote, and in Maine probate judges are elected but all others are appointed by the governor with the consent of an executive council.

Objections to Popular Election of Judges

Popular election of judges is considered undesirable for a number of reasons: (a) the choice of judges actually rests with the politicians who control the nominating process and command the most votes; (b) many competent persons, who would serve if appointed, are unwilling to compete for an elective office; (c) voters lack dependable information concerning the comparative fitness of candidates for a position that requires legal learning and a proper temperament; (d) emphasis is placed on party affiliation even in those states, about fifteen, that provide for a non-partisan election; and (e) judges, because of their usual desire for re-election, are likely to be influenced by partisan considerations and public opinion in exercising their judicial powers.

Arthur T. Vanderbilt, a famous jurist, conceded that there is no foolproof way of selecting jurists. He asserted, however, that "no system of selection could be worse . . . than popular elections on party tickets along with a host of other national, state, and local party candidates running for a variety of offices." [128]

Objections to Legislative Selection

Opposition to legislative selection usually is based on the claim that the results are likely to differ little from those

[128] *Ibid.*, p. 181.

attained in popular elections. Political maneuvering and intrigue occur on a substantial scale and leading politicians within and outside the legislature dominate the selective process. Responsibility for the action taken is dispersed among a multiplicity of legislators.

Merits of Executive Appointment

Opponents of both popular election and legislative selection prefer executive appointment on the ground that this mode of choice is more likely than the other two to produce a competent judicial personnel. Although poor appointments may be made by the chief executive, as has sometimes been the case, and although partisan considerations may be given considerable weight, as evidenced by Presidential appointments to the national judiciary,[129] the proponents of executive appointment believe that this mode of selection is less subject to abuse than choice by either the voters or the legislature. The chief executive can canvass the personnel market for judicial talent and responsibility for the appointments made rests solely with him, unless legislative approval of his selections is requisite.

Executive Appointment and Popular Endorsement

A method of selection now used in seven states combines executive appointment with an eventual popular vote enabling the electorate to terminate the services of an appointee if dissatisfied with his performance on the bench. The details of this procedure differ in the several states.

[129] *Supra,* p. 332–333.

(1) THE MISSOURI PLAN In Missouri, whenever a vacancy occurs in the courts to which this type of plan applies, a nominating commission submits the names of three persons to the governor. He is required to appoint one of the three. After the appointee has served for a trial period of at least one year, the voters decide whether he is to remain in office for a regular full term. His name appears on the ballot without party designation and the electorate merely votes "yes" or "no" on the question of his retention in office. If the noes outnumber the yeses, the resultant vacancy is again dealt with through the nominating and appointive process just described.

Two types of nominating commission are provided. One is an appellate judicial commission of seven members—three laymen appointed by the governor (one from each appellate court district), three lawyers (one from each appellate district chosen by the lawyers of the district), and the chief justice of the court of last resort, who acts as chairman. The other type is a commission for each circuit affected by the plan. These circuit nominating commissions consist of two resident laymen per circuit appointed by the governor, two resident lawyers chosen by the lawyers residing in the circuit, and the presiding judge of the court of appeals of the district in which the circuit is located.

(2) THE CALIFORNIA AND OTHER PLANS In California, the first state to use this combination of gubernatorial appointment and popular endorsement, no provision is made for nominating agencies. Instead, the governor's appointees are subject to the approval of a commission on judicial appointments.

The only check on the governor's appointive power in

Maryland is the requirement of an endorsing type of election after at least one year of service. Five other states, Alaska, Iowa, Kansas, Nebraska, and Utah, follow the Missouri plan of having a nominating commission of some type. The judicial council of Alaska serves in this capacity.

Most of these states require voter approval or disapproval of an appointee after he has been on the bench for a designated period of time. They also provide for a non-partisan and non-competitive election if a judge, having obtained office through appointment and subsequent popular endorsement, seeks re-election. He runs on his record. If he fails to gain majority support, the consequent vacancy is filled in the manner that has been described.

(3) THE MODEL CONSTITUTION'S PLAN The 1963 *Model Constitution* of the National Municipal League provides for the appointment of judges by the governor with the advice and consent of the legislature (unicameral), but also endorses an alternative arrangement which requires the governor to make his selections from a list of nominees presented by judicial nominating commissions. An earlier *Model Constitution* (1948) provided for the appointment of judges by an elected chief justice of the court of last resort. No state has used this method.

Although some methods of selecting judges seem more promising than others, no mode of choice so far devised will automatically insure a top quality judicial personnel. The best safeguard against incompetence on the bench is probably the development of a tradition in support of adherence to high standards in the choice of members of the judicial branch.

The Removal of Judges

All of the states provide one or more methods of removing judges from office prior to expiration of the terms for which elected or appointed. Provision for removal is a precautionary measure in the event that particular judges demonstrate unfitness for the discharge of judicial functions.

The longer the term of office, the greater the need for some method of removal. If terms are short, an incompetent jurist can soon be eliminated by refusal to re-elect or re-appoint him, but there are situations in which it is undesirable to permit a judge to remain on the bench even for a limited period of time.

(1) BY IMPEACHMENT AND TRIAL   A nearly universal mode of removing judges is through the process of impeachment and subsequent conviction of the charges brought against them. Impeachment by one house and trial by the other, as in the case of the national government, is the usual procedure in the bicameral states. As a rule, resort to the impeachment method is confined to accusations of criminal misbehavior.

(2) BY THE LEGISLATURE   Some states permit removal of judges by the legislature without holding a trial. An extraordinary majority vote is commonly required. A related mode of removal is by the governor following the passage of a concurrent resolution by the legislature. A legislative majority like two-thirds of each house is necessary for the adoption of such a resolution.

These two methods, unlike the impeachment process, may ordinarily be used to remove judges for various reasons in addition to misconduct falling in the criminal category. The new Michigan Constitution, for example, provides as follows: "For reasonable cause, which is not sufficient ground for impeachment, the governor shall remove any judge on a concurrent resolution of two-thirds of the members elected to and serving in each house of the legislature."

(3) MISCELLANEOUS MODES OF REMOVAL Nearly one-fifth of the states authorize removal by popular vote following the filing of a recall petition signed by a designated minimum number of qualified voters. In a few states, judges of inferior courts are removable by higher tribunals.

A comparatively recent innovation in several states is the establishment of courts-on-the-judiciary or commissions on judicial qualifications. These agencies investigate complaints against judges, conduct hearings, and either remove, suspend, or retire judges for cause, or, usually, merely recommend that such action be taken by a specified authority, such as the court of last resort or the legislature.

In Ohio, for instance, complaints concerning a judge are brought to the supreme court. It may remove, suspend, or retire him if a commission of five judges appointed by the highest court concludes that the charges against him are valid. California has a similar plan. A commission on judicial qualifications consisting of nine members (five judges, two attorneys, and two laymen) investigates complaints and may recommend retirement or removal by the supreme court unless an unfit judge can be persuaded to resign.

The *Model Constitution* provides two methods of removal. One is through the impeachment process. The other is removal by the supreme court for such cause and in such manner as may be provided by law.

Functions of the Judiciary

The Settlement of Legal Controversies

The primary responsibility of courts is the settlement of legal controversies. This task requires the performance of a number of distinguishable functions. Each of them is normally involved in the process of resolving disputes between the parties to cases.

(1) DETERMINATION OF THE FACTS Determination of the facts in a case is an important phase of adjudication. If the facts are in dispute, the court in which action has been instituted reaches a conclusion on the basis of the evidence presented to it.

(2) DECIDING WHICH LAW IS APPLICABLE A second function is to decide what law is applicable to a particular controversy. Sometimes two or more laws appear relevant to a given situation and the task confronting a court is that of deciding whether to apply the provisions of a constitution, a statute, an administrative regulation, a local ordinance, or a rule of common law.

(3) INTERPRETING THE LAW A related judicial responsibility is interpretation of the applicable law. The meaning of a law often is uncertain due to ambiguities, the various senses in which words are used, the generality of provisions, and the impossibility of drafting laws so as to cover every conceivable circumstance. A court's conclusions concerning the intent of the lawmaking authority are controlling in a particular case.

(4) and (5) APPLYING THE LAW TO THE FACTS AND MAKING A DECISION   A fourth function is application of the law to the facts of a case. This step in the process of adjudication leads to the making of a decision which disposes of the controversy and constitutes the fifth of the several functions involved in the settlement of disputes.

Administration of Property

Courts undertake the administration of property in certain kinds of cases in which the ownership and use of property is in dispute. Until the respective rights of the contestants in such cases are finally determined, the property in dispute is managed by a court-appointed agent under such directions as the court issues. The administration of property by courts commonly occurs in connection with bankruptcy proceedings and with settlement of the estates of deceased persons.

Handling Affairs of Incapable Persons

Courts also assume responsibility for handling the affairs of persons incapable of looking out for their own interests. Examples are orphaned minors and individuals who are mentally deficient. Guardians appointed by and answerable to the courts frequently are provided for such persons.

Criminal and Civil Cases

Another way of looking at the functions of judicial tribunals is from the standpoint of the purposes served by their decisions. In criminal cases, courts impose penalties for the crimes of which defendants have been found guilty; in civil actions, their decisions are designed to rectify the infringement of rights, e.g., by awarding damages for a breach of contract, or to prevent rights from being violated if infringement is threatened, e.g., by the issuance of a writ of injunction.

Non-Judicial Functions

The non-judicial functions of courts vary in character. Among them may be the appointment and/or removal of designated officials, the issuance and revocation of licenses, the granting of citizenship to aliens, approval of proposed annexations of territory by political subdivisions, and service by judges on administrative bodies, e.g., a board of election commissioners. The assignment of responsibilities of the foregoing type depends on the particular state.

Courts are sometimes authorized to prescribe rules of pleading, practice, and procedure. This power, when granted, is limited by controlling constitutional and statutory provisions. The preferred policy is to confer such rule-making authority on the court of last resort and to subject the rules it formulates to disapproval by the legislature. A number of states have taken this step.

The Administration of Justice: Factors Determining Its Quality

Many factors have a bearing on the administration of justice. Of major importance are the character of the court system and the calibre of judges. However, effective organization and a high quality personnel are insufficient in themselves to insure the proper settlement of controversies by the courts.

Juries

Juries as well as judges are involved in the disposition of many cases, unless the right of trial by jury is waived by the parties to disputes falling in the "jury trial" category. Without honest and intelligent juries, miscarriages of justice are likely.

In some states the selection of juries takes place in ways that are not conducive to the seating of jurors of sufficient competence and integrity for satisfactory discharge of a jury's responsibilities. Jury systems are often defective in other respects. For example, in a few states juries may decide questions of law as well as of fact. Many persons question the advisability of using juries in the process of deciding cases.

Rules of Pleading, Practice, and Procedure

Another factor affecting the functioning of courts is the character of the rules of pleading, practice, and procedure. These rules are extremely complicated in some states, largely because of their prescription on a piece-meal basis by the legislature.

Powers of Judges

In various states the powers of judges are unduly restricted. They are denied the right to question witnesses, or to comment on the testimony of witnesses, or to organize the evidence in their charges to the jury. Under such circumstances the judge's role in the process of adjudication amounts to little more than that of an umpire in a contest in which the principal participants are the attorneys for the plaintiff and the defendant.

Delays

One of the common criticisms directed against the judicial branch is excessive and unnecessary delay in the disposition of cases. This delay may be due to various causes, such as poor organization of the courts, procedural technicalities, an insufficient number of judges, and the failure of judges to decide cases promptly.

However, delays blamed on the courts are often attributable to the bad habits of lawyers. Honorable and well-educated attorneys, effective organization of the bar, and adherence to a high standard of professional ethics are just as essential to the administration of justice as a sound system of courts, capable judges and juries, and appropriate rules of procedure.

Public Attitudes

Attitudes of the public toward litigation influence the administration of justice. Too many people conceive of a trial as a contest that should be dominated by opposing attorneys primarily and properly desirous of emerging as victors rather than losers. The fact that a trial is supposed to be an unbiased search for the truth is forgotten. An unfortunate misconception of many participants in the judicial process is that laws and courts exist for the benefit of such servants of the law as judges, court officers, and lawyers rather than for the benefit of litigants and the state.[130]

Just Laws

The administration of justice also depends on the existence of just laws. Unjust and otherwise undesirable laws often account for unpopular court decisions. The rules of common law are judge-made, but the written law consists of constitutional provisions, statutes, local ordinances, and administrative regulations.

If the written law is unfair or poor in quality, the courts must nevertheless adhere to its provisions in deciding cases brought before them. Written laws supersede the rules of common law in the event of conflict.

As for the common law, that may also be defective in various respects. It is up to the courts to eliminate its inequities without awaiting corrective legislative action. Al-

---

[130] A. T. Vanderbilt, *op. cit.* Much of the material concerning factors determining the quality of the administration of justice is based on Vanderbilt's Article.

though the rules of common law undergo change, the tendency of courts is to resist departure from precedents of long standing—no matter how unsatisfactory a particular rule has become.

Local Government:
Counties,
Towns & Townships,
Special Districts

CHAPTER ☆ THIRTEEN

State Constitutional Provisions Pertaining to Local Government
    Home Rule
    Restrictions on Special Legislation
    Miscellaneous
Types of Control Exercisable by State Governments
    Legislative; Judicial; Administrative
Number and Types of Local Units
    Proposals for Decreasing the Number
County Government
    County Functions
    Structure of County Government
        Usual County Officials
        The County Board
        Organizational Defects of County Government
        Better Forms of County Government
            Manager Plan
            Appointed Chief Administrator

Elected Chief Executive
Dominant County Board
Other Defects of County Government
Personnel Policies
Administrative Procedures and Methods
Townships and New England Towns
Townships
Functions
Organization
Uncertain Future of the Township
New England Towns
Functions
Organization
Special Districts

☆ ☆ ☆ ☆ ☆ ☆ ☆ ☆ ☆ ☆ ☆ ☆ ☆

The establishment of systems of local government is a function of the states. Each state decides on the number and character of its political subdivisions, defines their powers and duties, usually prescribes their organization and procedure, and controls them to whatever extent it deems expedient.

The Supreme Court has declared that units of local government possess no privileges and immunities under the Constitution of the United States which may be invoked *by them* in opposition to the will of the state that creates them. In exercising their plenary power over local governments, the states, of course, are under obligation to respect the limits by which their authority in general is circumscribed by the national constitution. No state, for example, when controlling local units, may encroach on the constitutionally guaranteed rights of individuals or authorize local officials to exercise powers vested exclusively in the national government.

All of the states possess the same degree of legal competence in dealing with local units. However, the authority of a *state government* is subject to whatever restrictions the state's constitution imposes on its various governmental agencies. What the state as a body politic may do, on the one hand, and what its legislature, courts, chief executive, and administrative agencies may do, on the other, are by no means necessarily the same. No state gives its government a completely free hand in the local government field.

Some features of state policy with respect to local government are embodied in the state constitution. Insofar as this is done, the discretionary power of the state government is correspondingly reduced. Moreover, constitutional limitations in addition to those referring specifically to local units have restrictive effects. Thus state governments in controlling local authorities must avoid violation of the rights guaranteed by state constitutions to private persons and corporations. In a few states, too, the courts have held that constitutional guarantees of private rights afford direct protection, under some circumstances, to certain local bodies, e.g., municipal corporations when acting in a proprietary capacity.

State Constitutional Provisions Pertaining to Local Government

State constitutional provisions concerning local government are ordinarily restrictive in type. Usually, the restrictions are directed against the state government, particularly the legislature, because of past abuses of power, but some limitations are designed to prevent local governments from taking certain action. Even if a constitutional stipulation is obviously intended to limit local discretion, it serves indirectly as a restraint on the state government's authority.

State constitutional provisions are sometimes permissive in character. Examples are the granting of authority to the legislature to provide optional forms of government for counties and to delegate power to cities to adopt zoning ordinances or to own and operate specified public utilities. Frequently, the purpose of this type of grant is to modify previously imposed restrictions or to overcome the adverse effects of judicial decisions.

Home Rule

The most drastic method of restricting the power of a state government in relation to local units is through establishment of a home rule system by constitutional provision. Home rule, in the technical sense of the phrase, signifies the right of local units to devise their own forms of government and also, in some but not all of the home-rule states, to be free from legislative control in matters of local concern. Cities have been the chief beneficiaries of the home rule movement. About half of the states have provided for municipal home rule, but only a small number have extended the privilege to counties.

Restrictions on Special Legislation

Most state constitutions either impose severe restrictions on the power of the state legislature to enact special laws pertaining to particular local units or require conformity to a more difficult procedure, sometimes involving local approval, than is established for the enactment of general laws, i.e., laws applying to all local units or to all of a designated class.

A fairly common stipulation is that special acts may not be passed if general laws are applicable. Under this type of restraint, final decision as to the applicability of general laws to particular situations rests with the courts in some states and with the legislature in others.

Practically all state constitutions forbid the passage of special acts dealing with specified subjects, such as the location of county seats, the changing of county boundaries, the incorporation of cities, and the creation of local offices. Restrictions on the power of special legislation are designed to prevent arbitrary discrimination and to lessen state interference in local affairs.

Miscellaneous Provisions

State constitutions contain various other provisions relative to local government. Only a few will be mentioned.

Many constitutions specify that certain county officials are to be chosen by popular vote, or guarantee local selection of officers and employees of local governments. The establishment of state-appointed special commissions to take charge of local affairs is often prohibited. A substantial number of constitutions prescribe a procedure for creating new counties and altering county boundaries which limits, if it does not eliminate entirely, the discretionary power of the state legislature in regard to this matter. A few constitutions direct the legislature to provide a uniform system of county government.

Provisions limiting local governments are fairly common. Examples are the establishment of maximum permissible tax rates and amounts of indebtedness for local purposes; specification of the type and life of bond issues; and prohibition of the lending or granting of money to private interests.

Types of Control Exercisable by State Governments

Most regulation of local units of government is achieved through action by the state government rather than by constitutional provisions. The forms of state governmental control are three in number, viz., legislative, judicial, and administrative.

Legislative control is exercised by the state legislature chiefly through the enactment of statutes that are binding on local functionaries. Judicial control is wielded by the courts when enforcing the laws of the state through the process of litigation. Administrative control includes the different devices by means of which state administrative agencies supervise, regulate, or influence the functioning of local authorities. Legislative control is primary; judicial and administrative control supplementary.

Legislative Control

In every state the number and nature of local units of government and their organization, procedures, powers, and duties are largely determined by statutes enacted by the state legislature. Conformity to these laws by local officials may be secured by instituting civil or criminal actions against them in the ordinary courts. This combination of legislative and judicial control still constitutes the chief method by which state regulation of local government is accomplished. Administrative controls of various types are growing in importance as auxiliary regulatory techniques.

Legislative control of local units has proved unsatisfactory in many respects, but the need for its continuation is unquestionable. The problem is to improve its quality and to prevent it from being used unwisely or for the purpose of exploiting local communities for the benefit of seekers of special privileges. Local autonomy should not be curtailed beyond the point necessary for the protection of legitimate state interests.

Judicial Control

Judicial control occurs when courts are resorted to for the purpose of compelling local authorities to conform to the laws of the state. If a local unit or its agents overstep the boundaries of their delegated powers, disregard procedures prescribed by law, or fail to fulfill legal obligations, remedial actions may be instituted in the proper courts. Court decisions are enforceable by such appropriate means as judicial tribunals have at their disposal.

Judicial control is effective merely as a technique for

compelling local units to abide by laws which apply to them. Local authorities may embark on ill-advised public improvement programs, purchase supplies of inferior quality at unnecessarily high prices, or employ a mediocre personnel—without running the risk of intervention by the courts. Courts are legally incompetent to control the discretionary powers of the legislative and administrative organs of local governments, provided that these are exercised in good faith, in conformity to law, and without fraud, corruption, gross abuse, or manifest oppression.

Administrative Control

Administrative control includes all controls, direct or indirect, which state administrative departments and officers are authorized to exercise over local agencies. The forms and extent of this type of control vary from state to state and also within particular states with respect to the local functions subject thereto. It has been developed to the greatest degree in the fields of finance, health, education, highways, and social welfare.

The forms of administrative control include the requirement of reports; the collection and dissemination of information; the giving of advice; the rendition of services; the investigation and inspection of local conditions and services; enforcement of conditions prescribed in connection with grants-in-aid; approval of contemplated action; review of action which has been taken; the issuance of ordinances and orders; the appointment and removal of local officials; and substitute administration, i.e., state performance of a given activity normally administered by local officers.

Many of these controls are non-compulsory in character but nevertheless enable state officials to influence the functioning of local governments. A substantial number, however, permit state administrative agencies to take action which is binding on local officials.

(1) ADVANTAGES The chief advantages of administrative as compared with legislative control are its continuity, flexibility, and superior quality. Many legislatures are in session only for short periods of time at infrequent intervals, whereas administrative officers are on the job day after day. The greater flexibility of administrative control arises from its various forms and from the fact that these forms permit special treatment of problems peculiar to particular local units. The superior quality of administrative control is attributable to the inclusion of experts, specialists, and trained technicians among the officials and employees of administrative agencies. Another reason for the superiority of administrative control is that it permits face-to-face contacts between state and local officials.

(2) DISADVANTAGES Administrative control may result in undue interference in local affairs, as has been the case with legislative control. It also may be exercised by state officials whose competence is questionable, especially in states that have failed to establish a personnel policy based on the merit principle. There is the risk, too, that the flexibility of administrative control will result in discriminations against particular local units just as objectionable as those which occurred during the era of special legislation applying to designated communities.

Number and Types of Local Units

A large proportion of local units serve the dual purpose of acting as agencies for the local administration of state policies and as organs for the satisfaction of essentially local needs. In the case of incorporated municipalities, for instance, the latter role is primary. Counties, townships, school districts, and various other local units are chiefly engaged in administering state-established policies. More often than formerly, however, local units of this type are functioning to an increasing extent as agencies for the solution of problems of local concern.

According to the Bureau of the Census the number of counties in 1970 was 3,069—including the parishes of Louisiana. The figure for 1967 was 3,049 and for 1962, 3043.

Townships (known as towns in New York, Wisconsin, and New England) cover all or part of the rural area in nearly one-half of the states—assignable principally to the northeastern, north central, and central groups of states. The number reported by the Census Bureau for 1970 was 20,884 (17,299 civil townships and 3,585 towns). These subdivisions numbered 17,144 in 1962 and 17,107 in 1967.

Incorporated municipalities (variously known as cities, boroughs, villages, and towns) amounted to 18,666 in 1970. The reported figure for 1962 was 17,997, and for 1967, 18,051.

School districts decreased from 34,678 in 1962 to 21,782 in 1967, and to 17,498 in 1970. In addition, there were 560 non-operating districts in 1970. Other varieties of special districts increased in number from 1962 to 1967, viz., 18,323 for 1962 and 21,264 for 1967. At present no figure is available for 1970. Most special districts perform a single function, such as soil conservation, drainage, fire protection, housing and urban renewal, water supply, sewerage, and highways.

For the period 1962 to 1970 the total number of local units decreased—primarily because of school district mergers which reduced the number of operating districts by nearly fifty percent. As noted above, however, the 1970 figures for counties, townships, and incorporated municipalities are somewhat larger than in 1967. In all probability, too, the number of special districts has increased since that year.

Proposals for Decreasing the Number of Local Units

The continued existence of thousands of local government units has been challenged for a long time on the general ground that better and more economical service could be rendered by local instrumentalities designed to function under twentieth rather than nineteenth century (horse and buggy) conditions. Improved modes of communication and transportation permit an increase in the size of the effective administrative area. Fewer units of larger size with more adequate financial resources could result in the reduction of overhead expenses, higher personnel standards, the more effective use of equipment, areas corresponding to the scope of the problems to be solved, and a much more satisfactory allocation of functions among units of local government than is now the case.

Specific proposals for decreasing the number of local units include the following: (1) reduction in the number of counties, (2) abolition or consolidation of townships,

(3) further consolidation of school districts or transfer of the function of school administration to city and county governments, (4) elimination of many special districts and assumption of their functions by the state or by an appropriate local unit, and (5) the establishment of suitable governmental machinery for metropolitan areas which are now governed by an excessive number of independent units. The legal and political barriers to reforms of this type are numerous and difficult to overcome. Relatively little progress along these lines has been made up to the present time.

County Government

The county is an important unit of local government in all sections of the country other than New England and Alaska. In the New England states the town performs most of the functions which elsewhere are assigned to the county and the county serves chiefly as a judicial district.

Counties differ in their social character. Some are classifiable as rural, some as rural-urban, and others, a minority, are assignable to the urban category.

County Functions

The functions of the county vary considerably throughout the United States, depending on the state and the social complexion of particular counties, i.e., whether primarily rural or urban in character.

Among the nearly universal or fairly common functions are (1) participation in the administration of justice through courts, constituting part of the state judicial system, which are financed from county funds, served by the sheriff and a clerical staff composed of county officials and employees, and conducted by judges who are usually elected by popular vote in the county or a combination of counties; (2) the enforcement of state criminal law within the county through the offices of the prosecuting attorney, the sheriff and/or a county police force; (3) the maintenance of a jail or workhouse for the detention of persons awaiting trial and for the imprisonment of criminals serving short-term sentences; (4) administration of the correctional function of probation; (5) the issuance of various licenses, such as hunting, fishing, and marriage; (6) the assessment of property for taxation, the collection of taxes, and the custody of public funds; (7) the recording of deeds, mortgages, wills, and other documents; (8) the performance of welfare services, among them outdoor relief, assistance to the aged, the blind, and dependent children, and institutional care of the poor, the aged, and the defective; (9) the administration of various health services; (10) educational activities, sometimes involving the direct management of rural schools but usually only supervisory in character; (11) the construction and maintenance of such public works as secondary highways, drains, bridges, and public buildings; and (12) the administration of elections, including the preparation of ballots, selection of polling places, the appointment of election officials, and the canvassing of votes. In performing the foregoing functions, most of which have been discharged by counties for many decades, the county acts primarily as an agent for the local administration of general policies established by the state government.

A substantial number of counties, chiefly those with an urban or semi-urban character, render additional services. Among the newer county activities are the provision of parks, playgrounds, and other recreational facilities; the establishment of libraries; the operation of hospitals; the maintenance of airports; fire protection and forest fire control; various activities pertaining to agriculture and conservation; water and sewerage systems; housing; zoning; and the distribution of electricity. The gradual assumption of activities of the foregoing type, particularly in counties that are becoming urbanized, increases the importance of the county as an organ for the satisfaction of local needs.

Structure of County Government

In most states the more important county offices are provided for by constitutional provision, but determination of their powers and duties, as well as the creation of other positions, is almost always left to the discretion of the state legislature. A few states have granted all or some counties the privilege of determining their own governmental structure; and a larger number, still a small minority, have provided a choice of forms of government through legislative enactment of optional laws.

In many states all counties are organized under the same general laws; in some, counties are classified according to population and the organization of a particular county is determined by the general laws applicable to the class to which it belongs; and in states which still permit special legislation, special acts pertaining to particular counties are often enacted, with the consequence that the specifics of organization are likely to vary from county to county.

Despite variations in detail from state to state and often among the counties of a particular state, county governments in general, with exceptions to be considered below, conform to the same basic structural pattern. Its distinguishing features are extreme division of authority and responsibility; lack of a chief executive; popular election of many, if not most, of the officials heading county departments; and the existence of a county board which, though limited in power, is nevertheless more powerful than any other single agency of county government.

(1) THE USUAL COUNTY OFFICIALS   Among the officials ordinarily associated with the county board are many of the following: the sheriff, prosecuting attorney, coroner or medical examiner, treasurer, controller or auditor, tax collector, assessor, register of wills, recorder of deeds, surveyor, county clerk, court clerks, superintendent of schools, and the members of various boards and commissions.

Of these major officers, six or more are usually chosen by popular vote; the remainder are appointed by the county board or some other agency. Minor officials and employees are selected by the board and the sundry elective officers.

Although the county board is charged with the management and supervision of county affairs, its powers are too restricted for this purpose. It is unable to exercise effective control over the various elected officials who are accountable to the electorate rather than to the board.

Most county governments are describable as a hodgepodge of officers largely independent of one another in the performance of their specified functions. Of all forms of government in the United States (national, state, and local), the usual county organization is the least commendable.

(2) THE COUNTY BOARD   The first ranking organ of government in practically all counties is a county board which is most commonly entitled the Board of County Commissioners. Other titles in use are Board of Supervisors, the County Court, e.g., Missouri, the Fiscal Court, as in Kentucky, the Board of Freeholders in New Jersey, and by different names in several states. Titles are misleading. Thus what is labeled "County Court" in Missouri and two other states is not a court of the judicial variety—merely a county board.

With rare exceptions, the members of county boards are chosen by popular vote. Two- or four-year terms are the most common, but sometimes the designated period of service is three or six years.

(a) SMALL BOARDS   A small county board of three, five, and occasionally seven or nine members is provided for in most of the states, especially those of the South, Southwest, and West, but also in such Eastern or North Central states as Pennsylvania, Ohio, and Indiana. The members of these boards are elected from the county at-large in some states, by districts in others, and by some combination of election-at-large and by districts in a number of states.

(b) LARGE BOARDS   Large county boards range in size from about twenty members (usually) to as many as fifty and occasionally more. Most of them are found in certain North Central states, a few Southern states, and several states in the Middle West. The large boards of such states as Michigan, New York, and Wisconsin are attributable to the plan of according representation to townships and cities. Each township's voters choose a supervisor; one or more supervisors are selected by the voters of cities. Neither townships nor cities have received representation in proportion to their population. Departure from this long-established policy has become necessary because in *Avery v. Midland County* (1968) the Supreme Court ruled that disproportionate representation of districts in local policy-determining bodies, as well as in state legislatures, conflicts with the equal protection clause of the Fourteenth Amendment.

(c) POWERS AND DUTIES The powers and duties of county boards are essentially administrative rather than legislative in character. Such is the case because the county is engaged for the most part in the administration of laws enacted by the state legislature.

As a policy-determining body the board decides questions pertaining to the financing of county activities, the construction of public works, the care and use of county property, the type of equipment to be used, and the management of such institutions as poor farms, jails, and hospitals. County boards, especially in the urban counties, are gradually acquiring authority to enact police, health, and zoning ordinances, building codes, and fire prevention regulations; to undertake sewerage and water supply projects; and to render various services of the type required by the inhabitants of densely populated areas.

Other powers commonly possessed by county boards are the awarding of contracts; the purchase of equipment, materials, and supplies for some county offices; participation in the administration of charitable and other welfare activities; the issuance of licenses of various kinds; the supervision of election machinery; and the appointment and control of sundry minor officials and employees.

The financial authority of county boards usually includes the authorization of expenditures, the levying of taxes, the borrowing of money, the review and equalization of assessments, and the determination of salaries and other forms of compensation. Even in these matters, however, their discretionary power is often limited by state-wide statutes designating permissible sources of revenue, making certain expenditures mandatory, fixing the remuneration of various officials, and requiring the performance of specified services to be paid for by the county.

Due to the diversity of county government throughout the United States, what has been said above about the powers of the county board is subject to numerous exceptions and qualifications in the case of particular counties and groups of counties. Generally speaking, the powers of county boards are more restricted than they ought to be.

As for the functions of county officers other than the board, the general character of the work performed by many of them is indicated by their titles. Examples are the register of wills, the recorder of deeds, the surveyor, the treasurer, the assessor, and the prison warden.

Organizational Defects of County Government

The prevailing form of county government is defective because of a more or less haphazard distribution of powers and responsibilities among a substantial number of officials largely independent of one another. No agency possesses sufficient authority to insure cooperative and coordinated action. Without a chief executive, efficient and effective administration is seldom attainable.

In practically all of the more than three thousand counties, each of the many elected officials, responsible only to the voters, reigns supreme in his own office. If he appoints incompetent persons to subordinate positions, tolerates slipshod methods of administration, and refuses to cooperate with other county agencies, there are no adequate ways of compelling him to change his policies. Even the financial powers of the county board afford no long-range opportunity for effective control. Once the board has fixed the tax rate and appropriated money for the use of various officials, it can do little to prevent the exhaustion of funds prior to expiration of the fiscal year or to insure economy and wisdom in the expenditure of appropriations.

Better Forms of County Government

(1) THE MANAGER PLAN A small proportion of counties no longer operate with the disintegrated type of structure so far described. Nearly fifty are included in the International City Management Association's directory of cities and counties operating under the council-manager plan. Inclusion in this directory occurs only if a manager, selected by the county board, possesses the power to appoint and remove department heads and to prepare the budget for presentation to the board.

In no counties are the powers of the manager as extensive as recommended in the *Model County Manager Law* sponsored by the National Municipal League. However, the manager plan in somewhat modified form is operative in some of the counties of a number of states, mostly in North Carolina (the leader in adoptions of the plan), Virginia, California and Georgia, but also in a few counties of Maryland, Florida, Montana, Nevada, New Mexico, New York, South Carolina, and Tennessee.

(2) AN APPOINTED CHIEF ADMINISTRATOR Approximately fifty counties have created the office of chief administrator. This official is appointed by the county board but his powers are too limited to qualify him as a "manager." Ordinarily, various administrative positions in these counties remain "elective" and the chief administrator's powers with respect to personnel and other phases of administration are too restricted to enable him to function as the effective general manager of *all* of the county's administrative services. Even so, creation of the office of chief administrator, despite its limited authority, represents a significant improvement on the prevailing pattern of county government.

(3) AN ELECTED CHIEF EXECUTIVE A third alternative to this pattern is the establishment of an elected chief executive possessing authority to administer policies adopted by the county board or established by the state legislature. This arrangement resembles the well-known form of mayor-council government for cities, usually the weak rather than the strong mayor variety. An elected executive is provided for in a small number of counties, among them Nassau and Westchester counties of New York, Baltimore County, Maryland, and Milwaukee County, Wisconsin.

The extent of the powers of the elected executive vary among the few counties in which this office exists. Powers of appointment, removal, and supervision, usually limited in various ways, are commonly conferred. In some instances the elected executive, like the mayors of cities, is granted a veto power with respect to acts of the county board.

(4) A DOMINANT COUNTY BOARD Another substitute for the typical variety of county government is to extend the powers of the county board to enable it to exercise complete control over both the determination and administration of county policy. The board would be authorized to appoint and remove the heads of departments and other officials as well. Among the few counties possessing county boards with extensive power over county affairs are Shelby and Moore counties in Tennessee.

Other Defects of County Government

The principal defects of county government in addition to poor organization are unsound personnel policies and unsuitable administrative procedures. These two shortcomings are largely attributable to the organizational defects to which attention has been directed.

(1) PERSONNEL POLICIES Generally speaking, the personnel policies of county governments are anything but commendable. Although some progress toward application of the merit principle has occurred in recent times, as in New York state which has made the merit system compulsory for all local units, the spoils system still predominates in most counties. The situation is aggravated by the popular election of officials holding important administrative positions and by the common legal requirement that both officials and employees must be selected from the resident population. Spoils practices account for a rather high rate of turnover which prevents the public from being served by an experienced personnel and also discourages competent persons from seeking county employment.

(2) ADMINISTRATIVE PROCEDURES AND METHODS The administrative procedures and methods employed by most county governments fall far short of the best practices that have been developed in the public field. Sound budgeting systems, proper accounting methods, other effective controls over departmental spending, and efficient and economical purchasing procedures are conspicuous by their absence in a large majority of counties. Poor organization and a mediocre personnel are largely responsible for these and other deficiencies in administration, but far too often county officials are unable to resort to remedial measures because of restrictive laws which only the state legislature can modify or repeal.

The major defects of county government have received attention. Many others, such as the fee system of compensating various officials and the excessive number of counties, are in need of correction. The county problem in all of its aspects cannot be solved satisfactorily without a complete overhauling of the entire system of local government.

Townships and New England Towns

Townships in the group of states extending westward from New York, New Jersey, and Pennsylvania to the Dakotas are overshadowed by the county. With the exception of a few urbanized townships, they have lost their former significance. In New England, towns are an important unit of local government.

Several reasons account for this difference in status of townships and the New England towns. The latter are natural units of local government inasmuch as their boundaries, almost always irregular, conform fairly closely to socially unified areas, whereas townships, with some exceptions, have been laid out more or less arbitrarily without reference to community interests, particularly in the Middle West where the six-mile-square Congressional township prevails. A second reason is that New England towns furnish services for the village or villages contained within their limits—not merely for their rural inhabitants. The village is an integral part of the town and seldom is separately organized for governmental purposes. In the township states, villages are commonly incorporated and often excluded from the area to which the jurisdiction of township authorities extends. Thirdly, the importance of New England towns is enhanced because they perform most of the functions which elsewhere are assigned to the county.

Townships

(1) FUNCTIONS Ordinarily, the functions of townships are limited in scope and amount to little more in practice than the construction and maintenance of minor roads, bridges, and drains, the administration of outdoor poor relief, sanitary inspection, the establishment of quarantine, the assessment of property for taxation, the collection of state, county, and township taxes, and the administration of elections.

The powers delegated to townships often extend to other matters, among them parks, playgrounds, and libraries, and some townships, such as the first-class townships of Pennsylvania which are essentially urban in character, perform many of the functions of a village or city government.

In a few states the township serves as an area of school administration. If so, the township school district usually functions independently of the township as a governmental unit for other purposes.

(2) ORGANIZATION The governmental organization of townships is difficult to describe because of variations among the several states in which this unit of local government survives. One point of difference is that in some states provision is made for a township meeting of qualified voters, a feature shared with the towns of New England, whereas in other states the township meeting is not included among the agencies of township government.

(a) THE TOWNSHIP MEETING PLAN As part of the machinery of government in such states as Michigan, Illinois, Minnesota, and the Dakotas, the township meeting of qualified voters elects township officers, authorizes expenditures, levies taxes, enacts police and other regulations, and performs miscellaneous functions of minor importance. As a rule these township meetings are poorly attended.

The most important township official is variously known as the supervisor, township chairman, or township trustee. Whatever his title, he is the chief administrative officer of the township and also a member of the township board. In some of the states in this group, he represents the township on the county board.

The township board in these "township meeting" states is ordinarily an *ex officio* body composed of the supervisor, the town clerk, and justices of the peace, or of some similar combination of township officials. Its most important and usual function is to assist and check the supervisor, i.e., the chief administrative officer, whatever his title may be.

Among other township officers, some elected and others

appointed, are the treasurer, the clerk, the assessor, overseer of the poor, road commissioners, and constables. In some townships the duties of one or more of these offices are performed by the supervisor.

(b) THE TOWNSHIP BOARD PLAN No provision is made for the township meeting in Pennsylvania, Ohio, Indiana, and four other states. The most important organ of government in this category of states is the township board which is likely to be entitled the board of supervisors or the board of trustees. Its few members, usually three in number, are commonly chosen by popular vote for short terms. The board decides questions of policy in regard to township activities, appropriates money, levies taxes, and often acts as a general administrative authority, frequently administering poor relief and controlling road construction and maintenance. It is generally associated with a number of elective officers, such as the treasurer, clerk, assessor, tax collector, constable, and sometimes an auditor or auditors.

In some townships of this type, there is a chief official, e.g., the township trustee, who occupies about the same position as the supervisor in the township meeting states. A number of townships employ a township manager with sufficient authority to be listed among the units of local government operating under the "manager" plan.

(3) UNCERTAIN FUTURE OF THE TOWNSHIP The future of the township is uncertain. With some exceptions, e.g., the urbanized township, its few remaining functions probably should be transferred to the county.

The chief merit of the township is that its officials are closer to the public, more readily contacted, and more re-

sponsive to the representations of the residents of particular
localities than the officers of county and state governments
whose relations with the people have become increasingly
impersonal. These considerations are offset by the greater
administrative efficiency and economy realizable through
the functioning of local units of larger size with more adequate financial resources. However, elimination of the township, without substantial improvement in the quality of
county government, is unlikely to produce the results which
in theory are attainable through the substitution of larger
for smaller units of local government.

New England Towns

(1) FUNCTIONS   The towns of New England perform
a greater variety of functions than most of the townships
of other states. Their authority usually comprehends the
construction and maintenance of such public works as street
pavements, roads, bridges, drains, sewers, waterworks, lighting plants, and parks; the collection and disposal of garbage,
ashes, and rubbish; the administration of poor relief; the
enactment of regulations for the promotion of health and
safety; and the management and operation of schools. Furthermore, the towns are required to act as agents of the
state in the recording of vital statistics, deeds, and wills;
the enforcement of health laws; the assessment and collection
of state taxes; and in other matters that in most states are
assigned to counties.

This enumeration of town powers and duties is neither
complete nor indicative of the scale of operations of particular towns. What individual towns actually do depends
for the most part on the density and distribution of their

population. Urban and semi-urban towns perform a far greater variety of functions than towns which are primarily rural in character. As stated above, New England towns furnish governmental services for the inhabitants of villages contained within their limits as well as for their rural populations.

(2) ORGANIZATION: (a) TOWN MEETINGS One of the noteworthy features of the governmental organization of New England towns is survival of the town meeting as an instrument of direct democracy. Qualified voters of the town are eligible to participate in the annual or special meetings held in the town hall. However, the increase in population of some towns has brought about the "limited" meeting which involves the selection of delegates from voting precincts. Only the delegates are permitted to vote in the transaction of town business, even though voters in general are allowed to attend and participate in discussion.

The town meeting, whatever its composition, elects officers, enacts by-laws, appropriates money, levies taxes, authorizes the creation of indebtedness, and decides questions of policy. Advisory committees are often used for the preliminary consideration of financial and other matters.

(b) THE SELECTMEN AND OTHER OFFICIALS The officials commonly chosen for a short term by the town meeting include the selectmen, a town clerk, a treasurer, a tax assessor, an overseer of the poor, a constable, a school board, and a road commissioner. In some towns other officers and boards are elected and in all of them various minor officials and employees are appointed by the selectmen and other elective officers.

The selectmen vary in number from three to nine, usually three, and function as an administrative board which, as directed by the town meeting, undertakes the general supervision of town affairs. A large number of towns, especially in Maine, have provided for a town manager who directs and supervises administration. This official is appointed by the board of selectmen.

The town clerk is a particularly important officer who acts as secretary of the town meeting and custodian of town archives; issues marriage licenses; records vital statistics; and performs various duties elsewhere assigned to county clerks. If re-elected frequently, as is commonly the case, he becomes an extremely influential person in the governmental processes of the town. In towns not employing a manager, by far the great majority, the clerk in practice shares much of the responsibility for managing town business with the board of selectmen.

Special Districts

Over fifty percent of the local units of government in the United States fall in the "special district" category. Slightly fewer than half of them are school districts. The remainder deal with such matters as highways, bridges, tunnels, ports, sewage collection and disposal, water supply, flood control, irrigation, housing and urban renewal, fire protection, and soil conservation. Most special districts are single-functional; multi-functional districts are few in number.

The creation of special districts is due to a number of reasons. Among them are (1) the limited area and re-

sources of other local units, (2) avoidance of the opposition certain to arise against more drastic and comprehensive measures for reforming the local government system,
e.g., consolidation of existing units and abolition of some,
(3) the desire to evade tax and debt limitations commonly
imposed on local governments, and (4) the contention,
rarely substantiated by experience even in the field of education, that a special district stands a better chance of escaping the impact of partisan politics.

The validity of these reasons depends on the type of
district and the pertinent circumstances in particular cases.
Generally speaking, however, the special district plan is a
makeshift arrangement pending the time when the entire
system of local government can be overhauled in consideration of contemporary social conditions and governmental
needs. The prospects for such an overhaul seem dim.

The governing authority of a special district is usually a
board or commission generally chosen by popular vote but
sometimes appointed by a state agency, e.g., the governor,
or by the governing bodies of the several local units included within the district boundaries. These boards decide
questions of policy, raise money, appoint subordinate officials and employees, and either direct and supervise administration themselves or select a secretary, manager, or superintendent for this purpose. Of all special districts, the school
district is best known. Its characteristic organization includes an elective board and a board-appointed superintendent of schools.

Local Government: Municipalities

CHAPTER ☆ FOURTEEN

Urban Population
Legal Status of Cities
City Charters
    Legislative Charters: Special Acts; General Laws; Optional Charter Plan
    Home Rule Charters: Initial Adoption or General Revision; Partial Amendment
Home Rule Systems
Forms of City Government
    Mayor-Council Plan
        Weak and Strong Mayors
        Strong Mayor with a Managing Director
    Commission Plan: Its Features and Defects
    Council-Manager Plan
        The Council
        The Mayor
        The Manager: Administrative Powers and Role in Policy-Determination
    Comparison of Strong Mayor-Council and Council-Manager Plans
Governmental Problems of Metropolitan Areas
    Nature of a Metropolitan Area
        Causes of Origin and Growth

Political Decentralization

Matters of Metropolitan-Wide Concern: Illustrations

Opposition to Termination of Excessive Governmental
    Decentralization

Legal Obstacles

Slowness of the Reorganization Movement

Partial Solutions of the Metropolitan Governmental
    Problem

Comprehensive Solutions

    Single Government Plan

    Federal Plan

    City-County Separation and City-County Consoli-
    dation

☆ ☆ ☆ ☆ ☆ ☆ ☆ ☆ ☆ ☆ ☆ ☆

In 1970 73.5% of the inhabitants of the United States dwelt in places classified as urban by the Bureau of the Census. The proportion was 5.1% in 1790, 39.7% in 1900, 52.2% in 1920, 64% in 1950, and 69.9% in 1960. Urban-rural population percentages by states are more significant than the figure for the country as a whole. Thus each of ten states (New York, New Jersey, Massachusetts, Rhode Island, Illinois, California, Florida, Utah, Nevada, Hawaii) had an urban population exceeding 80% in 1970, whereas in eight states (North and South Dakota, Alaska, Mississippi, West Virginia, Vermont, North and South Carolina) the urban percentage ranged from 32% to 48%.

As of 1970 most urbanites lived in incorporated places

with a population of 2,500 or more. The remainder dwelt in
densely populated unincorporated territory adjacent to cities
having a population of 50,000 or more; in incorporated
communities with fewer than 2,500 inhabitants; in urban
towns and townships; or in other territory with a population
concentration meeting the minimum established by the Census Bureau's definition of an urban place. *For the first time
the suburban population was greater than that of either the
central cities or the non-metropolitan parts of the country.*

Of the total of urban incorporated places, six had a population exceeding 1,000,000, twenty were inhabited by
500,000 to 1,000,000 persons, thirty fell in the 250,000 to
500,000 category, and ninety-seven had populations in the
100,000 to 250,000 range. The number of incorporated places
with a population from 2,500 to 100,000 was nearly seven
thousand. About two-thirds of these had a population between 2,500 and 10,000. Only a few unincorporated places,
towns, and townships had more than 100,000 inhabitants.

In 1970 over two-thirds of the United States population
dwelt in 243 standard metropolitan statistical areas as defined by the Census Bureau. However, in late 1971 the
Office of Management and Budget issued a revised set of
criteria for determining metropolitan status. Consequently
the total number of standard metropolitan statistical areas
recognized officially in 1972 is 264 rather than 243. The
new definition established the following criteria: (a) at
least one city with 50,000 or more inhabitants, or (b) a
population density of at least 1,000 per square mile in an
area having a population composed of the inhabitants of a
city of 25,000 or more plus the residents of contiguous
places, provided that the city and the contiguous places
constitute a single community for general economic and

social purposes with a combined population of 50,000 or above, and provided also that the one or more counties in which the city and contiguous places are located have a total population of at least 75,000.[131] Later in this chapter another definition of metropolitan areas will be presented in conjunction with a discussion of their various governmental problems.

The Legal Status of Cities

For governmental purposes, cities are organized as municipal corporations with definite territorial boundaries. The principal reason for their incorporation is to promote the interests and contribute to the convenience of the inhabitants of a locality by establishing the right and the power of local self-government. In addition to functioning as organs for the satisfaction of local needs, municipal corporations serve as agencies of the state for the local administration of state-established policies. The former role is primary, the latter secondary.

As corporations, municipalities possess such common law powers as the authority to sue and be sued, to grant or receive in the corporate name, to purchase and hold lands, to have a common seal, and to make by-laws for the better government of the corporation. In addition, they possess whatever powers are delegated to them by the state.

The general legal rule concerning the powers of municipal corporations is that they possess only such powers as have

---

[131] This summation of the new definition is based on Bureau of the Census, Supplementary Report, *Population of Standard Metropolitan Statistical Areas established since the 1970 Census for the United States,* May 1972.

been granted them in express terms, or by necessary and
fair implication from express grants, or by inference from
their nature as corporations and the objects and purposes of
their creation. In drawing inferences with respect to the
delegation of powers, the courts ordinarily pursue a policy
of strict construction. Doubts concerning the possession of
power are usually resolved against municipal corporations.

City Charters

The powers and duties of a municipal corporation attach to it in its corporate capacity. These, together with the
details of its organization, are for the most part enumerated
in a charter which is considered an indispensable element
of every municipal corporation. Charters not only prescribe
the form of city government and the powers and duties of
municipal officials, but frequently establish the procedures
to be followed in the exercise of various powers and sometimes define the details of policy with respect to important
municipal problems.

From the standpoint of legal origin, two kinds of city
charters are distinguishable, viz., legislative charters and
home rule charters. The former are acts of the state legislature and the latter are drafted and adopted by duly authorized agencies of the city.

(1) LEGISLATIVE   CHARTERS: (a) SPECIAL   ACTS
In the absence of constitutional restrictions, the state legislature may pass a *special act* which constitutes the charter
of the particular city named therein. This method of providing charters prevailed until the middle of the nineteenth
century. Thereafter it was prohibited by constitutional pro-

vision in one state after another and today it may be utilized in only a small minority of the states.

(b) GENERAL LAWS In states which have banned special act charters, the legislature may enact a *general law* which serves as the charter of all cities in the state, or may *classify* cities on a population basis and provide a general law type of charter for each of the several classes established. No state now requires all cities to operate under a single general code. A majority use the classification plan, but not always to the exclusion of other methods of providing city charters.

(c) OPTIONAL CHARTER PLAN Another course of action pursuable by state legislatures is to grant cities the privilege of choosing one of two or more legislative charters incorporated in general laws applying to all cities or to all of a designated class. This method is known as the *optional charter plan*. A substantial majority of the states provide optional charters for either some cities or for practically all.

(2) HOME RULE CHARTERS Home rule charters are those which cities draft and adopt in states that have granted this right either by constitutional or by statutory provision. Almost half of the states have established "home rule" in this sense by constitutional guarantees of the following type: "cities may frame and adopt charters for their own government consistent with, and subject to, the constitution and laws of the state." Sometimes the qualifying phrase is worded differently, viz., "subject to the constitution and general laws of the state." Either wording is open to various interpretations. Other constitutions contain expressions to

the effect that cities may govern themselves in matters of
municipal or local concern.

A number of states included within the constitutional
home rule group confer the right to draft and adopt charters on all cities. Many, however, extend the privilege only
to cities with a designated minimum population, such as a
size greater than 5,000 or 10,000.

Some states, few in number, have granted the right to
draft and adopt charters by *statutory* provision. Statutory
home rule, being merely a matter of legislative policy, may
be terminated whenever the state legislature sees fit to do
so.

Despite variations in detail, the methods of preparing,
ratifying, revising, and amending home charters are basically
the same everywhere. Usually, the process for either the
initial preparation and adoption or the subsequent revision
of home rule charters differs from that established for partial
amendment.

(a) INITIAL ADOPTION OR GENERAL REVISION   An
elective local charter commission or board of freeholders is
commonly utilized for the drafting of a new charter or for
its subsequent general revision. Such a commission is brought
into being in several ways, viz., by passage of an ordinance
by the existing city council, by the filing of a petition signed
by a designated minimum number of voters, or by a popular vote following the enactment of an ordinance or the
filing of a petition.

The final step in the charter-making process is submission
of the commission's charter to the voters. An ordinary majority of those voting on the proposed charter is sufficient
for ratification in nearly all of the states, but an extraor-

dinary majority or an ordinary majority of those voting at the election is required in some states.

(b) PARTIAL AMENDMENT The methods for partial amendment of home rule charters are essentially the same in all of the states. Ordinarily, amendments may be proposed either by the city council or by a petition signed by some specified percentage of the qualified voters. Proposed amendments must be ratified in most jurisdictions by a simple majority of those voting *thereon* at a general or special municipal election. Exceptions to this usual procedure are established in some states.

Home Rule Systems

Constitutional home rule systems involve more than the simple right of drafting and adopting charters. An exceedingly important aspect concerns the scope of home rule powers and the extent of freedom from state legislative control. From this standpoint, four general types of home rule system are distinguishable.

One system enables cities to exercise *exclusive* control over matters of purely local concern by virtue of an express or implied constitutional grant of authority. Under another, although power to deal with matters of local concern is likewise conferred by constitutional provision, the state legislature possesses concurrent power to control such affairs by laws which apply uniformly to all cities. The other two systems have one feature in common, viz., the legislature retains authority to prescribe the powers of home rule cities. In one of these two, however, if a granted power pertains to local matters, state legislative control over them is inapplicable until such time as the power is withdrawn, whereas under the other system state legislation not only determines the powers of municipalities but also supersedes the conflicting provisions of charters and local ordinances in all matters, whether of state or local concern. The single common feature of the four varieties of constitutional home rule is the right of cities to draft, adopt, and amend their charters under whatever conditions are established by constitutional or statutory provisions, usually both.

Generally speaking, the original motive behind the home rule movement was to free cities from unwarranted intervention in their affairs by the state legislature, to provide them with adequate authority to solve their own problems, and to enable them to choose their own form of government. The extent to which these aims have been realized depends on the type of home rule system and on the rulings of courts with respect to the line of demarcation between matters of local concern and those of state concern. This line is difficult to establish, especially because of the changing conditions and needs of a dynamic society. Fewer and fewer problems are of concern to but one level of government.

Forms of City Government

The several patterns of city government in the United States are distinguishable from the standpoint of the relationship between the organs charged with the performance of legislative, executive, and administrative functions. Since courts which operate in urban areas are integral parts of the state judicial system, arrangements made for the administration of justice need not be taken into consideration. Each of the prevailing forms of city government is characterized by a controlling principle with respect to the functional distribution of power and responsibility.

The Mayor-Council Plan

Most cities operate under the mayor-council plan which is based on the doctrines of separation of powers and checks and balances. In its essential features this plan bears resemblance to the national and state governments. Powers are divided between an elective mayor and an elective council. Two varieties of mayor-council government are identifiable, viz., the strong mayor and the weak mayor types.

(1) WEAK AND STRONG MAYORS The weak mayor form provides for a mayor who is the nominal chief executive but shares control over administration with the council, with a varying number of elective officials, and with other agencies which, for one reason or another, he is unable to direct effectively. A weak mayor's administrative function is largely confined to the giving of advice and to supervision.

The distinguishing attributes of "strong mayors" in the legal sense are broad authority to appoint and remove department heads and other subordinate administrative officials, the power to prepare the budget, and possession of various other means of exercising effective control over the functioning of administrative agencies. Consequently, the role of the strong mayor is directive and managerial with respect to administration.

The position of "strong mayors" resembles that of the President of the United States. "Weak mayors" occupy an

office that is very much like the governor's post in the
structure of most state governments.

Weak and strong mayors possess essentially the same
legal powers in relation to the formal process of policy-
determination. Practically all mayors are authorized to make
recommendations to the council and to call special council
meetings. Most of them possess a suspensive veto over ordinances and resolutions adopted by the council. In addition,
many mayors preside over council meetings, a substantial
majority may vote in case of a tie, and a few are full-fledged
council members. Of the mayors who neither preside nor
hold regular seats in the council, some have the right to
attend meetings and take part in discussion. A few have the
privilege of introducing ordinances for council consideration.

Although strong and weak mayor varieties of the basic
pattern of mayor-council government are distinguishable,
this differentiation tends to over-simplify the actual situation because the degree of power possessed respectively by
mayors and councils varies so much from place to place that
it is often difficult to decide whether the government of a
particular mayor-council city is assignable to the strong
mayor or the weak mayor category.

The controlling consideration is the extent of the mayor's
power in regard to administration. In extreme cases his administrative authority is so restricted that the form of
government is more accurately describable as "council-
manic" rather than "mayor-council," provided that the
council possesses sufficient authority to exercise effective
control over all other agencies of city government.

(2) THE STRONG MAYOR PLAN WITH A MANAGING
DIRECTOR A comparatively recent innovation in connec-

tion with the strong mayor plan is the addition of a "managing director" selected by and responsible to the mayor. In Philadelphia, one of the few cities that have taken this step, the managing director exercises supervision over the departments whose heads he appoints and over the boards and commissions connected with these departments. With the approval of the mayor, the managing director appoints the following commissioners (department heads): police, health, fire, streets, recreation, welfare, water, public property, licenses and inspections, and records. This arrangement and a few other features of the Philadelphia plan are designed to lighten the heavy work load of a strong mayor in an urban community of large size, without, however, reducing his ultimate responsibility for administrative results.

The Commission Plan

The commission plan is mainly a twentieth century development. After its establishment in Galveston, Texas, in 1901, it spread fairly rapidly, but reached the peak of its popularity during the decade from 1910 to 1920. Although losing ground today, it remains one of the standard plans of city government in the United States.

(1) THE COMMISSION: ITS DOMINANT ROLE The commission type of government is characterized by the concentration of policy-determining and administrative power in a small group of persons, usually three or five in number, elected by the voters. This commission legislates and also functions as a plural executive. As individuals, its members act as the heads of administrative departments and in this capacity are responsible to the entire commission and subject to its control.

The two principal ways of determining the departmental assignments of the commissioners are by action of the commission or by popular election. If the latter method is used, candidates for the commission seek election as commissioners in charge of particular departments.

(2) THE MAYOR One of the commissioners is a mayor, sometimes entitled president or chairman of the commission. The mayor is elected directly as mayor-commissioner in some cities, but chosen by the commission from its own membership in others. In a few cities the candidate polling the highest vote at the popular election of commissioners becomes the mayor, and occasionally, in connection with a staggered term arrangement under which one commissioner retires from office annually, each commissioner acts as mayor during his last year in office.

The mayor serves as the official and ceremonial head of the city government, presides over the commission's meetings, and ordinarily heads an administrative department. In addition, he is authorized to call special meetings of the commission, usually is required to prepare an annual report covering the activities of the city government, and frequently is charged with the exercise of general supervision over administration.

This last-mentioned responsibility means little because no mayor can supervise effectively without powers of compulsion and without appropriate tools of management. The powerless mayor-commissioner is seldom able to exert significant influence over departments headed by commissioners who have been chosen by the voters and who are legally responsible only to the entire commission, of which the mayor is merely one member.

(3) DEFECTS OF THE COMMISSION PLAN Lack of a chief administrator has proved to be a major defect of the commission plan. Although the commission is supposed to function as a plural executive, what usually occurs is that each commissioner is permitted to manage his own department as he pleases. Another defect is that the elected commissioners are unlikely to be properly qualified for service as department heads. A third principal shortcoming is the rigidity of administrative organization. The number of administrative departments depends on the size of the commission, e.g., five commissioners and therefore five departments.

The Council-Manager Plan

The council-manager plan dates back to 1908 when the council of Staunton, Va., enacted an ordinance creating an officer entitled "General Manager" to be selected by its two-chambered council for a one-year term, subject to removal by the council at any time. This official was placed in control of the various administrative departments of the city which, at the time, had a government of the weak mayor-council variety.

The Staunton experiment was followed by the abortive Lockport plan. It was drafted by Richard S. Childs who is generally recognized as the father of council-manager government. This plan served as a model for council-manager charters. Council-manager government was initially established by *charter* provision for Sumter, S. C., in 1913 and thereafter, during the same year, for a few other cities.

A major milepost in the council-manager movement was adoption of the plan by Dayton, Ohio. Its charter became effective January 1, 1914. Dayton was the first large city to install council-manager government. The plan's marked success in this city gave impetus to its rapid spread in subsequent years.

In 1971, 2,163 municipalities were operating under this plan. The largest cities were Dallas (844,401), San Diego (696,769), San Antonio (654,153), Phoenix (581,562), Kansas City, Mo. (507,330), and Cincinnati (452,524). Most council-manager municipalities had fewer than 50,000 inhabitants. The total number over 10,000 was 1,029; from 5,000 to 10,000—505; and below 5,000—629.[131a]

(1) THE COUNCIL   The controlling principle of the council-manager form is a concentration of authority and responsibility in the council in combination with a division of functions between the council and the manager. Complete council control over both policy-determination and administration is attained by requiring the adoption of policies by the council and by granting it power to appoint the manager and dismiss him at pleasure. In selecting a manager the council is free to search far and wide for a capable person because of the usual charter provision that the manager need not be a local resident at the time of his appointment.

Most councils are small in size and seldom have more than three or five members. However, larger councils are by no means inconsistent with the council-manager idea. Thus Cincinnati, a city in which the plan has functioned successfully, has a council of nine members.

[131a] *Municipal Year Book, 1972*, derived from Tables 1/4, 1/5, 1/6.

Councilmen are chosen by popular vote for a definite term which is either two or four years in most cities. A substantial majority of communities provide for election-at-large rather than by districts.

(2) THE MAYOR Among the members of the council is a mayor.[132] This officer is ordinarily chosen in one of two ways, either by the council from its own membership or by direct popular election to the position of mayor-councilman. The mayor is official head of the city government and the council's presiding officer. Neither the mayor nor the council is supposed to engage in the administration of policies. Such action is commonly prohibited by express charter provision. The council may deal with administrative matters only by ordinance or resolution.

The mayor, a voting member of the council, may call special meetings of that body. He does not possess a veto power. Since he is titular head of the government and chairman of the council, the mayor is the logical spokesman for the council in the political field. Some mayors have been notably successful in providing political leadership in the initiation of new policies, in the development of support for them, and in the defense of established policies whenever the occasion for defending them arises. The manager is not supposed to undertake the responsibility of political leadership. That function should be discharged by the mayor and other council members.

---

[132] Some communities use the title "president" or "chairman" instead of "mayor."

(3) THE MANAGER   The manager is the administrative agent of the council. Being appointed by the council and removable at its pleasure, he lacks the independence of the elected mayor under the mayor-council form. The manager also plays an important part in policy-determination as an expert adviser to the council and often as a civic leader. Whether it is desirable for the manager to assume community, as distinguished from political, leadership is a delicate and highly controversial question.

(a) ADMINISTRATIVE POWERS   As administrative head of the city government, the manager possesses a variety of important powers. Among them are direction, control, supervision, and coordination of the administration of city services; the appointment and removal of department heads and other subordinate officials; investigation of the affairs of any administrative agency; preparation of a budget and execution of the budget eventually adopted by the council; and the enforcement of laws and ordinances. Powers of the foregoing type, as well as some others of lesser importance, enable the manager to function effectively as the general or over-all manager of agencies engaged in the administration of city services.

(b) ROLE IN POLICY-DETERMINATION   The role of the manager in regard to policy-determination by the council is merely advisory and informative. His specific powers and/or duties include the making of policy recommendations, the provision of information, preparation of the business requiring council consideration, and, in some cities, calling special council meetings.

Despite the limited nature of these powers, the manager's influence is likely to be substantial because of his prestige as the chief specialist in municipal affairs. As long as the council retains the services of a particular manager, the presumption that it has confidence in his judgment seems warranted.

Comparison of the Strong Mayor-Council and Council-Manager Plans

No form of government is sufficient in itself to guarantee satisfactory results, but some types of organization are more likely than others to promote higher standards of performance. Of the patterns of city government identifiable in the United States, the most desirable, as evidenced by experience, are the council-manager and strong mayor-council plans. The commission and weak mayor forms have proved defective in too many respects to entitle them to a satisfactory rating.

The strong mayor-council and council-manager plans meet the requirements of democratic government. Both also provide for a chief administrator with sufficient power to function effectively as general manager of the administrative services. Mayors are chosen by popular vote for fixed terms, whereas managers are appointed by an elective council to serve at the latter's pleasure.

The weight of available evidence indicates that managers in general are better qualified than mayors in general for service as chief administrators. Elected mayors are persons who have voter appeal, enjoy participation in election campaigns, are politically-minded in the partisan sense, and are laymen without greater competence for the task of general administrative management than many of their fellow citizens. The prospects for continuous service as mayors are usually slim.

Managers are appointed for indefinite periods of service, need not possess vote-gathering ability or be local residents at the time of selection, and as a group are professional rather than amateur administrators. Their outlook is non-partisan rather than partisan, as that of elective mayors must almost always be. Of course, some managers have been no better than the average mayor and some mayors have been superior to the average manager. Even so, an appointed chief administrator is more likely to be well-qualified for this post than an elected mayor.

A shortcoming of the mayor-council plan is the division of responsibility between an elected mayor and an elected council. Conflicts and deadlocks often develop between these two major agencies of city government and each is inclined to blame the other for such misgovernment as occurs. Under the council-manager plan ultimate responsibility for results rests with the council which is free to dismiss the manager whenever it concludes that his services are no longer satisfactory.

An advantage of the mayor-council form is that the mayor is expected to provide political leadership. Being an elected official it is proper for him to do so. The appointed manager, however, is not supposed to engage in partisan politics. If he does, his dismissal is inevitable; if he does not, and the mayor-councilman and other members of the council fail to provide such leadership, an important need of many urban communities (particularly those of large size) remains unfilled. One of the major criticisms of the council-manager plan is that its successful operation is endangered unless the mayor and council prove equal to the task of furnishing effective political leadership.

The steady increase in the number of council-manager cities is indicative of its success. Comparatively few communities have abandoned it. Despite the opposition of persons who for various reasons prefer an elected chief administrator, more and more cities will probably adopt the council-manager form. Those which retain or adopt the strong mayor-council plan are likely to provide for a managing director of the Philadelphia type who is selected by and responsible to the strong mayor.

The Governmental Problems of Metropolitan Areas

Nature of a Metropolitan Area

A metropolitan area is a densely populated region, predominantly urban in character, which has developed a substantial degree of unity in its social and economic life. Ordinarily, by far the greater part of its population is assembled in an aggregate of distinctly urban communities which are so closely related to one another, geographically as well as economically and socially, that they constitute a complex super-community with a number of distinguishable centers of population. This super-community also includes the rural or semi-rural areas adjacent to, and socially and economically dependent on, its component urban centers.

Generally, but not necessarily, the urban portion of a metropolitan area consists of one relatively large and dominant city associated with neighboring urban concentrations of smaller size that are often described as suburbs and satellites. New York, Chicago, Philadelphia, Los Angeles, and Detroit, to cite but a few examples, dominate the areas of which they are an integral part. Sometimes, as in the case of the Allentown, Bethlehem, and Easton area of Pennsylvania, none of the three major cities is considerably larger than the others.

Causes of Origin and Growth

The origin and growth of metropolitan areas is essentially a story of the increase and distribution of population as affected by technological developments in the production of wealth and in the modes of communication and transportation. Precise determination of the boundaries of metropolitan areas is difficult because the influence wielded by the dominant city or cities and the degree of social and economic interdependence between the central and outlying sections decreases gradually and imperceptibly, rather than abruptly and obviously, as the distance from the center or centers of population increases. A shifting of these boundaries occurs continuously.

Political Decentralization

Extreme governmental (political) decentralization prevails in metropolitan areas despite their more or less unified economic and social structure. With few exceptions, metropolitan areas lack a government with area-wide jurisdiction endowed with adequate authority to solve all of the many problems of metropolitan concern. Instead, each of the units of local government, such as cities, villages, towns, counties, townships, school districts, and sundry other special districts, undertakes the task of providing necessary services for that portion of the metropolitan area falling within its legal boundaries.

The number of these units is large in numerous metropolitan areas. For example, as reported by the Bureau of the Census in 1967, the Chicago statistical metropolitan area included 1,113; Philadelphia, 876; Pittsburgh, 704; New York, 557; and St. Louis, 474. Each of these areas has a population exceeding 2,000,000. In metropolitan areas with a population under 100,000, the number of local units is considerably smaller, ranging in 1962 (except in one case) from 2, 4, and 5 to 40, 47, and 48. The exception was 155, including 119 school districts, in the Sioux Falls, S. D., area. However, there is no definite relation between the number of local units and the size of a metropolitan area in either population or territorial extent.

Matters of Metropolitan-Wide Concern: Illustrations

Experience has demonstrated that conditions of life in metropolitan areas create many problems that can be solved properly only by taking into account the needs and interests of the entire area. Considerations of effectiveness, efficiency, economy, and convenience necessitate comprehensive and coordinated plans of action instead of the diverse and unrelated policies which usually result from the narrowly local approach of a multiplicity of governments with limited jurisdiction.

Among the matters of metropolitan-wide concern are the planning of general growth and development; transportation facilities; a system of arterial highways; traffic regulation; water supply; sewerage; light and power service; public health; police and fire protection; educational and recreational facilities and programs; housing; and the financing of governmental operations. A brief consideration of a few of these problems will indicate the benefits to be derived from the establishment of metropolitan programs of action.

(1) TRANSPORTATION   The constant flow of persons and goods into and out of a metropolitan area and from one section to another necessitates a variety of transportation facilities. Provision must be made for effective means of mass transportation, for the free and easy movement of automobiles and trucks, and for adequate terminal facilities to accommodate passengers and freight transported by land, water, and air. Unless the several modes of transportation are properly coordinated and capable of meeting peak demands, tremendous losses in time, effort, and money are suffered, congestion becomes acute, and the potential advantages of life in a metropolitan community are only partially realized. Although transportation has its strictly local aspects, the problem as a whole is too complex and extensive to be solved through the individual and unrelated efforts of numerous governmental agencies operating within restricted areas and handicapped by limited financial resources.

(2) SEWERAGE   Sewerage systems are indispensable for the collection and disposal of house and storm sewage. To avoid pollution it is almost always necessary to subject house sewage to treatment before ultimate discharge into some body of water. The design and construction of a sewerage system, the type of sewage treatment plants to be provided, and the selection of proper points of discharge into available bodies of water are engineering problems that should be solved without taking into consideration the artificial territorial limits of the numerous governmental units within a metropolitan area.

(3) WATER SUPPLY An adequate supply of pure water must be furnished the inhabitants of urban communities for domestic, manufacturing, and public purposes. If each of the separately incorporated municipalities in a metropolitan area provides its own system, water costs become unnecessarily high because of unneeded plant duplications and the higher operating expenses per gallon of water due to small-scale service. The proper solution of this problem requires a metropolitan rather than a narrowly local approach.

(4) GERMS AND CRIMINALS One of the chief obstacles to public health protection and to a more effective enforcement of criminal law is the existence of numerous independent and uncoordinated health and police agencies. Neither germs nor criminals behave as they should in view of the decentralized political organization of metropolitan areas. Misgovernment in one or more communities becomes a menace to the entire metropolitan district.

(5) FINANCE The financial factor looms large in the adequate solution of these and other problems of metropolitan-wide concern. Since taxable wealth is unevenly distributed throughout a metropolitan area, some of its component parts cannot afford to render as high a quality of service as the promotion of public welfare in its many aspects requires, e.g., the construction of expensive public works. Governmental arrangements which permit tapping the full resources of a metropolitan community for the benefit of all of its inhabitants are urgently needed.

Opposition to the Termination of Excessive Governmental Decentralization in Metropolitan Areas

Opposition, open or surreptitious, to the ending of excessive governmental decentralization in metropolitan areas comes from many quarters. Local officeholders and political leaders generally oppose any movement which may result in the elimination of units of local government and in a reduction of the number of public offices and employments, or in a curtailment of their political influence. Various private interest-groups, such as contractors and supply dealers, who benefit in specific ways from extreme governmental decentralization usually are found in the ranks of the opposition. Local pride, ignorance of the benefits derivable from integration, a strong desire for local autonomy, and distrust of centralizing tendencies motivate many individuals and groups.

Legally independent municipalities with a low tax rate fear that their tax burden will be increased. This fear blinds them to the opportunities for reducing the hazards, the inconveniences, and other costs of living in a metropolitan district through establishment of an effective area-wide governmental organization. The inhabitants of these communities are usually unwilling to pay for the functioning of a government other than that of the place wherein their homes are located, even though they are beneficiaries of the services rendered by the government, for example, of the central city in which a large proportion of them work.

Fear of an increased tax burden as a consequence of metropolitan reorganization also causes the opposition of sundry elements of the populations of the central city or cities of a metropolitan area. Many people fail to realize that the cost of community life is not merely a matter of the dollars spent in support of a particular unit of local government.

Legal Obstacles

Another factor contributing to the difficulty of establishing satisfactory metropolitan governments consists of legal obstacles, both constitutional and statutory. Examples of legal barriers are the frequent need of constitutional amendments or the obtainment of favorable state legislation; the common requirement that either a majority or all of the existing units of government in a metropolitan area must assent to a proposed reorganization; and, if a metropolitan district is included within the boundaries of two or more states (as some of them are), the necessity of negotiating interstate agreements subject to Congressional approval.

Slowness of the Reorganization Movement

So far, little headway has been made toward a *complete* solution of the governmental problems of metropolitan areas in the United States. Practically all comprehensive plans have failed to progress beyond the proposal stage. With few exceptions, the only measures that have been put into effect are classifiable as partial remedies of a makeshift or stop-gap variety. Disagreement concerning the proper remedy for the political ailments of metropolitan areas, if not a cause of inaction, strengthens the opposition to particular proposals.

The outlook for the future seems somewhat brighter than it has been in the past because of a growing realization that something will have to be done to bring governmental arrangements into line with the realities of metropolitan living conditions. Encouraging signs include steps taken by the national government, among them the creation of a Department of Housing and Urban Affairs, a Department of Transportation, and the expansion of conditional grant-in-aid programs for urban areas; the enactment of state legislation in many states removing some of the legal barriers to improvement of the governmental situation in metropolitan districts; an increase in the number of investigations and recommendations concerning the metropolitan problem; and the development of a better organized leadership than was forthcoming in preceding decades. However, opposition to the termination of excessive governmental decentralization in metropolitan areas remains formidable.

Partial Solutions of the Metropolitan Governmental Problem

Solutions of the partial and makeshift variety, which have been resorted to in many metropolitan areas, include the granting of extra-territorial powers, the transfer of functions from one unit of government to another, intergovernmental cooperation, and the creation of special districts.

(1) EXTRA-TERRITORIAL POWERS Cities are often delegated power to exercise some measure of control over unannexed, outlying areas with respect to such matters as the plotting of land, zoning, the prohibition of nuisances, and health regulations. In addition to such extra-territorial power of a compulsory type, authority is frequently granted to construct certain public works outside the city limits and to render service to neighboring communities on a cooperative basis.

(2) TRANSFER OF FUNCTIONS The transfer of functions from one unit of local government to another is occurring with increasing frequency. For instance, the operation of parks in Rochester, N. Y., has been transferred to Monroe County and Louisville's welfare activities have been shifted to Wake County in Kentucky.

(3) INTERGOVERNMENTAL COOPERATION Intergovernmental cooperation has been discussed in a preceding chapter. It involves not only the rendition of service by one unit of government for others but also the undertaking of joint enterprises and the policy of an exchange of services or mutual aid. Cooperative action of one type or another occurs in an impressive range of municipal functions. However, the number of such arrangements remains small in proportion to the opportunities for cooperation.

(4) SPECIAL DISTRICTS A more effective way of dealing with some of the governmental problems of metropolitan areas is by the creation of special districts for the purpose of coping with one or more matters of metropolitan-wide concern. Most special districts are single-functional, such as a metropolitan water district or a metropolitan park commission. A few are multi-functional. An example is the Massachusetts Metropolitan District Commission, an agency of the state government, which executes projects with respect to water supply, sewerage, and parks in the Boston area. A large proportion of special districts qualify as independent units of *local government*.

As a solution of the governmental problems of metropolitan areas, the establishment of special districts is in general undesirable. In the first place, only a few of the many matters of metropolitan concern have been entrusted to these special agencies. Secondly, if a special district authority were established for the discharge of every function of metropolitan significance, an already cumbersome and complex governmental machinery would become even more complicated. A comprehensive and coordinated program of action for solution of the numerous problems of metropolitan areas is not likely to be developed and executed by a large number of independent governmental agencies with narrowly restricted powers.

The chief value of the special district device is its utility as a makeshift and temporary means of meeting the most urgent needs of metropolitan communities. Since the creation of special districts does not endanger the survival of existing governmental units, opposition thereto is less intense than in the case of more drastic but superior remedies. Largely for this reason, the number of special districts operating in metropolitan areas is increasing steadily.

Comprehensive Solutions of the Metropolitan Governmental Problem

(1) THE SINGLE GOVERNMENT PLAN   The creation of a single government for a metropolitan area involves complete centralization. This plan requires abolition of all governmental units except one, viz., the central city and its government. The boundaries of the central city would be extended to include all territory comprising the metropolitan district.

Whatever the merits of the single government idea (a controversial question), its chances of adoption are virtually nil. Its achievement would require state action or the successful outcome of such annexation and consolidation proceedings as are prescribed by state law. Although many municipalities within metropolitan areas are extending their territorial limits through the process of annexing territory, a common requirement is consent of the inhabitants of areas to be annexed. The likelihood of obtaining it in the case of already incorporated municipalities is decidedly slim. Unincorporated areas are more inclined to endorse proposed annexations.

(2) THE FEDERAL PLAN   A federal type of organization, along the lines of those established in the Canadian metropolitan areas of Toronto and Winnipeg, appears to be the most feasible comprehensive solution. The only example of a plan involving the federal principle in the United States is the Dade County-Miami (Florida) organizational arrangement. Federal plans proposed for the Cleveland, Pittsburgh, and St. Louis areas, for example, were defeated many years ago.

Metropolitan government of the federal variety involves a division of legislative, financial, and administrative powers between a central government and the governments of the several component communities of the metropolitan area. In principle, problems of metropolitan-wide scope fall within the jurisdiction of the central metropolitan government, whereas matters of essentially local concern, which can be handled without disadvantage on a sectional basis, are placed under control of the governments of local units. Within the field of its allocated functions, each government is authorized to formulate, adopt, finance, and administer such policies as it deems expedient. The division of powers between the central metropolitan government and the governments of component communities is achieved by charter provisions which are not alterable by action of the central authorities alone.

(3) CITY-COUNTY SEPARATION AND CITY-COUNTY CONSOLIDATION City-county separation and city-county consolidation are sometimes listed among the various plans for solving the governmental problems of metropolitan areas. Both involve a reduction in the number of governments functioning within a specific area.

In the case of separation, the separated city's government discharges both county and city governmental functions within the city's boundaries. The government of the county from which the city is separated continues to operate in the remaining portion of the county's territory. Adding county functions to those of the city's government eliminates an unnecessary layer of government in the city but accomplishes nothing by way of ending extreme political decentralization in the metropolitan area of which the city is a component part.

Under certain circumstances, city-county consolidation qualifies as a means of solving the governmental problems of a metropolitan area. The circumstances are that the county includes the entire metropolitan district and that smaller units of government within the county either be abolished or survive and share governmental powers with the consolidated government of the county. If powers are shared on the basis of a distinction between matters of county-wide and local concern, the consolidated arrangement qualifies as a federal plan. About one-third of the metropolitan areas of the United States include two or more counties. In these cases, something more than city-county consolidation is needed to solve their governmental problems.

A promising city-county consolidation in a one-county metropolitan area became effective in 1963 with merger of the governments of Nashville and Davidson County in Tennessee. One of its features is a two-district system. The entire county constitutes a *general services* district. In addition there is an expandable *urban services* district. Initially, the latter's boundaries coincided with those of Nashville. The Metropolitan Government of Nashville and Davidson County renders designated area-wide services in the general services district and also provides the additional services of an essentially urban type needed and paid for by the inhabitants of the urban district. Six suburban municipalities, separately incorporated, are located in the general services district and remain outside the urban services section of the county. A similar plan for Chattanooga and Hamilton County of Tennessee was rejected by the voters of these areas in 1964.

The day may come when the governmental problems of metropolitan areas will be solved through adoption of a comprehensive plan, probably one of the federal type. Until then, the most likely remedies are intergovernmental cooperation in its various forms, the transfer of functions from smaller to larger units of government, city-county consolidations in some areas, and the creation of additional special districts. The entire system of local government in the United States needs overhauling. If that were to occur, perhaps in the remote future, the metropolitan problem would undoubtedly receive major consideration. Pressure from the national government through the device of conditional grants-in-aid may hasten the process of modernizing local governmental institutions.

Public Expenditures and Revenues

CHAPTER ☆ FIFTEEN

The Growing Tax Burden: Shall Governmental Services be Curtailed or Eliminated?

Facts Requiring Consideration

Budgets and Budgeting Systems

Nature of a Budget

Importance of Sound Budgeting

Budgetary Systems

Preparation of the Budget

Legalization: Itemized or Lump Sum Appropriations

Execution: Means of Controlling Departmental Spending

Post-Auditing

Barriers to Sound Budgeting

Expenditures

National Government: Totals and Distribution by Functions

State and Local: Totals and Functional Distribution

Public Revenues and Indebtedness

Revenues

Requirements of a Satisfactory Revenue System

Variety of Taxes

Other Sources of Revenue

Comparative Importance of Different Revenue
    Sources
Revenue Raising Limitations: On National Gov-
    ernment; on States and Local Units
Indebtedness
    Guides to Sound Borrowing
    Pay-As-You-Go
    Indebtedness of the National Government, States,
        and Local Units
Constructive Measures of Economy

☆ ☆ ☆ ☆ ☆ ☆ ☆ ☆ ☆ ☆ ☆ ☆ ☆

The *Growing Tax Burden: Shall Governmental
Services be Curtailed or Eliminated?* Complaints about the
growing tax burden in the United States have become commonplace and often are accompanied by demands for re-
trenchment. Many people believe that the remedy is a discontinuance or drastic curtailment of various activities of the
national, state, and local governments. This solution is
sound only if these governments are rendering many socially unnecessary services. Otherwise, the elimination or
limitation of governmental activity may prove to be a measure of destructive rather than constructive economy. Several significant facts are overlooked by those who think
solely in terms of a curtailment of public service.

Facts Requiring Consideration

(1) BOTH PUBLIC AND PRIVATE SERVICES CONSTI-
TUTE COMMUNITY COSTS The expense of services rendered by either public or private agencies is borne by the
community. With respect to the cost in community resources, it is immaterial, assuming equal efficiency and effectiveness in performance, whether a needed service is
paid for from the proceeds of taxation or in the form of a
price paid over the counter by the aggregate of consumers.
For example, an unquestionably necessary service is the
collection and disposal of garbage, ashes, and rubbish. The
inhabitants of the community foot the bill, regardless of the
agency that does the collecting, be it a government department or a private contractor.

(2) PRIVATE VERSUS PUBLIC SERVICE The foregoing illustration suggests another question that has an important bearing on the problem of community costs, viz.,
whether a particular service can be performed more effectively and economically by a government or by private
interests. From the consumer's point of view, it makes no
difference which agency is used, provided that an adequate
standard of service is maintained at a reasonable cost.

Fair comparisons of a general character between governmental and private service are difficult to make. Adequate
criteria for comparative appraisals of performance records
are lacking. In private enterprise the test of profit is frequently relied on to determine the operational efficiency of
a particular concern, but even an inefficient and wasteful
enterprise may be conducted at a profit.

The profit criterion is inapplicable to most governmental

undertakings because their purpose is the creation of social benefits rather than the making of money. Good housing for the lowest income group, public education, police and fire protection, public health services, and social welfare programs—these are but a few of numerous governmental activities which cannot be placed on a self-supporting basis without sacrificing highly desirable social objectives.

In comparing the cost of public and private rendition of a service, the expense of public regulation is a legitimate charge against private enterprise whenever such regulation becomes necessary to prevent abuses detrimental to the public welfare. Such has been the case, for example, with the functioning of privately-owned and operated public utilities. The profit-seeking motive in private business frequently proves incompatible with considerations of social service. Under such circumstances, the solution lies in either governmental enterprise or effective regulation of the private interests in question.

Both community costs and the relative merits of public and private enterprise should be taken into account by advocates of the discontinuance or curtailment of governmental services for the purpose of lightening the tax burden. Transferring services to private agencies will not bring about a reduction in community costs unless private performance proves superior or equal in quality and less expensive than governmental action.

(3) ELIMINATION OR CURTAILMENT OF SERVICES MAY PROVE COSTLY As for the discontinuance or contraction of governmental services, the consequence may be an increase rather than a decrease in community costs. Thus failure to maintain streets in proper condition causes an in-

crease in transportation expenses because of the greater wear and tear on vehicles, higher gasoline consumption, greater traffic hazards, and the like; a lowering of the standard of fire protection results in a rise in fire insurance rates and in an increase in loss of life and property; and a curtailment of public health activities and police protection promotes the spread of disease and an increase in the crime rate. The foregoing are examples of destructive rather than constructive measures of economy.

(4) CONSTRUCTIVE MEASURES OF ECONOMY Practical ways of economizing can be resorted to in the governmental field without abandoning or curtailing needed services. Whatever the number and scope of governmental activities, a major objective should be attainment of a maximum return of satisfactory service for every dollar spent by public officials. Economizing in this way is constructive, whereas eliminating or cutting down on socially necessary governmental functions is a destructive method of achieving a reduction of governmental expenditures.

At the end of this chapter consideration will be given to ways and means of ending *unnecessarily high* governmental outlays. In all probability governmental expenditures will continue to increase year after year, but even so steps can be taken to reduce the cost of doing whatever the people desire the government to do.

Budgets and Budgeting Systems

Nature of a Budget

A budget is a financial plan for a definite period, usually for a year but sometimes for a number of years, as in the case of a capital improvement program. It is concerned with probable expenditures and the revenues needed to meet them.

On its expenditure side a budget is a work or activities program expressed in monetary terms. An estimate of future expenses necessarily requires determination of what a government intends to do and what the cost of doing it will be. Due consideration should be given to what a community can afford in the way of public services.

As for the revenue side of budgeting, available sources of income need to be kept in mind and the yield from particular sources estimated in deciding on the taxes to be levied, the rate of taxation, service charges to be made, and the desirability of incurring long-term indebtedness. The revenue raising policy should not only provide needed income but also be fair in distributing the burden of financing governmental activity among the inhabitants comprising the membership of the body politic, be convenient to the taxpayers, and keep the cost of collecting revenue as low as possible.

Importance of Sound Budgeting

Sound budgeting is essential to the efficient and effective utilization of the resources which a community is able and willing to devote to governmental purposes. The goal to be achieved is the maintenance of high standards of service at a minimum cost. Proper budgeting preserves an approximate balance between income and outgo and promotes the distribution of expenditures among governmental services according to their relative social importance.

The creation of deficits and the wasteful expenditure of funds are largely preventible through appropriate budgetary practices. However, deficit financing is sometimes practiced and justified as a means of stimulating a private enterprise economy by injection of additional purchasing power in time of an economic slump or depression. The wisdom of such a policy is controversial. This technique is associated with an English economist, John Maynard Keynes, who advocated use of a government's fiscal powers for the purpose of influencing a country's economy.

Budgetary Systems

A budgetary system involves four stages. In the order of their occurrence, the first is preparation of the budget; the second, its legalization or adoption; the third, its execution; and the fourth, post-auditing of the financial transactions that occurred during the period of execution.

(1) PREPARATION OF THE BUDGET: PREFERABLY BY THE CHIEF EXECUTIVE Ultimate responsibility for preparation of the budget and for its submission to the legislature ought to be placed on the chief executive, as it is in the case of the President, the governors of most states, and the mayors or managers of numerous municipalities. Various bodies politic, however, arrange for preparation by a board of administrators, by a legislative committee, or by a board composed of both administrators and members of the legislative assembly.

(a) MERITS OF EXECUTIVE PREPARATION Preparation by the chief executive is generally considered the best plan for a number of reasons. As general manager of the administrative services, the executive is equally concerned about the affairs of all departments and likely to be well-in-

formed in regard to the extent and relative importance of
the financial needs of different administrative agencies. Another merit of executive preparation is that the chief executive's hand is strengthened in dealing with the department
heads who are supposed to be subject to his direction and
control. Furthermore, since the chief executive is held accountable for administrative results, considerations of fairness require that he be given the opportunity to recommend
(to the legislature) a financial program which represents his
judgment of the needs of the administrative branch. An
additional reason, in the case of the single type of chief
executive agency which prevails in the United States, is that
responsibility for preparation is located in one person.

(b) PREPARATION PROCEDURE For governments engaged in extensive activities, preparing a budget is a task of
great magnitude that necessarily involves the participation
of numerous officials. The initial estimates are made by the
operating units. If these were accepted as final, the budget,
instead of being a unified and well-balanced plan, would be
nothing more than a collection of estimates emanating from
officers with narrow interests and biased in favor of their
own particular activities and responsibilities. The existence
of a budget agency responsible to the chief executive and
acting in his behalf prevents this sort of thing from occurring.

Such an agency, e.g., the Office of Management and
Budget in the Executive Office of the President, specializes
in the task of obtaining pertinent information, reviewing
departmental requests, and working with the chief executive
and the departments in developing a properly balanced program. The chief executive in jurisdictions providing for

executive preparation assumes full responsibility for the budget that eventually is transmitted to the legislature in the form of a proposal. All of the activities necessary to budget preparation take place prior to beginning of the fiscal year.

(2) LEGALIZATION Legalization of a financial program requires passage of appropriation and revenue acts by the legislative authority. Unless the budget is both prepared and adopted by the legislature, which is the case, for example, under the commission plan of city government, the function of authorizing expenditures and raising revenues is discharged by officials other than those responsible for preparation of the budget. The financial program finally adopted may differ from the one initially prepared. What happens depends largely on the degree to which the legalizing authority possesses confidence in the preparing agency.

Congress often makes changes in the budget submitted by the President but, as a rule, drastic alterations are exceptional. There are so many state and local governments, especially the latter, that sufficient information warranting a generalization of any kind is lacking. The legislature ought to possess adequate information of its own in checking the requests of administrative agencies. It also should devise a satisfactory procedure for examining the budget recommended by the preparing agency. Progress along these lines remains to be made in the United States.

(a) APPROPRIATIONS—ITEMIZED OR LUMP SUM In authorizing expenditures, legislative bodies may pursue either of two general policies. One is to pass appropriation acts in which the amounts to be spent for particular activities are itemized in considerable detail, e.g., so much for equipment, so much for traveling expenses, and so forth. The other is to grant funds for major purposes with few, if any, strings attached concerning the objects of expenditure. Legislatures pursuing this "lump sum" policy, which is preferable in many respects to itemized appropriations, sometimes stipulate that the money appropriated for departments shall become available for disbursement only on approval by the chief executive. This device is a means of preventing department heads from spending money unwisely, in disregard of their asserted needs at the time of budget preparation, or in such a way as to exhaust their resources long before expiration of the fiscal year.

(3) EXECUTION With commencement of the fiscal year, the budget passes into the stage of execution. The financial program adopted by the legislature is binding on the administrative branch to the extent that appropriation acts and revenue laws fix the amounts and purposes of expenditures and the means of obtaining revenue. Expenditures in excess of legislative authorization are illegal; those in excess of actual need because of poor administration are inexcusable.

(a) ROLE OF THE CHIEF EXECUTIVE AND THE BUDGET AGENCY Experience has demonstrated that the spending departments should be subject to effective control by the chief executive during the fiscal year. The budget agency again is capable of rendering invaluable service to the chief executive and department heads by studying departmental operations, suggesting measures of economy, and approving the release of funds for departmental use if the periodic allotment plan of enabling the chief executive to control departmental expenditures is in effect.

(b) PRE-AUDITING A device for preventing illegal expenditures and the creation of deficits is the pre-audit. Pre-auditing means passing on proposed outlays prior to the creation of binding obligations. Approval of contemplated expenditures is withheld unless the proposed spending is legally authorized and unless the necessary money resources are available.

The official who performs the pre-auditing function, i.e., the controller, should be responsible to the chief executive. In many jurisdictions, however, such is not the case because the controlling function is assigned to an official elected by the voters or selected by the legislature.

(c) OTHER DEVICES FOR CONTROLLING DEPART-MENTAL SPENDING Other devices for either the direct or indirect control of departmental spending are available. Among them are adequate accounting and reporting; salary standardization on the basis of a position-classification plan; centralized purchasing; and the issuance of directives by the chief executive. Only too often, especially at the local government level, accounting and other record-keeping practices fall far short of the standards that ought to be maintained.

(d) PROPER LEADERSHIP AND A COMPETENT PERSON-NEL Apart from formal controls of one type or another which are designed to promote efficiency and economy in the making of expenditures, much depends on the quality of leadership furnished by the chief executive, on his objectives, and on the calibre of the administrative personnel in

general. A capable chief executive who is desirous of securing satisfactory results at a minimum cost can inspire his
subordinates to strive continuously for the attainment of
both economical and effective administration.

(4) POST-AUDITING   Post-auditing is an important feature of an adequate budgetary system. It occurs continuously or periodically *after*, rather than before, financial
transactions have been completed. The final post-audit is an
examination and verification of the entire record of expenditures made or payable and of income received or receivable
for the completed fiscal year. It helps to reveal illegal and
fraudulent transactions, provides evidence of the efficiency
of administration, and discloses the government's financial
condition. Its informative value depends, of course, on the
adequacy of the accounts and records which are maintained.

A post-audit by an agency independent of the chief executive and the administrative branch is desirable. Specific
arrangements vary. In some bodies politic the post-auditing
function is entrusted to an official, e.g., an auditor general,
who may be elected by the voters or appointed by either
the legislature or the chief executive. If selected by the chief
executive, the auditor's independence of the latter should be
assured by an adequate guarantee of tenure, as in the case of
the Comptroller General of the United States.[133]

[133] The Comptroller General is appointed by the President with
the advice and consent of the Senate for a fifteen-year term. He is
removable only by a joint resolution of the two houses of Congress.
Unfortunately, the General Accounting Office headed by the
Comptroller General exercises powers, such as pre-auditing and the
prescription of accounting systems, which in the judgment of many
qualified persons, including successive Hoover Commissions, should
be assigned to an agency responsible to the President of the United
States.

Prior to the 1930s local government expenditures amounted to about half of the total governmental outlay, those of the national government slightly over one-third, and those of the states comprised the remainder. By 1938 the national proportion had risen to 46% and from 1948 to 1964 it averaged in the neighborhood of 62%. During the years of participation in World War II it was much higher, e.g., 92% in 1944. For 1971 the expenditure total was distributed approximately as follows: national government—67%; state and local units—33%, with the local outlay exceeding that of the state governments.[134]

National Government Expenditures

(1) TOTALS The national government's expenditures amount to billions of dollars annually. Prior to 1968 three different budget concepts were utilized in presenting expenditure figures to Congress and the public. In 1964, for example, the *administrative budget* total was 97.7 billions; that of the *national income accounts budget*, 118.5 billions; and that of the *cash budget* (payments), 120.3 billions.[135] The figure for the *administrative budget* is the smallest because of exclusion of nearly the entire outgo of trust and various public enterprise funds and also the disbursements under some credit programs.

---

[134] For 1963 the expenditure total was distributed approximately as follows: national government—60%; state and local units—40%, with the local outlay nearly double that of the state governments, *Congress and the Nation, 1945–1964* (Washington, Congressional Quarterly Service, 1965), p. 1378.

[135] *Ibid.*, p. 392. For an explanation of the three federal budgets, see pp. 387–392 of this publication.

A new *unified budget* format has been substituted for the three-budget picture previously utilized. For the fiscal year 1969 the "unified budget" total of expenditures was approximately 183 billions. This total included amounts formerly excluded from the *administrative budget* expenditure figures. The total for 1971 was about 234 billions.

The billion dollar budgets of recent times contrast sharply with expenditures of 734 million in 1916 and 694 million in 1910. 1917 is the year in which the billion dollar era began —the year of entry into World War I.

(2) DISTRIBUTION BY FUNCTIONS The distribution of national government expenditures by major functions differs from time to time. For illustrative purposes, items in the budgets of 1968 and 1970, stated in approximate percentages, are presented, *viz.*,[135a]

	1968	1970
National defense	45%	40.8%
International Affairs and Finance	2.6	1.8
Space Research and Technology	2.6	1.9
Agricultural and Rural Development	3.3	3.2
Natural Resources	1.0	1.3
Commerce and Transportation	4.5	4.8
Community Development and Housing	2.3	1.5
Education and Manpower	3.9	3.7
Health	5.4	6.6
Income Security	18.9	22.3
Veterans' Benefits and Services	3.8	4.4
Interest	7.7	9.3
General Government	1.5	1.7
Special Allowance and Undistributed	−2.5	−3.3

By far the largest proportion of expenditures is for national defense purposes. That probably will continue to be

[135a] As reported by the Office of Management and Budget.

the case for the indefinite future. If expenditures for veterans' benefits and services and interest payments on indebtedness incurred for war purposes are added to the defense figure, nearly 60% of national government expenditures are attributable to war and its consequences.

State and Local Expenditures

For 1967-68 the direct expenditures of state and local governments amounted to about 115 billions—state governments 44 billions and local governments 71 billions. The major expenditures were for education at both the state and local levels. A few years ago state governments spent more for highways than for education. The proportionate allocation of direct expenditures for different purposes, as shown below, is for *all* state governments, *all* local units, and *all* cities. Proportions for particular governments are likely to vary from the percentages indicated. Furthermore, changes in percentages from year to year will occur in the future as has been the case in the past.

PROPORTIONATE ALLOCATIONS OF DIRECT EXPENDITURES[136]

State Governments, 1967–1968

Education	24.7%	Financial	
Highways	22.2	administration	1.83
Insurance trust	10.4	Employment	
Public welfare	11.6	security	1.36
Hospitals	7.3	Health	1.35
Natural resources	4.4	Police	1.17
Liquor stores	2.8	General control	1.16
Interest	2.55	Miscellaneous	5.3
Corrections	1.85%		

[136] *Book of the States* 1970–1971, pp. 202, 203, *Municipal Year Book,* 1970, pp. 226, 227

Local Governments, 1967–1968

Education	42%	General control	2.14%
Utilities	9.35	Parks, recreation	1.96
Highways	6.49	Sanitation	1.35
Public welfare	6.6	Insurance trust	1.43
Police	4.0	Natural resources	.71
Hospitals	4.23	Financial	
Interest	2.97	administration	1.1
Sewerage	2.41	Gen'l public bldgs	1.06
Fire protection	2.24	Health	.92
Housing, urban		Libraries	.72
renewal	2.24	Miscellaneous	5.7

All Cities, 1967–1968

Utilities	16.9%	Insurance trust	3.0%
Education	12.7	Interest	3.0
Highways	8.0	General control	2.2
Sanitation, sewerage	7.6	Financial	
Police	8.4	administration	1.3
Fire	5.2	Library	1.3
Health, hospitals	5.8	Gen'l public bldgs	1.2
Public welfare	6.5	Airports	1.0
Parks, recreation	3.7	Miscellaneous	8.7
Housing, commun. dev.	3.5		

Public Revenues and Indebtedness

Revenue sources of the national, state, and local governments include taxes of various types, charges for current services, earnings of public enterprises (e.g., an electric power plant or a water supply system), intergovernmental contributions (grants-in-aid), and insurance trust income. Of the foregoing, taxes are by far the most important.

Funds are also obtainable by borrowing, i.e., by the creation of indebtedness. Although borrowing is a means of securing money, it is not a source of revenue in the sense that taxes are. The issuance of government bonds, for example, creates an obligation to repay the amount borrowed and also to pay interest in accordance with the terms of the issue. Fulfillment of this responsibility requires the obtainment of income through taxation, charges for services rendered, and other revenue sources.

Revenues

(1) REQUIREMENTS OF A SATISFACTORY REVENUE SYSTEM Among the requirements of a satisfactory revenue system are (a) adequacy, (b) equitableness, (c) ease of administration and low administrative costs, (d) convenience for taxpayers, and (e) synchronization of the revenue sources of the several levels of government, viz., national, state, and local. Some of these requirements are also pertinent to an appraisal of particular revenue sources.

(a) ADEQUACY A revenue system that fails to provide the amount of money which governments need is obviously defective. Available sources should be of such a character that adequate funds are always obtainable.

(b) EQUITABLENESS The quality of equitableness is essential. Since everyone benefits in one way or another from the provision of governmental services, all should bear a fair share of the cost. Particular taxes may fall more heavily on one group than another, but the system as a whole should distribute the expense burden fairly. It is difficult, of course, to obtain agreement on the subject of what is fair or unfair. In the United States the "ability to pay" theory has received widespread support.

(c) EASE OF ADMINISTRATION Ease of administration promotes more effective collections and lowers administrative costs. Methods of raising revenue which involve difficulty in making collections, e.g., a personal property tax, encourage evasions and add so greatly to the expense of administration that the net yield is materially reduced.

(d) CONVENIENCE FOR THE TAXPAYER Convenience for the taxpayer simplifies the work of tax-collecting authorities; reduces either miscalculation or falsification of the amount of tax to be paid if a particular tax necessitates calculations, at least initially, by the taxpayer, as in the case of a complicated income tax; and helps avert development of a hostile attitude on the part of taxpayers towards the government. The antagonism of taxpayers is easily aroused in any event and especially if particular ways of raising revenue require undue sacrifice of time and effort on their part.

(e) SYNCHRONIZATION OF REVENUE SOURCES Finally, the revenue system of any unit of government should be correlated with the systems of other governments that exercise jurisdiction over the same persons and property. Harmony and balance between related systems are essential to the equitable production of adequate revenue. Much remains to be done along this line in the United States.

(2) VARIETY OF TAXES A great variety of taxes are levied by the many governments of this country. *Individual income taxes* are resorted to by the national government, by about two-thirds of the states, and by a comparatively small number of local units. The national government and nearly four-fifths of the states also tax *corporate income*. *Property taxes*, both general and selective, are the major source of revenue for local units but account for only a small percentage of the tax receipts of state governments. A general property tax is one imposed on real and personal property according to its assessed value.

Among other categories of taxes are *estate* and *gift* taxes; *manufacturers' excise taxes*, such as those on gasoline, oil, tires, and motor vehicles; *retailers' excise taxes*, e.g., on luggage and jewelry; *special excise taxes*, as on tobacco and alcoholic beverages; *general sales taxes; license taxes* of various types levied on the right to exercise a business or non-business privilege; *customs duties* (national government only); and *special assessments* levied against real property in return for a special benefit in the form of an increase in value attributable to the construction of public improvements like street pavements, sewers, water supply lines, and parks.

The foregoing list, although incomplete, gives adequate indication of the many kinds of taxes that furnish income for the national, state, and local governments. Not all of the taxes mentioned are levied by every government.

The "tax" categories identified differ in some respects from classifications used by various authorities in the field of public finance. For example, a general sales tax is a type of excise tax if excises are defined as indirect taxes levied on goods produced or consumed within certain territorial limits, but not if an excise is considered a duty imposed on the process of manufacturing. Customs duties fall outside the excise category whether either of the foregoing definitions is used. Customs duties are commonly defined as indirect taxes levied on goods imported into or exported from certain territories. They are collected from the trader rather than from the manufacturer.

(3) OTHER SOURCES OF REVENUE Other sources of revenue are grants-in-aid, charges for current services, and the earnings of public enterprises. Grants-in-aid represent money given by one government to another for either specific or general purposes. Charges for current services are exemplified by the billing of property owners for sewerage service, for the collection of garbage, ashes, and rubbish, and for the lighting of streets. By the earnings of public enterprises are meant the general revenue receipts derived from such governmentally-owned and operated enterprises as water supply systems, electric power plants, port facilities, and the postal service.

(4) COMPARATIVE   IMPORTANCE   OF   DIFFERENT REVENUE SOURCES The comparative importance of different major sources of revenue for the national, state, and local governments is presented in tabular form in the next paragraph—for the national government in 1968 and 1970, for state and local governments in the 1967–1968 period. Statistics for a single year or period fail to reveal trends or variations, but the proportions indicated have not changed significantly for several years. Obviously, the state and local percentages do not reveal differences among the fifty states and the great number of local units.

National Government—Revenue Receipts, 1968 and 1970
Percentages from Different Sources

	1968	1970
Individual income tax	44.7%	46.7%
Corporate income taxes	18.7	16.9
Employment taxes	22.5	23.3
Estate and gift taxes, customs duties	3.3	3.3
Excise taxes (alcohol, tobacco, manufacturer's, retailer's, miscellaneous)	9.2	8.1
Miscellaneous receipts (interest, sales of property, royalties, etc.)	1.6	1.7

State and Local Governments—Revenue Receipts, 1967–1968
Percentages from Different Sources

	State	Local
From national government (grants)	22.5%	2.8%
From state governments (grants)		29.0
Revenue from own sources		
Taxes		
Individual income	9.2	1.53
Corporation income	3.7	
Sales and gross receipts		
General	15.5	1.71
Selective	15.6	1.03
Property	1.35	38.3
Other taxes, e.g., license taxes	8.5	1.89
Charges and miscellaneous	10.0	13.8
Utility revenue		8.1
Liquor store revenue	2.3	.37
Insurance trust funds	11.4	1.48

Of the total revenue receipts of the states in 1967–1968, 53.85% was obtained from taxes. Sales and gross receipts

[137] Percentage calculations based on amounts from different sources published by the Office of Management and Budget.

[138] Percentage calculations based on amounts from different sources published in *The Book of the States, 1970–71* (Chicago, Council of State Governments, 1970), p. 202.

taxes accounted for 57.8% of the proceeds from taxation; income taxes, 17.2%. Only 2.59% of the tax revenue was derived from taxes on property.

In 1967–1968 local governments as a whole received 44.46% of their total revenue receipts from taxes. Taxes on *property* provided 86.3% of this tax income. The proportion varies greatly among local units. For all cities it was 68.8% in 1967–1968 but for particular cities selected at random it was nearly 61% for New York, 41% for Philadelphia, nearly 82% in the case of Cleveland, and slightly under 58% for Denver.

(5) REVENUE RAISING LIMITATIONS: (a) ON THE NATIONAL GOVERNMENT The revenue raising power of the national government is legally restricted in several ways, but practically all of the restrictions are of minor significance. Probably the most important restraint is the requirement of a public purpose. As stated in the Constitution, "Congress shall have power to lay and collect taxes, duties, imposts and excises, to pay the debts and provide for the common defence and general welfare of the United States."

Other specific constitutional limitations are as follows: no tax or duty shall be laid on articles exported from any state; no capitation or other direct tax shall be laid, unless in proportion to population; no preference shall be given by any regulation of revenue to the ports of one state over those of another; vessels bound to or from one state shall not be obliged to enter, clear, or pay duties in another; and all duties, imposts, and excises shall be *uniform* (geographically) throughout the United States.

Implied limitations include the following: the national government may not tax the states and their instrumentalities when engaged in the performance of governmental functions and the taxing power may not be used either to deprive the states of their reserved powers or in violation of the constitutionally guaranteed rights of individuals.

Despite the number of express and implied restrictions on the revenue raising power of the national government, this power is extremely broad with respect to the choice of sources of revenue and the rate of taxation. The principal prohibited source of revenue is export duties. No limitation on tax rates is incorporated in the Constitution.

(b) ON THE STATES AND LOCAL UNITS The states, as distinguished from their governments, also possess broad discretionary power in regard to the raising of revenue. Except for a few restrictions, either express or implied, the Constitution of the United States permits states to raise revenue in whatever ways seem expedient to them.

The only express limitation is that no state, without the consent of Congress, shall lay any duties on imports or exports, or any duty on tonnage. Duties on imports or exports may be levied, without the consent of Congress, only to the extent absolutely necessary for executing state inspection laws. The net produce shall be for the use of the national government.

By implication, the states may not tax the national government and its instrumentalities; directly tax interstate commerce, the agencies of that commerce, or the right to engage therein; and use their taxing power in disregard of the constitutionally guaranteed rights of individuals or in violation of their intergovernmental obligations.

State governments are subject to the additional restrictions of state constitutions. These vary from state to state. Local governments also are bound by whatever constitutional stipulations apply to them, e.g., limitations on the general property tax rate. Moreover, they possess only such revenue raising powers as are granted them, either by constitutional or by statutory provision, usually by the latter but sometimes by both.

Indebtedness

The Constitution of the United States places no limitations on the power of the national government and the states to incur indebtedness. However, the borrowing authority of state governments is frequently restricted by the provisions of state constitutions and local units may incur indebtedness only to the extent and by the ways which the states permit.

Guides to Sound Borrowing

(1) LONG-TERM BORROWING Generally speaking, long-term borrowing by governments is justified only if a government is faced with extraordinarily large expenditures for permanent assets or on the occasion of great emergencies, such as war, a serious economic depression, or an earthquake.

A cardinal rule to be observed in long-term borrowing for permanent improvements is that the life of a bond issue should not extend beyond the useful life of the project for which debt is incurred. The issuance of thirty-year bonds, for example, to pay for an improvement which will have outlived its usefulness in fifteen or fewer years is an unsound practice. It not only is inequitable but eventually leads to financial disaster. Additional borrowing for a new permanent improvement becomes necessary before the cost of the old one has been met. The proper term for a debt depends on the purpose for which it is incurred.

Emergencies for which long-term borrowing may be warranted are those of a type that occur infrequently. War is an example in the case of the national government. The cost of war is so great that borrowing, if not essential because of limited resources, may be preferable, for various reasons, to a pay-as-you-go policy. A different type of emergency is one which arises because of a serious and protracted economic depression. The falling off of revenues and the necessity of providing relief for the unemployed may create a condition for which borrowing affords the most feasible remedy. As for states and local units, an earthquake, a flood, a tornado, or a fire may prove disastrous enough to require the expenditure of huge funds for relief and rebuilding purposes. The same situation may arise as a consequence of war, e.g., the destructive bombing of cities, or because of large-scale unemployment due to an economic crisis.

(2) SHORT-TERM BORROWING A circumstance which warrants short-term borrowing is an immediate need for funds that are momentarily unavailable. This situation may arise if tax payments fall due too long after the beginning of the fiscal year or come in slowly for one reason or another; if unforeseen developments require expenditures in excess of anticipated needs; or if proceeds from the sale of duly authorized bonds for financing a permanent improvement are not immediately available.

Except for temporary or short-term borrowing under the

special conditions just mentioned, the incurrence of indebtedness to meet ordinary current expenses is absolutely unjustifiable. Such a policy, common enough in the United States, is conclusive evidence of misgovernment.

Pay-As-You-Go

An objective of wise financial management is to keep indebtedness as low as possible, both for the sake of economy and to preserve the credit of a particular government. A partial or complete pay-as-you-go policy reduces costs through the reduction or elimination of interest payments and at the same time helps to maintain credit at a point which enables a government to borrow at lower interest rates on occasions when the incurrence of indebtedness is really necessary.

A pay-as-you-go policy from the proceeds of a government's current revenues is desirable in the case of governments that regularly construct permanent improvements of various types. For example, a state may annually pave so many miles of highways and a municipality may lay approximately the same length of sewer and water pipes every year. On the other hand, improvements of an expensive variety that occur only occasionally are appropriately financed through the issuance of bonds, e.g., a sewage treatment plant or a water filtration system.

A project representing an unusual and costly undertaking for a small body politic may constitute a normal capital outlay for a large one. Small municipalities, for instance, find it necessary to construct school buildings only infrequently. A drastic increase in tax rates to cover the expense of construction would place too heavy a burden on current taxpayers. Under such circumstances borrowing on a long-term basis is clearly justified. In the case of a large municipality, the construction of a school building may occur every year. If so, the project falls in the category of regularly recurring improvements which should be financed on a pay-as-you-go basis from the proceeds of ordinary revenues.

Too many governments assume that all permanent improvements should be financed by borrowing. This attitude is partly attributable to the conviction that those who benefit from an improvement should share the cost. Although the plan of payment by those who benefit is sound in principle, it is not the only way of achieving equity between successive generations of taxpayers. A pay-as-you-go program may work out just as fairly if the annual outlay for permanent improvements remains reasonably constant from year to year. The amount expended in a given year measures the burden of that year's taxpayers and with careful planning major variations in the year-to-year burden can be avoided. Equity in regard to successive years of taxpayers is primarily a matter of comparative burdens. Whether the taxpayers' contribution is used to finance one improvement or another is a matter of secondary importance.

Indebtedness of the National Government, States, and Local Units.

Statistics concerning the extent of indebtedness of governments in the United States are presented below. The figures fail to reveal the purposes for which debt has been incurred or the relationship between the indebtedness of a government and the resources of the community wherein it functions. A special investigation of the financial policies of particular governments is essential to determination of the soundness of the policies pursued.

Debt Outstanding at End of Fiscal Year
(in billions of dollars)

Year	National	State and Local
1940	42.9	20.3
1942	72.4	19.7
1944	201.0	17.4
1950	257.3	24.1
1955	274.3	44.2
1960	286.3	69.9
1965	317.2	99.5
1966	319.9	107.0
1967	326.2	113.6
1968	347.5	121.1
1969	353.7	133.5

The indebtedness of the national government increased drastically in 1943 and 1944. World War II was the cause. Thereafter the rise became gradual, with occasional years showing a slight decrease in the total outstanding debt. In 1970 this debt reached 370.9 billions; in 1971, 398.1 billions. An increase to 450 billions has been authorized by Congress but the executive branch recommends that this figure be raised to 465 billions.

The outstanding debt total for the states rose from about 3.5 billions in 1940 to 35.6 billions in 1968. Of this amount 33.6 billions was for long-term indebtedness—over 94%. In 1940 the outstanding debt of local units was over 16.5 billions; in 1968 it exceeded 85 billions—all but about 6.4 billions (7.4%) consisting of long-term indebtedness.

Constructive Measures of Economy

Only an optimist anticipates a future reduction of public expenditures. The outlook is for an increase rather than for a decrease. However, governmental expenses in the United States are higher than necessary. By resorting to various measures of constructive economy, the services rendered could be furnished at a lower cost. Maximizing the return on every tax dollar is an objective to be sought at all times, whatever the number and scope of governmental activities.

Reduction in Number of Local Units

One reason for needlessly high governmental costs is the existence of too many units of local government. An undue multiplication of counties, townships, municipalities, and special districts results in unnecessary overhead expenses, overlapping jurisdictions, duplication of activities, small scale operations which are relatively costly as well as ineffective, and a division of responsibility that constitutes a major obstacle to coordinated government.

Proper Distribution of Functions

Closely related to the problem of reducing the number and variety of governmental units is that of a proper distribution of functions. Each function should be assigned to the level of government (national, state, or local) best qualified to perform it. Care should be exercised to insure a correspondence between functional responsibilities and financial capacity for the maintenance of adequate service standards. Of course, no activities should be allocated exclusively to one jurisdictional level unless a problem is one of sole concern to it. As social conditions change, a redistribution of functions may be required to achieve more effective and economical government.

Better Organization

Another measure of constructive economy is the improvement of organizational arrangements. Proper organization is an important factor in the operation of any enterprise, public or private, but despite general recognition of this fact, poorly organized governments survive in many jurisdictions. The worst examples are found in the counties which are served by governments characterized by an excess of elective officials, lack of a chief executive, and a poorly conceived assignment of activities to administrative agencies. As for cities, a substantial majority still operate under the weak mayor-council form which is unquestionably the least effective of the several plans of city government found in the United States. The basic structure of most state governments is defective in various respects and that of the national government is by no means entirely satisfactory.

The administrative organization of the national and state governments can be improved upon in many ways. Local units, too, are handicapped by unsatisfactory organization of their administrative services.

The essentials of sound organization are much the same for all levels of government. Among them are avoidance of a dispersion of power and responsibility, provision for a chief executive equipped with the powers necessary for effective general management of the administrative services, a well-integrated and manageable administrative organization, and the appointment, rather than the election, of officials other than the members of legislative bodies and, in some jurisdictions, the chief executive. The case for an appointed chief administrator is impressive, but it is unlikely that the firmly established policy of electing the President and state governors will be abandoned.

Better Administrative Practices

The establishment of sound administrative methods and procedures is an additional measure of constructive economy. Without a satisfactory budgeting system plus adequate accounts and records, effective planning and control of expenditures are unattainable. Too many governments in the United States have failed to adopt the best practices of this type. Such is also the case with respect to the purchasing of equipment, supplies, and materials. Savings are realizable through centralized purchasing, but departmental buying still survives in numerous jurisdictions. A proper combination of centralized and departmental purchasing is essential to achievement of the most satisfactory results.

Better Public Personnel

In the field of personnel, the spoils system still prevails in many jurisdictions. The greatest progress toward substitution of a merit for a spoils policy has been made by the national government and by the cities; the least by state and county governments. A merit-based system of selection, promotion, and dismissal from public service, together with such other features of a sound personnel policy as in-service training and adequate compensation, increases the likelihood of more effective and economical government. It is high time that governmental service be placed on a career basis.

The Alternative to Constructive Measures of Economy

Constructive measures of economy, like those above-mentioned and others as well, lower the cost of rendering public service. The only other way of reducing governmental expenditures is by discontinuing various services or by limiting their scope. This alternative is defensible only in the case of unneeded services or services that have been expanded beyond the point necessary for promotion of the general welfare.

Of all governmental activities, the most costly are war and preparation for defense against possible attack. The elimination of war and the constant threat thereof would be a boon to mankind in ways too numerous to mention. If this were to occur (which seems unlikely), a substantial reduction in governmental expenditures could be achieved. Either that, or the money now spent directly or indirectly for war purposes could be used to gain worthwhile objectives, such, for example, as "the great society."

☆ APPENDIX

Glossary

Absentee Voting. Qualified voters are permitted to cast ballots in an election if their anticipated absence on election day is unavoidable, provided that all legal requirements have been fulfilled within prescribed time limits.

Administration. All operations or activities involved in the fulfillment or enforcement of public policy.

Administrative Adjudication. The settlement of controversies by administrative agencies through a process including the giving of notice, the holding of a hearing, the presentation of evidence, and the handing down of a decision.

Administrative Law. The body of law regulating relations among public officials and between governmental agencies and private individuals in connection with the administration of public policies.

Administrative Legislation. The issuance, by administrative agencies, of rules having the force of law that prescribe or affect the rights of individuals.

Alien. A person who, from the standpoint of one country, owes permanent allegiance to another.

Amnesty. A blanket "pardon" extended to whole classes of persons exempting them from prosecution and/or punishment for the offense or offenses covered by the proclamation of amnesty.

Appellate Jurisdiction. The authority of a court to review the decisions of a lower or inferior court.

Apportionment. The function of allocating representatives among the groups of persons, commonly the inhabitants of designated areas, to whom representation is accorded.

Appropriation Act. A legislative act authorizing the expenditure of public funds for specified purposes.

At-Large Election. Choice of an official or officials by all of the qualified voters of a body politic or designated electoral area. For instance, United States Senators are chosen by the entire body of voters of a particular state. The alternative would be to divide the state into two districts and permit each district to select one Senator. Presidential electors also are elected at-large. Consequently, every voter of a particular state is eligible to participate in the choice of all of the presidential electors to which his state is entitled. A permissible alternative would be the creation of districts equal in number to the number of a state's presidential electors, with one elector being chosen by the voters of each district.

Attainder, Bill of. A legislative act imposing punishment without a judicial trial.

Australian Ballot System. The principal features of this system are (1) an official ballot provided by governmental authorities at public expense, (2) distribution of ballots within the polling place by government officials, and (3) adequate provision for secret voting.

Auxiliary Functions. The various activities of a government undertaken solely for the purpose of enabling it to achieve its primary objective of serving the people in sundry ways, e.g., the selection of officials and employees, the keeping of accounts and records, and the purchasing of equipment, materials, and supplies.

Biennial Sessions. Sessions held every other year rather than annually.

Bond Issue. The borrowing of money by selling bonds providing for interest payments and for repayment of the principal at a designated time.

Budget. A financial program of contemplated expenditures and anticipated revenues for a definite period of time, usually a year. On its expenditure side a budget is a work or activities program stated in monetary terms.

Bureau. A commonly used title or designation for subdivisions of an administrative department.

Career Service. A personnel policy providing for entrance on a merit basis, adequate opportunity for advancements in pay and promotions in rank for competent employees, and protection from demotion or dismissal for reasons other than incompetence.

Centralization. In the governmental field, this term usually signifies the transfering of powers and services from a lower to a higher level of government, e.g., transfering the functions of counties to the state government.

Centralized Purchasing. The purchasing of equipment, materials, and supplies for all departments by an agency created especially for that purpose—a substitute for departmental buying.

Checks and Balances. An organizational arrangement which enables each of the coordinate branches of a government to exercise some degree of control over the others, e.g., the power of the chief executive to veto acts of the legislature.

Civil Law. The body of law, distinguished from criminal law, which prescribes the rights and duties of private persons in their various relationships.

Civil Rights. The entirety of rights, other than those of a political character, possessed by individuals with respect to one another and the government.

Civil Service. The civilian as distinguished from the military personnel of governments.

Classified Service. Includes all positions placed under the jurisdiction of a central personnel agency in connection with the administration of a merit system. Other positions fall in the "unclassified" service. Not to be confused with "position-classification."

Closure or Cloture. A device for ending debate in a legislative assembly. The procedure for achieving closure is prescribed by the rules of the assembly.

Committee of the Whole. The entire membership of a legislative chamber sitting as a committee under procedural rules that differ from and are more informal than the rules of procedure in accordance with which the chamber ordinarily transacts its business.

Common Law. Rules of law developed through a process of judicial decision and adherence to established precedent with respect to spheres of individual and group activity unregulated by the provisions of written laws. In the event of conflict between statutory stipulations and the rules of common law, the former prevail.

Commutation of Sentence. The substitution of a less severe penalty for the punishment initially imposed on a person adjudged guilty of committing a crime.

Conference Committee. A committee created to iron out differences between the two houses of a bicameral legislature in regard to the bills each has passed concerning a particular problem. Sometimes referred to as a "conciliation" committee.

Constitution. The various media or instrumentalities through which the basic features of a governmental system are established. Among these media are documents, understandings, traditions, customs, and usages. In a narrower sense, a constitution is a document which creates the principal governmental institutions of a particular body politic. Some countries, for example Great Britain, do not have a documentary constitution.

Constitutional Convention. A gathering of delegates for the sole purpose of drafting, revising, or proposing amendments to a documentary constitution.

Constitutional Court. A court created by Congress under authority granted it by Article III of the Constitution.

Constituent Power. The power to participate in the formulation, adoption, revision, or amendment of a constitution.

Convention, Partisan. A gathering of selected party members or delegates for the purpose of nominating candidates and/or drafting a party platform.

Court of First Instance. A court in which cases are first commenced, i.e., a court of original jurisdiction.

Crime. A legally forbidden act considered an offense against the public for the commission of which punishment is imposed.

Criminal Law. The body of law which defines "crimes" and stipulates the punishment to be imposed on persons found guilty of committing them.

Cumulative Voting. The voter is granted one vote for each seat to be filled, with the privilege of casting the entire number for one candidate or of distributing his votes among two or more candidates in whatever way he desires.

Delegation of Power. The granting of power by one organ of government to another; also the conferment of power to agencies of government by constitutional provision.

Department. A major unit or subdivision of the administrative branch of government.

Direct Legislation. Legislation by direct popular vote, either through the initiative or the petition referendum.

Division. A title sometimes used for either a major or minor subdivision of an administrative department.

Double Jeopardy. Being tried twice by the same government for commission of a crime on a particular occasion.

Dual Committee System. Each house of a bicameral legislature establishes its own set of standing committees.

Due Process of Law. As interpreted by the Supreme Court, the due process clauses of the Fifth and Fourteenth Amendments prohibit the national government and the states from depriving any person of life, liberty, or property by unreasonable, arbitrary, or capricious action.

Electoral College. A body of individuals selected for the purpose of choosing an official, e.g., the presidential electors, collectively considered, who select the President of the United States.

Electorate. The body of qualified voters.

Eminent Domain, the Power of. The power of a government to take private property for public use, subject in the United States to the payment of just compensation.

End of Session Rush. This phrase refers to the congestion of business and hasty consideration of bills in the closing days of a legislative session, due in large measure to limitation of the frequency and length of sessions of state legislatures.

Equal Protection of the Laws. As interpreted, this clause of the Fourteenth Amendment prohibits arbitrary, unreasonable, and invidious discrimination against individuals and classes of individuals.

Equity. Rules of equity, historically originating in England through the settlement of disputes by the King's Chancellor, afford relief to persons with respect to infringement of rights when no adequate remedy is obtainable in a common law proceeding. Equity provides remedies to prevent the threatened violation of a right or to compel discharge of a legal obligation. Common law remedies are available only after rights have been infringed.

Ex Officio. By reason of holding a particular office, e.g., the mayor of a city is made an *ex officio* member of the city planning commission.

Ex Parte. An uncontested judicial proceeding by or for a particular individual.

Ex Post Facto Law. A law that is given retroactive effect, being made applicable to action taken prior to, as well as after, its enactment. The *ex post facto* laws forbidden by the Constitution of the United States are criminal laws which prove disadvantageous to persons accused of crime.

Executive. The function of administering or carrying out the policies of a government; also, an official empowered to direct and control the administration of policies.

Executive Agreement. An agreement entered into by the President with a foreign country without subsequent submission to the Senate, as required in the case of treaties.

Executive Order. A directive issued by a chief executive commanding performance of an act by his subordinates.

Executive Ordinance. Rules and regulations issued by an executive pertaining to the conduct of subordinate officials or private persons.

Extraordinary Majority. A majority exceeding more than half of the votes cast on a proposition or for the candidates competing for a particular office, e.g., a two-thirds or a three-fourths majority.

Federal System. A system of government featured by a constitutional division of powers between a central government and the major political subdivisions of a body politic. Both the central government and the major political subdivisions derive their powers from the same source, viz., the constitution.

Filibuster. A "minority group" strategy of prolonging debate and resorting to various delaying tactics until a legislative chamber withdraws a measure from consideration.

General Property Tax. A tax levied on both real and personal property according to its assessed value.

Gerrymandering. The political party in control of a legislative assembly devises an electoral district layout which, by reason of the geographical distribution of partisan voting strength, will result in the defeat of its opponents in at least a majority of the districts.

Grand Jury. A body of from twelve to twenty-three persons that hears evidence presented by a prosecuting attorney against persons suspected of serious crimes and eventually decides whether the evidence is sufficient to justify an "indictment," i.e., a formal accusation which warrants holding the accused for trial.

Grant-in-aid. A grant of money by one government to another, either conditionally or unconditionally, i.e., with or without specification of the purposes for which the money is to be spent or the establishment of performance standards to be fulfilled.

Habeas Corpus, Writ of. An order issued by a court to an officer who has taken an individual into custody directing that the arrested individual be brought before the court and that the officer show cause for the arrest and detention.

Home Rule. A system of permitting local units to devise their own forms of government and to be free from external control in matters of local concern.

Impeachment. The formal presentation of charges against a public official for the purpose of bringing about his subsequent trial and, if convicted, removal from office. At the national level the power of impeachment is vested in the House of Representatives and the power to try an impeached officer is granted to the Senate.

Incorporated Territory. A territorial possession of the United States to which the Constitution has been extended by Congress, with the result that Congress, in governing such a territory, is bound by all pertinent constitutional provisions. In governing an "unincorporated" territory, Congress is restricted only by what the Supreme Court has described as the fundamental, rather than the formal, parts of the Constitution.

Independent Establishment. An administrative agency located outside the departments (now eleven) of the national government.

Injunction, Writ of. A writ used to restrain acts unauthorized by or in violation of law which would cause irreparable damage to private rights or to property. Issued by courts only if there is no adequate remedy at law.

Integrated Organization. An administrative organization is "integrated" if ultimate power and responsibility are located in the office of chief executive and if lines of authority and control run downward from this office and lines of responsibility run upward and converge in the chief executive's office.

Interstate Commerce. Commerce involving the crossing of state boundary lines, even if the commerce begins and ends in the same state.

Interstate Rendition. The deliverance of a fugitive from justice by one state at the request of the executive authority of another state.

Intrastate Commerce. Commerce within a state which at no time involves the crossing of state boundary lines.

Item Veto. The power of a chief executive to veto parts of a bill, usually only items in appropriation acts.

Joint Committee. A committee composed of members of both houses of a bicameral legislature.

Joint Committee System. A single set of committees serves both houses of a bicameral legislature, with members of each house on every committee.

Judicial Activism. Signifies an attitude and readiness on the part of Supreme Court judges to construe the Constitution in such a way as to promote attainment of approved social and political objectives.

Judicial Review. The doctrine that the judicial branch has the right of final decision concerning the constitutionality of governmental action whenever the issue of constitutionality is necessarily involved in the settlement of a legal controversy.

Judicial Self-Restraint or Passivism. Signifies the attitude of Supreme Court judges who disapprove of constitutional interpretations based primarily on the social and political predilections of members of the Court. The reluctance of judges to use their power in a positive way to promote the attainment of desired objectives.

Jurisdiction. The right to exercise official authority over individuals or territory.

Jus Sanguinis. The principle or rule that the nationality of a child is determined by the nationality of its parents.

Jus Soli. The principle that the place of birth determines the nationality of a child, regardless of the status of its parents.

Justiciable. A controversy is "justiciable" if it can be settled in accordance with rules of law.

Legislative Calendar. A schedule of bills for consideration by a legislative chamber.

Legislative Courts. Courts created by Congress in the exercise of powers conferred by Article I rather than by Article III which deals with the judicial branch of the national government. The provisions of the third article pertaining to the tenure and compensation of judges are not binding on Congress with respect to "legislative" courts.

Limited Voting. An election method which denies the voter the privilege of voting for as many candidates as there are legislative seats to be filled.

Line Functions. Those functions of government discharged for the direct benefit of the public. Examples are police protection, the construction of public works, and the regulation of traffic.

Lobbyist. An individual or agent of an interest-group who endeavors to influence the determination of public policy by presenting information to individual legislators, legislative committees, and other public officials or by resorting to other techniques of persuasion.

Local Government. The government of localities by public officials, usually locally selected, who are authorized to deal with problems of local concern.

Majority. More than half. To define a majority as one more than half is correct only if the total vote is an even number, for example, 50. In that case 26 is a majority—one more than half of 50. However, if the total vote is an odd number, for example 49, 25 is a majority and 25 is not one more than half of 49. Half of 49 is 24½.

Mandamus, Writ of. A writ issued by a court and directed to an official commanding the performance of a duty made imperative by law, provided no other adequate legal remedy is available. For example, the writ may be issued to compel payment of an employee's salary or compel the holding of an election provided for by law.

Martial Law. The establishment of military control over a civilian population in an emergency situation, with the consequence that military decrees supersede civilian law and military courts replace civilian courts in the area with respect to which martial law has been proclaimed.

Merit System. As a personnel policy, the merit system is characterized by emphasis on competence in the selection and subsequent treatment of governmental employees.

Metropolitan Area or District. A densely populated region, predominantly urban in character, which has developed a substantial degree of unity in its social and economic life. By far the greater part of such an area's population is assembled in an aggregate of distinguishable urban communities, so closely related, geographically as well as socially, as to constitute a complex super-community.

Minority. Fewer than half.

Naturalization. The process of converting an alien into a citizen.

Obiter Dicta. Statements in a court opinion that are not strictly pertinent to the issues involved in a particular case—not essential to the court's reasoning and decision.

Office Block Ballot. A form of ballot on which the names of candidates are grouped according to the office for which they are competing.

Open Partisan Primary. A partisan nominating primary in connection with which no attempt is made to check a voter's claim to party membership; no evidence of party affiliation is required.

Original Jurisdiction. The original jurisdiction of a court consists of the kind of cases that may be brought before that court prior to consideration by any other tribunal; authority to hear a case in the first instance.

Pardon. A grant of exemption from the legal consequences of a crime either before trial, during trial, or after trial and conviction. A pardon frees the individual from whatever disabilities have been incurred by him as a consequence of criminal behavior.

Party Column Ballot. A type of ballot on which the names of a party's candidates for all offices are arranged in the form of a vertical column under the party's official title.

Petit Jury. A presumably impartial body of individuals, usually but not necessarily twelve in number, charged with the responsibility of hearing evidence and passing judgment on charges presented in civil and/or criminal cases—a trial jury.

Plurality. More votes than any other competing candidate, i.e., the most votes regardless of the proportion of the total number of votes cast for the several candidates competing for a particular office.

Pocket Veto. A veto that is absolute rather than suspensive because of legislative adjournment prior to expiration of the time allowed for exercise of the executive's suspensive veto while the legislature remains in session.

Police Power. The power of a government to restrict individual freedom of action and the use of property in order to safeguard or promote the general welfare.

Political Question. A question which the courts consider nonjusticiable and therefore decidable only by the political branches of the government, i.e., the legislative and executive branches.

Political Rights. Rights of direct or indirect participation in the formal process of government, e.g., the right to vote, the right to hold office, the right to organize and join political parties.

Position-Classification. The classification of positions according to functions, qualifications, and responsibilities as an aid to the systematic handling of most personnel problems, including salary standardization, establishment of lines of promotion, and transfering employees from one branch of service to another.

Post-audit. A checking process that occurs periodically or continuously after financial transactions have been *completed.* A final post-audit is an examination and verification of the entire record of outlay and income for the fiscal year.

Pre-audit. Pre-auditing is the function of passing on proposed expenditures prior to the creation of binding obligations. Consideration is given to the purpse of a contemplated expenditure and to the availability of funds.

Pressure-group. Any organized group of individuals which endeavors to influence the course of governmental action by bringing pressure to bear on public officials.

Previous Question, Motion of. This motion, if adopted by a legislative chamber, terminates all debate on the issue under consideration and requires an immediate vote on that issue.

Private Law. The body of law, established and enforceable by governmental authorities, which prescribes the rights and duties of private individuals in their relations with one another. Among its subdivisions are the law of property, the law of contracts, and the law of domestic relations.

Procedural Rights. The rights of individuals (a) to resort to specific procedures for the redress of wrongs and (b) to be dealt with by public officials in conformity with prescribed modes of action. Examples are the right of access to the courts, the right to compel the attendance of witnesses and to question them, and the right to notification of the charges if an individual is the defendant in a criminal prosecution.

Public Law. The body of law establishing rights and duties to which the body politic is one of the parties. Its principal subdivisions are constitutional law, administrative law, and criminal law.

Quasi-judicial. Bearing resemblance to but not identical with a strictly judicial function.

Quasi-legislative. The function of rule-making by administrative agencies closely resembling but not precisely the same as the lawmaking function of a legislature.

Recall. An election held for the purpose of enabling voters to remove an official prior to expiration of his legal term. The filing of a petition demanding this type of election is prerequisite.

Reprieve. Postponement of the execution of sentence in a specific case.

Reserved or Residual Powers. A phrase indicative of the historical fact that the states retained all powers not delegated exclusively to the national government or denied to the states.

Resulting Power. A power of the national government inferable from a combination of two or more expressly granted or implied powers.

Search and Seizure Warrant. A judicial writ or order authorizing a search and describing the place to be searched and the person or things to be seized.

Self-incrimination. The revelation of facts by an individual which may result in criminal proceedings against him.

Senatorial Courtesy. The Senatorial practice of withholding consent to Presidential appointments to federal positions located in a state if the Senators of that state, members of the President's party, object to the appointees. Consent may also be withheld if a Senator belonging to the Presidential party objects to a nominee who is a resident of the Senator's state.

Seniority Rule. A rule generally adhered to by both houses of Congress and by various state legislatures in designating committee chairmen, viz., the majority member of longest continuous service on a committee becomes chairman of that committee. Seniority as determined by length of continuous House or Senate membership also receives consideration, along with sundry other factors, in making assignments to standing committees.

Separation of Powers. An organizational arrangement featured by the distribution of powers among two or more mutually independent and coordinate branches of government, with each branch free to exercise its powers without being under obligation to submit to the dictates of the other branches. Legislative power is commonly assigned to one branch, executive power to another, and judicial power to a third.

Short Ballot. A ballot on which only a few decisions are required of voters—few officials to be chosen and few propositions, if any, to be voted on.

Special or Select Committee. A legislative committee established for a special purpose and only for such time as is required for the discharge of its responsibility.

Staff Functions. The investigatory, planning, and advisory activities undertaken by staff officers to aid the chief executive, department heads, and other high officials in the exercise of managerial authority.

Standing Committee. A committee established for the duration of a legislature and assigned jurisdiction over a designated category of bills for the purpose of giving them preliminary consideration.

Stare Decisis. The rule that previous decisions of a court are binding upon it in disposing of subsequent cases involving precisely the same issues.

Substantive Rights. The rights of persons to take action for the satisfaction of personal desires or needs. Rights enabling individuals to do something, e.g., to own and operate an automobile, to choose one's place of residence, to travel from place to place. Freedom of speech, freedom of religion, and the right to marry are other examples of substantive rights.

Torts. Infringements of private rights other than rights derived from contracts.

Treaty. A formal agreement between two or more states of the world community, such as the U.S.S.R., Great Britain, Switzerland, and the United States.

Unincorporated territory. See the explanation of incorporated territory.

Unitary System. A governmental system under which the central government of a body politic determines the number, nature, and powers of major and minor political subdivisions, i.e., units of regional and local government. The regional and local units are creatures of the central government.

Veto Power. The power of a chief executive to disapprove legislative acts within a designated period of time following their submission to him for consideration. A veto is suspensive, if the legislature may override it; otherwise it is absolute.

Cases Cited in Text

CASE	PAGE
Abington School District v. Schempp, 347 U. S. 203	96, 586
Apodaca et al v. Oregon, 40 Law Week 4528 (1972)	102, 590
Argersinger v. Hamlin, 40 Law Week 4679	101, Note 51b, 589
Ashe v. Swenson, 397 U. S. 436	88, Note 40b
Avery v. Midland County, 390 U. S. 474	390, 471
Bailey v. Drexel Furniture Co., 259 U. S. 20	41, Note 15
Baker v. Carr, 369 U. S. 186	28, Note 6; 198, 579
Barron v. Baltimore, 7 Peters 243	20, 573
Barrows v. Jackson, 346 U. S. 249	106, Note 57
Benton v. Maryland, 395 U. S. 784	88, Note 40a, 587
Beys Afroyim v. Dean Rusk, 387 U. S. 253	70, 71, 72, 577
Bloom v. Illinois, 20 L Ed 2d 522	101, 102, 589
Bolling v. Sharpe, 347 U. S. 497	104, Note 53, 105, 580
Bond v. Floyd, 385 U. S. 116	395, 584
Boynton v. Virginia, 364 U. S. 454	106, Note 56a
Branch v. Texas, 40 Law Week 4923	90, Note 40c
Branzburg v. Hayes, 40 Law Week 5025	95, Note 44b
Brown v. Board of Education, 347 U. S. 483	105, 580
Buchanan v. Warley, 245 U. S. 60	106, Note 57
Bullock v. Carter, 31 L Ed 2d 92	132, Note 60a
Burns v. Richardson, 384 U. S. 73	381
Burstyn v. Wilson, 343 U. S. 495	95, Note 44
Camara v. Municipal Court of City and County of San Francisco, 387 U. S. 523	87, 587
Chimel v. California, 395 U. S. 752	86, Note 38a, 587
Cipriano v. Houma, 23 L Ed 2d 647	116
Chisholm v. Georgia, 2 Dallas 419	21, 341
Cohens v. Virginia, 6 Wheaton 264	p. 570
Colegrove v. Green, 328 U. S. 549	197, 578
Coleman v. Miller, 307 U. S. 433	26, Note 5, 569
Cooley v. Board of Wardens, 12 Howard 299	49, 571
Coyle v. Smith, 221 U. S. 559	52, Note 23, 575
Dennis v. United States, 341 U. S. 494	93, Note 41
Dred Scott v. Sanford, 19 Howard 393	338, 341
Duncan v. Louisiana, 20 L Ed 2d 491	101, 589
Dunn v. Blumstein, 40 Law Week 269	118, 578
Eakin v. Raub, 12 Sergeant & Rawle (Pa) 330	337, 344
Engle v. Vitale, 370 U. S. 421	96, 586
Escobedo v. Illinois, 378 U. S. 478	84, Note 37
Everson v. Board of Education, 330 U. S. 1	97, 586
Ex Parte Grossman, 267 U. S. 87	271, Note 89, 272, Note 90
Fletcher v. Peck, 6 Cranch 87	339

Forston v. Dorsey, 379 U. S. 433   419, 576

Forston v. Morris, 385 U. S. 231   396

Furman v. Georgia, 40 Law Week 4923   90, Note 40c

Gayle v. Browder, 352 U. S. 906   106, Note 56a

Gibbons v. Ogden, 9 Wheaton 1   571

Gilbert v. California, 388 U.S. 263   586

Gitlow v. New York, 268 U. S. 652   93, Note 41, 583

Gordon v. Lance, 29 L Ed 2d 273   116, Note 59b

Gravel v. United States, 40 Law Week 5053   95, Note 44c

Grosso v. United States, 19 L Ed 2d 906   589

Hadley v. Junior College District, 397 U. S. 50   390, 580

Hammer v. Dagenhart, 247 U. S. 251   29

Hans v. Louisiana, 134 U. S. 1   319, Note 95

Harper v. Virginia Board of Election, 383 U. S. 663   116, 578

Harris v. New York, 401 U. S. 223   85, Note 37a

Harris v. Washington, 30 L Ed 2d 212   88, Note 405

Haynes v. United States, 19 L Ed 2d 923   589

Helvering v. Davis, 301 U. S. 619   40, Note 14

Henderson v. United States, 339 U.S. 816   106, Note 56a

Holmes v. Atlanta, 350 U. S. 879   106, Note 56a

Humphrey's Executor (Rathbun) v. United States, 295 U. S. 602   259, 260, 261, 574

In Re Gault, 387 U. S. 1   103, Note 25g, 590

In Re Pappas, 40 Law Week 5025   95, Note 44b

In Re Winship, 397 U. S. 358   103, Note 52h, 590

Jackson v. Georgia, 40 Law Week 4923   90, Note 40c

James v. Valtierra, 402 U. S. 137   106, 581

Johnson v. Louisiana, 40 Law Week 4524 (1972) p. 153   102, 590

Kennedy v. Mendoza-Martinez, 372 U. S. 144   71

Kentucky v. Dennison, 24 Howard 66   56, 576

Kilbourn v. Thompson, 103 U. S. 168   209

Kirby v. Illinois, 40 Law Week 4607   101, Note 51b, 588

Korematsu v. United States, 323 U. S. 214   43, 246, 574

Kramer v. Union Free School District, No. 15, 395 U. S. 621   116, 578

Loving v. Virginia, 388 U. S. 1   108, Note 58, 581

Lucas v. Colorado General Assembly, 377 U. S. 713   392, 579

Luther v. Borden, 7 Howard 1   576

Mahon v. Justice, 126 U. S. 700   56, Note 26

Malloy v. Hogan, 378 U. S. 1   p. 84, Note 36, 588

Mapp v. Ohio, 367 U. S. 643   87, 587

Marbury v. Madison, 1 Cranch 137   336, 344, 569

Marchetti v. United States, 19 L Ed 2d 889   589

Mayor & Council of Baltimore v. Dawson, 350 U. S. 977   106, Note 56a

McCulloch v. Maryland, 4 Wheaton 316 — 37, 570

McGrain v. Daugherty, 273 U. S. 135 — 209

McKeiver v. Pennsylvania, 29 L Ed 2d 647 — 103, Note 52i, 590

Minersville School District v. Gobitis, 310 U. S. 586 — 98

Miranda v. Arizona, 384 U. S. 436 — 84, Note 37, 588

Missouri v. Holland, 252 U. S. 416 — 42, 572

Monaco v. Mississippi, 292 U. S. 313 — 319, Note 96

Moose Lodge No. 107, Appellant v. Irvis, 40 Law Week 4715 — 107, 582

Murdock v. Pennsylvania, 319 U. S. 105 — 98, 585

Murray v. Curlett, 374 U.S. 203 — 587

Myers v. United States, 272 U. S. 52 — 259, 260, 573

Near v. Minnesota, 283 U. S. 697 — 94, 583

New York Times Company v. United States, 29 L Ed 2d 822 — 95, Note 44a, 584

O'Callahan v. Parker, 23 L Ed 2d 291 — 103, Note 52e

Oregon v. Mitchell, 27 L Ed 2d 272 — 117

Pacific States Telephone & Telegraph Co. v. Oregon, 223 U. S. 118 — 52, 53, 576

Palko v. Connecticut, 302 U.S. 339 — 587

Palmer v. Thompson, 29 L Ed 2d 438 — 106, Note 56a

Patsone v. Pennsylvania, 232 U. S. 138 — 80, Note 35

Perez v. Brownell, 356 U. S. 44 — 70

Phoenix v. Kolodziejski, 26 L Ed 2d 523 — 116, 578

Plessy v. Ferguson, 163 U. S. 537 — 105, Note 54, 580

Pollock v. Farmers' Loan & Trust Co., 158 U. S. 601 — 341, Note 106

Powell v. McCormack, 395 U. S. 486 — 195, 573

Reitman v. Mulkey, 387 U. S. 369 — 106, 581

Relford v. Commandant, 28 L Ed 2d 102 — 103, Note 52f

Reynolds v. United States, 98 U. S. 145 — 97, 584

Reynolds v. Sims, 377 U. S. 533 — 28, Note 6, 355, 389, 390, 57

Rogers v. Bellei, 401 U. S. 815 — 70, 72, 577

Schechter Poultry Corporation v. United States, 295 U. S. 495 — 206, Note 71; 575

Schenk v. United States, 249 U.S. 47 — 582

Schneider v. Rusk, 377 U. S. 163 — 71, 72

See v. City of Seattle, 387 U.S. 541 — 587

Shaffer v. Valtierra, 402 U. S. 137

Shelley v. Kramer, 334 U. S. 1 — 106, Note 57

Slaughter House Cases, 16 Wallace 36 — 78, 577

Slochower v. Board of Education, 350 U. S. 551 — 85, Note 38

Southern Pacific Co. v. Arizona, 325 U. S. 761 — 49, Note 22; 571

Steward Machine Co. v. Davis, 301 U. S. 548 — 40, Note 14, 572

Texas v. White, 7 Wallace 724 — 46, Note 20

Tilton v. Richardson, 29 L Ed 2d 790 — 97, Note 47b

Times Film Corporation v. Chicago, 365 U. S. 43   95, Note 44

Trop v. Dulles, 356 U. S. 86   70

United States v. Caldwell, 40 Law Week 5025   95, Note 44b

United States v. Curtiss-Wright Export Corporation,   43, 206, 570, 595
299 U. S. 304

United States v. Darby, 312 U. S. 100   29, Note 7; 39, 572

United States v. Wade, 388 U. S. 218   101, Note 51b, 588

United States v. Washington Post Co., 29 L Ed 2d 822   95, Note 44a

United States v. Wong Kim Ark, 169 U. S. 649   68, 577

Virginia v. Tennessee, 148 U. S. 503   62, Note 27

Walz v. Tax Commission of City of New York,   97, Note 47a, 586
397 U. S. 664

Washington v. Texas, 388 U.S. 14   589

Wesberry v. Sanders, 376 U. S. 1   28, Note 6; 197, 198, 579

West Virginia State Board of Education v. Barnette,   98, 585
319 U. S. 624

Whitcomb v. Chaves, 29 L Ed 2d 363   396, 579

Whitney v. California, 274 U.S. 357   583

Wickard v. Filburn, 317 U. S. 111   39, 40, 572

Wiener v. United States, 357 U. S. 349   259, 261, 574

Williams v. Florida, 399 U. S. 78   102, Note 52b, 589

Wisconsin v. Yoder, 20 Law Week 4476   98, 99, 585

Wolf v. Colorado, 338 U. S. 25   87, Note 40

Woods v. Miller, 333 U. S. 138   265, Note 88

Yates v. United States, 354 U.S. 289   584

Youngstown Sheet & Tube Co. v. Sawyer,   246, 247, 574
343 U. S. 579

Digest of Selected Supreme Court Cases

* Indicates Cases of Major Importance
** Indicates Cases of Lesser Importance

JUDICIAL REVIEW

* *Marbury v. Madison*, 1 Cranch 137 (1803). In this famous case the Supreme Court maintained that it had the power to pass judgment on the constitutionality of an act of Congress. The Judiciary Act of 1789 increased the original jurisdiction of the Supreme Court beyond that enumerated in Article III of the Constitution. Chief Justice Marshall's opinion sets forth the reasons why the Court is duty-bound to refuse enforcement of any act of Congress in conflict with constitutional provisions.

AMENDING THE CONSTITUTION OF THE
UNITED STATES

* *Coleman v. Miller*, 307 U. S. 433 (1939). In 1924 the Child Labor Amendment was proposed by Congress and submitted to the states for ratification. The Kansas legislature *rejected* the proposal in 1925 but *ratified it* in 1937.

With respect to amendment of the Constitution, the Supreme Court held that "political questions" (subject to final determination by Congress rather than by the judiciary) include the following; whether a state which has rejected a proposed amendment may subsequently change its vote to the affirmative; whether an affirmative vote may later be replaced by a negative vote; whether reasonable time limits for ratification of specific proposals should be established; and whether, by lapse of time, a proposed amendment has lost its vitality and is no longer subject to ratification.

The Court pointed out that the policy of Congress has been to count changes from the negative to the affirmative; to disregard changes from the affirmative to the negative; to prescribe time limits for the ratification of several proposed amendments; and, in the case of the 1924 proposed child labor amendment, to permit ratification until Congress withdraws the proposal.

Note: the Child Labor Amendment is still ratifiable by the states.

NATIONAL GOVERNMENT: POWERS AND SUPREMACY

** *Cohens v. Virginia,* 6 Wheaton 264 (1821); *Martin v. Hunter's Lessee* 1 Wheaton 304 (1816). The Judiciary Act of 1789 provided for Supreme Court review of the decisions of state courts in three classes of cases involving questions of federal law. In the *Cohens* and *Martin* cases, the Supreme Court upheld the constitutionality of this provision of the Judiciary Act and clearly established the Court's power to review federal questions arising in state courts.

* *McCulloch v. Maryland,* 4 Wheaton 316 (1819). This case arose because of creation of the Second Bank of the United States by act of Congress and the enactment of a law by Maryland levying a tax on notes issued by banks not chartered by the state itself.

Issues: Could Congress incorporate a bank, even though not expressly authorized to do so? Could a state tax an instrumentality of the national government?

The Court held that Congress possessed the power by *implication.* It construed the "necessary and proper" clause broadly as meaning appropriate, useful, and convenient. The creation of a bank is an appropriate means of implementing various expressly granted powers.

The Maryland tax was declared unconstitutional. By reason of the "supremacy" clause of Article VI, states have no power, by taxation or otherwise, to retard, impede, burden, or in any manner control the functioning of the national government within the sphere of its delegated authority, whether granted expressly or by implication.

* *United States v. Curtiss-Wright Corporation et al,* 299 U. S. 304 (1936). In this case the Supreme Court asserted that a fundamental difference exists between the powers of the national government in respect to foreign or external affairs and those pertaining to domestic or internal affairs. In the field of internal affairs, the doctrine of delegated powers is categorically true. Not so in the field of foreign affairs." . . . the investment of the federal government with the powers of external sovereignty did not depend upon the affirmative grants of the Constitution. The powers to declare and wage war, to

conclude peace, to make treaties, to maintain diplomatic relations with other sovereignties, if they had never been mentioned in the Constitution, would have vested in the federal government as necessary concomitants of nationality. . . ."

* *Gibbons v. Ogden*, 9 Wheaton 1 (1824). A broad construction was placed on the power of Congress to regulate foreign and interstate commerce. Chief Justice Marshall, speaking for the Court, defined commerce as intercourse—not merely as buying and selling, or the interchange of commodities. The word describes the commercial intercourse between nations and parts of nations in all of its branches, including navigation. Commerce among the states concerns more states than one. It does not stop at the external boundary line of each state but may be introduced into the interior. The power to regulate is to prescribe the rules by which commerce is to be governed. This power is complete in itself and may be exercised to its utmost extent. The acts of a state must yield to the laws of Congress when Congress exercises its power to regulate foreign and interstate commerce.

** *Cooley v. Board of Wardens of the Port of Philadelphia*, 12 Howard 299 (1852). A Pennsylvania statute of 1803 established a system of regulations affecting pilotage in the port of Philadelphia. Money penalties were imposed for failure to comply with the regulations. This statute was challenged as unconstitutional on the ground that Congress possesses exclusive authority over foreign and interstate commerce.

In upholding the state law, the Supreme Court asserted that exclusive legislation by Congress is required with respect to subjects of the "commerce power" that are in their nature "national," or admit of only one uniform plan of regulation, but "local aspects," such as pilotage regulations which demand diversity, may be dealt with by the states until superseded by Congressional legislation.

* *Southern Pacific Co. v. Arizona*, 325 U. S. 761 (1945). An Arizona law prohibited the operation of trains within the state of greater length than 70 freight or 14 passenger cars. No act of Congress limited train lengths.

The Arizona statute was declared unconstitutional by the Supreme Court on the ground that if the length of trains is to be regulated at all, national uniformity in the regulation adopted, which only Congress can prescribe, is practically indispensable to the operation of an efficient and economical national railway system.

* *United States v. Darby*, 312 U. S. 100 (1941). The Fair Labor Standards Act of 1938 prohibited the shipment in interstate commerce of products produced in the United States under labor conditions defined by Congress as "substandard."

Although conceding that manufacturing and labor conditions fall outside the meaning of the term "commerce," the Court held that the power of Congress to regulate interstate commerce extends to the control, through legislative action, of intrastate activities which have a *substantial effect* on that commerce or the exercise of Congressional power over it.

* *Wickard v. Filburn*, 317 U. S. 111 (1942). This case involved the Agricultural Adjustment Act of 1938 which endeavored to stabilize agricultural production. Wickard had exceeded the wheat acreage quota assigned him but contended that his excess wheat production was to be consumed only on his farm and not shipped in interstate commerce.

The Court held that even if Wickard's activity was local and could not be regarded as commerce, Congress could control it inasmuch as it had a *substantial economic* effect on interstate commerce. Any matter having a substantial effect on interstate commerce is controllable by Congress.

* *Steward Machine Co. v. Davis*, 301 U. S. 548; *Helvering v. Davis*, 301 U. S. 619 (1937). The Social Security Act of 1935 and its subsequent amendments provide for old-age benefits, unemployment compensation, hospital and medical insurance, and aid to dependent children and for maternal and child welfare. Cost of the program is met by taxes levied on employers, employees, and self-employed persons.

The Supreme Court upheld the constitutionality of the Social Security Act of 1935, inasmuch as the tax is levied for a *public purpose;* no unlawful invasion of the reserved powers of the states is involved; and the states are neither compelled to participate in the security program nor coerced into abandoning governmental functions that they are not permitted to surrender.

* *Missouri v. Holland*, 252 U. S. 416 (1920). The Supreme Court upheld a 1918 act of Congress providing protection for migratory birds in pursuance of a treaty entered into with

Great Britain for that purpose in 1916. Legislation by Congress in 1913 had been declared unconstitutional by the lower federal courts on the ground that control of bird life was not covered by powers granted to Congress.

The Court declared that both the treaty and the law passed by Congress to give it effect were constitutional. In the words of the Court, "it is obvious that there may be matters of sharpest exigency for the national well-being that an act of Congress could not deal with, but that a treaty followed by such an act could. . . ."

THE FEDERAL BILL OF RIGHTS

** *Barron v. Baltimore*, 7 Peters 243 (1833). The Supreme Court recognized that the first eight amendments to the Constitution of the United States were intended to restrict the exercise of national rather than state power.

CONGRESS: QUALIFICATIONS OF MEMBERS

* *Adam Clayton Powell v. John W. McCormack*, 395 U.S. 486 (1969). Congress, in judging the qualifications of its members, is limited to the specific qualifications prescribed in the Constitution, viz., citizenship, age, and residence. Neither House can exclude a duly elected member who possesses the stipulated qualifications. The power of each house to expel members is not affected by this ruling.

PRESIDENTIAL POWERS

* *Myers v. United States*, 272 U.S. 52 (1926). Myers, postmaster of Portland, Oregon, was removed from office by executive order of President Wilson in disregard of an act of Congress of 1876 requiring Senate approval of the removal of first, second, and third class postmasters.

The Supreme Court ruled that the removal power of the President is inferable from his position as chief executive, his duty to execute the laws, and his power of appointment. Congress lacks authority to limit the President's power to remove executive officers appointed by him with the advice and consent of the Senate.

* *Humphrey's Executor (Rathbun) v. United States*, 295 U. S. 602 (1935)

President Roosevelt removed Humphrey from the Federal Trade Commission solely on the ground that his views and Humphrey's differed on questions of policy and administration. The statute creating the Federal Trade Commission merely authorized Presidential removal for inefficiency, neglect of duty, or malfeasance in office.

The Court held that the President had exceeded his authority in removing Humphrey. It asserted that Congress may place limitations on the Presidential removal power *with respect to officials performing quasi-legislative or quasi-judicial functions*, as distinguished from purely executive functions, such as those of a postmaster.

* *Wiener v. United States*, 357 U. S. 349 (1958). President Eisenhower removed Wiener from a War Claims Commission for the purpose of replacing him with a man of his choice. The statute creating the Commission made no provision for removals.

The Supreme Court decided that the President lacked the power to remove Wiener because the War Claims Commission was an *adjudicating* body and the failure of Congress to deal with the question of removals indicated its intention to withhold this power from the President.

* *Youngstown Sheet and Tube Co. et al v. Sawyer*, 343 U. S. 579 (1952). A few hours before a strike deadline President Truman issued an executive order authorizing the Secretary of Commerce to seize and operate the steel mills. The President based his action on his constitutional authority as chief executive and commander-in-chief of the armed forces.

The Presidential order was declared invalid by the Supreme Court for two reasons: (1) Congress had not authorized the President to do what he did and (2) the possession of executive power by the President is insufficient constitutional justification for the action that was taken.

* *Korematsu v. United States*, 323 U. S. 214 (1945). The Supreme Court upheld the action of President Roosevelt and Congress in placing individuals of Japanese ancestry, even though United States citizens, in "war relocation centers." This action during World War II was based on a Presidential executive order authorizing the creation of military areas from which any or all persons might be excluded. Penalties for violation of the military orders and regulations were subsequently established by Congress. The Court refused to conclude that the action taken was beyond the war power of Congress and the Executive.

DELEGATION OF POWERS

* *Schechter Poultry Corporation et al v. United States*, 295 U. S. 495 (1935). The National Industrial Recovery Act of 1933 was declared unconstitutional on two grounds: (1) as an attempted regulation of intrastate transactions which affect interstate commerce only indirectly and (2) as an attempted delegation of unfettered lawmaking discretion to the President. Note that the Court no longer uses the direct and indirect effects test—replaced by the criterion of "substantial effect," as in *United States v. Darby*.

The rule against delegation of the *essence of legislative power* remains unviolated only as long as Congress establishes a general policy and prescribes standards limiting the discretion of the governmental agency to which rule-making authority is delegated.

** *United States v. Curtiss-Wright Corporation et al*, 299 U. S. 304 (1936). With respect to the delegation of lawmaking authority, the Supreme Court took the position that congressional legislation which is to be made effective through negotiation and inquiry within the *international field* must often accord to the President a degree of discretion and freedom from statutory restriction which would not be admissible were domestic affairs alone involved.

EQUALITY OF STATES

* *Coyle v. Smith*, 221 U. S. 559 (1911). Oklahoma, having been admitted as a state, disregarded the terms of the enabling act of 1906 which required that the state capital be located in Guthrie at least until 1913. An agreement to this effect had been ratified by the Oklahoma voters. In 1910, however, the Oklahoma legislature provided for immediate removal of the capital to Oklahoma City.

The Supreme Court upheld Oklahoma's action. A new state is admitted to the Union with all of the powers of sovereignty and jurisdiction pertaining to the original states and these powers may not be constitutionally diminished by any conditions, compacts, or stipulations embraced in the act of admission that would be invalid if the subject of Congressional legislation after admission. One such power is locating the state's seat of government.

SELECTION OF STATE GOVERNOR

** *Forston v. Morris*, 385 U. S. 231 (1966). No provision of the Constitution of the United States prevents a state from providing for legislative selection of its governor.

INTERSTATE RENDITION OF FUGITIVES
FROM JUSTICE

** *Kentucky v. Dennison*, 24 Howard 66 (1861). The constitutional provision concerning interstate rendition of fugitives from justice is merely declaratory of a moral obligation, even though the wording of this stipulation of Article IV appears to be mandatory. There is no way of compelling a state executive to abide by this constitutionally declared obligation.

LEGITIMACY OF A STATE GOVERNMENT

** *Luther v. Borden*, 7 Howard 1 (1849). Dorr's rebellion in Rhode Island raised the question of which of two contending governments in that state was its lawful government.

The Supreme Court decided that determination of which of the two competing governments was the lawful one was a responsibility of the President and/or Congress—not of the courts. The issue was "political" rather than "justiciable."

* *Pacific States Telephone & Telegraph Co. v. Oregon*, 223 U. S. 118 (1912). The government of Oregon was claimed to be non-republican because of that state's establishment of the initiative and the referendum. Congress had seated Representatives and Senators from Oregon.

The Supreme Court ruled that the question of "republican character" is "political" rather than "justiciable" and that the courts are bound by the stand taken by the political branches of the government, viz., Congress and/or the President.

CITIZENSHIP

* *United States v. Wong Kim Ark,* 169 U. S. 649 (1881). Any person born within the United States and subject to the jurisdiction thereof, regardless of his race, color, or the status of his parents (whether aliens or citizens) acquires United States citizenship solely because of the place of birth. Wong's parents were subjects of the Emperor of China and at that time ineligible for citizenship, but Wong, being born in the United States, acquired United States citizenship.

Examples of persons born within but not subject to the jurisdiction of the United States are the children of visiting heads of foreign countries, of foreign ambassadors and other diplomatic representatives accredited to the United States, and of members of foreign armed forces in occupation of United States territory.

* *Beys Afroyim, Petitioner, v. Dean Rusk, Secretary of State,* 35 Law Week 4502 (1967). Congress has neither express nor implied power to expatriate a citizen, natural-born or naturalized, *without his assent.* Only voluntary expatriation is permissible.

* *William P. Rogers v. Aldo Mario Bellei,* 401 U. S. 815 (1971). The Fourteenth Amendment definition of citizenship is restricted to the combination of three factors, viz., birth in the United States, naturalization in the United States, and subject to the jurisdiction of the United States. This definition does not apply to a person born abroad of an American parent, as was Bellei. The acquisition and loss of citizenship not covered by the Fourteenth Amendment depends on Congressional policy. Involuntary expatriation is permissible in such cases.

PRIVILEGES AND IMMUNITIES OF
UNITED STATES CITIZENSHIP

* *The Slaughter House Cases,* 16 Wallace 36 (1873). The Fourteenth Amendment prohibits the states from making or enforcing any law abridging the privileges and immunities of citizens of the United States. This provision refers only to privileges and immunities owing their existence to the relationship between the citizen and the national government and to the provisions of national laws and treaties.

Privileges and immunities of state citizenship, as prescribed by the laws of particular states, are excluded from the meaning of this limitation on the power of the states. The privileges and immunities of United States citizenship protected by the Fourteenth Amendment *do not comprehend ordinary civil rights.*

VOTING QUALIFICATIONS

* *Harper v. Virginia Board of Elections,* 383 U. S. 663 (1966). The equal protection clause of the Fourteenth Amendment is violated by the states whenever the *affluence* of the voter or payment of any fee is established as a qualification for voting, e.g., payment of taxes and/or the ownership of property.

**Phoenix v. Kolodziejski,* 399 U. S. 24 (1970). The exclusion of non-property owners from elections for approval of the issuance of general obligation bonds violates the Equal Protection clause of the Fourteenth Amendment.

**Kramer v. Union Free School District, No. 15,* 395 U. S. 621 (1969). A New York statute barred persons from voting in school district elections, outside cities, unless they *owned or leased real estate* or had *children in the public schools.* Declared unconstitutional in violation of the equal protection clause.

* *Dunn v. Blumstein,* 40 Law Week 4259 (1972). Tennessee's residence requirements for voting were one year in the state and three months in the county. The Equal Protection clause of the Fourteenth Amendment is violated by such requirements. In the majority opinion the Court stated that thirty days appears to be ample for completion of administrative tasks for prevention of fraud. A state would have to establish a sufficient compelling interest to justify long residence requirements as a means of preventing fraudulent practices or of securing an informed electorate. Tennessee failed to do so.

CONGRESSIONAL DISTRICTS

** *Colegrove v. Green,* 328 U. S. 549 (1946). In this case (overruled in 1964) the Court held that the Constitution confers exclusive authority on Congress to prevent unfairness by state legislatures in establishing districts for the selection of members of the popular chamber of Congress, viz., the House of Representatives. No judicial remedy is available.

* *Wesberry v. Sanders*, 376 U. S. 1 (1964). Congressional districts must be substantially equal in population. The Court based its ruling on the provision of Article I that representatives are to be chosen by the people of the several states and apportioned among the states on a population basis. Emphasis was placed on the one-man-one-vote idea.

APPORTIONMENT—STATE LEGISLATURES

* *Baker v. Carr*, 369 U. S. 186 (1962). The Supreme Court decided that a justiciable controversy, subject to settlement by the federal courts, arises under the "equal protection" clause of the Fourteenth Amendment when the constitutionality of a state's legislative apportionment plan is challenged on the ground that it debases, dilutes, and consequently impairs the right to vote of citizens.

Abandoning a long-standing view that the issue of legislative apportionment is "political," the Court asserted that the non-justiciableness of a political question is primarily a function of the separation of powers. In previous "political question" cases, the relationship between the judiciary and coordinate branches of the Federal Government was involved—not the federal judiciary's relationship to the states, as in the present case concerning malapportionment in Tennessee.

The Court summarized the circumstances under which an issue is actually non-justiciable. It concluded that an allegation of denial of equal protection (Fourteenth Amendment) presents a justiciable question.

* *Reynolds v. Sims*, 377 U. S. 533 (1964). The equal protection clause of the Fourteenth Amendment requires that members of state legislatures (bicameral or unicameral), unless all are elected at-large, must be apportioned among the component subdivisions of a state in proportion to their populations. Representation must be population-based.

* *Lucas v. Colorado General Assembly*, 377 U. S. 713 (1964). Even if approved by the voters of a state, any plan of apportioning seats in the state's legislature is unconstitutional unless provision is made for population-based representation.

** *Whitcomb v. Chaves*, 29 L Ed 2d 363 (1971). Multi-member electoral districts are subject to challenge if the circumstances of a particular case may have the effect of minimizing or canceling out the voting strength of racial or political elements of the voting population, especially if a voting district is large and elects a substantial proportion of the seats in either house of a bicameral legislature, or if multi-membered districts are used for both chambers of the legislature, or if no provision is made for at-large candidates running from particular geographical sub-districts.

*Hadley Junior College District of Metropolitan Kansas City, 397 U. S. 59 (1970). This decision extended the rule of one man —one vote to school boards. Previously, in Avery v. Midland County, 390 U. S. 474, the Supreme Court ruled that disproportionate representation of districts in local policy-determining bodies, as well as in state legislatures, conflicts with the equal protection clause.

In the Hadley case the court asserted that, as a general rule, if a state or local government decides to select persons by popular election to perform governmental functions, the equal protection clause requires that each qualified voter must be given an equal opportunity to participate in that election—and if the members of an elected body are chosen from separate districts, the districts must be so established as to ensure, as far as is practicable, that an equal number of voters can vote for proportionately equal numbers of officials.

RACIAL DISCRIMINATION

** Plessy v. Ferguson, 163 U. S. 537 (1896). In this case (no longer authoritative), the Supreme Court upheld a Louisiana statute requiring railroads to furnish separate but equal accommodations for white and colored people. The Court asserted that a law authorizing or requiring separation of the two races cannot be considered unreasonable or obnoxious to the Fourteenth Amendment (equal protection clause).

* Brown et al v. Board of Education, 347 U. S. 483 (1954). Segregation of children in public schools of the states, solely on the basis of race, is prohibited by the equal protection clause of the Fourteenth Amendment. Separate educational facilities, even though the physical facilities and other tangible factors may be equal, are inherently unequal and therefore unconstitutional.

* Bolling v. Sharpe, 347 U. S. 497 (1954). Segregation in

schools of the District of Columbia on the basis of race conflicts with the due process clause of the Fifth Amendment. The equal protection provision of the Fourteenth applies only to the states—not to the national government. Segregation in public education imposes a burden on Negro children that constitutes arbitrary deprivation of liberty in violation of the due process clause.

* *Loving v. Virginia*, 387 U. S. (1967). A Virginia law prohibited and punished marriages in conflict with a racial classification. This anti-miscegenation statute was declared unconstitutional as an invidious racial discrimination of the type prohibited by both the equal protection and due process clauses of the Fourteenth Amendment.

* *Reitman v. Mulkey*, 387 U.S. 369 (1967). An amendment to the California constitution prohibited state and local legislation denying or limiting the right of any person to refuse to sell, lease, or rent real property for residential purposes to anyone to whom he did not wish to sell, rent, or lease such property.

This provision, according to the Supreme Court, involved the state in racial discrimination in violation of the equal protection clause. The effect of the amendment was to authorize private discrimination on racial grounds in the housing market. Such authorization *by the state* falls within the category of state action prohibited by the Fourteenth Amendment.

* *James v. Valtierra*, 402 U. S. 137 (1971). Article 34 of the California constitution provides that no low-rent housing project shall be developed, constructed, or acquired in any manner by a state public body until the project is approved by a majority vote in a city, town, or county referendum. The term "low-rent housing" was defined as a development providing living accommodations for persons of low-income financed in whole or in part by the Federal Government or the state.

The Court held that this provision did not violate the equal protection clause or other stipulations of the national constitution. It did not rest on racial distinctions. Low-income persons were not *singled out* for *mandatory referenda*. Mandatory referenda are required for various decisions in California, e.g., constitutional amendments, general-obligation bond issues, and annexations. Provision for referenda demonstrates devotion to democracy—not to bias, discrimination, or prejudice. A law-making procedure that "disadvantages" a particular group does not always deny equal protection.

Three judges dissented. They considered the low-rent, low-income provision to be an explicit and invidious discrimination between the well-to-do and the poor in violation of the equal protection clause.

Moose Lodge No. 107, Appellant v. Irvis, 40 Law Week 4715 (1972). Irvis, a Negro guest of a member of the Moose Lodge which is a private club, was refused service at the club's dining room and bar solely because of his race. He contended that the discrimination was state action in violation of the equal protection clause because the Pennsylvania liquor board had issued a private club liquor license to the lodge. The Court held that the issuance of the license did not implicate the state *sufficiently* in the lodge's discriminatory practices to make the state a party to this action. There was no indication in the record that the state's regulation of the sale of liquor is intended overtly or covertly to encourage discrimination.

A lower federal three-judge panel had ruled in favor of Irvis's contention. At that time the constitution of the lodge merely contained discriminatory membership provisions. Subsequent to the lower court decision the lodge's discriminatory guest practices were incorporated in its by-laws. The liquor board's regulation required that "every club licensee shall adhere to all provisions of its constitutions and by-laws." Failure to do so could result in revocation of the license. The Supreme Court stated that this regulation, in effect, placed state sanctions behind the discriminatory practices of the lodge, but it held that enforcement of the regulation should be enjoined only to the extent that it *requires* the lodge to adhere to its discriminatory practices.

FREEDOM OF SPEECH AND OF THE PRESS

* *Schenck v. United States,* 249 U. S. 47 (1919). "The question in every case is whether the words used are in such circumstances and are of such a nature as to create a clear and present danger that they will bring about the substantive evils that Congress has a right to prevent. It is a question of proximity and degree. When a nation is at war things that might be said in time of peace are such a hindrance to its effort that their

utterance will not be endured as long as men fight, and that no court could regard them as protected by any constitutional right."

* Gitlow v. New York, 268 U. S. 652 (1925). The principal significance of this case is the Supreme Court's assertion that freedom of speech and of the press—protected by the First Amendment from abridgment by Congress—are among the fundamental personal rights and liberties protected by the due process clause of the Fourteenth Amendment from impairment by the states.

In this case the Court applied the "bad tendency" rather than the "clear and present danger" test in upholding the conviction of Gitlow. Gitlow had advocated, advised, and taught the duty, necessity, and propriety of overthrowing government by force. His defense was an absence of evidence that concrete results had flowed from his publications.

* Whitney v. California, 274 U. S. 357 (1927). ". . . although the right of free speech and assembly are fundamental, they are not in their nature absolute. Their exercise is subject to restriction, if the particular restriction proposed is required in order to protect the state from destruction or from serious injury, political, economic, or moral. That the necessity which is essential to a valid restriction does not exist unless speech would produce, or is intended to produce, a clear and imminent danger of some substantive evil which the state constitutionally may prevent, has been settled."

* Near v. Minnesota, 283 U. S. 697 (1931). "It is no longer open to doubt that the liberty of the press, and of speech, is within the liberty safeguarded by the due process clause of the Fourteenth Amendment from invasion by state action. . . . In maintaining this guaranty, the authority of the State to enact laws to promote the health, safety, morals, and general welfare of its people is necessarily admitted."

". . . liberty of the press, historically considered and taken up by the Federal Constitution, has meant principally although not exclusively, immunity from previous restraints or censorships. . . ."

". . . the principle as to immunity from previous restraint is stated too broadly, if every such restraint is deemed to be prohibited. . . ."

". . . the protection even as to previous restraint is not absolutely unlimited. But the limitation has been recognized only in exceptional instances."

*New York Times Company v. United States, United States v. Washington Post Company, 29 L Ed 822 (1971). An injunction was denied the United States government against the publication by newspapers of the contents of a classified study entitled "History of United States Decision-Making Process on Vietnam Policy" (Pentagon Papers) because the government failed to show justification for imposition of a prior restraint of expression. Any system of prior restraint of expression bears a heavy presumption against its constitutional validity.

* Yates et al v. United States, 354 U. S. 289 (1957). "The distinction between advocacy of abstract doctrine and advocacy directed at promoting unlawful action is one that has been consistently recognized in opinions of this Court. . . . those to whom that advocacy is addressed must be urged to do something, now or in the future, rather than merely to *believe* in something."

** Bond v. Floyd, 385 U. S. 116 (1966). The lower house of the Georgia legislature refused to seat Julian Bond because of his comments on Vietnam and the draft. This action was invalidated by the Supreme Court on the ground that the freedom of speech guarantee of the national constitution (due process clause of the Fourteenth Amendment) requires that legislators be given the widest latitude in expressing their views on issues of policy.

FREEDOM OF RELIGION; ESTABLISHMENT
OF A RELIGION

** Reynolds v. United States, 98 U. S. 145 (1878). The Supreme Court upheld the conviction of Reynolds, a Mormon, under an act of Congress making polygamy a punishable crime in the territory of Utah. Reynolds, whose religion at that time sanctioned a plurality of wives, was prosecuted for having more than one wife.

In rejecting Reynolds's contention that his religious freedom had been abridged, the Court pointed out that this freedom does not include the right, in the name of religion, to commit acts of an immoral or criminal character. No one is exempt from obedience to criminal law merely because of his religious convictions.

Wisconsin v. Yoder et al, 40 Law Week 4476 (1972). Yoder and others were convicted of violating Wisconsin's compulsory school attendance law which requires attendance until age sixteen. The Amish refused to send their children to public or private school after graduation from the eighth grade on the grounds that to do so would endanger their own salvation and that of their children and that high school attendance is contrary to the Amish religion and way of life.

The Supreme Court upheld their contention that application of the Wisconsin law to them violated their rights under the free exercise of religion clause of the First Amendment as binding on the states through the Fourteenth. In the opinion of the Court a regulation neutral on its face may, in its application, nevertheless offend the constitutional guarantee of religious freedom. Wisconsin failed to show, with more particularity, how its concededly strong interest in compulsory education would be adversely affected by granting an exemption to the Amish.

* *West Virginia State Board of Education v. Barnette,* 319 U. S. 624 (1943). The issue in this case was the constitutionality of a compulsory flag salute which the West Virginia Board of Education had ordered as a regular part of the program of activities in the public schools. All teachers and pupils were required to participate. Refusal to do so was an act of insubordination to be dealt with by expulsion. Parents of an expelled child were liable to fine and imprisonment.

Children of Jehovah's Witnesses refused to participate on religious grounds. The Court held that requiring the children to do so and subjecting them and their parents to the penalties above-mentioned violated the guarantee of religious freedom (embraced by the due process clause of the Fourteenth Amendment).

* *Murdock v. Pennsylvania,* 319 U. S. 105 (1943). A local ordinance required procurement of a license and payment of a fee by all persons canvassing or soliciting orders for merchandise of any kind or delivering such articles under orders so solicited and obtained.

Jehovah's Witnesses, without obtaining the required license

or paying a fee, went from door to door distributing literature and soliciting people to purchase certain religious books and pamphlets. The ordinance was declared invalid in its application to the distribution and sale of religious literature. *No tax can be levied on exercise of the right of religious freedom.*

* *Everson v. Board of Education,* 330 U. S. 1 (1947). A township board of education authorized reimbursement to parents of money expended for the bus transportation of their children to school, including parochial as well as public schools.

The New Jersey statute empowering school districts to take such action was challenged as a "law respecting an establishment of religion." This contention was rejected by the Court on the ground that the statute and the township policy were designed to promote the welfare of the general public, in particular, school children and their parents. The law and policy did not have the purpose or effect of providing financial aid in support of a religious institution or religious sect.

Walz v. Tax Commission of the City of New York, 397 U. S. 664 (1970). The religious clauses of the First Amendment are binding on the states through the due process clause of the Fourteenth Amendment. These restrictions do not prohibit a state from granting real property tax exemptions to religious organizations for religious purposes if (a) the legislative purpose is not aimed at establishing, sponsoring, or supporting religion and if (b) the effect of the exemption is not an excessive government entanglement with religion. The Court pointed out that the exemption applied to real property owned not only by religious organizations but also by hospitals, libraries, scientific, and historical groups, among others.

* *Engel v. Vitale,* 370 U. S. 421 (1962). This case concerned the constitutionality of state authorization of daily recital, in school, of a prayer composed by state officials. The Court held that this state policy violated the constitutional ban on the enactment of laws establishing a religion (applicable to the states through the due process clause of the Fourteenth Amendment).

* *Abington School District v. Schempp,* 374 U. S. 203 (1963). A Pennsylvania statute required the daily reading in school, without comment, of at least ten verses from the Holy Bible. This law was declared unconstitutional because the policy

amounted to the *establishment of a religion*. The fact that individual pupils were free to absent themselves upon parental request failed to save the statute.

** *Murray v. Curlett*, 374 U. S. 203 (1963). A Maryland law provided for reading in school, without comment, of a chapter of the Holy Bible and/or use of the Lord's Prayer. This statutory provision was declared unconstitutional as a policy in conflict with the ban on establishment of a religion.

CRIMINAL PROCEDURE

*Benton v. Maryland, 395 U. S. 784 (1969). The Supreme Court held that the double jeopardy clause of the Fifth Amendment applies to the states through the Fourteenth Amendment. This case overruled *Palko v. Connecticut*, 302 U. S. 319 (1937). In *Palko* the Court decided that placement in double jeopardy by a state is not inconsistent with the due process clause of the Fourteenth Amendment.

* *Mapp v. Ohio*, 367 U. S. 643 (1961). The due process provision of the Fourteenth Amendment prohibits the use of evidence, gathered on the occasion of illegal searches and seizures by public officials, in state prosecutions for the commission of crimes prohibited by state law.

Chimel v. California, 395 U. S. 752 (1969). The Court declared that the Fourth Amendment command against unreasonable searches and seizures protects individuals against sweeping searches of their homes when placed under arrest. Searches without warrants must be confined to the arrested individual's person and to the area from within which said individual might have obtained a weapon or something which could have been used as evidence against him.

* *Camara v. Municipal Court of the City and County of San Francisco*, 387 U.S. 523 (1967). Search warrants are necessary to valid inspections of residential dwellings by health, fire, and other inspectors. Warrantless inspection without the occupant's consent is prohibited by the due process clause (Fourteenth Amendment)

** *See v. City of Seattle*, 387 U.S. 541 (1967). The compulsory inspection of business premises for the purpose of ascertaining conditions detrimental to the public health or safety requires the issuance of search warrants.

* *Malloy v. Hogan*, 378 U. S. 1 (1964). The due process clause of the Fourteenth Amendment comprehends the privilege against self-incrimination.

* *Miranda v. Arizona*, 384 U. S. 436 (1966); *Escobeda v. Illinois*, 378 U. S. 478 (1964). Involuntary confessions are inadmissible as evidence against a person accused of crime. Confessions or other incriminating statements will be considered involuntary unless various procedural safeguards are heeded by law-enforcing agencies. Among these safeguards are informing a suspect of his right to remain silent and his right to counsel; no police interrogation prior to retention or appointment of counsel; questioning to be conducted in presence of counsel; and no coercion, such as threat or infliction of physical harm or questioning of prolonged duration.

* *United States v. Wade* 388 U.S. 218 (1967); *Gilbert v. California*, 388 U.S. 263 (1967). The presence of counsel is a constitutional essential *at any critical stage* of the prosecution of an accused person, formal or informal, in court or out, if counsel's absence might detract from the accused's right to a fair trial.

After Wade had been indicted for bank robbery and after counsel had been appointed to represent him, federal agents, without notice to the defendant's attorney, conducted a lineup at which two bank employees indentified Wade as the robber. The identification was held inadmissible as evidence because Wade and his counsel should have been notified of the impending lineup and counsel's presence should have been requisite to conduct of the line-up. For Wade, the post-indictment lineup was a *critical stage* of the prosecution.

In the *Gilbert* case the Court ruled that the admission of in-court identifications without first determining that they were untainted by an illegal lineup, but independent in origin, is a "constitutional error."

***Kirby v. Illinois*, 40 Law Week 4607 (1972). The Supreme Court ruled that the presence of counsel is unnecessary in connection with identification of a suspect in a police station show-up that occurred *before* the defendant had been indicted or otherwise formally charged with a criminal offense. The right to counsel applies only *at* or *after* the initiation of adversary judicial criminal proceedings.

Argersinger v. Hamlin, 40 Law Week 4679 (1972). Indigent defendants possess the right to assistance of counsel in criminal prosecutions, whether or not the offense is a felony or a misdemeanor and whether or not a jury trial is required. No accused person may be deprived of his liberty, if denied counsel, as the result of any criminal prosecution.

** *Marchetti v. United States,* 19 L. Ed. 2d, 889 (1968); *Grosso v. United States,* 19 L. Ed. 2d 906 (1968); *Haynes v. United States,* 19 L. Ed. 2d 923 (1968). The privilege against self-incrimination is violated by federal conviction for failure to register and pay an occupational tax for engaging in the business of accepting wagers (Marchetti case); for failure to register and pay a wagering excise tax (Grosso case); and for failure to register the possession of a sawed-off shotgun (Haynes case).

* *Washington v. Texas,* 388 U.S. 14 (1967). The Sixth Amendment right of the accused to compulsory process for obtaining witnesses in his favor is enforceable against the states through the due process clause of the Fourteenth Amendment.

Duncan v. Louisiana, 20 L Ed 2d 491 (1968). The Sixth Amendment, through the due process clause of the Fourteenth, guarantees a right to jury trial in *serious* state criminal prosecutions. The penalty is of major relevance in determining seriousness. Crimes carrying penalties up to six months do not require a jury trial if they otherwise qualify as petty offenses.

**Bloom v. Illinois,* 20 L Ed 2d 522 (1968). The Fourteenth Amendment through the due process clause guarantees the right to a jury trial in serious criminal contempt cases, e.g., a criminal contempt punishable by a two-year prison term. Only petty contempts may be tried without a jury. Criminal contempt is a petty offense unless the punishment makes it a serious one.

Williams v. Florida, 399 U.S. 78 (1970). The traditional twelve-man jury in criminal cases is not required by either the Sixth Amendment or the due process clause of the Fourteenth. Florida's six-member jury system was upheld. A state may settle on any number of jurors as long as the "common-sense judgement of a group of laymen" stands between the accused and his accusor.

Johnson v. Louisiana, 40 Law Week 4524 (1972). The Supreme Court asserted that jury unanimity never was held to be a requisite of due process of law. It upheld the conviction of a person accused of a crime that according to Louisiana law was necessarily punishable by hard labor. The jury vote was 9 to 3. Louisiana law provided for conviction of less serious crimes by a unanimous vote of a jury of five, or more serious crimes by at least nine of twelve jurors, and of most serious crimes by unanimous assent of twelve-man juries. This state policy with respect to jury trials was considered consistent with the requirements of both due process and equal protection of the laws.

Apodaca et al v. Oregon, 40 Law Week 4528 (1972). The Supreme Court ruled that the Sixth Amendment guarantee of a jury trial in criminal prosecutions, applicable to the states via the due process clause of the Fourteenth Amendment, does not prohibit conviction by a substantial majority jury vote, instead of by a unanimous vote, in state criminal cases. The Court divided five to four. The dissenters took the position that unanimous jury decisions are required in both federal and state criminal prosecutions. One of the five majority justices agreed that unanimity is essential in federal cases. As a result, unanimous jury decisions are unnecessary in state trials but are mandatory in federal prosecutions.

In Re Gault, 387 U. S. 1 (1967). Due process in juvenile court proceedings requires that a child, his parents, or guardian be given written notice of specific charges or factural allegations; be represented by counsel; be granted the privilege against self-incrimination; and enjoy the right of confrontation and cross-examination of witnesses.

In Re Winship, 397 U. S. 358 (1970). Due process requires that a twelve-year-old child (liable to confinement for as long as six years) must be found guilty beyond a reasonable doubt—not merely by a preponderance of the evidence.

McKeiver v. Pennsylvania, 29 L Ed 2d 647 (1971). Despite denial of a public trial, the Fourteenth Amendment due process clause does not assure trial by jury in the adjudicative phase of a state juvenile delinquency proceeding.

Examination Questions: Essay Type

CHAPTER 1

1. What were the defects of the Articles of Confederation?
2. Indicate the subject-matter of (a) Articles I to VII of the Constitution of the United States and (b) each of the twenty-five amendments.
3. What is the formal procedure for amending the Constitution of the United States?
4. What constitutional issues with respect to the amending process were involved in the case of *Coleman v. Miller?* How did the Supreme Court dispose of these questions and on what grounds?
5. Through what processes other than formal amendment have changes in the Constitution of the United States occurred?
6. Even though the powers of the national government, *as enumerated in the Constitution,* are essentially the same as in 1789, a great expansion of national authority has taken place. *Why* and *how?* (Also consult Chapter 2)
7. What is meant by "the living constitution"?

CHAPTER 2

8. What are the distinguishing features of a federal system of government?
9. What is meant by "the equality of the states in the Union"?
10. Discuss the limitations on the power of Congress to admit new states into the Union.
11. Explain each of the following: (a) express powers, (b) implied powers, (c) exclusive powers, and (d) concurrent powers.
12. What basic principles of constitutional law are applied by the courts in settling controversies concerning the respective powers of the national government and the states?
13. Why has the "commerce clause" become one of the most important grants of power to the national government?
14. Under what circumstances may Congress, when exercising its power to regulate foreign and interstate commerce, establish policies that supersede state legislation pertaining

to agriculture, manufacturing, mining, and intrastate commerce?

15. Discuss the circumstances under which state policies affecting foreign and interstate commerce are constitutional—despite the grant of power to Congress to regulate commerce of both types.

16. Why did the *Missouri v. Holland* case open the door to national control of various matters ordinarily subject to regulation only by the states?

17. What are the constitutional obligations of the national government to the states?

18. Indicate the circumstances under which the national government is constitutionally justified in dealing with domestic violence confined within the borders of one of the states.

19. What are the constitutional obligations of the states to one another?

20. What is the meaning of the "full faith and credit" clause?

21. Give three examples of cooperation between the national government and the states.

22. Discuss intergovernmental cooperation at the state and local government levels.

CHAPTER 3

23. Indicate the circumstances under which United States citizenship is (a) acquired and (b) lost.

24. What is the relationship between United States and state citizenship?

25. What are the privileges and immunities of United States citizenship safeguarded against abridgment by the states by the Fourteenth Amendment?

26. Discuss the meaning of the following provision of Article IV of the United States Constitution: "the citizens of each state shall be entitled to all privileges and immunities of citizens in the several states."

27. Submit evidence in support of the assertion that constitutionally guaranteed rights in the United States are limited rather than absolute in character. By what governmental processes are limitations on constitutionally guaranteed rights established?

28. Distinguish between substantive and procedural rights.

29. Discuss the circumstances under which the Supreme Court

considers a "confession" to be involuntary rather than voluntary.

30. What tests has the Supreme Court utilized in passing judgment on the constitutionality of restraints on freedom of speech? Which of these tests has been most often used?

31. What is the purpose of the guarantee against *establishment of a religion?* How does this restriction differ from the guarantee of a "free exercise of religion"?

32. Discuss the general meaning of (a) the due process and (b) the equal protection provisions of the Fourteenth Amendment.

33. Racial segregation in public schools was declared unconstitutional in 1954. *On what grounds?*

CHAPTER 4

34. What are the usual qualifications for voting in the United States?

35. Which provisions of the national constitution limit the discretion of the states in establishing voting qualifications?

36. Explain each of the following: (a) plurality rule, (b) cumulative voting, (c) limited voting.

37. What are the distinctive features of the "single transferable vote" system of proportional representation?

38. Explain the following methods of nomination: (a) closed primary, (b) open primary, (c) non-partisan primary, and (d) the petition plan.

39. What are the distinguishing characteristics of a "political party"? How does a "two-party" differ from a "multiple-party" system (situation)?

40. Describe the organization of political parties in the United States. What important functions are performed by these parties?

41. Account for the fact that the major political parties of the United States (Democratic and Republican) are very much alike both in organization and in their avowed principles and favored governmental policies.

42. What is a "pressure group"? Discuss the ways in which pressure groups endeavor to attain their objectives.

43. What part is played in the governmental process by the people of the United States (a) in theory and (b) in reality?

CHAPTER 5

44. Explain the doctrines of (a) separation of powers and (b) checks and balances.
45. In what ways has the role of the President of the United States become different from that probably anticipated by the framers of the Constitution? (Also consult Chapter 7)
46. Enumerate the legislative, executive, and judicial powers of the President. (Also consult Chapter 7)
47. What are the sources of Presidential power and influence over Congress? (Also consult Chapter 7)
48. Describe the various stages, both legal and extra-legal, in the process of selecting a President of the United States.
49. What is a "minority" President?
50. What are the claimed advantages and disadvantages of Presidential-Congressional government?

CHAPTER 6

51. What are the non-legislative powers and/or functions of Congress?
52. Compare representation of the states in the House of Representatives and the Senate.
53. What was the ruling in the *Wesberry v. Sanders* case with respect to the establishment of districts for the election of Representatives?
54. What are the "privileges" of members of Congress?
55. Distinguish between the "formal" and "informal" organization of the House of Representatives and the Senate.
56. Indicate the successive steps in the law-making process from the introduction of a bill to its final enactment as a statute of the United States.
57. Discuss the role of standing committees in the national and state lawmaking process. (Also consult Chapter 11)
58. What is the situation with respect to "leadership" in the House and the Senate?
59. What criteria are applied by the Supreme Court in deciding whether "legislative power" has been delegated to the President in violation of the doctrine of separation of powers?
60. Discuss the scope of the investigating power of Congress.

CHAPTER 7

61. How extensive is the President's power of appointment? To what limitations, either legal or extra-legal, is the exercise of Presidential discretion in making appointments subject?
62. Under what circumstances, if any, may Congress place restrictions on the power of the President to remove officials appointed by him with the advice and consent of the Senate?
63. What are the sources and extent of the President's power of subsidiary legislation?
64. What is meant by "institutionalization of the Presidency"?
65. Discuss the role of the President in the conduct of foreign relations.
66. Why is the question of peace or war for the United States largely a Presidential responsibility despite the possession by Congress of the power to declare war?
67. Compare the parts played by the President and the Senate in the making of treaties with foreign countries.
68. Discuss the veto power of the President.
69. What are the functions of the President's cabinet?
70. Why are Presidents usually able to function effectively as legislative leaders?
71. To what offenses does the pardoning power of the President extend? (Also consult Chapter 5)

CHAPTER 8

72. Why is "administration" so important?
73. Compare the powers of Congress, the President, and the courts with respect to control over "administration."
74. What is the difference between "departments" and "independent establishments"?
75. What are the principal weaknesses of the administrative organization of the national government?
76. What are the outstanding features of the "personnel policies" of the national government?
77. What are the functions of the Civil Service Commission and department personnel officers?
78. Distinguish between "administrative legislation" and "ad-

ministrative adjudication." What safeguards are desirable to prevent abuse of these powers?

CHAPTER 9

79. Compare the system of national courts with the structure of a typical state judicial system. (Also consult Chapter 12)
80. What classes of cases are placed within the jurisdiction of the national judiciary by Article III of the Constitution?
81. How do cases get into the national (federal) courts?
82. How are judges of the national courts selected? How may they be removed from office?
83. What was President Roosevelt's "court" proposal? Discuss the constitutionality of this proposal.
84. Summarize the arguments advanced by the Supreme Court in *Marbury v. Madison* to justify its conclusion that the judicial branch possesses authority to declare acts of Congress unconstitutional.
85. What have been the four stages in the nature and growth of the Supreme Court's power over legislation?
86. What reasons are advanced in support of the contention that the Supreme Court functions as a continuous constitutional convention?
87. Explain "judicial activism" and "judicial self-restraint."
88. What are the arguments for and against "judicial review" of legislation?
89. Comment on the significance of each of the following cases: *

    McCulloch v. Maryland (consult Chapter 2)
    Wickard v. Filburn (consult Chapter 2)
    Abington School District v. Schempp (consult Chapter 3)
    Brown v. Board of Education of Topeka (consult Chapter 3)
    Loving v. Virginia (consult Chapter 3)
    Everson v. Board of Education (consult Chapter 3)
    West Virginia State Board of Education v. Barnette (consult Chapter 3)
    Reynolds v. Sims (consult Chapter 11)
    Beys Afroyim v. Rusk (consult Chapter 3)

* See Digest of Supreme Court Cases in the Appendix

CHAPTER 10

90. What are the requirements of a satisfactory constitution? Why have state constitutions become unduly long?
91. What subjects ought to be excluded from a documentary constitution? Why?
92. What are the principal defects of state constitutions in general? Why is it difficult to secure needed revisions?
93. Describe the various methods of amending state constitutions.
94. What provisions of the national constitution, either directly or indirectly, limit the discretion of the states in organizing their governments?

CHAPTER 11

95. What are the arguments for and against bicameral state legislatures?
96. To what extent is state discretion in the organization of legislatures limited by the equal protection clause of the Fourteenth Amendment?
97. Compare the veto power of most state governors with that of the President of the United States.
98. Distinguish between "joint" and "dual" committee *systems*. What are the advantages of the former?
99. How are committee assignments made in state legislatures and in Congress? (Also consult Chapter 6)
100. What can and should be done to improve the organization and functioning of state legislatures?
101. What has been and still is the policy of many states with respect to the frequency and length of legislative sessions?
102. Discuss the "legislative leadership" situation in the several states.
103. Distinguish between the initiative and the petition referendum.
104. Account for the persistent lack of faith in state legislatures.

CHAPTER 12

105. How are state governors selected; for what terms of office; and how may they be removed prior to expiration of their terms?

106. Compare the usual powers of state governors with those of the President of the United States. (Also consult Chapters 6 and 7)

107. Discuss the appointive and removal powers of governors.

108. Why are governors more effective as legislative leaders than as chief administrators?

109. What are the principal reasons for the inability of most state governors to function effectively as general managers of state administration?

110. Why is administrative reorganization needed in many states?

111. How are judges in most of the states selected? What are the distinctive features of the Missouri and California plans?

112. What methods of removing judges are provided for in one or more of the fifty states?

113. What are the principal weaknesses of state judicial systems?

114. Discuss the composition and functions of judicial councils.

115. What are the features of a unified judicial system?

116. What factors are determinative of the quality of the administration of justice?

CHAPTER 13

117. What is the extent of state authority over local government?

118. How is state control over local units exercised?

119. Discuss the defects of county government in the United States. What remedies have been proposed?

120. Compare New England towns with the townships of other states in regard to their organization and functions.

121. What is a special district? Why have so many of them been created in the United States? What kinds of special districts are identifiable?

CHAPTER 14

122. Discuss the nature of municipal corporations, indicating their primary purpose and the source and extent of their powers.

123. Explain the several methods of providing cities with charters.

124. What is the meaning of "constitutional home rule" for cities? What different "home rule" systems are identifiable in the United States?
125. Distinguish between the commission, strong mayor-council, and council-manager plans of city government.
126. What is wrong with the government of metropolitan areas? What remedies have been proposed and/or adopted?
127. Why has so little progress been made toward solution of the governmental problems of metropolitan areas?

CHAPTER 15

128. What is a budget? What are the several stages of a budgetary system?
129. Distinguish between constructive and destructive measures of economy in the government field. Give examples.
130. What are the requirements of a satisfactory revenue system?
131. What are the principal sources of revenue of (a) the national government, (b) the states, and (c) local units of government?
132. What are the guides to sound borrowing?
133. What is meant by "pay-as-you-go"? Under what circumstances is a pay-as-you-go policy advisable? Why?

Multiple Choice Questions

Place the number of the statement which is correct or most nearly correct in the right-hand margin.

1. With respect to domestic affairs the national government may exercise: 1. all powers except those granted expressly to the states, 2. only those powers granted to it in express terms, 3. any powers not expressly denied to it, 4. only such powers as have been granted to it either expressly or by implication, 5. any power necessary to promotion of the general welfare.   1.___
2. The Constitution of the United States provides for the choice of Presidential Electors: 1. by popular vote from each state at-large, 2. by popular vote from districts equal in number

to the state's electoral quota, 3. in such manner as the legislature of each state may determine, 4. by the state legislature, 5. by the chief executive of the state.   2.____

3. In cases of conflict between national and state laws consistent with the Constitution, the courts are under constitutional obligation to enforce: 1. state laws, 2. national laws, 3. the law most recently enacted, 4. the law first enacted, 5. the law which the courts consider more desirable.   3.____

4. A bill vetoed by the President may be passed over his veto by: 1. an ordinary majority of each house of Congress, 2. a majority of the total membership of each house, 3. a two-thirds vote of those present in each house, provided there be a quorum, 4. a two-thirds vote of the total membership of each house, 5. a three-fourths vote of each house.   4.____

5. The 14th Amendment confers United States citizenship upon 1. all persons born or naturalized in the United States, 2. all residents of the states and incorporated territories, 3. all white persons and persons of African nativity or African descent born in the United States, 4. all persons whose ancestors were United States citizens at the time the 14th Amendment was ratified, 5. all persons born or naturalized in the United States and subject to the jurisdiction thereof.
                                                                               5.____

6. The Supreme Court passes judgment on the constitutionality of acts of Congress: 1. when requested to do so by the President or Congress, 2. only when necessary to decide a case presented to it in the ordinary course of litigation, 3. within a period of two weeks following the passage of an act of Congress, 4. only when the question of constitutionality is raised by one of the states, 5. only if the Attorney General of the United States recommends that it do so.   6.____

7. Proposed amendments become valid as part of the Constitution when ratified by: 1. the President, 2. a majority popular vote in three-fourths of the states, 3. the legislatures of two-thirds of the states, 4. the legislatures of three-fourths of the states or conventions in three-fourths of the states, as one or the other mode of ratification is specified by Congress, 5. the governors and legislatures of three-fifths of the states.   7.____

8. If the executive authority of a state refuses to surrender a fugitive from justice, the demanding state: 1. may request the President to intervene, 2. may obtain a writ of mandamus

from the federal courts, 3. may appeal to the Attorney General of the United States, 4. has no effective remedy, 5. has the right to resort to armed intervention. 8.___

9. United States citizenship may be lost: 1. only by voluntary expatriation, 2. by voting in a foreign election, 3. by desertion from the armed forces in time of war, 4. by residing abroad for more than ten years, 5. by refusing to serve in the armed forces of the United States. 9.___

10. The primary purpose of registration of voters is: 1. to insure secrecy in voting, 2. to solve the problem of non-voting, 3. to obtain information necessary to the collection of income taxes, 4. to permit only qualified persons to vote and to prevent such persons from voting more than once in a particular election, 5. to provide information for use in apportioning representatives among the states. 10.___

11. A "minority" President is one who: 1. belongs to a minority party, 2. polls a plurality of the electoral vote, 3. polls a majority electoral vote but receives fewer than half of the total popular vote, 4. is less than twenty-one years of age, 5. is one whose party holds a minority of the seats in Congress. 11.___

12. For the most part, national policies are administered by: 1. the state governments, 2. state, city, and county governments, 3. the Department of the Interior, 4. Congressional committees, 5. national officials and employees. 12.___

13. As interpreted by the Supreme Court, the equal protection clause of the 14th Amendment requires: 1. equal representation of counties in one chamber and population-based representation of localities in the other chamber of a bicameral state legislature, 2. limits the permissible size of state legislatures, 3. requires population-based representation in both houses; 4. endorses any plan of representation approved by the voters of a state, 5. permits direct representation of pressure groups in one house. 13.___

14. The function of standing committees of the House of Representatives is to: 1. approve or reject bills which the House has adopted, 2. give preliminary consideration to bills introduced in the House, 3. see to the proper wording of bills after adoption by the House, 4. advise the President concerning the exercise of his veto power, 5. supervise the enforcement of national laws. 14.___

15. Most of the rights guaranteed against invasive governmental action are enjoyed by: 1. United States citizens only, 2. only United States citizens and nationals, 3. all persons, 4. only registered voters, 5. adults only.   15.___

16. Members of the Senate are now chosen by: 1. the state legislatures, 2. popular vote from districts, 3. state electoral colleges, 4. popular vote from the state at-large, 5. by each state's representatives in the House of Representatives. 16.___

17. The size of the House of Representatives is fixed by: 1. the President, 2. the Senate, 3. the House itself, 4. express constitutional stipulation, 5. Act of Congress.   17.___

18. To be eligible for a seat in the House of Representatives, a person must be: 1. merely a qualified voter, 2. 25 years of age or over, at least seven years a citizen, and a legal resident of the Congressional district from which chosen, 3. 30 years of age or over and an inhabitant of the state by which elected, 4. 25 years of age or over, at least seven years a citizen, and an inhabitant of the state by which elected, 5. no older than 65 years or younger than 25.   18.___

19. The Speaker of the House of Representatives is: 1. an impartial moderator, 2. a figure-head with little or no influence in the lawmaking process, 3. a partisan officer whose legislative and political influence is very great, 4. an official whose primary function is to present the point of view of the House in the trial of impeached Presidents by the Senate.
                                                                19.___

20. Bills are submitted to the President for approval after: 1. adoption by the House, 2. adoption by the Senate, 3. adoption in identical form by two successive Congresses, 4. adoption in identical form by a majority vote in the House and a two-thirds majority of the Senate, 5. adoption in identical form by both the House and the Senate.   20.___

21. Powers possessed by the House of Representatives but not by the Senate are: 1. the power to try impeachments, 2. the power to approve treaties and Presidential appointments, 3. the power of impeachment and the power to originate revenue bills, 4. the power to originate appropriation acts, 5. the power to remove heads of administrative departments.
                                                                21.___

22. The most common term of service for members of state legislatures is: 1. one year, 2. 3 years, 3. 5 years, 4. 6 years, 5. 2 or 4 years.   22.___

23. Of the thirty-seven states admitted to the Union since 1789, only one was an independent body politic rather than a territorial possession at the time of admission, viz., 1. Louisiana, 2. Hawaii, 3. California, 4. Texas, 5. Maine.

23.___

24. The powers of the states are: 1. enumerated in the Constitution, 2. conferred by act of Congress, 3. specified in a compact negotiated by the national government and the states, 4. all powers not delegated exclusively to the national government nor denied the states, either expressly or by implication, by the Constitution, 5. powers designated by the President of the United States.

24.___

True and False Questions

1. The phrase "cooperative federalism" conveys the idea that the national government and the states should function as partners, rather than as antagonists, in promoting the welfare of the general public. 1.___

2. The first state constitutions placed few restrictions on the policy-determining authority of the legislature and most of them provided for selection of the governor by the legislature. 2.___

3. Only a few state constitutions are lengthy, replete with statutory materials and unnecessary restrictions on state governments, cluttered with obsolete and inconsistent statements, badly written and illogically arranged. 3.___

4. Cumulative voting is used in the selection of members of the lower house of the Illinois legislature. 4.___

5. Various states provide for a combination of multi-member and single-member districts for the selection of legislators. 5.___

6. Lieutenant governors are the presiding officers of state senates in all of the states. 6.___

7. All state legislatures have dual committee systems. 7.___

8. The governors of nearly all of the states may veto items in appropriation bills. 8.___

9. The Supreme Court has held that nothing in the Constitution of the United States prohibits a state from providing for

legislative selection of its governor either in the first instance or as a consequence of the failure of some other method to result in choice of a governor.   9.___

10. No state limits the number of terms a person may serve as governor or prohibits service for consecutive terms.   10.___

11. In many states the legislature in special session may consider only such matters as fall within the scope of the purposes of the session as declared by the governor.   11.___

12. Most of the states provide for popular election of four or more top-rank administrative officials in addition to the governor.   12.___

13. State governors, unlike the President of the United States, possess an absolute rather than a suspensive veto.   13.___

14. The Constitution of the United States requires popular election of state judges.   14.___

15. Loss of faith in state legislatures is a major cause of the general practice of incorporating desired governmental policies in state constitutions.   15.___

16. As of 1968, Nebraska is the only state having a unicameral state legislature.   16.___

17. In most counties of the United States the only elected officials are the members of the county board or commission.
                                                                17.___

18. The optional charter plan permits designated units of local government to select one of several forms of government prescribed by an act of the state legislature.   18.___

19. In the New England states the county is a more important unit of local government than the town.   19.___

20. Judges of state courts are chosen by popular vote in most of the states.   20.___

21. Although state governors are charged with the duty of law enforcement, their powers are too limited to enable them to carry out this responsibility effectively.   21.___

22. The spoils system still survives in many states.   22.___

23. Managers under the council-manager plan are more powerful officials than the mayors of cities having a strong mayor-council form of government.   23.___

24. The granting of home rule to cities and counties by constitutional provision necessarily prevents the state government from exercising control of any sort over them.   24.___

25. Most school districts are organized as units of government

that are uncontrollable by the governments of cities, townships, and counties. 25.____

26. Only a few states limit the frequency and length of legislative sessions. 26.____

27. The issuance of long-term bonds is ordinarily justified only for the purpose of financing costly permanent improvements. 27.____

28. The preamble of the Constitution is the source from which the implied powers of Congress are derived. 28.____

29. The sole permissible penalties in cases of impeachment and subsequent conviction are removal from office and disqualification from holding any office under the United States. 29.____

30. The veto power of the President of the United States extends to constitutional amendments proposed by Congress. 30.____

31. Congress may provide for the punishment of witnesses who refuse to appear and testify before Congressional committees that are investigating matters falling within the scope of the legislative power granted to Congress. 31.____

32. The Constitution expressly authorizes the Supreme Court to declare acts of Congress unconstitutional. 32.____

33. Any commerce which involves the crossing of state lines, even though beginning and ending in the same state, constitutes interstate commerce. 33.____

34. All state laws which affect interstate commerce, even though only incidentally, are unconstitutional. 34.____

35. The "necessary and proper" clause in the last paragraph of Section 8, Article I, has been interpreted to mean "reasonably appropriate, convenient, useful." 35.____

36. An *ex post facto* law is a legislative act which imposes punishment without judicial trial. 36.____

37. Congress lacks authority to levy taxes or duties on articles exported from any state. 37.____

38. Congress may provide for the expenditure of money for public purposes falling outside the scope of its regulatory authority. 38.____

39. The pardoning power of the President extends to offenses against the United States and also against the states. 39.____

40. The Constitution stipulates that presidential electors shall be chosen by popular vote. 40.____

41. Congress may authorize the President to appoint inferior officers without the advice and consent of the Senate. 41.____

42. The Supreme Court has ruled that determination of whether or not a state has a republican form of government is a political rather than a justiciable question.   42.____

43. A person who has committed an act in violation of both national and state law is placed in double jeopardy if prosecuted by either the national government or the state after acquittal by one or the other of the two governments. 43.____

44. The due process of law clauses of the 5th and 14th amendments have been construed to prohibit arbitrary, capricious, and oppressive governmental action.   44.____

45. The "equal protection" clause of the 14th Amendment is a limitation on private persons as well as on the states. 45.____

46. The "equal protection" clause requires that all persons have precisely the same legal rights and duties.   46.____

47. Although the first ten amendments are binding only on the national government, the Supreme Court has held that many of the rights guaranteed by these amendments are protected against infringement by the state because of the 14th amendment's stipulation that no state shall deprive any person of life, liberty, or property without due process of law.   47.____

48. In appointing judges of the national courts, Presidents have seldom given consideration to the "political party" affiliations of prospective appointees.   48.____

49. Debate in the Senate is limited to two hours per Senator.
                                                                   49.____

50. Most positions in the classified service of the national government have been placed there by order of successive Presidents under authority delegated by Congress.   50.____

Examples of Other Types of Questions

Completion Type
The blank spaces in each sentence should be filled in with the proper word or words.

1. Additional states may be admitted to the Union by ....
   ....

2. Amendments to the Constitution of the United States may be proposed either by .... or by a national ....
   ....

3. The Director of the Office of Management and Budget is appointed by the President ....

4. United States citizenship is acquired either by .... or by ....

5. Each house of Congress may .... its members by a .... vote.

6. All state governors are chosen by ....

7. The jurisdiction of justices of the peace is confined to petty .... and/or .... cases.

8. With few exceptions the government of metropolitan areas is excessively ....

9. City managers need not be .... of the city at the time of their appointment.

10. Population-based representation in both houses of a state legislature is required by the .... clause of the Fourteenth Amendment.

11. No person may be deprived of life, liberty, or property without ....

12. One of the principal defects of nearly all county governments is lack of a ....

Identification Type

Identification is to be accomplished by a brief statement of the meaning or significance of each enumerated item.

1. *Gibbons v. Ogden*
2. *McCulloch v. Maryland*
3. *United States v. Darby*
4. *Engle v. Vitale*
5. *United States v. Wong Kim Ark*
6. *Korematsu v. United States*
7. *Plessy v. Ferguson*
8. *Brown v. Board of Education of Topeka*
9. *Loving v. Virginia*
10. *In Re Gault*
11. Open primary
12. Electorate
13. Personal registration
14. Proprietary colony
15. Lump sum appropriation
16. *Ex post facto* law

17. Pre-audit
18. Government Career Service
19. Implied power
20. Impeachment
21. Committee of the Whole
22. Party whip
23. Committee on Committees
24. Conference committee
25. Executive agreement
26. Pocket veto

Association or Matching Type

The items in the right-hand column are numbered. Select the item in this column most closely associated with each of the enumerated words or phrases in the left-hand column. Place the number of the selected item opposite the appropriate word or words in the left-hand column.

( ) Presiding officer of the Senate
( ) Political questions
( ) Income taxes
( ) Independent establishment
( ) Self-incrimination
( ) Presidential disability
( ) Direct democracy
( ) Clear and present danger
( ) Republican form of government
( ) Permanent allegiance

1. Sixteenth Amendment
2. Twenty-Fifth Amendment
3. Vice President
4. New England towns
5. Representative government
6. *Baker v. Carr*
7. Involuntary confession
8. Freedom of speech
9. Federal Trade Commission
10. National
11. Referendum
12. Expatriation
13. Pay-as-you-go
14. Spoils system
15. Secretary of State
16. Pressure group
17. Majority floor leader
18. Chief Justice of the Supreme Court

Suggested Supplementary Reading

Abraham, H. J., *The Judiciary* (Boston, Allyn & Bacon, Inc., 1965)

Abraham, H. J., *The Judicial Process* (New York, Oxford University Press, 1962)

Adrian, C. R., *Governing Our Fifty States and Their Communities* (New York, McGraw-Hill Book Co., 1963)

Adrian, C. R., *State and Local Governments,* 2nd ed. (New York, McGraw-Hill Book Co., 1966)

Anderson, P., *The President's Men* (Garden City, Doubleday, 1969)

Bachrach, P. & Baratz, M. S., *Power and Poverty: Theory and Practice* (New York, Oxford University Press, 1970)

Baker, J. W., *Member of the House* (New York, Charles Scribner's Sons, 1962)

Banfield, E. C., *Big City Politics* (New York, Random House, Inc., 1965)

Barber, J. D., *Political Leadership in American Government* (Boston, Little, Brown & Co., 1964)

Barber, A. J., *The American Corporation: Its Powers, Its Money, Its Politics* (New York, Dutton, 1970)

Barker, L. J. & Barker, T. W., *Freedoms, Courts, Politics* (Englewood Cliffs, Prentice-Hall, Inc., 1965)

Berger, R., *Congress and the Supreme Court* (Cambridge, Harvard University Press, 1969)

Berle, A. A., *Power* (New York, Harcourt, Brace and World, 1969)

Berman, D. M., *A Bill Becomes a Law: The Civil Rights Act of 1960* (New York, The Macmillan Co., 1962)

Berman, D. M., *In Congress Assembled* (New York, The Macmillan Co., 1964)

Berman, D. M., *It is So Ordered* (New York, W. W. Norton & Co., 1966)

Black, C., *Perspectives in Constitutional Law* (Englewood Cliffs, Prentice-Hall, Inc., 1963)

Blair, G. S., *American Local Government* (New York, Harper & Row, 1964)

Brock, P., *Twentieth Century Pacifism* (New York, Van Nostrand, Reinhold, 1970)

Brown, S. G., *The American Presidency: Leadership, Partisanship, and Popularity* (New York, Macmillan Co., 1966)

Burns, J. M., *Presidential Government: The Crucible of Leadership* (Boston, Houghton Mifflin Co., 1965)

Childs, R. S., *The First 50 Years of the Council-Manager Plan of Municipal Government* (New York, American Book-Stratford Press, Inc., 1965)

Claude, R., *The Supreme Court and the Electoral Process* (Baltimore, The Johns Hopkins Press, 1969)

Congressional Quarterly Service, *Congress and the Nation, 1945–1964* (Washington, Congressional Quarterly Service, 1965)

Corson, J. J. & Harris, J. P., *Public Administration in Modern Society* (New York, McGraw-Hill Book Co., 1963)

Cox, A., *The Supreme Court: A Constitutional Decision as an Instrument of Reform* (Cambridge, Harvard University Press, 1968)

Cushman, R. E. & Cushman, R. F., *Leading Constitutional Decisions*, 13th ed. (New York, Appleton-Century-Crofts, 1966)

Dahl, R. A., *Pluralist Democracy in the United States* (Chicago, Rand McNally & Co., 1967)

Dishman, R. B., *The State of the Union* (New York, Charles Scribner's Sons, 1965)

Dixon, R. G., *Democratic Representation* (New York, Oxford University Press, 1968)

Dye, T. R., *Politics, Economics, and the Public* (Chicago, Rand McNally & Co., 1966)

Dye, T. R. & Hawkins, B. W., *Politics in the Metropolis* (Columbus, Charles E. Merrill Books, Inc., 1967)

Egger, R., *The President of the United States* (New York, McGraw-Hill Book Co., 1967)

Egger, R. & Harris, J. P., *The President and Congress* (New York, McGraw-Hill Book Co., 1963)

Fein, L. J., *American Democracy, Essays on Image and Realities* (New York, Holt, Rinehart & Winston, 1964)

Fiszman, J. R., ed., *The American Political Arena* (Boston, Little, Brown & Co., 1962)

Frost, R. T., ed., *Cases in State and Local Government* (Englewood Cliffs, Prentice-Hall, Inc., 1961)

Goldman, R. M., *The Democratic Party in American Politics* (New York, Macmillan Co., 1966)

Grad, F. P., *The State Constitution: Its Function and Form for Our Time* (New York, National Municipal League, 1968)

Greenstein, F. I., *The American Party System and the American People* (Englewood Cliffs, Prentice-Hall, Inc., 1963)

Haight, D. E. & Johnston, L. D., *The President: Roles and Powers* (Chicago, Rand McNally & Co., 1965)

Hamilton, H. D., ed., *Reapportioning Legislatures* (Charles E. Merrill Books, Inc., 1967)

Hargrove, E. C. *Presidential Leadership, Personality, and Political Style* (New York, Macmillan Co., 1966)

Harris, J. P., *Congress and the Legislative Process* (New York, McGraw-Hill Book Co., 1967)

Heard, A., ed., *State Legislatures in American Politics* (Englewood Cliffs, Prentice-Hall, Inc., 1966)

Herring, P., *The Politics of Democracy* (New York, W. W. Norton & Co., 1965)

Holcombe, A. N., *The Constitutional System* (Chicago, Scott, Foresman & Co., 1964)

Hyneman, C. S. & Gilbert, C. E., *Popular Government in America* (New York, Atherton Press, 1966)

Hyneman, C. S., *The Supreme Court on Trial* (New York, Atherton Press, 1966)

Jewell, M. C., *Metropolitan Representation: State Legislative Districting in Urban Counties* (New York, National Municipal League, 1969)

Jones, C. O., *The Republican Party in American Politics* (New York, Macmillan Co., 1965)

Kaufman, H., *Politics and Policies in State and Local Governments* (Englewood Cliffs, Prentice-Hall, Inc., 1963)

Key, V. O., *American State Politics* (New York, A. A. Knopf, 1956)

Key, V. O., *Public Opinion and American Democracy* (New York, A. A. Knopf, 1961)

Konvitz, M. R., *Expanding Liberties* (New York, The Viking Press, 1966)

MacIver, R. M., *The Ramparts We Guard* (New York, The Macmillan Co., 1952)

Manley, J. F., *The House Committee on Ways and Means* (Boston, Little, Brown, 1970)

Martin, R. C., *The Cities and the Federal System* (New York, Atherton Press, 1966)

McCandless, C. A., *Urban Government and Politics* (New York, McGraw-Hill, 1970)

McKay, R. B., *Reapportionment: The Law and Politics of Equal Representation* (New York, 20th Century Fund, 1966)

Millet, J. D., *Government and Public Administration* (New York, McGraw-Hill Book Co., 1959)

Monsma, S. V. & Henry, P. B., *The Dynamics of the American Political System* (Hinsdale, Dryden Press, 1972)

National Municipal League, Model City Charter, 6th ed. 1964 Model State Constitution, 6th ed., 1963.

Peabody, R. L., & Polsby, N. W., *New Perspectives on the House of Representatives* (Chicago, Rand McNally & Co., 1963)

Peltason, J. W. & Burns, J. M., eds., *Functions and Policies of American Government*, 2nd ed. (Englewood Cliffs, Prentice-Hall, Inc., 1962)

Penniman, H. R., *The American Political Process* (Princeton, Van Nostrand Co., 1962)

Perkins, D., *The Evolution of American Foreign Policy*, 2nd ed. (New York, Oxford University Press, 1966)

Pierce, N. R., *The People's President: The Electoral College in American History and the Direct Vote Alternative* (New York, Simon & Schuster, 1968)

Plano, J. & Greenberg, M., *The American Political Dictionary* (New York, Holt, Rinehart & Winston, 1967)

Pollock, J. K., *Making Michigan's New Constitution* (Ann Arbor, George Wahr Publishing Co., 1962)

Pomper, G., *Nominating the President* (New York, W. W. Norton & Co., 1966)

Powell, T., *Democracy in Action* (New York, The Macmillan Co., 1962)

Press, C. & Williams, O. P., *Democracy in the Fifty States* (Chicago, Rand McNally & Co., 1966)

Pritchett, C. H., *The American Constitutional System* (New York, McGraw-Hill Book Co., 1963)

Pritchett, C. H. & Westin, A. F., eds., *The Third Branch of Government* (New York, Harcourt, Brace and World, Inc., 1963)

Pusey, M. J., *The Way We Go to War* (Boston, Houghton, Mifflin, 1969)

Reedy, G. E., *The Twilight of the Presidency* (New York, World Publishing Co., 1970)

Reynolds, H. W., ed., "Intergovernmental Relations in the United States," *Annals of the American Academy of Political and Social Science*, Vol. 359, May 1965.

Ripley, R. B., ed., *Public Policies and Their Politics* (New York, W. W. Norton & Co., 1966)

Rogow, A. A. & Lasswell, H. D., *Power, Corruption, and Rectitude* (Englewood Cliffs, Prentice-Hall, Inc., 1963)

Ross, R. M. & Millsap, K. F., *State and Local Government and Administration* (New York, Ronald Press, 1966)

Rossiter, C., *American Presidency*, rev. ed. (New York, Harcourt, Brace and World, 1967)

Rourke, F. E., ed., *Bureaucratic Power in National Politics* (Boston, Little, Brown, & Co., 1965)

Rowat, D. C., ed., *The Ombudsman, Citizen's Defender* (Toronto, University of Toronto Press, 1965)

Sanford, T., *Storm over the States* (New York, McGraw-Hill Book Co., 1967)

Schattschneider, E. E., *The Semi-Sovereign People* (New York, Holt, Rinehart & Winston, 1960)

Sharkansky, I., *Regionalism in American Politics* (Indianapolis, Bobbs-Merrill, 1970)

Snider, C. F., *American State and Local Government*, 2nd ed. (New York, Appleton-Century-Crofts, 1965)

Solberg, W. U., *The Federal Convention and the Formation of the Union* (New York, Bobbs-Merrill Co., 1958)

Sorauf, F. J., *Political Parties in the American System* (Boston, Little, Brown & Co., 1964)

Sturm, A. L., *Thirty Years of State Constitution Making* (New York, National Municipal League, 1970)

Sweet, E. C., *Civil Liberties in America* (Princeton, Van Nostrand Co., 1966)

Tresolini, R. J., *Constitutional Decisions in American Government* (New York, The Macmillan Co., 1965)

Tresolini, R. J., *Justice and the Supreme Court* (Philadelphia, J. B. Lippincott Co., 1963)

Tussman, J., *The Supreme Court on Church and State* (New York, Oxford University Press, 1962)

Tussman, J., ed., *The Supreme Court on Racial Discrimination* (New York, Oxford University Press, 1963)

Van Dyke, V., *Human Rights, the United States and World Community* (New York, Oxford University Press, 1970)

Westin, A. F., *The Uses of Power* (New York, Harcourt, Brace and World, 1962)

Wheeler, J. P., ed., *Salient Issues of Constitutional Revision* (New York, National Municipal League, 1961)

Woll, P., *American Government, Reading and Cases*, 2nd ed. (Boston, Little, Brown & Co., 1965)

Articles of Confederation

Excerpts

Article I The stile of this confederacy shall be "The United States of America.

Article II Each State retains its sovereignty, freedom and independence, and every power, jurisdiction and right, which is not by this confederation expressly delegated to the United States, in Congress assembled.

Article III The said States hereby severally enter into a firm league of friendship with each other, for their common defence, the security of their liberties, and their mutual and general welfare. . . .

Article IV . . . the free inhabitants of each of these States . . . shall be entitled to all privileges and immunities of free citizens in the several states; and the people of each State shall have free ingress and regress to and from any other State. . . .

If any person guilty of, or charged with treason, felony, or other high misdemeanor in any State, shall flee from justice, and be found in any of the United States, he shall upon demand of the Governor or Executive power, of the State from which he fled, be delivered up and removed to the State having jurisdiction of his offence.

Full faith and credit shall be given in each of these States to the records, acts and judicial proceedings of the courts and magistrates of every other State.

Article V . . . delegates shall be annually appointed in such manner as the legislature of each State shall direct, to meet in Congress on the first Monday in November, in every year, with a power reserved to each State, to recall its delegates, or any of them, at any time within the year, and to send others in their stead, for the remainder of the year.

No State shall be represented in Congress by less than two, nor by more than seven members; and no person shall be capable of being a delegate for more than three years in any term of six years; . . .

In determining questions in the United States, in Congress assembled, each State shall have one vote.

Freedom of speech and debate in Congress shall not be impeached or questioned in any court, or place out of Congress, and the members of Congress shall be protected in their persons from arrests and imprisonments, during the time of their going to and from, and attendance on Congress, except for treason, felony, or breach of the peace.

Article VI   No State without the consent of the United States in Congress assembled, shall send any embassy to, or receive any embassy from, or enter into any conference, agreement, alliance or treaty with any king, prince or state. . . .

No two or more States shall enter into any treaty, confederation or alliance whatever between them, without the consent of the United States in Congress assembled. . . .

No State shall engage in any war without the consent of the United States in Congress assembled, unless such State be actually invaded . . . or the danger of invasion is so imminent as not to admit of a delay, till the United States in Congress assembled can be consulted: . . .

Article VIII   All charges of war, and all other expenses that shall be incurred for the common defence or general welfare . . . shall be defrayed out of a common treasury, which shall be supplied by the several States, in proportion to the value of all land within each State. . . .

The taxes for paying that proportion shall be laid and levied by the authority and direction of the Legislatures of the several States. . . .

Article IX   The United States in Congress assembled, shall have the sole and exclusive right and power of determining on peace and war, . . . of sending and receiving ambassadors— entering into treaties and alliances, provided that no treaty of commerce shall be made whereby the legislative power of the respective States shall be restrained from imposing such imposts and duties on foreigners, as their own people are subjected to, or from prohibiting the exportation or importation of any species of goods or commodities whatsoever—of establishing rules for deciding . . . what captures on land or water shall be legal. . . . —of granting letters of marque and reprisal in times of peace—appointing courts for the trial of piracies and felonies committed on the high seas and establishing courts for receiving and determining finally appeals in all cases of captures. . . .

The United States in Congress assembled shall also be the last resort on appeal in all disputes and differences now subsisting or that hereafter may arise between two or more States concerning boundary, jurisdiction or any other cause whatever. . . .

The United States in Congress assembled shall also have the sole and exclusive right and power of regulating the alloy and value of coin struck by their own authority, or by that of the respective States—fixing the standard of weights and measures. . . . —regulating the trade and managing all affairs with the Indians, not members of any of the States, provided that the legislative right of any State within its own limits be not infringed or violated—establishing and regulating post-offices from one State to another. . . . —appointing all officers of the land forces, in the service of the United States, excepting regimental officers—appointing all the officers of the naval forces. . . . —making rules for the government and regulation of the said land and naval forces, and directing their operations.

The United States in Congress assembled shall have authority to appoint a committee, to sit in the recess of Congress, to be denominated "a Committee of the States," and to consist of one delegate from each State; and to appoint such other committees and civil officers as may be necessary for managing the general affairs of the United States under their direction—to appoint one of their number to preside, provided that no person be allowed to serve in the office of president more than one year in any term of three years; to ascertain the necessary sums of money to be raised for the service of the United States, and to appropriate and apply the same for defraying the public expenses—to borrow money, or emit bills on the credit of the United States. . . . —to build and equip a navy—to agree upon the number of land forces, and to make requisitions from each State for its quota, in proportion to the number of white inhabitants in such State; which requisition shall be binding, and thereupon the Legislature of each State shall appoint the regimental officers, raise the men and cloath, arm and equip them in a soldier like manner, at the expense of the United States; . . .

The United States in Congress assembled shall never engage in a war, nor grant letters of marque and reprisal in time of peace, nor enter into any treaties or alliances, nor coin money, nor regulate the value thereof, nor ascertain the sums and expenses necessary for the defence and welfare of the United States, or any of them, nor emit bills, nor borrow money on the credit of the United States, nor appropriate money, nor agree upon the number of vessels of war, to be built or purchased, or the number of land or sea forces to be raised, nor appoint a commander in chief of the army or navy, unless nine States assent to the same; nor shall a question on any other point, except for adjourning from day to day be determined, unless by the votes of a majority of the United States in Congress assembled. . . .

Article X The committee of the States, or any nine of them, shall be authorized to execute, in the recess of Congress, such of the powers of Congress as the United States in Congress assembled, by the consent of nine States, shall from time to time think expedient to vest them with; provided that no power be delegated to the said committee, for the exercise of which, by the articles of confederation, the voice of nine States in the Congress of the United States assembled is requisite.

Article XI Canada acceding to this confederation, and joining in the measures of the United States, shall be admitted into, and entitled to all the advantages of this Union; but no other colony shall be admitted into the same, unless such admission be agreed to by nine States.

Article XIII Every State shall abide by the determinations of the United States in Congress assembled, on all questions which by this confederation are submitted to them. And the articles of this confederation shall be inviolably observed by every State, and the Union shall be perpetual; nor shall any alteration at any time hereafter be made in any of them; unless such alteration be agreed to in a Congress of the United States, and be afterwards confirmed by the Legislatures of every State. . . .

. . . Done at Philadelphia in the State of Pennsylvania the ninth day of July in the year of our Lord one thousand seven hundred and seventy-eight, and in the third year of the independence of America.

CONSTITUTION OF THE UNITED STATES

General objectives of the Constitution

WE THE PEOPLE of the United States, in Order to form a more perfect Union, establish Justice, insure domestic Tranquility, provide for the common defence, promote the general Welfare, and secure the Blessings of Liberty to ourselves and our Posterity, do ordain and establish this CONSTITUTION for the United States of America.

ARTICLE I · LEGISLATIVE DEPARTMENT

A bicameral Congress

SECTION 1. All legislative Powers herein granted shall be vested in a Congress of the United States, which shall consist of a Senate and House of Representatives.

Selection and term of Representatives

SECTION 2. ¹The House of Representatives shall be composed of Members chosen every second Year by the People of the several States, and the Electors in each State shall have the Qualifications requisite for Electors of the most numerous Branch of the State Legislature.

Qualifications of Representatives

²No person shall be a representative who shall not have attained to the Age of twenty five Years, and been seven Years a Citizen of the United States, and who shall not, when elected, be an Inhabitant of that State in which he shall be chosen.

NOTE:—This text of the Constitution follows the engrossed copy signed by Gen. Washington and the deputies from 12 States. The superior number preceding the paragraphs designates the number of the clause; it was not in the original.

³[Representatives and direct Taxes shall be apportioned among the several States which may be included within this Union, according to their respective Numbers, which shall be determined by adding to the whole Number of free Persons, including those bound to Service for a Term of Years, and excluding Indians not taxed, three fifths of all other Persons.].* The actual Enumeration shall be made within three Years after the first Meeting of the Congress of the United States, and within every subsequent Term of ten Years, in such Manner as they shall by Law direct. The Number of Representatives shall not exceed one for every thirty Thousand, but each State shall have at Least one Representative; and until such enumeration shall be made, the State of New Hampshire shall be entitled to chuse three, Massachusetts eight, Rhode-Island and Providence Plantations one, Connecticut five, New-York six, New Jersey four, Pennsylvania eight, Delaware one, Maryland six, Virginia ten, North Carolina five, South Carolina five, and Georgia three.

⁴When vacancies happen in the Representation from any State, the Executive Authority thereof shall issue Writs of Election to fill such Vacancies.

⁵The House of Representatives shall chuse their Speaker and other Officers; and shall have the sole Power of Impeachment.

SECTION 3. The Senate of the United States shall be composed of two Senators from each State, [chosen by the Legislature thereof,]** for six Years; and each Senator shall have one Vote.

---

*The part included in heavy brackets was changed by section 2 of the fourteenth amendment.

**The part included in heavy brackets was changed by section 1 of the seventeenth amendment.

Apportionment of Representatives among states—see Section 2 of Fourteenth Amendment; a decennial census; maximum and minimum size of House

Filling of vacancies

Choice of Speaker and other officers; sole power of impeachment

Composition of Senate; see Seventeenth Amendment for selection of Senators.

Terms of Senators—
overlapping

²Immediately after they shall be assembled in Consequence of the first Election, they shall be divided as equally as may be into three Classes. The Seats of the Senators of the first Class shall be vacated at the Expiration of the second Year, of the second Class at the Expiration of the fourth Year, and of the third Class at the Expiration of the sixth Year, so that one third may be chosen every second Year; [and if Vacancies happen by Resignation, or otherwise, during the Recess of the Legislature of any State, the Executive thereof may make temporary Appointments until the next Meeting of the Legislature, which shall then fill such Vacancies].*

Vacancies—see
Seventeenth Amendment

Qualifications

³No Person shall be a Senator who shall not have attained to the Age of thirty Years, and been nine Years a Citizen of the United States, and who shall not, when elected, be an Inhabitant of that State for which he shall be chosen.

Vice President to preside;
choice of other officers

⁴The Vice President of the United States shall be President of the Senate, but shall have no Vote, unless they be equally divided.

⁵The Senate shall chuse their other Officers, and also a President pro tempore, in the Absence of the Vice President, or when he shall exercise the Office of President of the United States.

Trial of impeachments by
Senate; penalties if
impeached and convicted.

⁶The Senate shall have the sole Power to try all Impeachments. When sitting for that Purpose, they shall be on Oath or Affirmation. When the President of the United States is tried, the Chief Justice shall preside: And no Person shall be convicted without the Concurrence of two thirds of the Members present.

---

*The part included in heavy brackets was changed by clause 2 of the seventeenth amendment.

[7]Judgment in Cases of Impeachment shall not extend further than to removal from Office, and disqualification to hold and enjoy any Office of honor, Trust or Profit under the United States: but the Party convicted shall nevertheless be liable and subject to Indictment, Trial, Judgment and Punishment, according to Law.

Times, places and manner of holding Congressional elections.

SECTION 4. [1]The Times, Places and Manner of holding Elections for Senators and Representatives, shall be prescribed in each State by the Legislature thereof; but the Congress may at any time by Law make or alter such Regulations, except as to the Places of chusing Senators.

Congressional sessions— see Twentieth Amendment

[2]The Congress shall assemble at least once in every Year, and such Meeting shall [be on the first Monday in December,]** unless they shall by Law appoint a different Day.

Judging elections and qualifications; size of a quorum; expulsion of members of Congress

SECTION 5. [1]Each House shall be the Judge of the Elections, Returns and Qualifications of its own Members, and a Majority of each shall constitute a Quorum to do Business; but a smaller Number may adjourn from day to day, and may be authorized to compel the Attendance of absent Members, in such Manner, and under such Penalties as each House may provide.

[2]Each House may determine the Rules of its Proceedings, punish its Members for disorderly Behavior, and, with the Concurrence of two thirds, expel a Member.

Rules of proceedings and keeping of journal.

[3]Each House shall keep a Journal of its Proceedings, and from time to time publish the same, excepting such Parts as may in their Judgment require

_____

**The part included in heavy brackets was changed by section 2 of the twentieth amendment.

Secrecy; and the Yeas and Nays of the Members of either House on any question shall, at the Desire of one fifth of those Present, be entered on the Journal.

Adjournment

⁴Neither House, during the Session of Congress, shall, without the Consent of the other, adjourn for more than three days, nor to any other Place than that in which the two Houses shall be sitting.

Compensation and immunities of members of Congress

SECTION 6. ¹The Senators and Representatives shall receive a Compensation for their Services, to be ascertained by Law, and paid out of the Treasury of the United States. They shall in all Cases, except Treason, Felony and Breach of the Peace, be privileged from Arrest during their Attendance at the Session of their respective Houses, and in going to and returning from the same; and for any Speech or Debate in either House, they shall not be questioned in any other Place.

Limitations on appointment of members of Congress to civil offices; no national office-holder to be a member of Congress

²No Senator or Representative shall, during the Time for which he was elected, be appointed to any civil Office under the Authority of the United States, which shall have been created, or the Emoluments whereof shall have been encreased during such time; and no Person holding any Office under the United States, shall be a Member of either House during his Continuance in Office.

Origin of revenue bills

SECTION 7. ¹All Bills for raising Revenue shall originate in the House of Representatives; but the Senate may propose or concur with Amendments as on other Bills.

Veto power of President: overriding of veto

²Every Bill which shall have passed the House of Representatives and the Senate, shall, before it become a Law, be presented to the President of the

United States; If he approve he shall sign it, but if not he shall return it, with his Objections to that House in which it shall have originated, who shall enter the Objections at large on their Journal, and proceed to reconsider it. If after such Reconsideration two thirds of that House shall agree to pass the Bill, it shall be sent, together with the Objections, to the other House, by which it shall likewise be reconsidered, and if approved by two thirds of that House, it shall become a Law. But in all such Cases the Votes of both Houses shall be determined by Yeas and Nays, and the Names of the Persons voting for and against the Bill shall be entered on the Journal of each House respectively. If any Bill shall not be returned by the President within ten days (Sundays excepted) after it shall have been presented to him, the Same shall be a Law, in like Manner as if he had signed it, unless the Congress by their Adjournment prevent its Return, in which Case it shall not be a Law.

³Every Order, Resolution, or Vote to which the Concurrence of the Senate and House of Representatives may be necessary (except on a question of Adjournment) shall be presented to the President of the United States; and before the Same shall take Effect, shall be approved by him, or being disapproved by him, shall be repassed by two thirds of the Senate and House of Representatives, according to the Rules and Limitations prescribed in the Case of a Bill.

Enumerated powers of Congress:
Taxation

SECTION 8. ¹The Congress shall have Power To lay and collect Taxes, Duties Imposts and Excises, to pay the Debts and provide for the common Defence and general Welfare of the United States; but all Duties, Imposts and Excises shall be uniform throughout the United States;

Borrowing of money	²To borrow Money on the credit of the United States;
Regulation of commerce	³To regulate Commerce with foreign Nations, and among the several States, and with the Indian Tribes;
Naturalization and bankruptcy	⁴To establish an uniform Rule of Naturalization, and uniform Laws on the subject of Bankruptcies throughout the United States;
Coining of money; weights and measures	⁵To coin Money, regulate the Value thereof, and of foreign Coin, and fix the Standard of Weights and Measures;
Punishment of counterfeiting	⁶To provide for the Punishment of counterfeiting the Securities and current Coin of the United States;
Postal service	⁷To establish Post Offices and post Roads;
Patents and copyrights	⁸To promote the Progress of Science and useful Arts, by securing for limited Times to Authors and Inventors the exclusive Right to their respective Writings and Discoveries;
Creation of courts	⁹To constitute Tribunals inferior to the supreme Court;
Piracies and high seas felonies	¹⁰To define and punish Piracies and Felonies committed on the high Seas, and Offences against the Law of Nations;
Declaration of War	¹¹To declare War, grant Letters of Marque and Reprisal, and make Rules concerning Captures on Land and Water;
Provide armed forces and for calling forth and organizing the militia	¹²To raise and support Armies, but no Appropriation of Money to that Use shall be for a longer Term than two Years;
	¹³To provide and maintain a Navy;
	¹⁴To make Rules for the Government and Regulation of the land and naval Forces;
	¹⁵To provide for calling forth the Militia to execute the Laws of the Union, suppress Insurrections and repel Invasions;

¹⁶To provide for organizing, arming, and disciplining the Militia and for governing such Part of them as may be employed in the Service of the United States, reserving to the States respectively, the Appointment of the Officers, and the Authority of training the Militia according to the discipline prescribed by Congress;

¹⁷To exercise exclusive Legislation in all Cases whatsoever, over such District (not exceeding ten Miles square) as may, by Cession of particular States, and the Acceptance of Congress, become the Seat of the Government of the United States, and to exercise like Authority over all Places purchased by the Consent of the Legislature of the State in which the Same shall be, for the Erection of Forts, Magazines, Arsenals, dock-Yards, and other needful Buildings;—And

¹⁸To make all Laws which shall be necessary and proper for carrying into Execution the foregoing Powers, and all other Powers vested by this Constitution in the Government of the United States, or in any Department or Officer thereof.

SECTION 9. ¹The Migration or Importation of such Persons as any of the States now existing shall think proper to admit, shall not be prohibited by the Congress prior to the Year one thousand eight hundred and eight, but a Tax or duty may be imposed on such Importation, not exceeding ten dollars for each Person.

²The Privilege of the Writ of Habeas Corpus shall not be suspended, unless when in Cases of Rebellion or Invasion the public Safety may require it.

³No Bill of Attainder or ex post facto Law shall be passed.

*⁴No Capitation, or other direct, Tax shall be laid, unless in Proportion to

_____
*See also the sixteenth amendment.

Congress to govern the District of Columbia and other places owned by national government

Necessary and proper (elastic) clause

Express limitations on national government— Congress in particular

Express limitations on
national government—
Congress in particular

the Census or Enumeration herein before directed to be taken.

⁵No Tax or Duty shall be laid on Articles exported from any State.

⁶No Preference shall be given by any Regulation of Commerce or Revenue to the Ports of one State over those of another: nor shall Vessels bound to, or from, one State be obliged to enter, clear, or pay Duties in another.

⁷No Money shall be drawn from the Treasury, but in Consequence of Appropriations made by Law; and a regular Statement and Account of the Receipts and Expenditures of all public Money shall be published from time to time.

⁸No Title of Nobility shall be granted by the United States: And no Person holding any Office of Profit or Trust under them, shall, without the Consent of the Congress, accept of any present, Emolument, Office, or Title, of any kind whatever, from any King, Prince, or foreign State.

SECTION 10. ¹No State shall enter into any Treaty, Alliance, or Confederation; grant Letters of Marque and Reprisal; coin Money; emit Bills of Credit; make any Thing but gold and silver Coin a Tender in Payment of Debts; pass any Bill of Attainder, ex pcst facto Law, or Law impairing the Obligation of Contracts, or grant any Title of Nobility.

²No State shall, without the Consent of the Congress, lay any Imposts or Duties on Imports or Exports, except what may be absolutely necessary for executing it's inspection Laws: and the net Produce of all Duties and Imposts, laid by any State on Imports or Exports, shall be for the Use of the Treasury of the United States; and all such Laws shall be subject to the Revision and Controul of the Congress.

[3]No State shall, without the Consent of Congress, lay any Duty of Tonnage, keep Troops, or Ships of War in time of Peace, enter into any Agreement or Compact with another State, or with a foreign Power, or engage in War, unless actually invaded, or in such imminent Danger as will not admit of delay.

ARTICLE II · EXECUTIVE DEPARTMENT

Executive power vested in President; term of office— see Twenty-second Amendment

SECTION 1.   [1]The executive Power shall be vested in a President of the United States of America. He shall hold his Office during the Term of four Years, and, together with the Vice President, chosen for the same Term, be elected as follows

Selection of Presidential electors and number per state

[2]Each State shall appoint, in such Manner as the Legislature thereof may direct, a Number of Electors, equal to the whole Number of Senators and Representatives to which the State may be entitled in the Congress: but no Senator or Representative, or Person holding an Office of Trust or Profit under the United States, shall be appointed an Elector.

Replaced by Twelfth Amendment

[The Electors shall meet in their respective States, and vote by Ballot for two Persons, of whom one at least shall not be an Inhabitant of the same State with themselves. And they shall make a List of all the Persons voted for, and of the Number of Votes for each; which List they shall sign and certify, and transmit sealed to the Seat of the Government of the United States, directed to the President of the Senate. The President of the Senate shall, in the Presence of the Senate and House of Representatives, open all the Certificates, and the Votes shall then be counted. The Person having the greatest Number of Votes shall be the President, if such Number be a Majority of the whole Number of

Electors appointed; and if there be more than one who have such Majority, and have an equal Number of Votes, then the House of Representatives shall immediately chuse by Ballot one of them for President; and if no Person have a Majority, then from the five highest on the List the said House shall in like Manner chuse the President. But in chusing the President, the Votes shall be taken by States, the Representation from each State having one Vote; A quorum for this Purpose shall consist of a Member or Members from two thirds of the States, and a Majority of all the States shall be necessary to a Choice. In every Case, after the Choice of the President, the Person having the greatest Number of Votes of the Electors shall be the Vice President. But if there should remain two or more who have equal Votes, the Senate shall chuse from them by Ballot the Vice President.]*

³The Congress may determine the Time of chusing the Electors, and the Day on which they shall give their Votes; which Day shall be the same throughout the United States.

⁴No Person except a natural born Citizen, or a Citizen of the United States, at the time of the Adoption of this Constitution, shall be eligible to the Office of President; neither shall any Person be eligible to that Office who shall not have attained to the Age of thirty five Years, and been fourteen Years a Resident within the United States.

⁵In Case of the Removal of the President from Office, or of his Death, Resignation, or Inability to discharge the Powers and Duties of the said Office, the Same shall devolve on the Vice President, and the Congress may by Law provide for the Case of Removal, Death, Resignation or Inability, both of the

*This paragraph has been superseded by the twelfth amendment.

Replaced by
Twelfth Amendment

Congress to determine the
time of choosing electors
and the casting of
electoral votes

Required qualifications
of President

Succession to the
Presidency; also see the
Twenty-fifth Amendment

President and Vice President declaring what Officer shall then act as President, and such Officer shall act accordingly, until the Disability be removed, or a President shall be elected.

Compensation of the President

⁶The President shall, at stated Times, receive for his Services, a Compensation, which shall neither be encreased nor diminished during the Period for which he shall have been elected, and he shall not receive within that Period any other Emolument from the United States, or any of them.

Presidential oath of office

⁷Before he enter on the Execution of his Office, he shall take the following Oath or Affirmation:—"I do solemnly swear (or affirm) that I will faithfully execute the Office of President of the United States and will to the best of my Ability, preserve, protect and defend the Constitution of the United States."

Powers of the President: Commander in Chief

SECTION 2. ¹The President shall be Commander in Chief of the Army and Navy of the United States, and of the Militia of the several States, when called into the actual Service of the United States; he may require the Opinion, in writing, of the principal Officer in each of the executive Departments, upon any Subject relating to the Duties of their respective Offices, and he shall have Power to grant Reprieves and Pardons for Offences against the United States, except in Cases of Impeachment.

Granting of pardons and reprieves

Treaty-making with advice and consent of Senate

Appointment of officials with advice and consent of Senate; appointment of inferior officers by President alone if Congress so provides

²He shall have Power, by and with the Advice and Consent of the Senate, to make Treaties, provided two thirds of the Senators present concur; and he shall nominate, and by and with the Advice and Consent of the Senate, shall appoint Ambassadors, other public Ministers and Consuls, Judges of the supreme Court, and all other Officers of the United States, whose Appointments are not herein otherwise provided for, and which shall be established by Law:

but the Congress may by Law vest the Appointment of such inferior Officers, as they think proper, in the President alone, in the Courts of Law, or in the Heads of Departments.

³The President shall have Power to fill up all Vacancies that may happen during the Recess of the Senate, by granting Commissions which shall expire at the End of their next Session.

SECTION 3. He shall from time to time give to the Congress Information of the State of the Union, and recommend to their Consideration such Measures as he shall judge necessary and expedient; he may, on extraordinary Occasions, convene both Houses, or either of them, and in Case of Disagreement between them, with Respect to the Time of Adjournment, he may adjourn them to such Time as he shall think proper; he shall receive Ambassadors and other public Ministers; he shall take Care that the Laws be faithfully executed, and shall Commission all the Officers of the United States.

SECTION 4. The President, Vice President and all civil Officers of the United States, shall be removed from Office on Impeachment for, and Conviction of, Treason, Bribery, or other high Crimes and Misdemeanors.

ARTICLE III · JUDICIAL DEPARTMENT

SECTION 1. The judicial Power of the United States, shall be vested in one supreme Court, and in such inferior Courts as the Congress may from time to time ordain and establish. The Judges, both of the supreme and inferior Courts, shall hold their Offices during good Behaviour, and shall, at stated Times,

---

Temporary filling of vacancies

Make recommendations to Congress and provide information

Call special sessions of Congress

Receive ambassadors and other public ministers

Enforce the laws

Civil officers, including President and Vice President, to be removed from office if impeached and convicted

Structure of national judiciary

Tenure and compensation of judges

receive for their Services a Compensation, which shall not be diminished during their Continuance in Office.

Jurisdiction of the national judiciary

SECTION 2. [1]The judicial Power shall extend to all Cases, in Law and Equity, arising under this Constitution, the Laws of the United States, and Treaties made, or which shall be made, under their Authority;—to all Cases affecting Ambassadors, other public Ministers and Consuls;—to all Cases of admiralty and maritime Jurisdiction;—to Controversies to which the United States shall be a Party;—to Controversies between two or more States;—between a State and Citizens of another State;*—between Citizens of different States,—between Citizens of the same State claiming Lands under Grants of different States, and between a State, or the Citizens thereof, and foreign States, Citizens or Subjects.

Original and appellate jurisdiction of the Supreme Court

[2]In all Cases affecting Ambassadors, other public Ministers and Consuls, and those in which a State shall be Party, the supreme Court shall have original Jurisdiction. In all the other Cases before mentioned, the supreme Court shall have appellate Jurisdiction, both as to Law and Fact, with such Exceptions, and under such Regulations as the Congress shall make.

Jury trial in criminal cases other than impeachment

[3]The Trial of all Crimes, except in Cases of Impeachment shall be by Jury; and such Trial shall be held in the State where the said Crimes shall have been committed; but when not committed within any State, the Trial shall be at such Place or Places as the Congress may by Law have directed.

Definition of treason and requisites for conviction

SECTION 3. [1]Treason against the United States, shall consist only in levying War against them, or in adhering to their Enemies, giving them Aid and

*This clause has been affected by the eleventh amendment.

Comfort. No Person shall be convicted of Treason unless on the Testimony of two Witnesses to the same overt Act, or on Confession in open Court.

[2]The Congress shall have Power to declare the Punishment of Treason, but no Attainder of Treason shall work Corruption of Blood, or Forfeiture except during the Life of the Person attainted.

ARTICLE IV · RELATION OF THE STATES TO EACH OTHER

SECTION 1. Full Faith and Credit shall be given in each State to the public Acts, Records, and judicial Proceedings of every other State. And the Congress may by general Laws prescribe the Manner in which such Acts, Records and Proceedings shall be proved, and the Effect thereof.

SECTION 2. [1]The Citizens of each State shall be entitled to all Privileges and Immunities of Citizens in the several States.

[2]A Person charged in any State with Treason, Felony, or other Crime, who shall flee from Justice, and be found in another State, shall on Demand of the executive Authority of the State from which he fled, be delivered up, to be removed to the State having Jurisdiction of the Crime.

[3][No Person held to Service or Labour in one State, under the Laws thereof, escaping into another, shall, in Consequence of any Law or Regulation therein, be discharged from such Service or Labour but shall be delivered up on Claim of the Party to whom such Service or Labour may be due.]*

---

*This paragraph has been superseded by the thirteenth amendment.

Punishment for treason

Interstate obligations: full faith and credit, privileges and immunities of citizens, rendition of fugitives from justice

Obsolete

Admission of new states

SECTION 3. ¹New States may be admitted by the Congress into this Union; but no new State shall be formed or erected within the Jurisdiction of any other State; nor any State be formed by the Junction of two or more States, or Parts of States, without the Consent of the Legislatures of the States concerned as well as of the Congress.

Government of territories

²The Congress shall have Power to dispose of and make all needful Rules and Regulations respecting the Territory or other Property belonging to the United States; and nothing in this Constitution shall be so construed as to Prejudice any Claims of the United States, or of any particular State.

Guarantee of republican form of government and protection against invasion and domestic violence

SECTION 4. The United States shall guarantee to every State in this Union a Republican Form of Government, and shall protect each of them against Invasion; and on Application of the Legislature, or of the Executive (when the Legislature cannot be convened) against domestic Violence.

ARTICLE V · AMENDMENTS

Proposal ard ratification of amendments

The Congress, whenever two thirds of both Houses shall deem it necessary, shall propose Amendments to this Constitution, or, on the Application of the Legislatures of two thirds of the several States, shall call a Convention for proposing Amendments, which, in either Case, shall be valid to all Intents and Purposes, as Part of this Constitution, when ratified by the Legislatures of three fourths of the several States, or by Conventions in three fourths thereof, as the one or the other Mode of Ratification may be proposed by the Congress: Provided, [that no Amendment which may be made prior to the Year One thousand eight hundred and eight shall in any Manner affect the first and fourth Clauses in the Ninth Section of the first Article; and]** that no State, without its Consent, shall be deprived of its equal Suffrage in the Senate.

ARTICLE VI · GENERAL PROVISIONS

[1]All Debts contracted and Engagements entered into, before the Adoption of this Constitution shall be as valid against the United States under this Constitution, as under the Confederation.

[2]This Constitution, and the Laws of the United States which shall be made in Pursuance thereof; and all Treaties made, or which shall be made, under the Authority of the United States, shall be the supreme Law of the Land; and the Judges in every State shall be bound thereby, any Thing in the Constitution or Laws of any State to the Contrary notwithstanding.

[3]The Senators and Representatives before mentioned, and the Members of the several State Legislatures, and all executive and judicial Officers, both of the United States and of the several States, shall be bound by Oath or Affirmation, to support this Constitution; but no religious Test shall ever be required as a Qualification to any Office or public Trust under the United States.

ARTICLE VII · RATIFICATION OF THE CONSTITUTION

The Ratification of the Conventions of nine States, shall be sufficient for the Establishment of this Constitution between the States so ratifying the Same. DONE in Convention by the Unanimous Consent of the States present the Seventeenth Day of September in the Year of our Lord one thousand seven

---

Validity of debts contracted prior to adoption of the Constitution

Supremacy of the national constitution, laws, and treaties

Oath of office to support Constitution: required of all officials, national and state; no religious qualification

Schedule

**Obsolete.

hundred and Eighty seven and of the Independence of the United States of America the Twelfth IN WITNESS whereof We have hereto subscribed our Names,

George Washington
President and Deputy from Virginia

[Signed also by the deputies of twelve States.]

New Hampshire
John Langdon
Nicholas Gilman

Massachusetts
Nathaniel Gorham
Rufus King

Connecticut
William Samuel Johnson
Roger Sherman

New York
Alexander Hamilton

New Jersey
William Livingston
David Brearley
William Paterson
Jonathan Dayton

Pennsylvania
Benjamin Franklin
Robert Morris
Thomas FitzSimons
James Wilson
Thomas Mifflin
George Clymer
Jared Ingersoll
Gouverneur Morris

Delaware
George Read
John Dickinson
Jacob Broom
Gunning Bedford, Jr.
Richard Bassett

Maryland

James McHenry

Daniel Carroll

Dan of St. Thomas Jenifer

Virginia

John Blair

James Madison, Jr.

North Carolina

William Blount

Hugh Williamson

Richard Dobbs Spaight

South Carolina

John Rutledge

Charles Pinckney

Charles Cotesworth Pinckney

Pierce Butler

Georgia

William Few

Abraham Baldwin

Attest: William Jackson, Secretary

RATIFICATION OF THE CONSTITUTION

The Constitution was adopted by a convention of the States on September 17, 1787, and was subsequently ratified by the several States, on the following dates: Delaware, December 7, 1787; Pennsylvania, December 12, 1787; New Jersey, December 18, 1787; Georgia, January 2, 1788; Connecticut, January 9, 1788; Massachusetts, February 6, 1788; Maryland, April 28, 1788; South Carolina, May 23, 1788; New Hampshire, June 21, 1788; Virginia, June 25, 1788; New York, July 26, 1788; North Carolina, November 21, 1789; Rhode Island, May 29, 1790.

ARTICLES IN ADDITION TO, AND AMENDMENT OF, THE CONSTITUTION OF THE UNITED STATES OF AMERICA, PROPOSED BY CONGRESS, AND RATIFIED BY THE LEGISLATURES OF THE SEVERAL STATES PURSUANT TO THE FIFTH ARTICLE OF THE ORIGINAL CONSTITUTION

ARTICLE I*

Freedom of religion, speech, and assembly

Congress shall make no law respecting an establishment of religion, or prohibiting the free exercise thereof; or abridging the freedom of speech, or of the press, or the right of the people peaceably to assemble, and to petition the Government for a redress of grievances.

ARTICLE II

Militia and the right to bear arms

A well regulated Militia, being necessary to the security of a free State, the right of the people to keep and bear Arms, shall not be infringed.

ARTICLE III

Quartering of soldiers

No Soldier shall, in time of peace be quartered in any house, without the consent of the Owner, nor in time of war, but in a manner to be prescribed by law.

*Only the 13th, 14th, 15th, and 16th articles of amendment had numbers assigned to them at the time of ratification.

ARTICLE IV

The right of the people to be secure in their persons, houses, papers, and effects, against unreasonable searches and seizures, shall not be violated, and no Warrants shall issue, but upon probable cause, supported by Oath or affirmation, and particularly describing the place to be searched, and the persons or things to be seized.

Unreasonable searches and seizures prohibited

ARTICLE V

No person shall be held to answer for a capital, or otherwise infamous crime, unless on a presentment or indictment of a Grand Jury, except in cases arising in the land or naval forces, or in the Militia, when in actual service in time of War or public danger; nor shall any person be subject for the same offence to be twice put in jeopardy of life or limb, nor shall be compelled in any criminal case to be a witness against himself, nor be deprived of life, liberty, or property, without due process of law; nor shall private property be taken for public use without just compensation.

Indictment by grand jury; no double jeopardy; due process of law; no self-incrimination; compensation for taking property

ARTICLE VI

In all criminal prosecutions, the accused shall enjoy the right to a speedy and public trial, by an impartial jury of the State and district wherein the crime shall have been committed; which district shall have been previously ascertained by law, and to be informed of the nature and cause of the accusation; to be confronted with the witnesses against him; to have compulsory

Guarantee of basic procedural rights in criminal prosecutions, e.g., jury trial, confrontation of witnesses process for obtaining Witnesses in his favor, and to have the Assistance of Counsel for his defence.

ARTICLE VII

In Suits at common law, where the value in controversy shall exceed twenty dollars, the right of trial by jury shall be preserved, and no fact tried by a jury shall be otherwise reexamined in any Court of the United States, than according to the rules of the common law.

Jury trial in common law suits

ARTICLE VIII

Excessive bail shall not be required, nor excessive fines imposed, nor cruel and unusual punishments inflicted.

Excessive bail or fines, cruel and unusual punishments prohibited

ARTICLE IX

The enumeration in the Constitution, of certain rights, shall not be construed to deny or disparage others retained by the people.

Retention of rights by the people

ARTICLE X

The powers not delegated to the United States by the Constitution nor prohibited by it to the States, are reserved to the States respectively, or to the people.

Reserved powers of the states

ARTICLE XI

The Judicial power of the United States shall not be construed to extend to any suit in law or equity, commenced or prosecuted against one of the United States by Citizens of another State, or by Citizens or Subjects of any Foreign State.

Immunity of states from suits by citizens or aliens in national courts

ARTICLE XII

The electors shall meet in their respective states and vote by ballot for President and Vice-President, one of whom, at least, shall not be an inhabitant of the same state with themselves; they shall name in their ballots the person voted for as President, and in distinct ballots the person voted for as Vice-President, and they shall make distinct lists of all persons voted for as President, and of all persons voted for as Vice-President, and of the number of votes for each, which lists they shall sign and certify, and transmit sealed to the seat of the government of the United States, directed to the President of the Senate; —The President of the Senate shall, in presence of the Senate and House of Representatives, open all the certificates and the votes shall then be counted;— The person having the greatest number of votes for President, shall be the President, if such number be a majority of the whole number of Electors appointed; and if no person have such majority, then from the persons having the highest numbers not exceeding three on the list of those voted for as President, the House of Representatives shall choose immediately, by ballot, the President. But in choosing the President, the votes shall be taken by states,

Replaces third paragraph of Section 1, Article II. Principal provision requires separate ballots for President and Vice President and a majority electoral vote. Procedure to be followed if no candidate obtains a majority

the representation from each state having one vote; a quorum for this purpose shall consist of a member or members from two-thirds of the states, and a majority of all the states shall be necessary to a choice. [And if the House of Representatives shall not choose a President whenever the right of choice shall devolve upon them, before the fourth day of March next following, then the Vice-President shall act as President, as in the case of the death or other constitutional disability of the President.]* The person having the the greatest number of votes as Vice-President, shall be the Vice-President, if such number be a majority of the whole number of Electors appointed, and if no person have a majority, then from the two highest numbers on the list, the Senate shall choose the Vice-President; a quorum for the purpose shall consist of two-thirds of the whole number of Senators, and a majority of the whole number shall be necessary to a choice. But no person constitutionally ineligible to the office of President shall be eligible to that of Vice-President of the United States.

Replaces third paragraph of Section 1, Article II. Principal provision requires separate ballots for President and Vice President and a majority electoral vote. Procedure to be followed if no candidate obtains a majority

ARTICLE XIII

SECTION 1. Neither slavery nor involuntary servitude, except as a punishment for crime whereof the party shall have been duly convicted, shall exist within the United States, or any place subject to their jurisdiction.

SECTION 2. Congress shall have power to enforce this article by appropriate legislation.

Slavery and involuntary servitude prohibited

*The part included in heavy brackets has been superseded by section 3 of the twentieth amendment.

ARTICLE XIV

SECTION 1.   All persons born or naturalized in the United States, and subject to the jurisdiction thereof, are citizens of the United States and the State wherein they reside. No State shall make or enforce any law which shall abridge the privileges or immunities of citizens of the United States; nor shall any State deprive any person of life, liberty, or property, without due process of law; nor deny to any person within its jurisdiction the equal protection of the laws.

SECTION 2.   Representatives shall be apportioned among the several States according to their respective numbers, counting the whole number of persons in each State, excluding Indians not taxed. But when the right to vote at any election for the choice of electors for President and Vice President of the United States, Representatives in Congress, the Executive and Judicial officers of a State, or the members of the Legislature thereof, is denied to any of the male inhabitants of such State, being twenty-one years of age, and citizens of the United States, or in any way abridged, except for participation in rebellion, or other crime, the basis of representation therein shall be reduced in the proportion which the number of such male citizens shall bear to the whole number of male citizens twenty-one years of age in such State.

SECTION 3.   No person shall be a Senator or Representative in Congress, or elector of President and Vice President, or hold any office, civil or military, under the United States, or under any State, who, having previously taken an oath, as a member of Congress, or as an officer of the United States, or as

Definition of United States and state citizenship; no state abridgment of privileges and immunities of United States citizens; no state denial of due process of law or equal protection of the laws to any person

Apportionment of Representatives among the states according to population, excluding untaxed Indians. Provision for reduction of representation under specified circumstances

Disqualification from office-holding by officials who, having taken an oath to support the Constitution, engage in rebellion against the United States a member of any State legislature, or as an executive or judicial officer of any State, to support the Constitution of the United States, shall have engaged in insurrection or rebellion against the same, or given aid or comfort to the enemies thereof. But Congress may by a vote of two-thirds of each House, remove such disability.

SECTION 4. The validity of the public debt of the United States, authorized by law, including debts incurred for payment of pensions and bounties for services in suppressing insurrection or rebellion, shall not be questioned. But neither the United States nor any State shall assume or pay any debt or obligation incurred in aid of insurrection or rebellion against the United States, or any claim for the loss or emancipation of any slave; but all such debts, obligations and claims shall be held illegal and void.

SECTION 5. The Congress shall have power to enforce, by appropriate legislation, the provisions of this article.

ARTICLE XV

SECTION 1. The right of citizens of the United States to vote shall not be denied or abridged by the United States or by any State on account of race, color, or previous condition of servitude.

SECTION 2. The Congress shall have power to enforce this article by appropriate legislation.

Validity of public debt incurred for suppressing rebellion not to be questioned. All indebtedness incurred in support of rebellion illegal and void

Right of citizens to vote not to be denied because of race, color, or previous condition of servitude

ARTICLE XVI

The Congress shall have power to lay and collect taxes on incomes, from whatever source derived, without apportionment among the several States, and without regard to any census or enumeration.

Congress empowered to levy income taxes without apportionment among states on a population basis

ARTICLE XVII

The Senate of the United States shall be composed of two Senators from each state, elected by the people thereof, for six years; and each Senator shall have one vote. The electors in each State shall have the qualifications requisite for electors of the most numerous branch of the State legislatures.

When vacancies happen in the representation of any State in the Senate, the executive authority of such State shall issue writs of election to fill such vacancies: *Provided,* That the legislature of any State may empower the executive thereof to make temporary appointments until the people fill the vacancies by election as the legislature may direct.

This amendment shall not be so construed as to affect the election or term of any Senator chosen before it becomes valid as part of the Constitution.

Popular election of Senators for six year terms by persons qualified to vote for members of the most numerous branch of the state legislature

Procedure for filling vacancies in Senate

ARTICLE XVIII

SECTION 1. After one year from the ratification of this article the manufacture, sale, or transportation of intoxicating liquors within, the importation thereof into, or the exportation thereof from the United States and all territory subject to the jurisdiction thereof for beverage purposes is hereby prohibited.

Prohibition Amendment; repealed by Twenty-first Amendment

Section 2. The Congress and the several States shall have concurrent power to enforce this article by appropriate legislation.

Section 3. This article shall be inoperative unless it shall have been ratified as an amendment to the Constitution by the legislatures of the several States, as provided in the Constitution, within seven years from the date of the submission hereof to the States by the Congress.*

ARTICLE XIX

Right of citizens to vote not to be denied because of sex

The right of citizens of the United States to vote shall not be denied or abridged by the United States or by any State on account of sex. Congress shall have power to enforce this article by appropriate legislation.

ARTICLE XX

Ending of terms of President, Vice President, Senators, and Representatives

Section 1. The terms of the President and Vice President shall end at noon on the 20th day of January, and the terms of Senators and Representatives at noon on the 3d day of January, of the years in which such terms would have ended if this article had not been ratified; and the terms of their successors shall then begin.

Beginning of required annual Congressional sessions

Section 2. The Congress shall assemble at least once in every year, and such meeting shall begin at noon on the 3d day of January, unless they shall by law appoint a different day.

_____
*Repealed by section 1 of the twenty-first amendment.

Procedure to be followed if President elect has died or no President has been chosen or qualified by beginning of the Presidential term. This amendment also deals with other contingencies

SECTION 3. If, at the time fixed for the beginning of the term of the President, the President elect shall have died, the Vice President elect shall become President. If a President shall not have been chosen before the time fixed for the beginning of his term, or if the President elect shall have failed to qualify, then the Vice President elect shall act as President until a President shall have qualified; and the Congress may by law provide for the case wherein neither a President elect nor a Vice President elect shall have qualified, declaring who shall then act as President, or the manner in which one who is to act shall be selected, and such person shall act accordingly until a President or Vice President shall have qualified.

SECTION 4. The Congress may by law provide for the case of the death of any of the persons from whom the House of Representatives may choose a President whenever the right of choice shall have devolved upon them, and for the case of the death of any of the persons from whom the Senate may choose a Vice President whenever the right of choice shall have devolved upon them.

SECTION 5. Sections 1 and 2 shall take effect on the 15th day of October following the ratification of this article.

SECTION 6. This article shall be inoperative unless it shall have been ratified as an amendment to the Constitution by the legislatures of three-fourths of the several States within seven years from the date of its submission.

ARTICLE XXI

SECTION 1. The eighteenth article of amendment to the Constitution of the United States is hereby repealed.

SECTION 2. The transportation or importation into any State, Territory, or possession of the United States for delivery or use therein of intoxicating liquors, in violation of the laws thereof, is hereby prohibited.

SECTION 3. This article shall be inoperative unless it shall have been ratified as an amendment to the Constitution by conventions in the several States, as provided in the Constitution, within seven years from the date of the submission hereof to the States by the Congress.

ARTICLE XXII

SECTION 1. No person shall be elected to the office of the President more than twice, and no person who has held the office of President, or acted as President, for more than two years of a term to which some other person was elected President shall be elected to the office of the President more than once. But this article shall not apply to any person holding the office of President when this Article was proposed by the Congress, and shall not prevent any person who may be holding the office of President, or acting as President, during the term within which this Article becomes operative from holding the office of President or acting as President during the remainder of such term.

SECTION 2. This article shall be inoperative unless it shall have been ratified as an amendment to the Constitution by the legislatures of three-fourths of the several States within seven years from the date of its submission to the States by the Congress.

ARTICLE XXIII

Allocation of presidential
electors to District of
Columbia

SECTION 1.   The District constituting the seat of Government of the United States shall appoint in such manner as the Congress may direct:

A number of electors of President and Vice President equal to the whole number of Senators and Representatives in Congress to which the District would be entitled if it were a State, but in no event more than the least populous State; they shall be in addition to those appointed by the States, but they shall be considered, for the purposes of the election of President and Vice President, to be electors appointed by a State; and they shall meet in the District and perform such duties as provided by the twelfth article of amendment.

SECTION 2.   The Congress shall have power to enforce this article by appropriate legislation.

ARTICLE XXIV

Right of citizens to vote in
national elections not to
be denied because of
failure to pay taxes

SECTION 1.   The right of citizens of the United States to vote in any primary or other election for President or Vice President, for electors for President or Vice President, or for Senator or Representative in Congress, shall not be denied or abridged by the United States or any State by reason of failure to pay any poll tax or other tax.

SECTION 2. The Congress shall have power to enforce this article by appropriate legislation.

ARTICLE XXV

Succession to the Presidency and Vice Presidency in case of vacancies

SECTION 1. In case of the removal of the President from office or of his death or resignation, the Vice President shall become President.

SECTION 2. Whenever there is a vacancy in the office of the Vice President, the President shall nominate a Vice President who shall take office upon confirmation by a majority vote of both Houses of Congress.

SECTION 3. Whenever the President transmits to the President pro tempore of the Senate and the Speaker of the House of Representatives his written declaration that he is unable to discharge the powers and duties of his office, and until he transmits to them a written declaration to the contrary, such powers and duties shall be discharged by the Vice President as Acting President.

Presidential disability: procedure for determining when and for how long disability exists. Vice President to act as President for duration of disability

SECTION 4. Whenever the Vice President and a majority of either the principal officers of the executive departments or of such other body as Congress may by law provide, transmit to the President pro tempore of the Senate and the Speaker of the House of Representatives their written declaration that the President is unable to discharge the powers and duties of his office, the Vice President shall immediately assume the powers and duties of the office as Acting President.

Thereafter, when the President transmits to the President pro tempore of the Senate and the Speaker of the House of Representatives his written declaration that no inability exists, he shall resume the powers and duties of his office unless the Vice President and a majority of either the principal officers of the executive department or of such other body as Congress may by law provide, transmit within four days to the President pro tempore of the Senate and the Speaker of the House of Representatives their written declaration that the President is unable to discharge the powers and duties of his office. Thereupon Congress shall decide the issue, assembling within forty-eight hours for that purpose if not in session. If the Congress, within twenty-one days after receipt of the latter written declaration, or, if Congress is not in session, within twenty-one days after Congress is required to assemble, determines by two-thirds vote of both Houses that the President is unable to discharge the powers and duties of his office, the Vice President shall continue to discharge the same as Acting President; otherwise, the President shall resume the powers and duties of his office.

ARTICLE XXVI

SECTION 1. The right of citizens of the United States, who are eighteen years of age or older, to vote shall not be denied or abridged by the United States or by any State on account of age.

SECTION 2. The Congress shall have power to enforce this article by appropriate legislation.

Citizens eighteen years or older not to be denied suffrage because of age

ARTICLE XXVII — PROPOSED

Equal legal rights for men and women

SECTION 1. Equality of rights under the law shall not be denied or abridged by the United States or by any State on account of sex.

SECTION 2. The Congress shall have the power to enforce this article by appropriate legislation.

☆ INDEX

Absentee voting, 121
Administration
Aids to general management
of, 251-253
Control of, by
Congress, 159, 278
Judiciary, 162, 279
Local assemblies, 471, 493,
494, 498
State legislatures, 422, 426,
428, 431
Direction and control of, by
Governors, 421-423, 426-
428
Local executives, 471, 474,
479, 482, 493-494, 495,
498-500
President, 251-254, 278
Importance of, 276-278
Administration of justice
Factors determining its quality,
451-454
Administrative adjudication, 311-
314
Administrative legislation, 310-
311
Administrative Office of the
United States Courts, 330-331
Administrative officers of states
Methods of selection, 422-423
Administrative offices of state
judicial systems, 441
Administrative organization
Appraisals of national,
Criticisms, 298
Major studies, 298
Results, 299-301
Features of national, 279-301
Reorganization Acts of Con-
gress, 279-280

State, 422, 427-428
Types of national administra-
tive agencies, 281-282
Admission of states, 51-52
Agricultural, Department of, 285
Amendment and revision of,
Constitution of the United
States, 19, 25-26
Home rule charters, 489-491
State constitution, 365-377
Amnesty, 270
Appendix, 551
Appointment, power of,
Governors, 423-424
Local executives, 469, 471,
478-479, 481, 493, 498, 500
President of United States,
256-258
Apportionment
House of Representatives (U.
S.), 196
State legislatures, 389-393
Appraisal of
National administrative orga-
nization, 298-301
Presidential-Congressional plan,
180-189
Appropriations
Itemized or lump sum, 525-
526
Articles of Confederation
Defects of, 14-16
Excerpts from, see Appendix
Governmental features of, 13-
14
Assembly, freedom of, 92-95
Atomic Energy Commission, 297
Attainder, bills of, 79, 80, 81, see
Glossary
Australian ballot system, 126-127

Bad tendency test, freedom of speech, 93
Ballots, types, 125-126
Barriers to sound budgeting, 529-530
Bicameral versus unicameral legislatures, 382-388
Birth, acquisition of citizenship by, 66-69
Budgeting systems, 523-529
Budget, Office of Management and, 179, 252, 254, 255, 524
Budgets
    Execution of, 526-528
    Legalization of, 525-526
    National budget concepts, 531-532
    Nature of, 521-523
    Post-auditing, 528-529
    Pre-auditing, 527
    Preparation of, 523-525

Cabinet, President's, 253-254
Calendars, legislative, 232
California plan for selecting judges, 444
Career service, 303
Cases cited in text, see Appendix
Caucus, 130
Checks and balances
    Congressional checks on executive and judiciary, 159-161
    Doctrine of, 153, 159-163
    Judicial checks on President and Congress, 162-163
    Local governments, 493
    Presidential checks on Congress and judiciary, 161-162
    State governments, 380
Cities, legal status of, 487-488
Citizenship
    Acquisition and loss of United States, 66-73
    Rights associated with,
        State, 75-76
        United States, 76-79

State, acquisition of, 73-74
City charters
    Legislative
        General laws, 489
        Optional charters, 489
        Special acts, 488
    Home rule, 489-491
City government, forms of,
    Commission, 495-497
    Comparison of strong mayor-council and council-manager plans, 501-503
    Council-manager, 497-501
    Mayor-council
        Philadelphia plan, 494-495
        Strong mayors, 493-494
        Weak mayors, 493-494
Civil Aeronautics Board, 291
Civil rights,
    Associated with citizenship, 75-79
    of all persons, 80-108
Civil Rights Act of 1964, 78
Civil Service Commission, 304-305
Civil service reform, 303-304
Clear and present danger test, freedom of speech, 93-94
Clear and probable danger test, freedom of speech, 93
Colonial political institutions
    General features, 3
    Governor, 5-6
    Judiciary, 8
    Legislature, 6-8
    Types of colonies, 4-5
Commerce, Department of, 286
Commerce power, 38-40
Commission plan, 495-497
Commissioners on Uniform State Laws, 63
Committee of the Whole, 220-221
Committees
    Conference, 221, 236
    Joint, 218
    Special, 218

Standing, 215-228

Committees on committees, 224, 226-227

Compliance with governmental policies, securing, 314-316

Comptroller General of the United States, 262, 299, 528

Compulsory voting, 110

Concurrent powers, determining factors, 47-50

Conditional grants-in-aid, 41, 60-61, 462

Conference committees, 221, 236

Conference of Chief Justices, 62

Conferences or caucuses, partisan, 222-223

Congress

Apportionment of Representatives, 196

Committees, 216-221

Compensation, 199

Composition of, 192-199

Equal representation of states in Senate, 193-194

Expulsion of members, 155

Functions of, as representative body, 204-205

Organization and procedure

Formal, 211-221

Informal, 221-228

Party agencies, 221-228

Powers of, 200-204

Privileges of members, 199-200

Qualifications for membership, 192, 194-195

Selection of members: *Wesberry* case, 177-178, 197

Size, 193, 196

Terms, 155

Congress in action

Passage of bills, 228-236

Conference committees, 221, 236

House procedure, 230-234

Senate procedure, 234-235

Constituent powers of Congress, 200

Constitution of the United States

Amendment procedure, 19, 25-27

Drafting of, 16-17

Main body of

Articles I-VII, 18-20

Preamble, 18

Twenty-six amendments, 20-25

Constitutional change, processes of

Amendment, 25-26

Auxiliary legislation, 30

Custom and usage, 29-30

Interpretation, 27-29

Constitutions, requirements of satisfactory, 355-357

Constitutions, state, 108-109, 352-378

Constructive measures of economy, 547-550

Contracts, impairment of obligation of, 90-92

Conventions, party

Composition of national, 170-172

Functions of, 173

Nominations by, 130-131, 170-173

Selection of delegates to, 172-173

Votes per delegate, 172

Cooperative federalism, 59, 64

Corporate or charter colonies, 4

Council of State Governments, 62

Council-manager plan, 497-501

Counties

Better forms of county government, 473-475

Defects, organizational and other, 472-473, 475-476

Functions of, 466-468

Structure of county government, 468-473

County Board and other officials, 470-472

Court of Claims, United States, 328

Court of Customs and Patent Appeals, United States, 328

Courts, national, 323-329; also see Judges and Judiciary
Administrative office of, 330
Constitutional and legislative, 323-324
Courts of Appeal, 325-326
District courts, 324-325
Federal Judicial Center, 330
Judicial conferences, 329-330
Special courts, 328-329
Supreme Court, 326-328

Courts, state, 432-438; also see Judges and Judiciary
Administrative offices of, 441
County and other courts, 434-435
Courts of last resort, 437-438
Intermediate appellate, 436
Judicial conferences, 440
Judicial councils, 440
Justices of the peace, 433-434
Major trial courts, 435-436

Cumulative voting, 123

Customs Court, United States, 329

Death Penalty, 89-90

Declaration of Independence, 8-10

Defense, Department of, 284

Delegation of powers, 205-207
Non-permissible, 206
Permissible, 206

Democratic party, organization of, 136-141

Departmental personnel offices, 305

Departments, national government
Agriculture, 285; Commerce, 286; Defense, 284; Health, Education, and Welfare, 288; Housing and Urban

Development, 288 ;Interior, 285; Justice, 284; Labor, 287; State, 282; Transportation, 289; Treasury, 289

Digest of Selected Supreme Court Cases, see Appendix

Direct legislation
Desirability of, 414-415
Initiative: direct and indirect, 412-413
Petition or protest referendum, 413-414

Direct primaries
Non-partisan, 129-130
Partisan
Closed, 128
Open, 128-129

Director of Office of Management and Budget, 179

Disability, Presidential, 240-241

Disintegrated judicial administration, 438-439

Dismissals from national service, 307-309

Disqualifications for voting, 120

Districts
Congressional, 196-198
Multi-member, 395
Single-member, 396

Domestic violence, protection against, 53-54

Double jeopardy, 88-89

Dual committee systems, 402

Dual system of courts, 318, 432

Due process of law, 100-104

Duties of individuals, 109-111

Economy, constructive measures of, 547-550

Election methods
Ballot, types of, 125-126
Cumulative voting, 123
Limited voting, 123
Majority choice, 122-123
Proportional representation
List system, 123-124

Single transferable vote, 124-125
Safeguards against fraud and intimidation, 126-127
Single choice-plurality, 122
Elections, 114-127
Elective officers, 114-115
Electoral college
Criticisms of, 175-176
Electors per state, 156
Proposals for change, 176-177
Selection of electors, 153, 173, 174
Electoral powers of Congress, 201
Entrance appointments, 306
Equal protection of the laws, 104-108
Ethical obligations, 110
Ex post facto laws, 79, 80, 81, see Glossary
Examination questions, see Appendix
Exclusive powers, 47-50
Executive agreements, 269-270
Executive appointment of judges, merits, 443
Executive branch, 155-157, 237-274, 418-432
Executive Office of the President, 252-253
Executive powers of Congress, 201
Expatriation
Involuntary, 70-72
Voluntary, 73
Expenditures, public, 519-534
Express powers, 36-37
Expulsion of Senators and Representatives, 155

Federal Administrative Procedure Act of 1946, 207, 311, 313
Federal Bureau of Investigation, 60, 284

Federal Communications Commission, 292-293
Federal district courts, 324-325
Federal Maritime Commission, 291
Federal Power Commission, 293
Federal Register, 207, 311
Federal system of government, 34-35
Federal Trade Commission, 291-292
Federalism, cooperative, 59, 64
First state constitutions, 10-12, 357-358
Floor leaders, party, 223-224
Foreign affairs, source of national power over, 43
Foreign policy, 265-270
Freedom of religion, 96-100
Freedom of speech, press, assembly, 92-95
Fugitives from justice, 55-56
Full faith and credit clause, 54-55
Functions of judiciary, 448-450
Fundamental rights, significance of
Double jeopardy, 88-89
Due process of law, 100-104
Equal protection of the laws, 104-108
Freedom of religion, 96-100
Freedom of speech, press, assembly, 92-95
Impairment of obligation of contracts, 90-92
Self-incrimination, 84-85, 87
Unreasonable searches and seizures, 85-88
Writ of *habeas corpus*, 83

General Services Administration, 295
Georgia, selection of governor, 418

Gerrymandering, 198, Note 70, 392
Glossary, see Appendix
Governmental powers
    Commerce power, 38-40
    Exclusive and concurrent, 47-50
    Express, 36-37
    Foreign affairs, 43
    Implied, 37-38
    Limitations on, 43-44, 46
    Local governments, 50
    National government, 35-43
    Reserved or residual, 45-46
    Resulting, 37
    States, 44-46
    Taxing power, 40-41, 48, 536-538
    Treaty-making, 42, 268-269
    War, 42-43, 262-265
Governmental process
    Realities of, 150-151
    Role of the people, 113-115, 150
Governors
    Administrative role of, 421-427
    Appointive power, 423-424
    Compensation, 419-420
    Law enforcement, 425
    Legislative powers and influence, 420-421
    Management of administrative services, obstacles to, 426-427
    Pardoning power, 429-430
    Qualifications, 419
    Removal of, 419
    Removal powers of, 424-425
    Selection, 418-419
    Term, 419
Grants-in-aid, 41, 60-61, 462
Guarantees of rights
    State constitutions, 108-109
    United States Constitution, 74-108

Habeas corpus, writ of, 83
Health, Education, and Welfare, Department of, 288
Home rule systems, 489-492
House Committee on Rules, 219
Housing and Urban Development, Department of, 288

Impeachment process, 157, 158, 160, 201, 202, 419
Implied powers, 37-38
Indebtedness
    National government, 545-546
    Pay-as-you-go, 544-545
    Sound borrowing, 542-545
    State and local governments, 546
Independent establishments, 290-297
Individual rights and responsibilities, 65-111
Initiative, direct and indirect, 412-413
Institutionalization of the Presidency, 253
Interest-groups, 141-145
Intergovernmental cooperation
    Interlocal, 63-64
    Interstate, 61-63
    National-state-local, 60
    State-local, 61
Interior, Department of, 285
Interstate Commerce Commission, 290-291
Interstate compacts, 61-62
Invasion, protection against, 53-54
Investigatory power of Congress, 202, 208-211

Joint committee systems, 400-403
Joint committees, 218, 402
Judges
    California plan, 444

Compensation, 334-335, 436, 437
Missouri plan, 444
Model State Constitution, 445
Powers of, 452
Removal of
National, 334
State, 446-448
Selection of
National, 332-333
State, 441-445
Tenure of,
National, 334
State, 434-437
Judicial activism, 343-344
Judicial branch, 157-158, 317-351, 432-454
Judicial conferences, 329-330, 440
Judicial councils, 440
Judicial lawmaking, 207, 351
Judicial powers of Congress, 202
Judicial review
Advantages and disadvantages, 344-350
Curbing
Limiting appellate jurisdiction of Supreme Court, 340-341
Packing the Court, 341-343
Roosevelt plan, 342
Expansion of, 338-340
Improving, 349-350
Marbury v. Madison and *Eakin v. Raub*, 336-338
Nature of, 335
Ultimate center of legal reference needed, 350-351
Judicial self-restraint, 343
Judiciary; also see Courts
Functions of, 448-450
National
Jurisdiction, 318-323
Organization, 323-335
State
Jurisdiction, 321, 433-438
Organization, 432-439

Juries, 101, 451
Jurisdiction of courts
Congressional control over, 322-323
Exclusive and concurrent, 320-321
How cases reach national courts, 321-322
National, 318-321
State, 321, 433-438
Jury trial, 101-102, 451
Jus sanguinis, 67
Jus soli, 66
Just laws, 453-454
Justice, administration of, 451-454
Justice, Department of, 284

Labor, Department of, 287
Lawmaking procedure
Congress, 228-236
Realities of, 410-411
State legislatures, 405-408
Legislative councils, 409
Legislative powers of Congress, 202-204
Legislative selection of judges, objections to, 442-443
Legislative service agencies, 410
Legislatures, state, 379-415
Aids to legislative action, 408-410
Apportionment and *Reynolds* case, 389-393
Committee systems, 402-405
Compensation, 397-398
Gerrymandering, 392
Lawmaking procedure, 405-408
Methods of election, 395-397
Number of chambers, 382
Bicameralism versus unicameralism, 382-388
Occupations of members, 395
Performance records of, 411

Population-based representation, 389-391
Presiding officers, 400-402
Qualifications of members, 393-395
Realities of legislative process, 410-411
Sessions, frequency and length, 398-400
Size, 388-389
Terms, 397
Limitations on national and state powers, 43-44, 46
Limited voting, 123
Living constitution, 30-31
Local expenditures, 532-533
Local government
  Counties, 466-476
  Home rule, 458, 489-492
  Municipalities, 484-516
  New England towns, 480-482
  Special districts, 482-483
  Special legislation, 459
  State control of,
    Administrative, 462-463
    Judicial, 461-462
    Legislative, 461
  State constitutional provisions concerning, 458-460
  Townships, 476-480
Local units of government
  Number and types, 464-466
  Powers of, 50, 458, 487-488
  Proposals for decreasing number, 465-466
Loss of faith in state legislatures, 359-361

Major and minor parties in United States, 134
Majority choice elections, 122-123
Mayor-council plan, 493, 495, 501-503
Mediation boards, 294
Messages

Gubernatorial, 420
Presidential, 242
Metropolitan areas
  Causes of origin and growth, 504
  City-county consolidation, 515-516
  City-county separation, 514
  Comprehensive solutions
    Federal plan, 513-514
    Single government plan, 513
  Matters of metropolitan-wide concern, 505-507
  Nature of, 503-504
  Partial solutions, 510-512
  Political decentralization of, 504-505
  Opposition to reorganization of, 508-509
    Legal obstacles, 509
Michigan constitution, 108, 360-361, 363, 427, 447
Minority Presidents, 174-175
Missouri plan, selecting judges, 444
Model State Constitution
  Features, 361-362, 400
  Governorship, 429, 430-432
  Legislature, 388, 400
  Purpose, 361
  Removal of judges, 447-448
  Selection of judges, 445
  Unified judicial system, 439-440
Movers and voting, 119
Municipal corporations, 487
Municipalities, 484-516

Nashville-Davidson metropolitan government, 515
National Aeronautics and Space Administration, 296
National constitutional restrictions on state governmental organization, 354
National expenditures, 530-532

National government; also see
   Congress, Courts, Presidency
   Executive branch, 155-157,
      237-274
   Judicial branch, 157-158, 317-
      351
   Legislative branch, 154-155,
      190-236
   Powers of, 35-44
   Supremacy of, 35
   Unique features of, 152-189
National government in action
   Presidential leadership
      Causative factors, 164-168
      Fluctuations in influence,
         168-169
      Selecting a President, 155-157,
         169-175
         Criticism and proposals for
            change, 175-177
National Labor Relations Board,
   294
National officials and employees
   Methods of selection, 178-180
National party conventions,
   170-173
Naturalization
   Collective, 67-69
   Individual, 67-69
Nebraska, unicameral legislature
   of, 387
New England towns
   Functions, 480-481
   Organization, 481-482
Nomination methods
   Caucuses, 130
   Conventions, 130-131, 170-173
   Non-partisan primary, 129-130
   Partisan direct primaries
      Closed, 128
      Open, 128-129
   Petition plan, 131-132
   Self-announcement, 132
Non-partisan primary, 129-130

Obligation of contracts, impair-
   ment of, 90-92
Obligations of national govern-
   ment to states
   Invasion and domestic vio-
      lence, protection against, 53-
      54
   Republican form of govern-
      ment, guarantee of, 52-53
   Territorial integrity and legal
      equality of states, mainte-
      nance of, 51-52
Obligations of states to national
   government and the Union,
   58-59
Obligations of states to one an-
   other
   Full faith and credit, 54-55
   Privileges and immunities of
      state citizens, 56-58
   Rendition of fugitives from
      justice, 55-56
Office-block ballots, 125-126
Opinion-creation by public of-
   ficials, 150
Organization of Democratic and
   Republican parties
   National, state, and local or-
      gans, 136-140

Party-column ballots, 125
Pennsylvania constitution, 363-
   364
People, role of, 113-115, 150
Personal conferences, 249
Personnel offices, departmental,
   305
Personnel policies
   National government, 301-309
   Problems requiring solution,
      302
   State governments, 428-429
Persons, rights guaranteed to all,
   80-108
Petition, nomination by, 131-
   132
Petition referendum, 413-414

Police power, 45
Policy committees, partisan, 227-
    228
Political parties
    Functions of, 133-134
    Major and minor, 134
    Multi-party situation, 136
    Nature of, 133
    One-party situation, 136
    Organization of, 136-140
    Two-party situation, 136
        Reasons for, in United States,
        134-135
Popular election of judges, ob-
    jections to, 442
Port of New York Authority,
    62
Post-auditing, 528-529
Postal Service, 297
Powers of
    Local governments, 50
    National government, 35-44
    States, 44-46
Pre-auditing, 527
Presidency
    Cabinet, President's, 253-254
    Compensation, 157, 239
    Disability of Presidents, 240-
        241
    Executive Office of the Presi-
        dent, 252-253
    Institutionalization of the Pres-
        idency, 253
    Leadership, popular and poli-
        tical, 248
    President and lawmaking
        Legal basis
            Messages, 242
            Special sessions, calling
                of, 244-245
            Subsidiary legislation, 245-
                247
            Veto power, 243-244
        Political source of influence,
            247-250
            Coercive tactics, 249-250

Magnitude of influence,
    250
Personal conferences, 249
Political leadership, 248
Popular support, 248
Pressure-group support,
    249
Prestige of Presidency,
    248
President as chief executive
    Commander-in-chief and
        war-time powers, 262-265
    Determination of foreign
        policy, 265-270
    Direction and control of ad-
        ministration, 251-254
    Executive agreements, 269-
        270
    Law enforcement, 251
    Pardoning power, 270-272
    Power of appointment, 256-
        258
    Power of removal, 259-262
    Preparation and execution
        of budget, 254-255
    Treaty-making, 268-269
    Qualifications, 238
    Rating of Presidents, 272-274
    Removal of Presidents, 157
    Selecting a President, 155-159,
        169-177
    Succession to the Presidency,
        239
    Term, 157, 238
Presidential disability, 240-241
Presidential electors
    Choice of, 173-174
    Number per state and District
        of Columbia, 24, 156, 169
Presidential influence, fluctua-
    tions in, 168-169
Presidential leadership, causative
    factors, 164-168
Presidential preference primaries,
    172
Presidential-Congressional gov-
    ernment, appraisal of, 180-189

Press, freedom of, 92-95
Pressure-groups
Nature, 141-142
Techniques, 142-145
Pressure politics
Nature, 142-146
Extent, 146
Private associations, 141-142
Privileges and immunities of,
State citizens, 56-58
United States citizens, 76-79
Privileges of members of Congress, 199-200
Procedural rights, 79-82
Promotions, 306-307
Proportional representation election methods, 123-125
Proprietary colonies, 4
Public expenditures, 517-534
Public indebtedness, 542-546
Public opinion
Influence of, 148-150
Nature of, 147-148
Public revenues, 534-542

Rating of Presidents, 272-274
Reading, suggested supplementary, see Appendix
Realities of the governmental process, 150-151
Recognition of states and governments, 267-268
Referendum, petition or protest, 413-414
Registration of voters, 120-121
Religious freedom, 96-100
Removal power of,
Governors, 424-425
Local executives, 493, 495, 500
President, 259-262
Removal of judges, 334, 446-448
Representatives, choice of, 177-178, 196
Representatives, House of
Apportionment of representatives, 196

Committees, 216-221
Compensation, 199
Partisan composition, 198-199
Procedure, 230-234
Qualifications, 194-195
Reapportionment procedure, 196
Selection of members, 177-178, 196
Single-member districts, 177, 196-198
Wesberry case, 197-198
Size, 196
Term, 155
Republican form of government, guarantee of, 52-53
Republican party, organization of, 136-141
Requirements of a satisfactory constitution, 355-357
Reserved or residual powers, 45-46, 353
Restrictions on state governmental organization, 354
Revenues, public
Comparative importance of different sources, 538-540
Limitations on raising, 540-542
Requirements of satisfactory revenue system, 535-536
Sources of, other than taxes, 538
Taxes, variety of, 536-538
Reynolds case, apportionment requirements, 389-393
Rights associated with citizenship
State, 75-76
United States, 76-79
Rights guaranteed to all persons, 80-108
Role of the people in the governmental process, 113-115, 150
Royal colonies, 4
Rules, House Committee on, 219
Rules and Administration, Senate

Committee on, 219-220
Safeguarding elections, 126-127
Sanctions, 315-316
Searches and seizures, 85-88
Secrecy in voting, 126-127
Securities and Exchange Commission, 293
Segregation, banning of, 105-108
Self-announcement of candidacy, 132
Self-incrimination, 84-85, 87
Senate, United States
  Committees, 217
  Compensation, 199
  Performance as representative body, 194
  Personal characteristics of members, 193
  Powers, 201-202
  Procedure, 234-236
  Qualifications, 192
  Selection of members, 177, 194
  Size, 193-194
  Term of members, 155, 193
Senatorial courtesy, 258
Senators, choice of, 177, 194
Seniority rule, 224-226
Separation of powers, doctrine of, 153-159
Sessions
  Congress, 23, 244-245
  State legislatures, 398-400
Single choice-plurality elections, 122
Social Security Act, 40-41, 288
Speaker
  House of Representatives, 199, 214-215
  State legislatures, 400-402
Special committees, 218
Special courts, 328-329
Special districts, 482-483
Special legislation, restrictions on, 459
Special sessions, power to call
  Governors, 421
  Local executives, 494, 496, 499

President, 244-245
Speech, freedom of, 92-95
Spoils system, 302
Standing committees
  Functions, 216, 230, 404
  House of Representatives, 215-221
  Number of, 217, 404
  Selection of members, 224-227, 403-404
  Senate, 217, 219
  State legislatures, 402-405
State, Department of, 282
State citizenship, 73-74
State constitutions, 352-378
  Amendment and revision of, 365-377
    Constitutional conventions, 370-374
    Initiative petition, 369-370
    Legislative proposal, 367-369
      Revisory commissions, 374-375
  Chief defects of, 365
  Comparison of first, with today's, 357-358
  First, features of, 10-12
  Increased length, reasons for, 358-361
  Obstacles to revision of, 376-378
  Rights, guarantees of, in, 108
State control of local governments
  Administrative, 462-463
  Judicial, 461-462
  Legislative, 461
State expenditures, 533
State governments
  Executive branch, 418-432
  Judicial branch, 432-454
  Legislative branch, 379-415
  Restrictions on organization of, 354
State powers, 44-46
State revenues, 539-540
Sub-committees, 217-218

Subsidiary legislation, 245-247
Substantive rights, 79-82
Supremacy of national govern-
ment, 35
Supreme Court, United States
Compensation of members,
334-335
Jurisdiction of,
Appellate, 326-328
Original, 326
Selection of members, 332-333
Size, 326
Tenure, 334
Supreme Court Cases, Digest of
Selected, see Appendix

Tax burden, growing, 519-521
Remedies
Constructive measures of
economy, 521, 547-550
Curtailment of governmental
services, 520-521
Tax Court, 329
Taxes, variety of, 533-536
Taxing power, 40-41, 48, 536-
542
Tennessee Valley Authority, 296
Towns, New England
Functions, 480-481
Organization, 481-482
Townships, 464-468
Functions, 477
Organization, 478-479
Uncertain future of, 479-480
Transportation, Department of,
289
Treasury, Department of the, 283
Treaties, 35, 42
Treaty-making power and pro-
cedure, 42, 268-269

Types of ballot
Office-block, 125-126
Party-column, 125

Unicameral legislatures
Arguments for, 384-387
Nebraska, 387
Unified judicial systems, 439-440
Unitary system of government,
34
United States citizenship
Acquisition of, 67-69
Loss of, 70-74
Privileges and immunities of,
77-79
United States Courts of Appeal,
325-326
United States Postal Service, 297
Unorganized interest-groups, 145

Veterans Administration, 295-296
Veto power,
Governors, 407-408, 421
Mayors, 494
President, 243-244
Vice President
Compensation, 199
Presiding officer of Senate,
215-216
Selection of, 156, 169, 174
Vacancy in office of, 156
Voting qualifications and dis-
qualifications, 114-120

War powers, 42-43, 262-265
Wesberry case, 197-198
Whips, party, 224